William Hume Elliot

The Country and Church of the Cheeryble brothers

William Hume Elliot

The Country and Church of the Cheeryble brothers

ISBN/EAN: 9783337141080

Printed in Europe, USA, Canada, Australia, Japan

Cover: Foto ©ninafisch / pixelio.de

More available books at **www.hansebooks.com**

THE COUNTRY AND CHURCH

OF THE

CHEERYBLE BROTHERS

BY THE

REV. W. HUME ELLIOT

RAMSBOTTOM

SELKIRK

GEORGE LEWIS & SON

MDCCCXCIII

All Rights reserved

I Dedicate this Volume

TO

MY WIFE,

WITHOUT WHOSE CEASELESS SUNSHINE IN THE HOME,

AND SERVICE AMONG THE PEOPLE,

THE BOOK MIGHT NEVER HAVE BEEN WRITTEN.

PREFACE.

SINCE it was publicly announced, a few weeks ago, that this volume was in the press, communications have reached me from one and another, at a distance, interested in its subject; and one venerable and singularly vigorous octogenarian, from a neighbouring Lancashire town, honoured me with a visit on a point of much interest to him, relative to the actual prototypes of the "Brothers Cheeryble." He had known the Grants—had business transactions with them, cherished a generous estimate of their character and worth, but entertained the idea that, in portraying the Cheerybles in 'Nicholas Nickleby,' the novelist had his eye on two amiable bachelors who lived next door to himself in Devonshire Terrace and had an office in the city of London. Having met the present Mr Charles Dickens on one occasion, he received from him an answer to a question which, while not so intended, yet, not unreasonably, appeared to him to bear favourably on this view. After further investigation, he stated his case fully in a letter to Mr Dickens, who courteously replied; but the reply, dated 10th April 1893, contains the following sentences:—

"It is merely waste of time to argue about the prototypes of the Cheeryble Brothers. My father may be supposed to have known what he meant himself, and as he always distinctly said that the Cheerybles were taken from the Grants, the matter admits of no further discussion. Mr ——, who was my father's neighbour in Devonshire Terrace, had no more to do with the Cheerybles than you have. Indeed, the Brothers had appeared in 'Nickleby' months before my father went to live in Devonshire Terrace at all."

Still the honourable enthusiasm of my venerable visitor to claim the Cheerybles as natives of the good town of Rochdale was not extinguished, and he had journeyed hither to ask whether I possessed any documentary evidence bearing directly on the point. I put before him the words of the illustrious novelist himself (see footnote, p. 275 of this volume)—"The Cheeryble Brothers, with whom I never interchanged any communication in my life." He was satisfied, and with his sanction I give the above interesting quotation from the letter of Mr Charles Dickens *fils*.

A communication has just reached me as the last pages of this volume are leaving my hands. It comes from a gentleman at the head of a mercantile firm in Birmingham, and contains the following interesting and admirably characteristic incidents. He says:—

"At the Queen's coronation (1838) I was one of the children (my age four) in a long procession which proceeded to Nuttall Hall to partake of a treat given by the Grants—cake, wine, and fun. Being so young, I was one of the first to arrive, as we tapered off from the shortest to the tallest. One of the brothers—William or Daniel—gave a silver coin to each of the children, I believe. At all events, he came up to me and said, 'Here, take this, child, and show it to me again some day, and I'll put another on it,' giving me a new small silver coin. I looked well at him, and fastened the silver well in my little hand, the first probably that I ever had there. Some twelve years after this, being out of employment, I rambled to Manchester, and found myself one day looking in at Grant Brothers' warehouse in Cannon Street. An old gentleman came up behind me, aud getting a good grip of my left ear, said, 'Youngster, what does thee want here? That's not a cookshop.' 'No more it is; and that's not your lug you're pulling. I'd rather be inside than outside a cookshop just now,' I retorted. 'Well, well, has ti no change to buy a dinner?' said he, still holding my ear. 'Well, I've got the Queen's coronation money Mr Grant gave me when I was a little un—but I cannot part with that.' 'So, so—well, I never!' said he, letting go my ear; 'let's see it, lad—let's see it!' So I pulled it out from the centre of a piece of calico, black as ink. 'Ah! yes, yes, so it is! And what did Mr Grant say to thee when he gave it thee?' 'Why, he said he'd put another on t' top of it if I'd show it him again; and you are summat like that Mr Grant.' 'Well, did he now? Well, well, I'll just do it for him,'—and putting a gold coin on the top of the small silver one, and adding a shilling for my dinner, he entered Grant Brothers' warehouse."

This was, no doubt, Daniel, the younger Cheeryble. William was gone eight years before this time. The gentleman proceeds:—

"I recollect the circumstance of a visit of Lord Derby—grandfather, I think, of the present earl—or father. [It would be the latter.] However, I was about ten years old, and worked in the 'hanging-room,' where prints were dried at the old Square. Lord Derby was coming round to see the works, was the information conveyed to me by one, Ned Hamer, a well-known character at the Square, and manager of the steaming-rooms. Ned was leader of the Primitive Methodist choir, and a great prayer-meeting enthusiast. He liked to show off, and told me, on the occasion referred to, to keep a sharp look-out for Mr Grant, and call out when I saw him coming. He then sat down on his stool, and, as usual, fell fast asleep in a twinkling. I soon followed suit, tired out as I might well be, a child of my age, working from 6 A.M. to 10 P.M. I was woke up with a smart slap on my cheek, when I immediately sprang up and shouted out, 'Ned! the Lord's arrived!' 'Glory to God! Allelujer! Turn off steam!' shouted Ned, in an ecstasy, at the top of his voice. The exclamation was so sudden, and within a yard or two of Lord Derby and Mr John Grant, that these gentlemen went immediately into fits of merriment, which, I was told, continued all through their round of the works. Young William Grant who followed, seeing me rubbing my ear after the slap, gave me a coin,—as he said, 'to buy an eye-opener!'

"I also recollect, at one dinner-hour at the old Square, some more lads and myself had taken possession of some floating planks, and were rowing about on one of the lodges, when who should suddenly turn up but Mr John Grant! He came running towards us holding up a stick and calling out, 'Come off there, you young rascals!' I immediately made for the nearest bank, and the sudden run of the plank against it sent me backwards into the dam, which at the time, fortunately for me, was only half full. Mr Grant immediately slid down the bank up to his neck in water, and pulled me out, dragging me after him to the bank side. 'Now,' he said, 'I shall make thee remember giving me this wetting,' and thereupon he used his cane to some purpose on my back. Having finished, he said, 'Now, how do ti feel?' 'Very wet,' I said, 'and sore.' 'And has ti nothing to say for saving thy life?' 'Yes, you've made a hole in my coat by dragging me up there.' At this he burst out laughing, and handed me a coin to buy a new coat."

"These," the correspondent adds, "are but small instances of the thorough good-heartedness of the Cheerybles and their brother, Mr John Grant—'The three gentlemen of Lancashire,' as they were popularly called."

I have very cordially to acknowledge the courteous readiness with which J. Grant Lawson, Esq., M.P., gave me access to the art treasures in his possession, and thus enabled me to place likenesses of the venerable parents of the "Brothers Cheeryble," as well as that of Mr John Grant of Nuttall Hall, and "Ramsbottom in the beginning of the century," among the illustrations of this volume.

I was fortunate enough to possess a fine engraving of

each of the Cheerybles themselves. The original painting of the elder of the two, William, is in the possession of Mr Grant Lawson; but that of the younger, Daniel, so far as I have been able to ascertain, has unfortunately been lost sight of. It is probably somewhere in Manchester or its neighbourhood, and it will be a happy circumstance if this reference to it should result in bringing it to light.

To Major Grant I am indebted for much kindness, and especially for preparing the plan of the "Old Ground" buildings of the Peels and the Grants.

The cordial co-operation of Mr George Haworth, photographer, Ramsbottom, during many months, in procuring satisfactory pictures for the engraver, entitles him to my warmest acknowledgments. But for him, some of the likenesses would not have been discovered; while more than half of the entire number of illustrations in the volume have passed through his hands.

To all the other friends who have kindly furnished me with necessary pictures, or otherwise aided me in my task, I tender very cordial thanks.

I am also beholden to my friends, William Carruthers, Esq., F.R.S., of the British Museum, and the Rev. A. H. Drysdale, M.A., of Morpeth, author of the 'History of the Presbyterians in England,' for valuable counsel in connection with the second book of the volume. To the Rev. Robert Hunter, M.A., LL.D., F.G.S., of the 'Encyclopaedic

Dictionary'—whose Resident Tutorship in the Theological Hall in student days, and warm friendship ever since, have been among the highest privileges of my life—I am indebted for reading several chapters, and verifying some points of historic interest. And a very tender and grateful recollection will always remain with me of the characteristic kindness of the distinguished man to whom the MS. was first submitted just two years ago, and who, with other grateful words, wrote, "I am so much interested in the whole tale, that I would like to preach to your people." Alas! before the generous and revered wish could be gratified, the eloquent voice was suddenly hushed in its last silence: it was the late gifted and chivalrous minister of Marylebone, London—Dr Donald Fraser.

One thought specially impresses me in completing the volume—it is, that almost all the old friends, from whose lips it was my privilege to gather what perhaps may lend interest to some of its pages, have passed away. The age, in the aggregate, of six of these amounted to 522 years, an average of 87 for each. It would not be possible, starting *now*, satisfactorily to accomplish the task.

WM. HUME ELLIOT.

WOODHILL, RAMSBOTTOM,
 December 15, 1893.

CONTENTS.

BOOK I.

CHAPTER I.—TOPOGRAPHY.

PAGE

The landscape now and in prehistoric times — The Irwell Valley — Neighbouring towns — The Peel Monument — The view from the summit — The home of the De Notoghs — Park — Grant's Tower — Walmersley House — Springside, the Home of the Cheerybles — Chamber Hall — Tottington — Claremont — Watling Street — Ancient pillar marking middle point between London and Edinburgh — Turton Chapel — Edgeworth Homes — Entwistle Moor — Holcombe Range — The Pilgrim's Cross — Bull Hill — " Ellen Strange " — Robin Hood's Well — Stake Lane Bar — Ewood Hall — Windy Arbour — Horncliff — Cliff Towers — Edenfield — Dearden Moor — Fo' Edge and Waugh's Well — Whittle Pike — Scout — Facit — Fletcher Bank — Top o' th' Hoof — Horse-shoe formation of hills — Ramsbottom, ... 1

CHAPTER II.—PLACE NAMES.

Nomenclature of hills and dales interesting and instructive — Alderbottom, Barwood, Bass Lane, Buckden, Buckhurst, Carr, Crimble Wood, Dearden, Deeply, Dundee, Harden, Hartlee, Hawkshaw, Helmshore, Hey, Holcombe, Th' Hoof, Irwell, Kibboth Crew, Nuttall, Pikelaw, Quarleton, Radisher, Rake, Ramsbottom, Ravenshore, Rowlands, Shuttleworth, Stubbins, Tittleshow, Tor, Whittle Pike, ... 15

CHAPTER III.—HISTORICAL.

The Romans in Lancashire — The Segantii — Britons — Roman stations and roads—A tumulus—Watling Street—An interesting "find"—Carausius—First elements of civilisation—The dawn of Christianity—*Ad Veteres*—The Anglo-Saxon conquest—The Frisian and Celtic elements in the Lancashire vernacular—Progress of civilisation—Forest laws—Their penalties—Grant of Holcombe Forest in 13th century—Disforesting—General Monk rewarded—The Buccleuch family, . . . 28

CHAPTER IV.—NUTTALL VILLAGE.

The old home of the De Notoghs—Prehistoric lake—New owners of Nuttall estate—Purchase by Messrs Grant of Nuttall estate and Mr Alsop's mill — The Wilds — Mr William Grant — Clothing and entertaining of the workers—His views of the relations between employers and employed—Nuttall Memories—Owd Nutta-ites — The palmy days of Nuttall — Recollections of the village and the Grants, by old residents, in the native dialect—" Mr John wur a good maisther "—Jane Storey singing "The Prodigal Son" — Her reward — Courtings, marriages, births, christenings, funerals, school, Crowlum boggart, accidents, and marlocks—Kitty Hamer, Tom W., Jim B., and Nellie D.—Scene changed. 40

CHAPTER V.—HOLCOMBE VILLAGE.

Its situation—The coom—The Church—The Original Chapel—Tithes for it and Edenfield—The Bishop's arrangement—Edenfield Church tower—The Minister's Pathway—The incumbents of Holcombe—Cock-fighting suppressed—John o' Matty's and his loved bass — " Sing smo', sing smo' ! "— Rush-bearing or wakes — Origin and history — The rush-cart — Its adornments and journey—Adam and Eve—The custom explained—The sports—Donkey and other races, greasy-pole, Grinning match—Ralph Fish—His unique victory—Holcombe churchyard—

Quaint inscriptions—The Ramsbottom Cromptons in America—The Crompton Loom—Tower and clock—Dr Bates—Dr Woodcock—The very Rev. Jas. Wood, D.D.—Roger Worthington—The Howcum Weaver chap, &c., ... 51

CHAPTER VI.—CHEERYBLE BROTHERS.

The advent of the Grants to the valley—How their father was impressed—William Grant, the Cheeryble's reminiscences—Description of district at the time—Founding of the cotton industry at Ramsbottom—Apprenticeship of the Grants—Their industry and progress—Purchase of Sir Robert Peel's works—Top o' th' Brow—Grant Arms—George Goodrick—The parents of the Grants—M'Kenzies of Tumbrech—Recollections of Mrs Grant's maid—Mrs Grant's aphorisms—A genial pair—Topwood saved—Extent of foreign commercial connections—The Corn Laws—Relieving the poor—Reminiscences of the late John Slagg, M.P.—William reads Riot Act at Chatterton—Henshaw's Blind Asylum—The Cheerybles and Steam-hammer Naysmith—£500 "*and no security!*"—"A most-knowing wink"—Its explanation—Naysmith's gratitude—"Always be civil"—Unfailing courtesy tested—Daniel Grant, the younger Cheeryble—His characteristics—Illustrative incidents—"First to come first to go"—His severest rebuke—Springside—Egypt! Pharaoh! mummies!—Mosley Street, Manchester—Alfred Boot, Dickens's "apoplectic butler"—Tiffin at 2—"Alfred! Ruby! Lightning!"—Impulsive oration in St Andrew's Church on Daniel in the den of lions—The preacher appeased—John Roe and John Wardle's boy—Aversion to signing documents—Generosity—"A thing of honour"—The Grants' affection for their parents—Characteristic speech in 'Nicholas Nickleby'—"The memory of our mother!"—Franklin Haworth's recollections—Mr William Grant's death—Funeral Sermon by Dr MacLean—Inscription on tombstone—Mr William Grant's account of their coming to Lancashire, and their subsequent career—Death of Daniel Grant and the other members of the family—Pulpit references, . 70

CHAPTER VII.—RAMSBOTTOM (INDUSTRIAL).

Local Board—Its Chairmen—The cotton industry—Its origin —Inventive genius—Arkwright, Wyatt, Kay, Hargreaves, Crompton, Cartwright—Calico Printing—The Peels and Grants—"The old ground" works—Plan—Water Street—Crowtrees Farm—Boundaries—Wardrobe and Coffin—St Paul's Church—The Vicars—Rev. W. H. Corbould—Old Toll House—Peel Bridge—Patmos Chapel—Callender Yard—Water-wheel—"Pin-roller Nook"—Topwood—Barwoodlee—Crofters' wages—Festivities—Earliest Sunday-schools—Old ground buildings—Dungeon Row—Ailsa Thorrocks—Her dressed cats—Cricket-ground—Cawdaw Mill—The name—Orchard Mill—Houses in "old ground" times—Chapel Field—Carr Bank—Foot o' th' Rake Pane—Old Dun Horse—Grant Lodge flower-garden—Wesleyan Chapel—New Jerusalem—Rev. S. Pilkington—The only well—Bridge Street Brook—John Gray's Lodge—Baptist Chapel—Rev. R. Maden—An old track —Catholic Chapel—Rev. B. G. De Mullewie—New Primitive Methodist Chapel—The Square—Its form and dimensions—The genesis of the Square in 'Nicholas Nickleby'—Charles Grant and his horse "Wellington"—The architect of the Square—A memorable demonstration—Four Grants at the head—Grand banquet in a field—Bullock and sheep roasted—A storm—Alarming mishap—Charles Grant digs through the *débris*—Rescue—Charles in another character—John appears on the scene—An exciting chase—Death of Charles—A drastic chastisement—A melting march to justice—The equipment of the Square works—Testimony of Samuel Parkes—The Grants' managers—Messrs Hepburn—The Chatterton riot—The elder Cheeryble reads the Riot Act—Three riotous periods—Chartists —Great demonstration—Cap of liberty—Noah's dove—Pikes —Sam Bamford—Snatches in the vernacular—Owd Bassett the bellman—Robert Peel and Nellie Yates—A new industry —Stubbins Vale and Church—Industrial leaders and employers in Ramsbottom to present time—Cotton, Woollen, Engineering, Engraving, Chemical, Stone, Co-operation, &c.—Brooks-

CONTENTS.

bottom Mills—Shuttleworth—Works—The Vicar—Volunteers
—Major Grant—His successor—Mrs Wilson—A peaceful sunset, ... 103

BOOK II.

CHAPTER I.—GENERAL HISTORICAL INTRODUCTION.

Reformation forces—Puritanism—The Scottish Covenant—The
Westminster Assembly—Presbyterianism—Lancashire Presbyteries—Rev. Henry Pendlebury at Holcombe, Bass Lane, &c.,
1651-1695 — Rev. Edward Rothwell, 1699-1731, embracing
building and opening of Dundee Chapel—Bank Street Chapel,
Bury, and its history, &c.—Old Baptismal Records of Dundee
and Bank Street, ... 163

CHAPTER II.—1731-1811.

Fifteen ministers, from Rev. Edward Rothwell to Rev. Peter
Ramsay — The building and history of Park Chapel — The
advent to Dundee Chapel of the Grant family — Rebuilding
Dundee—The puzzle of the premises—An old leaf and its story
—The forcible extrusion of Mr Ramsay in 1811—Reasons—
Deardengate, Haslingden—Characteristic stories, . . . 215

CHAPTER III.—1811-1891.

SECTION I. (1811-1830).— Rev. Thomas Nelson—Auchtergaven,
Lord Nairne, and the Young Pretender—Peace thanksgiving
sermon, 1814—Waterloo, Napoleon, and St Helena—Rev. Dr
George Brown—His call, ordination, induction, &c., with
interesting documents — Tim Linkinwater—List of Members,
Elders, Deacons—Extracts from Session records, &c. — The
Associate Synod—Presbytery of London—Elaborate title—

Interesting explanation — Unique relation of Dundee Church to the Presbytery of Lancashire—Relation of the Cheeryble, William Grant, to the Congregation and Sabbath-schools—The vine and the palm—Rev. Grant Brown—The family record—The maid of the manse—Interesting duties—Birth of Princess Victoria—Dr Thomas Chalmers at Dundee Chapel—His visit to the Cheeryble Brothers—A Miniature of Daniel Grant by Dr Chalmers—Stocks House, Cheetham—J. Crossley, F.S.A., Harrison Ainsworth, and Charles Dickens—Did Dickens and the Cheerybles ever meet?—Dr Chalmers and the Cheerybles at Stockport—Great service for Sunday-schools—The Orchestra—Humour and electric eloquence of the great divine—Robert Dalglish, the future M.P. for Glasgow—Letter of Dr Chalmers.

SECTION II. (1830-1869)—Ministry of the Rev. Dr MacLean—Elders, William Grant and others—Sacred wish of the Grants' parents — Honoured by building St Andrew's Church — Picturesque Situation—Hymn sung at the laying of the foundation stone—Procession—The Cheerybles—Free-Masons, &c.—'Manchester Guardian' Report—Opening of St Andrew's Church—Minute of thanks by the Presbytery—The government of the church—Office-bearers—Forcible seizure of St Andrew's Church—Scene at the church—" Blunt wedges rive hard knots "—Meeting at Old Dundee Chapel—Resolutions—Death of Dr MacLean—Funeral sermon—The Bishop of Manchester — Reception of the church — Death of William Grant, the younger—"Consecration" of the church—Correspondence—Interview with the bishop—His offer declined—Claim for restitution,   .   246

CHAPTER IV.—1869-1891.

SECTION III.—Dundee property and the Grants' estate—Building of new St Andrew's Church—Cost—Debt removed—Forcible seizure of Old Dundee property—Protracted litigation—Remarkable discovery of deeds—Another tell-tale leaf—Congregational Union Secretary—Strange doings—Intimidation—Assize trial before Mr Justice A. L. Smith—His Lordship's judgment — Notes — Restoration of property —

Counterfeit Minute-book — Detection — Ejectments — St Andrew's (Dundee) congregation—Choir—Personal reminiscences—Joseph Strong—Medallist of Highland Society—Mrs Gray—Rescues of drowning children, ... 326

CHAPTER V.—Conclusion.

Presbytery and Parliament, 378

APPENDIX.

Appendix A.—New Testament Episcopacy,	385
Appendix B.—Group of Deeds,	395
Appendix C.—A Spurious Deed,	402
Appendix D.—"Going Home!"	404

LIST OF ILLUSTRATIONS.

FULL-PAGE ILLUSTRATIONS.

"The Cheeryble Brothers," . . .	. *Frontispiece*	
Mr John Grant of Nuttall Hall, . . .	*To face page*	100
Ramsbottom in 1893 (the Square in the foreground),	,,	102
St Paul's Church, Ramsbottom, . . .	,,	108
Old Ground Plan, Ramsbottom,	,,	112
Ramsbottom Cricket-Ground and Players,	,,	114
Stubbins Vale, ...	,,	148
Mrs Wilson in her 90th year, . .	,,	270
Rev. Andrew MacLean, D.D., . .	,,	302
St Andrew's (Dundee) Presbyterian Church, .	,,	326
St Andrew's (Dundee) Presbyterian Church Choir, .	,,	368

ILLUSTRATIONS IN TEXT.

Nuttall Hall, Park, and Grant's Tower,	6
Walmersley House, . .	7
Springside, . . .	8
Old Stone, . .	9
Ewood Hall, . . .	12
Waugh's Well, .	14
In Buckden Ghyll, . .	17
Crimble Wood, . .	41
Old Nuttall Hall Farm, ...	44
Ruins in Nuttall Village (octogenarian native in foreground),	48
Holcombe Church and The Rake, .	52

Holcombe Old Church,	55
Holcombe Church and Churchyard,	63
Dr Woodcock,	67
Mr Wm. Grant of Grant Lodge (Father of the Cheeryble Brothers),	74
Mrs Grant (Mother of the Cheeryble Brothers),	75
Ramsbottom in beginning of Century (showing Grant Lodge),	106
Rev. W. H. Corbould,	110
Foot o' th' Rake Pane,	116
Rev. Samuel Pilkington,	118
Rev. Robert Maden,	119
Rev. B. G. De Mullewie,	121
Mrs Wilson and her Minister,	125
Scene of Chatterton Riot (Stubbins Church in the distance),	131
Samuel Bamford,	136
Bassett the Bellman,	140
Sir Robert Peel,	142
Lady Peel (née Nellie Yates),	143
Mr Richard Ashton, J.P.,	144
Mr William Rumney,	145
Mr James Porritt, J.P.,	147
Mr Lawrence Stead,	149
Mr Henry Stead, J.P.,	150
Rev. Edwin Dyson,	153
Brooksbottom Mills (Rowlands Chapel in the distance),	155
Major Grant,	157
Park Chapel (built, 1798),	225
Dundee Chapel and Manse (built, 1712; renewed, 1809),	228
St Andrew's Church (now Episcopal),	299
The Little Gate,	319
Hymn, and important heading, (1832).	321
A Weapon,	344
Mr Robert Haworth,	358
Mr John Roe,	369
Mr William Stead,	371
Mr Joseph Strong (Strang),	373
Mrs Gray,	374

INTRODUCTION.

"HALLO! you're quite among the hills here. I didn't expect to find a country like this so near the great Cottonopolis. How far are you from Manchester?"

"About a dozen miles."

"So near the great centre?"

"Yes—and we are ourselves a bit of a centre, but of a different kind. In Edinburgh you have the *heart* of Mid-Lothian; here in Ramsbottom, and the ancient village yonder, perched higher than the Calton Hill or the grand old Castle rock of the Scottish capital, you see the *heart* of the ancient forest of Holcombe in the Royal Manor of Tottington."

"Well, but for the chimney-stalks and the streak of smoke, one *might* imagine himself in some northern strath, in the neighbourhood of the grouse and the deer!"

"Oh! we can produce grouse along our hills and moorlands, as well as calico in the cloughs and valleys. Of deer, in former ages, we had quite enough. Now we have something more useful. As for the chimney-stalks, we don't complain of them. They are what a facetious native, during the cotton famine, called the 'lilies of the valley.' Unfortunately, now, as then, too many of them 'toil not, neither do they spin.'"

"So I understand. But you energetic Lancashire folk *have* had good times; and, doubtless, they will come again. The sun eventually beats the fog. Your striking array of towers, and spires, and goodly residences on the crests and slopes of these hills, tell of prosperous times."

"We lack neither energy nor hope, substantial homes nor fine churches; and those towers, which crest the terminal hills on either side of the valley, like our staple industry, link us with the great world beyond."

"What are they?"

"The one to the *west*, on Holcombe Hill, is Sir Robert Peel's. It stands within sight of his birthplace, a little farther down the valley, and commemorates the great service he rendered to his toiling fellow-countrymen in connection with the repeal of the Corn Laws, which had been rendered practicable by the invincible genius of Richard Cobden and his illustrious coadjutor, John Bright. The other, with graceful pinnacles, crowning the crest of the hill on the *eastern* side of the valley, is the memorial tower of the Grants — the "Brothers Cheeryble" of Charles Dickens[1] — and commemorates the advent of their father and the elder of the two Cheerybles to the Valley of the Irwell, more than a century ago."

It is with the picturesque and interesting region referred to in the foregoing colloquy, and especially with something

---

[1] In 'Nicholas Nickleby.'

of its history, industrial and ecclesiastical, embracing brief personal sketches of prominent and noteworthy actors on the scene, that we propose to deal in this volume.

In Book I., through faint lingering vestiges, and obscure and unsuspected place-names — Saxon, Scandinavian, or Celtic — we shall briefly grope our way back to Roman and pre-Roman times, when dusky forests overspread the land, and formed a habitat of bulls and wolves and boars. We shall note the Saxon and Norman periods, to glance at the operation of barbarous and oppressive forest laws; the changes brought about by disforesting the territory, and giving scope to pastoral and agricultural pursuits; and the rise—in humble and ever-increasing homes, scattered along the valleys and adjacent hills—of that textile industry for which the Irwell Valley has since achieved renown. We shall see how the first Sir Robert Peel—the father of the illustrious Premier—founded, by his calico-printing works, the modern industrial life of Ramsbottom; how the Grants succeeded him, and found here a home, and the centre of their remarkable subsequent career; and how they here erected the great calico-printing establishment, which was considered at the time to be the best equipped in Europe. We shall make known, for the first time, the *genesis* of the unwonted form of that structure, whose name—"The Square"—with the "rusty and shattered blunderbuss," and the "two swords broken and edgeless above the chimney-piece of its old office," and which there "became emblems of mercy and forbearance," with "shipping announcements," "statements of charities," &c., translated to "the heart of a busy town like London" by the pen of Charles Dickens in 'Nicholas Nickleby,' became familiar throughout, and beyond, the English-speaking world. It will also appear how two partners in the firm who reared the Square, by their fine industrial and commercial instinct, marked individuality, and homely and genial generosity, furnished the great novelist with two of the most interesting characters in the picture-gallery of his genius. Of these remarkable men and other members of their family many illustrative incidents are here recorded, which were obtained mainly from octogenarian and nonagenarian friends with whom they had long been closely associated. A valuable sketch is also given of their coming to Lancashire, their progress and phenomenal success, written by the venerable elder Cheeryble, Mr William Grant, himself, and not hitherto published.

The ancient village of Holcombe and some of its vanished customs and characters, and the palmy days of the old village of Nuttall, under the Grants—" when it wur in it pomp "—do not escape attention, most of what relates to the latter village having been gathered in quaint vernacular from aged residenters, some of whom had lived far beyond the allotted span, and knew little outside the old village and its immediate environment. What relates to Holcombe Rushbearing came from persons who, in youthful days, witnessed what they narrated, and who, in after years, became distinguished and useful citizens, but have now, like the old-world scenes they described, passed for ever away.

The Ramsbottom of the first two decades of the century is portrayed, and an original plan of the " Old Ground " of the Peels and the Grants is furnished; while a record is given of these noted pioneers' contemporaries and successors, whose energy and business capacity subsequently promoted the industrial expansion of the neighbourhood. We shall also note the *birth* of a new branch of industry quite recently cradled amongst us.

But the locality has had an ecclesiastical history even more remarkable than its industrial. In Book II. of this volume, the singularly chequered history of the Puritan congregation of the district will be traced from the middle of the seventeenth century to the present time. The unique array of ejectments, extrusions, and usurpations which bestud its annals; its vicissitudes under the cruel prelatic Stuart dynasty; its struggle through the dreary decades of the eighteenth century, and peculiar perils at its close; the advent of the Grant family to "Dundee" chapel, and the rebuilding of the old sanctuary, followed by the violent expulsion of one minister and the cultured and consecrated pastorate of another, with its regrettable close, will claim our attention. The building of a new and costly church for the congregation by the senior "Cheeryble," one of its elders; its forcible seizure nearly thirty years after his decease; the death of the venerable minister three weeks after the untoward event; and, subsequently, the "consecration" of this Presbyterian sanctuary, and acceptance and appropriation of its cherished "Cheeryble" endowment to Episcopalian uses by a distinguished Anglican bishop and the Ecclesiastical Commissioners, will likewise fall to be set forth.

Within our scope will also come the erection of a new church by the congregation thus despoiled; the seizure by force, at a later date, of its "Old Dundee" chapel and manse; the introduction of such strange ecclesiastical embellishments as sledge-hammers, bludgeons, and other forms of intimidation; the quest for evidence of ownership, the remarkable recovery of trust-deeds and other documents from time to time, and, after obstinate resistance, the ultimate legal expulsion of the usurpers. The author has written this part of the work from a simple sense of duty, which, in the face of some reluctance, has proved persistent and imperious. He, therefore, ventures to hope that it will be found neither devoid of interest nor lacking in salutary influence.

One of the more startling episodes embraced has, already, had one happy result. It has led ecclesiastical authorities, in various quarters, to see to the legal security of their possessions. This record may repeat and emphasise that lesson, and also lead congregations everywhere to see to it that their trust-deeds are safely deposited, and not lost sight of. It may also make plain the urgent need of a relationship between sister Churches, such as should render doings like some we shall have to narrate practically impossible. And it may serve to remind the Ecclesiastical Commissioners of their part in the consummation of a great wrong, with the consequent claim for righteous restitution which sleeplessly stands against them, and which, under the deep-running spirit of justice characteristic of modern democracy, must sooner or later be met.

BOOK I.

THE COUNTRY OF THE CHEERYBLE BROTHERS.

THE COUNTRY OF THE
CHEERYBLE BROTHERS.

CHAPTER I.

TOPOGRAPHY.

IF a member of the race who roamed the East Lancashire hills in prehistoric times—traces and remains of whom have been dug up now and then, in sequestered clough or on wild moorland—could revisit the scene, he would discover, in most respects, a wonderful change; but, in some, he would find none. What Byron said of the Mediterranean,—

> "Time writes no wrinkles on thine azure brow,"—

is equally true of the great ethereal expanse. At night the planets would still be found glowing calmly in their orbits, and the stars pulsating with undiminished beauty in their spheres. The sun, on a summer morning, would still burst with its wonted splendour over these eastern hills, and set, unshorn of its ancient glory, behind the western, bequeathing now, as then,

"Twilight and evening star."

And although smiling fields had replaced the gloom and grace of virgin forests, and substantial homesteads and busy cities superseded wattled huts; yet the well-marked outlines of hill and stream and plain would be there to greet him substantially as he left them, say three or four millenniums ago.

Between two of these hills—the terminal eminences, in the Irwell Valley, of spurs thrust out from the central Pennine range—stands the town of Ramsbottom. Four miles north of Bury and twelve of Manchester, it has Accrington eight miles to the north, Rochdale seven miles to the south-east, and Bolton a like distance to the south-west. It is built mainly on the right bank of the river, where the land slopes up towards the Holcombe range. Above it, four hundred feet higher than the valley, and just under the wooded brow of the hill, nestles the ancient village of Holcombe; and higher still, by four hundred and fifty feet, up the steep face of the height, stands the square and massive monumental tower,[1] with the simple inscription in bold relief—" PEEL." Its upper gallery is reached by successive flights of stairs. From its summit, where for the present we may take our stand, the view up the valley, northwards, by Cribden and Hameldon, towards Pendle Hill—for ever fragrant of Harrison Ainsworth's ' Lancashire

---

[1] Built 1852, by public subscription, at a cost of about £1000. It is of millstone grit, quarried on the spot (1169 feet).

Witches'—or across the hills and dales and bleak moorlands towards Rivington Pike on the west, or Blackstone Edge on the east, well rewards the climb. Nearer at hand, to the north-east, lie the Rossendale Hills;[1] and to the east, flat-topped Knoll Hill, Rooley Moor, and the valleys beyond. In these regions, thanks to the genius of Edwin Waugh, fancy still can hear the cheery voice of Lobden Ben,[2] singing by the way,—

"Green grows the leaves on the hawthorn tree,"

or—

"Robin Lilter's here again,
Wi' th' merry bit o' timber!"

—and his old friend, blind Dan o' Tootler's, with *his* wonderful "bit o' timber," whose wail, in "the plaintive old forest tune," "Remember the Poor," sent the tears rolling down Ben's honest face, and "seemed to hush the wild birds," and subdue "the silvery tinkle" of the "rindle of water dribbling into the well hard by."

"Listening hinds would drop the spade,
Forgetful of their hardy trade;
And peeping maidens raised the latch,
The minstrel's melting lay to catch;
And the lone brook that crept along,
Bore on its breast the fiddler's song."

From the base of Holcombe Hill, southwards, stretches out the great plain of Lancashire, studded with towns, and lit up here and there by the lake-like "lodges"[3] of modern

---

[1] See Mr Newbigging's admirable 'History of the Forest of Rossendale,' and 'Rambles round Rossendale,' by J Marshall Mather

[2] Besom Ben: "Tufts of Heather"—vol. iv of Waugh's Works.

[3] Reservoirs of pure water stored for industrial purposes.

industry, gleaming sometimes like molten silver in the sunlight.

Looking down towards the river, we see, near at hand, the spot where the De Notoghs had their home five centuries ago. A high baronial tower has been erected over the gateway during the present century. A few hundred yards

NUTTALL HALL, PARK, AND GRANT'S TOWER.

beyond, on the farther side of the Irwell, opposite Ramsbottom, the modern Nuttall Hall, built by the Grants, stands embowered in trees and shadowy evergreens.[1] On the top of the hill behind—"the Hoof"—and above Park

---

[1] Opposite the principal approach a stone bears the Grant Arms with the motto "Stand Fast," and the date 1817.

Chapel and School, is seen Grant's Tower, fronted and flanked by a grove of hardy trees, and visible from afar. Like the Peel Monument on the opposite hill, it is a favourite resort of excursionists. A little to the south of "the Hoof" is Bass Lane, where, after his ejectment from Holcombe in 1662, Henry Pendlebury found a home, and a chapel, and died in 1695. Near by is Walmersley House, with its heart-

WALMERSLEY HOUSE.

some and bracing demesne, now the Robinson-Kay Home for Incurables. It was the benign gift of the elegant family residence by a generous daughter to the memory of her honoured parents, whose name it now bears. A mile or so down the valley is Springside, where the Cheeryble Brothers lived for many years, and where both of them died. Farther south about two miles, on the confines of Bury, is Chamber Hall, where the Premier Peel was born; and down at the river, near by, "the Ground," where his father mainly achieved his singular industrial success. To the south of Holcombe Hill lies the ancient manorial village of Tottington, now a growing industrial centre; while, nearer at hand, is Claremont, long the residence of the late William Hoyle, the temperance statistician of his time. Farther over, about three miles from Ramsbottom, is Affetside, on the old Watling Street. It has an ancient

SPRINGSIDE.

weather-worn stone shaft, which is said to mark the middle point between London and Edinburgh. A little farther to the west is Turton, where Humphrey Chetham, founder of the Chetham Library in Manchester, once lived. In Turton Church may still be perused the goodly folios given by him in 1655, and recently restored by kindly hands to their original condition. They are chained each to a

transverse iron rod for perusal on the spot. Works by
Jewell and Ussher; Calvin and Baxter; Burroughs and Foxe;
Gouge and Burgess; John White, of Eccles; Isaac Ambrose,
of Garstang; Robert Bolton, of Blackburn; and many others,

OLD STONE.

are embraced in the fifty-two volumes. The old dark oaken
case is surmounted by the carved inscription—"The gift of
Humphrey Chetham, Esquire, 1655."[1] North of Turton,

---

[1] At Gorton there is a similar case with fifty-six volumes. Like gifts
to the parish churches of Manchester, Bolton, and Walmsley have not
been preserved. (W. E. A. Axon, 'East Lancs. Review,' Nov. 1890.)

and a short distance to the west of Holcombe Hill, on the western verge of the ancient forest, is Edgeworth. The Children's Homes, founded there by the late Mr Barlow, accomplish, by well-regulated industries and Christian munificence, much beneficent work for hundreds of orphan and other destitute children, and have made a portion of the bleak upland literally "rejoice and blossom as the rose." The little ones are benignly *mother'd* in these admirable homes. Farther over a little is Entwistle Moor, where neolithic remains were found in 1886.[1]

Along the Holcombe range, northwards, rises Harcles Hill[2] (1216 feet), no doubt the "Arkilles" that appears in the word "Arkilleshow,"[3] nearly seven hundred years ago; and a little beyond stood the Pilgrim's Cross referred to, we apprehend, in the word "Pilgrimscrosschahe" of the same remote period. The "chahe," or schaw, has long since disappeared, and the shaft of the cross has also gone, but the massive stone socket remains on the moor. Not far off is the rifle-range of the Ramsbottom Volunteers. And close at hand is Bull Hill (1371 feet), the highest point in the Holcombe range, where neolithic remains have been found.[4] At a lonely spot away at the northern end

---

[1] By Mr T. Wilkinson: 'East Lancs. Review,' June 1890.

[2] Just under the crest of Harcles Hill the 88th Connaught Rangers were under canvas for some time after service in India, and preparatory to embarking for the Crimea. It is said that only eight of the brave fellows returned. One came back to Ramsbottom—Edward Lacy.

[3] Gift of the Forest of Holcombe to Monkbretton Monastery, Yorkshire, by Roger Montbegon, who died in 1225. "Arkilles" 'is probably for Ark-hill, suggested by its rude resemblance to an ark stranded on the top of the mountain range. (See illustration, Ramsbottom in 1893.)

[4] 'East Lancs. Review,' June 1890.

of the moor, on its eastern slope, near where the old road dips down into Stake Lane, is "Ellen Strange"—no doubt a corruption of Ellen's Cairn. Here a heap of stones has marked the spot where Ellen, at some remote period, met an untimely end. The ancient custom was for passers-by to cast a stone on the pile, now mostly vanished; but aged natives have been known, in recent times, on passing, to pay the simple memorial tribute. A few yards down Stake Lane is Robin Hood's Well, with an ancient well-hewn coping-stone over it of ample dimensions. Down this lane, in more barbarous times, bulls were staked for baiting; and near Stake Lane Bar, where four roads meet, a gibbet stood, where wretched criminals were hung in chains. To the north of the Holcombe range, beyond Alden Clough, towers the truncated conical hill called Musbury Tor[1] (1115 feet). It was the "Laund," or specially preserved hunting-ground, to furnish the table of kings and nobles in ancient royal forest days. Its boundaries marched with

---

[1] In a parish not a thousand miles from Musbury Tor a new vicar had just been settled, when, one day, he was requested to visit an aged parishioner, in his last illness. With prompt alacrity he went to the house. He was attired in the orthodox Anglican fashion. With eager zeal he urged the old man, if he had anything on his mind, or troubling his conscience, to tell it out freely to him, and all would be right, repeatedly informing him, as a reason for so doing, that he was his vicar—the *new* vicar of the parish. He magnified his office, however, in vain. For a considerable time not a spark of interest could he elicit. At length, standing by the bed, with the light falling on his smooth cassock-vested chest, he observed the desiderated interest kindling in the old man's eye, and took fresh courage. "That is right, my good man; don't hesitate, whatever it is—speak it out to your vicar." "Yeigh," said the aged pilgrim, moving a little towards him. "There—now—what is it?" said the vicar, bending the ear. The old man, with a curiously perplexed expression, answered slowly—"*Aw've been wonderin' however yo' got inside that westcoat o' yours bout* [without] *buttons up t' middle!*"

Holcombe Forest on the one hand and Rossendale on the other.

Down in the valley, nestling among trees and stately hollies and ivy, is Ewood Hall, with its fine mullioned windows. It bears—" 1641, C. G. I. G." The original hall was the home of Roger Gartsyde, whose grandson, Peter

EWOOD HALL.

Heywood, it is said, was the Justice of the Peace who arrested the notorious Guy Fawkes.

On the eastern side of the Irwell, and opposite the northern end of the Holcombe range, as seen from about Ramsbottom or Shuttleworth, the bluff hill end called Windy Arbour protrudes—concealing Horncliffe ridge, long noted for its flags and slates, with Cliff Towers gracefully commanding the valley from its bold sylvan side. The height overlooks Edenfield village, whose houses, faintly fringed with trees, picturesquely strike the sky-line between Windy Arbour and the eastern flank of Cribden (1317 feet). From Windy Arbour, Dearden Moor sweeps round behind Whittle Pike, the monarch of the region (1572 feet). On the southern slope of the moor stands Newhall, now old, with its weird traditions of plague and ghost and intramural sepulture; while beyond Whittle, on the bare green slope of Fo' Edge, still "tinkling" in the wild upland stillness, "drips" Edwin Waugh's lone well—a modern pilgrim-spot, where

> "A lonely, rindling fountain,
> Yonder moorland hills among,
> From the heather-breasted mountain,
> Tinkling drips its liquid song."

In front, bare and bold, are Scout and Facit. Between these is seen the crown of Whittle Pike. South of Shuttleworth brook, Harden Hill, with Fletcher Bank, famed for Millstone-grit, in front, leads the eye back to "Top o' th' Hoof." Waugh concludes one of his best stories with these words—"I had a fine starlight walk to 'Th' Top o' th' Hough' on that breezy October night. After a quiet supper in Owd Bob's little parlour, I took a walk round about the quaint farmstead, and through the grove upon the brow of the hill. The full moon had risen in the cloudless sky, and the view of the valley as I saw it from 'Grant's Tower' that night was a thing to be remembered for a man's lifetime."

As seen from the south, the hills that guard the valley present a majestic horse-shoe formation — Cribden, in the north, forming the toe; Top o' th' Hoof, one heel; and Holcombe Hill, the other. Between these two lies Ramsbottom.

From Ramsbottom, southwards, the ancient forest extended to Elton, now part of the municipality of Bury. Northwards, a few miles up the valley, it touched Musbury

WAUGH'S WELL.

and Rossendale. From east to west it stretched from three to four miles—from the district of Shuttleworth on the east, where the land sweeps up to Whittle Pike, right across the valley and the Holcombe range to Edgeworth, in the parish of Bolton, on the west.

CHAPTER II.

PLACE NAMES.

WHERE, through remote centuries, different races have successively held sway in a country, and ancient records are rare or altogether wanting in a district, it may be both interesting and instructive to consult the nomenclature of the hills and dales, and try, through familiar place-names, to shake hands with our predecessors in the "fable-shaded eras"[1] of a distant and otherwise unrecorded antiquity. It is to supply something illustrative of this, in a very limited sphere, that the writer furnishes the following notes on a few local place-names.

Alderbottom — often "Owlerbottom." — The holm or bottom where Alder trees abounded.

Barwood, in Barwoodlea, &c., means *Boar*wood—from the Anglo-Saxon *bár*, a boar—the wood infested with boars. This, and such other names as Bull Hill, Boarsgreave, Sowclough, Wolfstones, Wolfenden, Buckhurst, Dearden, &c., record unerringly the forest *fauna* of many centuries ago.

Bass Lane.—Bass might come (1) from *bass*, or *bast*, a fibrous bark from which ropes and mats are made—but

---

[1] Hawick's famous song, "Tyr-ibus ye Tyr ye Odin."

there is no trace of any such industry there; or (2) from *bass*, "shale found in coal." Shale amply cushions the millstone grit of the neighbouring hills, and abounds in the coal measures of the locality; and it appears plentifully in the deep wooded clough along the upper margin of which Bass Lane extends. From this word, therefore, in all likelihood, the name has sprung. But (3) there is another possibility in the *obsolete* word *bass*, a kiss, or to kiss; and thus some might find in Bass Lane an old equivalent of Lovers' Lane.

Buckden, the dell or glen of the bucks. From *buck*, a stag, and *den*, which, in place-names, means dell, dingle, or glen. *Dion*, in Gaelic and Irish, means a valley or sheltered place. The Saxon evidently got the word from the Celt.

Buckhurst, the thicket or grove of the bucks or stags. From *buck*, and old Norse *hrioster*, or Anglo-Saxon *hyrst*, a grove or thicket.

Carr, a name in the north-west portion of Ramsbottom— "Carr Street," or "The Carr," "Carr Fowt" or "Fold," "Carr Terrace," "Carr Barn," now "Carr Bank," &c.

Carr may come from the Danish *kaer*, the Icelandic *kiar* or *kaer*, or the old-Swedish *kaerr*, which alike mean a marsh, or marshy place. *Carse*, as in "The Carse o' Gowrie" or "The Carse of Stirling," meaning low-lying fertile land, is supposed to have a kindred origin. But one does not very readily associate "The Carr" at Ramsbottom, with its steep ascent, with either *marsh* or *carse*. We may, therefore, look for another root. The vernacular, "up t' ker," shows that the double r is no insuperable difficulty. Now Caer, or Car—as in *Car*lisle, *Car*narvon, *Caer*marthen,

*Car*munnock, and other names—in the language of the ancient Britons meant a city, a castle or fort, or place surrounded by a wall, or palisades, or a rampart. In this locality the *Caer* may have been of the most primitive

IN BUCKDEN GHYLL.

description, protected, perhaps, by palisades, and a natural rampart formed by an abrupt break in the side of the hill. But it is probable that a fortified place of some kind existed in pre-Roman times on the hill-side somewhere in this locality, whose name alone has survived in "the Carr." Right up Carr Street, and its continuation, "the Taper," a bluff buttress springs up just at the upper end of the straight ascent—the "top o' th' taper." On the summit of this eminence—"the tip o' th' top o' th' taper"—there is a considerable plateau, which, with the adjacent space above Topwood, and especially before the advent of the delphmen,[1] would be well adapted both for outlook and a place of strength. At the base, towards the valley, is "Carr-field"; and farther down, "Carr Fold" on the one hand, and "Kibboth Crew" on the other. On the north and south, alike, are flanking declivities; while behind, to the west, there is the long gradual ascent towards the top of the Holcombe range. Across the site of the Caer, or Car, would flow a mountain rill, whose track has now been quarried into a deep rocky gorge. If, then, Carr here comes from Caer, a portion of the ancient Britons had a home somewhere in the locality indicated, before Roman hatchets began to clear the virgin forest, where Manchester now stands, to found the *Mancunium*, or *Mamucium*, of the first century; and British heroes, with the patriot fire of ancient days, may have marched down the Car, or along the Coomb (cwm),[2] to pit their fierce untutored valour, under the brave British general, Venutius, against the well-compacted discipline of the martial might of Rome.

Crimble, in "Crimble Wood," the steep wooded bank below Nuttall village. *Crimell* in Cambro-Britannic or Welsh means a *sharp ridge*.

Dearden, in "Dearden Clough," and "Moor"—from *deer*

---

[1] Quarrymen.   [2] See Holcombe, p. 21, *infra*.

and *den*. Clough is Scandinavian, and means a narrow valley or ravine.

Deeply, in "Deeply Vale"—a corruption of Deerplay, or Deer-uplay. The upland vale where the deer lay, or used to sport and frolic. *Deer* and *play* are from Anglo-Saxon *deor* and *plega*.

Buckhurst—the thicket frequented by the bucks—lies just above Deeply Vale, in a group of little hills which flank its western side, stretching towards "Top o' th' Hoof." They are now stript of their sylvan beauty, but with rippling rill, grassy meadow, and secluded winding ways, possess a quiet charm of their own.

"DUNDEE," the name by which the old Presbyterian chapel at Ramsbottom is known, is supposed to be a corruption of DONUM DEI—the gift of God; or DOMUS DEI—the house of God,—words which, tradition says, were inscribed on the original building. The inscription is not found on the present structure.

The chapel stands well up the slope above Ramsbottom, to the west, and just below the prominent and picturesque height on which Holcombe Church is built. From its proximity to Holcombe, and also, perhaps, because its congregation was originally the ejected congregation of Holcombe in 1662, it was also called "Holcom,"[1] and "Holcombe Lower Chapel."[2]

Its graveyard and manse garden abut on Nuttall Lane —now in part "Dundee Lane"—which links the old village

---

[1] Dr Evans's list in Dr Williams's library—London, 1717-1729. Also Halley's 'Lancashire Puritanism,' vol. ii. p. 325.
[2] See Book II., *infra*.

of Nuttall with that of Holcombe; hence it was likewise known as Nuttall,[1] and Nuttall Lane Chapel.[2] In ancient records the Forfarshire town Dundee is written "Dundie," but the seal of that royal burgh bears "Dei Donum"; and it is written "Donum Dei" in a charter of Queen Mary, in reference to a church which had been built by a brother of King William the Lion, in the twelfth century.

Harden, in "Harden Hill," is, perhaps, a corruption of Hart-den—stag-dell. In Celtic *na hardibh* means the heights.

Hartlee, Hart Lees, or Hartlea. Hart is Anglo-Saxon *heort*, a stag; *lee* is Scandinavian, signifying sheltered—as the lee-side; *lea* or *lee* is also Anglo-Saxon, and means a meadow, or grass-land. Hartlee is the old name of what was long the Higher Public House in Holcombe, and the land adjacent. Its sign, painted on a slab of stone, linked it with the past, for it was a *White Hart*. Hartlee or Hartlea, therefore, means the sheltered or meadow-land pastured by the harts or stags. It was a likely spot, high up on the inner edge of the village. Certain fields in the farm opposite Dundee Chapel are also called "Hartlee," and "Hartlee Meadow," in an old deed.

Hawkshaw.—Oak trees abounded in this locality. The name is most likely a corruption of Oakshaw—from Anglo-Saxon *ac*, an oak, and *scua* or *scaga*, a small wood or thicket, a shaw. The sign of an old wayside inn, near Hawkshaw Lane, is a flourishing old oak tree, with the words, "Let the old oak stand!"

---

[1] 'Memoirs of Chalmers,' vol. ii. p. 333.
[2] See deed, 1722, Book II., chap. i., *infra*.

Helmshore.—Corruption of Elmshaw—a wood or thicket in which the *elm* predominated. Often pronounced Hel-shore; and "devilling"—tearing up the raw material—is a cotton-manufacturing process carried on there. This, on one occasion, led to a southern gentleman being greatly horrified by a youth gravely informing him, in answer to inquiries, that he lived at Hel-shore, and assisted his father to "tent" two devils! The youth, of course, did not observe the grim meaning of his words, and the visitor knew nothing of their local significance.

Hey, in Hey Mount and Hey House, is most likely from the Anglo-Saxon *hea* or *heh*, signifying *high*. The long section of Holcombe Hill, on which the Peel Tower stands, is called "Hey House Level." Hey House, rich internally with old oak panelling, is just at the south-east end of the hill; and well out in front, on a comely and conspicuous wooded height, stands the modern mansion, Hey Mount, now called Holcombe Hall. But *hey*, *hay*—as in Green*hay*, Green*heys*, Sheep*hey*, &c., is from French *haie*, a hedge, a palisade, a fence.

Thomas De Quincey says of "Greenhay" (now Greenheys Manchester), where he was born on 15th August 1785— "I ought, in justification of my mother, who devised the name to have mentioned that 'hay' was meant for the old English word (derived from the old French word *haie*) indicating a rural enclosure. Conventionally, a *hay* or *haie* was understood to mean a country house within a verdant ring-fence, narrower than a park."—'De Quincey's Works,' vol. xiv. p. 397.

Holcombe.—This word is evidently of very ancient origin. *Holl* is Saxon, and means hollow, how, deep; and the *cwm*, *coom*, of the Celtic Britons means a hollow, or the bosom of a hill, having a somewhat semicircular form. Holcombe, or Howcum Hill, therefore, is the *hollow*, how, or deep-bosomed Hill; and Holcombe village, the village situated in the coomb or bosom of the steep. It would be difficult to find a word more accurately descriptive of the place. From far and near, eastwards, the bay or coomb-like conformation, at the south-east end of the range, is manifest—Holcombe Church standing out in bold relief, on its commanding site, in front; and the village, almost entirely concealed, nestling in the *coomb* behind.

Let any one wishing a near view look from the street or field above the Ramsbottom Liberal Club, past old Dundee Chapel, and up the wooded dell lying immediately beyond, between the Kennel Knowe and Holcombe Burying-Ground, and he will get an admirable view of the *coomb* of the hill; or, let him climb the height, and stand at the entrance to Holcombe Church, and he will see distinctly marked, and close at hand, the semicircular formation curving round from right to left above the village, at whose north-eastern extremity is thrown out the bold buttress on which the church stands. Or let him in summer, or autumn, look across the vale from the eastern side, when the westering sun, from above the mountain top, silhouettes the trees along the grassy slopes, and, shooting its rays over the "holl" or "coomb," fills it with impressive shadows, while lighting into airy relief the sentinel-like church perched on its green rampart in front, and still brightening the diversified valley beneath and the far-extending plain beyond.

In Cornwall "*coom*" abounds—*e.g.*, Smallacombe, North

Comb, South Combe, Millcoome, Dewcomb. In Devonshire, we have Ilfracombe — pronounced Ilfra*coom* — and Hollacombe. The former is so named, no doubt, from its finely-sheltered harbour, formed by the semicircular sweep of craggy heights round three of its sides. Hollacombe is, we apprehend, formed, like Holcombe, from the Saxon *hol* and the British *cwm*. There are also *Holcombe* Rogus and *Holcomb* Burnel, Comb Martin, Challacombe, and others. In Somerset there is a *Holcombe*, some six miles from Shepton Mallet. In Gloucestershire we find Winchcombe; in Derbyshire, Comb's Moss and Comb's End; in Cumberland, Black Coom or Comb; in Northumberland, Comb Hill, near Haltwhistle, on the South Tyne; and, still farther north, the Teviotdale poet — Henry Scott Riddell — in "Johnnie Nip-nebs," writes, "On Cauldcleuch's wild haggs, roun' *the coome o' the steep*"—('Poetical Works,' vol. ii. p. 203). We thus find the old British word *cwm* still used, along the west, all the way from Cornwall to Teviotdale. Cornwall was "West Wales," and "Strathclyde" stretched from Warwick to beyond the river Clyde. These western regions were longest held by the Britons at the English Conquest. The Angles, from Suffolk to the Forth, invaded from the east. Whitaker says—"The composition of the word Holcombe is one instance among many of the combination of two or more syllables of local names, expressing the same idea in different and successive languages. Thus *cwm* in British and *hol* in Saxon—denote a bottom." —('History of Whalley,' vol. i. p. 326.)

Hoof, in "Top o' th' Hoof," on which Grant's Tower stands, is the local form of heugh, *heuch*, or *hewch*, which means a *steep hill* or *bank*, and also a *craggy steep*. Top o' th' Hoof, therefore, meant top of the steep hill or bank. Similarly, *seuch* or *sewch* is sometimes pronounced soof—a ditch or drain. Akin to this is Hay-moof, for Hay-mow.

Irwell, from Cambro-British *ir*, meaning fresh, and *gwili*, a winding stream. The "g" disappears in composition. Irwell, therefore, means the fresh-winding river. Although hard work has, during the present century, robbed the river of its pristine freshness, yet its windings are no doubt as marked to-day as when the ancient Britons fitly named it the fresh-winding stream.

Kibboth Crew.—This curious place-name has been a puzzle to all who have thought about it. Can it have anything to do with the old word *croo*, which meant a calf's crib? Or must we look further back for its constituent elements? *Cridden* or Cribden—the finely terraced hill which looks down the Ramsbottom valley from between Haslingden and Rawtenstall—according to Dr Whitaker, the historian of Whalley, is *Keirudon*—the hill of stags. Now knob-like parts of a mountain are sometimes called *Kipps*, and *kippie* means a little hill; while, in Celtic, *kippen* means a promontory.[1] Kibboth Crew is just at the extremity of a cape-like piece of land running out to a considerable distance from the base of a steep-wooded eminence on the hillside, and abruptly dipping down into the dell, where now Springwood Mill stands, with

---

[1] Thus we have Kippen in Stirlingshire, Kippenross in Perthshire, and Kippilaw in Roxburghshire; with various "Kips," also, throughout the country.

the deeply embanked lodge behind. One or other of these old words, *kip, kippie*, or *kippen* — may have been linked with *keiru*. And *Kippie*, or Kippen Keiru, might, in the course of centuries, be corrupted into Kibboth Crew, meaning the hill or cape-like resort of the stags. *Kip o' th' Keiru*, if permissible, would, phonetically, come very near *Kibboth Crew*. If *Crew*, as is possible, is a corruption of *Keiru*, then the name goes back to the time of the ancient Britons, and may have been applied here before the Romans appeared on the scene.

Nuttall.—De Notogh, transformed through Nutbaulgh, Nutshall, Newthal, Newthall, Nuthall, and Nuttal.

Pike*law*, often " Pike*low*," is a sub-height of Cribden. From Brit. *pic*, a point, and law. " Pikelaw," like " Holcombe," is an instance of the original British name having an Anglo-Saxon one, of like meaning, added.

Near Chetham Close, Turton, there are, close together, three small round hills. In the village we asked what they were called. One said " Three loaves," another " Three lows "—that is, three *laws*, from the Anglo-Saxon *hlaew*, a law or little hill. "Low" for "law" is interesting. It is an instance of the marked and impressive Frisian element which abounds in the Lancashire vernacular.

Quarleton. — In the 13th century it was written "Querendon." It is most probably formed from the Anglo-Saxon *cweorn*, a quern—that is, a stone handmill, used in old times for grinding corn; and *dun*, Gaelic and Anglo-Saxon for a hill or mound. Quarleton stands on the hill-top. Dunse in Berwickshire, and Dunsyre —the hill of the Seer—the termination of the Pentland Hills, in the Upper Ward of Lanark, are also formed from *dun;* so are Cribden and Hameldon, near at hand; Snowdon, in Wales; and the Eildons, near Melrose.

> "He cleft the Eil*don* Hills in three,
> And bridled the Tweed with a curb of stone."

Radisher Wood.—The Monkbretton Register, describing the boundaries of Holcombe forest as given to that monastery in the 13th century, has near this locality "the Lane of Robbers," from "Tittleshow towards the west." There may also have been a "Robbers-schaw," which would very easily become Radisher, the name now given to the bold and finely wooded southern slope of Holcombe Hill, as it breaks down into the Holcombe Brook, a mile to the south-west of Ramsbottom. The Ordnance Survey Map gives "Reddy Shore."

The Rake, the steep ascent from Ramsbottom to Holcombe Church and village.—*Rake* is Scandinavian, and signifies a steep slope or declivity, like the slope or *rake* of a mast.

Ramsbottom.—This name, in all likelihood, sprang up in the not very remote pastoral era, and means the low-lying ground where the rams grazed—from *ram*, and the Anglo-Saxon *bötm*, which means an alluvial hollow. Similarly, across the holm, we find Shipperbottom, which was most likely the *holm* or *bottom* where the shepherd lived. The site of the old farmhouse of Shipperbottom is now occupied by the statelier Nuttall Hall. Farther down we have Brooksbottom—the low-lying land where Holcombe and other brooks join the Irwell; and farther up, Alderbottom.

Ravenshore.—A corruption of Ravenshaw—the wood frequented by the *ravens*.

Rowlands,—perhaps a corruption of Roe-lands,—the lands pastured by the roe or roebuck in the distant past.

Shuttleworth.—From Icelandic *skutul*, or Anglo-Saxon *scyttels*, a shuttle; and *worth*, which, like *ham*, *cote*, and *ton*, means a homestead with its enclosure.

Stubbins.—*Stub*, from Anglo-Saxon *styb*, means the root of a tree; *to stub*, is to root out stumps; and *ing* means a meadow. Stubbings, now Stubbins, therefore, signifies the *stubbed* or *cleared meadows*—meadow land cleared from forest growths. Stubby Lee is a kindred name.

Tittleshow, Titles-howe, or Titlarks-how, may be from *titlark*, and *how* or *howe*, a hollow—meaning the hollow or low-lying meadow-land where titlarks abounded.

Tor.—*Tor* is the Cambro-British *twr*, meaning a lofty pile, a high pointed rock or hill. Tors abound in Devonshire, especially in the upper reaches of the river Dart —the ancient Royal Forest of Dartmoor. The word is also found in the High Peak, Derbyshire—*e.g.*, Mam Tor, Blakelow Tor.

Whittle Pike.—Whittle is probably a corruption of White-hill. The Pike is 1572 feet above sea-level, and snow is frequently seen on its crown when visible nowhere else in the neighbourhood. Pike, as already stated, is from Cambro-British *pic*, which means a pointed end or beak. The Gaelic *peac*, *peic*, means any sharp-pointed thing. We have Thievely Pike near Todmorden, Wardlow Pike in Derbyshire, Langdale Pike in Westmoreland, and, a few miles up the Irwell Valley, *Pike*law on the south side of Cribden. (See p. 25, *supra*.)

CHAPTER III.

HISTORICAL.

MORE than eighteen hundred years ago, *Anno Domini* 79—the year of the Emperor Vespasian's death, and nine years after his son and successor, Titus, captured Jerusalem—the Roman general, Agricola, invaded what we now call Lancashire, the country of the Segantii, and reduced the Britons there to subjection. These Segantii-Britons belonged to the native state of the Brigantes—the largest and most powerful of the British tribes—which eventually submitted to a foreign military environment. This the Romans effected by establishing a line of fortified camps and garrisons at well selected strategic points around them. Such Roman stations were planted where we now find Manchester,[1] Wilderspool,[2] near Warrington; Walton,[3] near Preston; Lancaster,[4] Ribchester,[5] Whalley,[6] Colne,[7] and Overborough.[8]

Roads were essential to the effectual conquest of the country, as well as to the continued maintenance of the im-

---

[1] Mancunium or Mamucium.   [2] Condate.   [3] Coccium.
[4] Bremetonacis.   [5] Rerigonium.   [6] Gallumo.
[7] Calumo.   [8] Ad Alaunam.

perial power. And the Romans, very wisely, proved themselves great road-makers. In this we see their purpose to grip the country firmly, and maintain their grasp. They had to cut their way through dense forests, in the face of a sleepless and heroic enemy. One of the forests through which they had thus to force their way northwards, after establishing themselves at Mancunium or Mamucium, was that of Holcombe. Leaving Manchester by Strangeways, Kersall Moor, Prestwich, and Radcliffe, the road strikes right along the crown of the Affetside ridge, on by Edgeworth to Ribchester and the north. A short distance above Hawkshaw Lane, and a little to the south of a lone moorland rill, there is what appears to be a sepulchral mound.[1] In the absence of definite knowledge about it, we may yield for a moment to conjecture. At this point the Romans in their northward advance, after leaving Manchester, would first approach the East Lancashire hills. The Britons there, on their favourite ground, would doubtless be on the alert, and, issuing from the neighbouring *coom* of Holcomb, or the *caer* that probably existed above Ramsbottom, may have swept round upon them through the forest, from the brow of the hill, to dispute the way; and the *tumulus* may mark the spot where some brave chieftain fell. The footprints of imperial Rome in Britain are indelible, and material remains abundant.[2] But those of an authentic character, in this immediate locality, are scanty. In addition, however, to the great Roman high-

---

[1] Marked on Ordnance Survey Map.
[2] See Horsley's 'Britannia Romana,' Dr Collingwood Bruce's 'Roman Wall,' and also his 'Lapidarium Septentrionale.'

way, or Watling Street,[1] we have an interesting *find* of coins and jewelry, which takes us back to the third century. On the eastern side of the valley, in a secluded little dell at Throstle Hillock, which lies between Grant's Tower and Buckhurst, a small earthen vessel was dug up by a farmer[2] in 1864. It contained silver bracelets, armlets, rings, &c., and "an amulet of silver, richly streaked with orange-coloured veins, and pierced so as to be suspended alone."[3] In addition to these relics, the urn contained upwards of five hundred Roman coins— extending from the reign of Gallienus (253-268) to that of Maximianus (286-310). Many of them bore the image and superscription of *Carausius*. This Carausius was appointed by the Roman Emperor Maximian to command the imperial naval force stationed at Boulogne. Soon after his appointment he revolted (287), and having secured the allegiance of the fleet, sailed over to Britain—at that time only slightly guarded—persuaded the Roman legion and auxiliaries there to embrace his party, assumed the imperial purple and the title Augustus, defied the Roman power, spread terror far and wide by his fleets, and usurped the rule of Britain for seven years. He was assassinated by his first minister, Allectus, who then succeeded him; but soon after, to the joy of the people, Allectus was overthrown by a Roman force under Asclepiodatus, and thus Constan-

---

[1] "In the star-strown track of the Milky Way, our fathers saw a road by which the hero-sons of Waetla marched across the sky, and poetry only hardened into prose when they transferred the name of Watling Street to the great trackway which passed athwart the island they had won."—Green, 'Making of England,' p. 166. Some think the name comes from *Stratum Vitellianum*.

[2] Mr. James Nuttall.   [3] 'History of Bury.'

tius recovered the island for imperial Rome in the year 296.¹

The obverse side of one of the coins which is in the writer's possession bears round the head, "Carausius P P Aug. Imp.—Carausius, pater patriæ, Augustus Imperator"—Carausius, father of his country, sacred or august, Emperor. These coins and other relics, perhaps deposited in flight, had, in all likelihood, lain in the sequestered spot where they were found for more than fifteen hundred years.

The first elements of civilisation that reached our dusky forest domain came with the conquering eagles of Imperial Rome. The alphabet we teach our children was hers. And it was during her supremacy that the light of Christianity began to dispel the prevailing heathen darkness. We have seen an altar, found farther north, on the line of the Roman Wall,² from the Tyne to the Solway, inscribed thus—*Ad Veteres* (to the old ones). It is just possible that it was reared by persons adhering to the old Roman deities, as a protest against the growing influence of Christianity. Perhaps, also, it might have a dash of facetiousness, such as would be found in the modern Lancashire equivalent, "To th' owd uns." The Emperor Constantius Chlorus, who favoured the Christians, died in the imperial palace of York—Eboracum—in the year 306. The coins of his son, Constantine the Great, bore the Christian emblem of the cross. Constantine and his successors held Britain till the second decade of the fifth century. By that time the Goths of Alaric had been within the gates of Rome, and

---

[1] Gibbon's 'Decline and Fall of the Roman Empire.'
[2] Hadrian's Wall.

the Roman legions in Britain were recalled in 411 to protect the centre of what had become a tottering empire.

After the departure of the imperial forces, the civilisation wrought through three centuries and a half was practically obliterated by the Anglo-Saxon conquest. Angles, Saxons, Jutes, Frisians, and others, like successive waves, moved westward over the land, and Roman Britain bowed

"to swift decay,
As ocean sweeps the labour'd mole away."

Her cities, palaces, laws, industries, customs—civil, social, and domestic alike—seem to have crumbled to pieces under the force and fury of successive onslaughts. The conquering warrior-husbandmen preferred a "stead" or "wick," a "ham" or "ton" or "worth" on the open plain or slope, to elegant Roman villas or fortified Roman towns, and they evidently would have none of them. But the elements of civilisation, literature, and art, which thus vanished before the invader, after the withdrawal of the protecting sword of Rome, returned, two centuries later, with her messengers of the *Cross*. It was, however, to a different people. Her military and civil dominion, so far as it extended in the island, had been over the Britons; her ecclesiastical was organised among the English. Where her legions left the Celt, Augustine found the Saxon. The southern Celt, after long-continued and heroic defence, retreated to Cornwall and Wales; the northern still remained supreme beyond the Forth and the Clyde.

After the English conquest, the Frisian element appears to have been strong in south Lancashire; and this explains much in the local dialect, especially the peculiar use of the *o* for the *a* sound, as in *mon, con, lond, stond, sond, cromp, domp, gron*'feyther, *gron*'mother, &c.; while it is also literally true that

"'Good butter' and 'good cheese'
Are good English and good Friese."

Dr Whitaker says that South Lancashire "may be considered the Friesland of Britain." It may be accounted for in this way. A Frisian cohort[1] seems to have been stationed at Manchester, as part of the Roman auxiliary force, for probably about three centuries. This body of nearly six hundred men would, according to the Roman military custom, be recruited from its native shores during that long period; and, by the fifth century, the families and descendants of this cohort must have formed an important part of the whole community. It is not likely that Rome would withdraw these Teutonic auxiliaries with her own native legions, and, doubtless, they would fraternise with their invading kinsmen from Schleswig, Jutland, and their native Friesland. Before these the Britons, to a great

---

[1] Dr Whitaker, in his 'History of Manchester' (vol. i. p. 63), has preserved the inscription of an interesting Frisian relic of the Roman occupation, dug up in Castle Field, in the seventeenth century. It runs thus:—

COHO. I. FRISIN
⊃ MASAVONI S
P   XXIII.

That is—

COHORS PRIMA FRISINORUM
CENTURIONI MARCO SAVONI
SEPULCHRUM POSUIT
[VIXIT ANNOS] XXIII,

—and may be translated thus: "The first Frisian Cohort erected this monument to the Centurion Marcus Savo [who lived] twenty-three [years]." Unlike ourselves, the Romans on their monuments did not state when a man *died*, but *how long he lived*.

extent, disappeared. But many of them, no doubt, remained, mingled with the general population. This, in itself, was probable; and the Celtic element in the vernacular speech, and in the names borne by the more prominent natural features of this district, affords confirmation. Of *hills*, "Cribden," "Tor," "Combe," in Holcombe; "Pike," in Pikelaw and Whittle Pike; and the name of the river Irwell, are British. Some of these, it is interesting to notice—such as Holcombe, Whittle Pike, and Pikelaw—unite the Celtic with the Saxon. But in the case of other hills, as "Bull Hill," "Th' Hoof," "Fo' Edge," and "Knoll Hill," and on the plains and upland slopes, as well as in the vales and dens and cloughs, the Teutonic holds unquestioned sway—Buckden, Dearden. Buckhurst, Hart Lees, Hawkshaw, Stubbins, Shuttleworth. Ox Hey, Sheep Hey, Deeply Vale, Tottington, Ramsbottom, Helmshore, &c. In the vernacular, to *punse* and to *purr*, as well as their more widely known synonym, to *kick*; *boggart*, a spectre or ghost; *cob*, to strike, fling, excel, as— "He cob'd me on th' head," "He cob'd a stone at me," or, "That cobs o';" *cut* and *cuts*, as "to draw cuts"—a lot; *addle*, to earn, as well as *addle*, to rot; *cleaw*, a watergate; *goyt*, a water-channel, or drain; and many others in common use, are Celtic, and have come down to us from the Britons. In adverse circumstances—and with such the brave Britons were familiar—a man, at the present time, says, "Everything goes *colleywest* with me." "Colleywest" is Celtic, from *coll*, loss, destruction, and *gwestwng*, to go down.[1] *Gam*, crooked or infirm,—"Awm

---

[1] 'Philolog. Soc. Trans.,' 1885.

just nursing this *gam* leg o' mine,"—is also Celtic; so is *file*, one who is astute and cunning—"He's an old *file;*" and so also is *awse* or *oss*, to offer or attempt, as in Waugh's familiar couplet—

> "A man that plays a fiddle weel,
> Should never *awse* to dee."

The only word in the vernacular with a *Roman* element in it which occurs to us as worthy of remark is "*circumsnivvie*." It was, as we heard it, used to describe a cold blustering wind, that seemed to assail the speaker from all the four points of the compass at once—"It's quite a *circumsnivvie* wynd."[1] "*Applecumplex*," for "apoplectic stroke"—"He wur took off sudden wi' an *applecumplex*"—is also worthy of note; and "*connywest*" for in a slightly westerly direction.

The Anglo-Saxons found fertile fields and rich and attractive domains, yet the country, for the most part, was uncultivated. They were confronted by vast forests and scrub, bog and moorland. By hard toil these soldier-husbandmen cleared their way, reared houses of the felled timber, and formed their homes and townships. "The cluster of such farmers' houses, each set in its own little croft," formed "the unit of social life," and "made up the township or the tun," which was "surrounded by an earthen mound tipped with a stockade or quickset hedge, as well as defended externally by a ditch."[2] The common law, among them, was coextensive in its range with the

---

[1] See an example of this phrase at p. 45, *infra*.
[2] Green, 'Making of England,' p. 180.

area of land under cultivation. Beyond that, over marsh, moorland, and woodland, the king was absolute — "The common law ran only where the plough ran."[1] As, through successive generations and centuries, the woodman's axe and the farmer's plough advanced, and busy homesteads and townships multiplied, the area under the absolute sway of the sovereign retreated. Hence, eventually, the forest laws. Forest rights were exercised by the Saxon kings, and the Danish Canute is said to have published a forest charter — *constitutiones de foresta* — in 1016.[2] But it was not till after the Norman Conquest (1066) that the laws became cruel and oppressive. Then Saxon and Dane alike writhed under the iron grip of the haughty and relentless Norman. The king assumed the ownership of all the game in the realm, and no one was allowed to hunt even on his own property. For killing a deer, the penalty was death; for taking a boar, the eyes of the offender were torn out; for hunting a fox, a human limb was lopped off; and for taking even a hare, a fine was inflicted tantamount to ruin. For two centuries, with lessening rigour, these laws continued. They were abolished and a more clement code inaugurated by Henry III. and Edward I.[3] (1272-1307). Fine, imprisonment, or exile was

---

[1] Green, 'History of English People,' p. 63.
[2] Lord Coke questioned the authenticity of this document—Inst. iv. 320.
[3] Referring to the *forest law*, Blackstone, in his Commentaries (pub. 1765-1769), says: "From this root has sprung a bastard slip, known by the name of the game laws, now arrived to and wantoning in its highest vigour, both founded upon the same unreasonable notions of permanent property in wild creatures, and both productive of the same tyranny to the commons, but with this difference, that the forest laws established only one mighty hunter throughout the land, while the game laws have raised a little Nimrod in every manor."—Vol. iv.

severity enough, but henceforth "no one was to lose life or limb for killing deer."

In regard to Holcombe, Roger de Montbegon, who, we are told, was "mesne lord under the Lacies,"[1] and died in 1225, gave to the Monk Bretton Monastery in Yorkshire—

"The whole forest of Holcombe, and the pasture within the bounds underwritten, namely — As far as the forest extends in length and breadth towards Querendon, and ascending by the bounds of the forest up to Langschahehevet [Langshawhead], and thence across as the path divides into Holcomhehevet [Hol. head] across to Arkilleshow up to Pilgrimscrosschahe [Pilgrims-cross-shaw], and thence descending to the road which leads through the middle of Tittleshow, following the said road up to Caldwell, following Caldwell sike to the water of Yrewell, and thence descending to Titleshoubroc [Titles-howe-brook], and descending by Titleshoubroc to the way which leads through the middle of Titleshow, and thence towards the west, following the lane called 'the Lane of Robbers' as far as Salterbrigge, and from Salterbrigge to the road of Oskellie."

A century later, we get a glimpse of what was going on.

"In 7 Edward II. the Earl of Lancaster[2] makes complaint—'That several malefactors and disturbers of the peace, by force and arms, have entered his free chases[3] in Penhull, Trouden, Acrington, Rossendale, Hoddesden, Romesgrene, and Todinton, in the county of Lancaster, and his free chases of Boweland and Marchedan, &c., without his leave; and chased, taken and carried away his wild animals, besides perpetrating other great enormities therein.'"[4]

---

[1] Baines, 'History of Lancaster,' vol. i., p. 524.
[2] While the privilege of forest belonged to the monarch alone, it might be granted by him in favour of a subject.
[3] A chase was a smaller forest in the hands of a subject.
[4] Newbigging, 'History of Forest of Rossendale,' p. 60.

At the dissolution of the monasteries, Holcombe was granted by letters patent, under seal of Henry VIII., to John Braddyll of Whalley, Gent.[1]

The disforesting, in the Irwell region, appears to have taken place in the sixteenth century, in the time of Henry VII. and Henry VIII.

> "The said kings gave in commandment, and caused not only that the said deer should be killed and destroyed, but also that the ground within the said forrest should be letten out to such of the inhabitants as wod take the same, and had made thereof to the intent the same forrest might, for the great increase of God's glory and the commonwealth of this realme, be inhabited. . . . So that where before that time was nothing else but deer and other savage and wild beasts, there is since then, by the industry and labour of the inhabitants, grown to be a very good and fertile ground, . . . become very populous, and replenished with a great number of people."[2]

As in Rossendale, so also in the adjacent forests, the old order was changed. The words of Tennyson, descriptive of a much earlier period—

> "And so there grew great tracts of wilderness,
> Wherein the beast was ever more and more,
> But man was less and less,"[3]

might now once more be reversed. The *man*, henceforth, "was ever more and more." And as time went on, pastoral and agricultural pursuits went hand in hand with spinning and weaving, in increasing homesteads and hamlets, and thus was laid the foundation of the great textile industry

---

[1] Baines.
[2] Decree of the Chancellor of the Duchy of Lancaster, 4 Edward VI., in Newbigging's History, pp. 113, 114.
[3] "The Coming of Arthur."

which, now for more than a century, has distinguished the locality.

In the 17th century we find another royal bestowal of the territory. In the time of Charles II., Holcombe forest formed part of the reward bestowed on General Monk—Duke of Albemarle—for the part he had played in restoring the Stuart dynasty to the British throne. In 1664, Albemarle built a courthouse at Holcombe, which was also "sometimes used to teach a school in."[1] This courthouse was demolished in 1864, and, since that time, the Halmot Court has sat in Ramsbottom.

By the marriage, in 1767, of Henry, the third Duke[2] of Buccleuch, to Lady Elizabeth Montagu, only daughter of the Earl of Cardigan, the Albemarle possessions, and amongst them Holcombe Forest, passed to the Buccleuch family. On the death of the fifth Duke, in 1884, the Honor of Clitheroe, of which Holcombe, in the manor of Tottington, forms a part, went to his second son, Lord Henry Scott. He has since been created Baron Montagu of Beaulieu, the beautiful demesne in the New Forest, Hants, where he resides, thus reviving the old name and title held by the family of his great-grandmother, the duchess above-named.

---

[1] Notitia Cestriensis.
[2] This Duke was called by Sir Walter Scott "the good Duke." He was one of the best administrators of large estates of his time. In youth he had as his travelling companion for three years (1763-1766) Dr Adam Smith, who at the time was collecting materials for his great work, 'The Wealth of Nations.' Dr Smith resigned his chair in Glasgow University to accompany the young Buccleuch. A lifelong friendship resulted. The Duke settled on him £300 a-year, and this no doubt helped him to accomplish his *magnum opus*, to which modern commerce owes so much.—'Upper Teviotdale and the Scotts of Buccleuch,' by J. Rutherford Oliver.

CHAPTER IV.

NUTTALL VILLAGE.

A FEW hundred yards down the valley from Ramsbottom, and at the lower extremity of the "S" which the sinuous course of the Irwell forms in crossing the holm below Nuttall Hall, stands the old village of Nuttall. On the higher ground overlooking it, on the west, is the old home of the De Notoghs,[1] and about 450 yards up the eastern side of the holm—the river spanned by a bridge intervening—is the modern Nuttall Hall. The village is close to the point where, in the far remote past, the river

---

[1] There are said to be many descendants of De Notogh living—some in Ireland, others in America. One of the latter—Dr Geo. H. F. Nuttall—visited Nuttall about 1886. "When at Kingstown, in Ireland, his luggage was found to contain several revolvers, and other weapons. He was arrested under the Irish Crimes Act, and taken before the local magistracy. Mr Nuttall stated his position, and showed that his purpose in visiting Europe was to collect materials for a history and genealogy of the Nuttalls of Nuttall Hall, Lancashire. He was closely questioned by the presiding magistrate, and after the two had had a conversation, which caused uncommon interest in court, the magistrate and prisoner shook hands warmly, and afterwards left the court together. Prisoner and the magistrate were cousins, both descendants of De Notogh, and both named Nuttall."—T. H. Hayhurst in 'East Lancashire Review, October 1890.

has gradually ploughed its way through the superincumbent deposits, right down to its present rocky bed, and thus drained the holm and the ground on which the lower part of Ramsbottom is built. Before the ridge between Nuttall

CRIMBLE WOOD.

and Brooksbottom was thus penetrated, a lake must have extended from Crimble Wood, just below the village, well up the Ramsbottom valley.

In the time of Richard II. (1377-1399) Richard de Notogh is said to have resided in the old hall. It remained in the hands of the De Notoghs, or Nuttalls, as they came to be called, till 1698. Afterwards it passed, by marriage, to Mr Miles Lonsdale of Fieldhouse, and, subsequently, to the Rev. Richard Formby of Formby, by his marriage, about 1790, to Ann, only daughter of Mr Henry Lonsdale. From Mr Formby the estate was purchased by Messrs William Grant & Brothers. Inside Nuttall farmhouse, on the site of the old hall, may be seen portions of the original oak panelling; and over the front entrance, on a stone with armorial bearings, there is the date MCCCCXXIX.[1] The high baronial tower over the gateway to the spacious farmyard — said to be a restoration of part of the original structure — was built by the late Mr John Grant.

In 1812, Messrs Grant purchased the factory which at that time existed at Nuttall. Referring to the event, Mr William Grant wrote, in 1839—

"In consequence of the death of Mr Alsop, the workpeople had been long short of employment, and were very destitute. We ordered the manager to get new machinery of the first-rate construction, and greatly extended the building; and before we began to spin or manufacture, we clothed the whole of the hands at our own expense, prepared an entertainment for them, and observed that the interests of masters and servants are bound up together; that there are reciprocal duties to perform; that no general or admiral could be brave unless he was supported by his men; that we knew how to reward merit, and would give constant employment and liberal wages to all our faithful servants—and I am happy to say that they, as well as those at our printing establishment,

---

[1] May have been copied from the original.

with very few exceptions, have conducted themselves with great propriety."[1]

The *village of Nuttall* has memories of its own, to which "owd Nutta-ites" cling with great affection and tenacity. For fifty years or more after it came into the hands of the Grants, it was a busy, thriving, populous village, long tended in all its interests, with a kind of paternal care, by Mr John Grant of Nuttall Hall. Mrs Grant, kindly and generous-hearted as her husband, likewise, for much of that time, took a genuine interest in its people.[2] We have often heard old residenters, who knew it in its palmy days, expatiate with enthusiasm on its charms. To such there was no place, in days of yore, to be compared with Nuttall. By the following snatches from their homely and often picturesque utterances made from time to time in conversation with us, we shall allow them to speak of the old village for themselves.

---

[1] The mill at Nuttall, bought by Messrs Grant in 1812, was, we believe, run for a time by Mr Robert Wild of Nuttall, who came from Rochdale in the latter part of last century. He married a daughter of Mr Barcroft of Nuttall Hall farm, where he afterwards resided. He was the father of John and Thomas Wild, who were long well known in the district, and grandfather of Dr Thomas Wild and the late Mr Edward Wild; and the great-grandfather, on the mother's side, of Mr John and Mr William Wild, and Mr James Wild, solicitor, Ramsbottom, and Mr Tom Markland, solicitor, Manchester; and also the great-grandfather, on the father's side, of Dr Robert Wild of Manchester. The parents of Mr James Wild united the Wilds of Nuttall with the Wilds of Shuttleworth; and his great-grandfather, on the father's side, ran the carding mill, which—long since transformed into dwelling-houses—is known as "The Old Engine."

[2] A trusted almoner of Mrs Grant's was Thomas Whittle. Here is a copy of one of the tickets he freely dispensed in Nuttall, and elsewhere: "Sir, please to let the bearer have to the value of 4s. in what is desired.—THOS. WHITTLE."

"Fro' Nutta' farm, o' t' way threaw t' village to Nutta' Ho',[1] aw durnt think as yo' could a' feawnd a loase stone on t' road t' size ov a pidgen's *egg*; an' it wur beautiful, fair beautiful o' reawnd abeawt i' them days."

We remarked that the country about Nuttall was beautiful still.

OLD NUTTALL HALL FARM.

"Yeigh! gradely, happen gradely as it wur, but yo see aw've no sich seets *neaw*; an' lyin' here i' th' nook, neet an' day, wi' *th' leet gwon fro' th' een*,[2] aw see th' *owd* [old] picturs an' th' owd *foak*, wi' o' th' owd pranks an'

---

[1] Nuttall Hall.
[2] Light gone from the eyes—blind.

camplin din o' th' younger end, fain to be wick¹—it's o' clear an' breet to me neaw, an' awm fain it's so. . . .

"An' yo're reet, misther, yo're reet—t' darkest cleawd has leet aboon. We han to wait—to wait, an' t' cleawds get sliftered² a bit, an' then t' leet cooms threaw. . . .

"Misther John wur a good maister—*a better wur never laid low*. He mut 'ave o' things clen an' nice, yo' know'n. He gaen o' th' women what we co'd a *shoulder-bishop*³ apiece every year, an' we had to get another ersels. We co'ed him *Jacky* sometimes, but that wur becose we liked him. He wurn't a fratchin' an' frownin' man. We could go whoam to pap t' chylt, or put t' dough i' th' oon,⁴ an' nought wur said. They knowed we wouldn't wrang 'em. . . .

"At *first* t' women weyved i' one room, an' t' men in another, i' t' cellar. . . . They [the Grants] wur kind to th' foak abeawt 'em. They help'd th' owd crayters, an' wur good to th' young uns, in many mak' o' ways—wi' schoo's an' sich like. . . .

"Misther John gaen Jane Storey a sovereign one neet, for singin' t' Prodigal Son⁵ to 'im in her feyther's heawse. Jane wur a gradely singer. Hoo said, 'Eh! muther, it's a suvreign he's gaen me. Aw can do noughts wi' 't—*tha* tek it!' Hoo *did, fain,* an' Jane ne'er saw it *agen*. Hoo wur a gradely lass. . . .

"Yo' ne'r saw Nutta in it *pomp*. It wur a lively place, wi' plenty o' wark, tha knows; but we wur o' kind wi' one another, and al'ays helpful and neighbourly. When ought wur t' matter, we *did* t' one for t' other, an' *look'd for nought*. It's noan so neaw. An' there wur al'ays summat stirrin'—Quwortin's, marryin's, and sometimes buryin's; and oft' births and christnin's wur amung it as weel. But, bless yo! things were different i' them days fro' neaw. There wur no grond *coaches* then. Foak ne'er thowt ov ought but *walkin'* to t' church *to get wed*. Wet or dry, snow and frost, or circumsnivvie⁶ wynd and sturm,

---

¹ Living—quick. ² Slit, rent, opened.
³ A large apron, with bib and shoulder-straps. ⁴ Oven.
⁵ "I will arise," &c.
⁶ A blustering wind that seems to assail one from "a' the airts the wind can blaw" at one and the same time. We never heard the word used but by one person, and that was a "Nutta-ite."

they cared nought—off they set up Golinder Broo' to t' Bury Church, and got wed, and coom whoam again. Th' bride and bridegroom met to have a sup tay wi' a tothree friends, at *her* feyther's heawse, and then they set off quietly to th' neest. . . . An' t' *buryin's* wur different. Say it wur at Howcum. On t' way back, t' foak broke off to their own heawses, at Tanners, or Nutta Lone, or Ramsbottom, or Shepsters Row, or th' owd Bridge, as t' case met be; an' o' but t' mourners had left before *they* got whoam. There wur no feastin's an' grond carriages at funerals i' them days—noan o' them *lubrigubry*[1] *felleys*, wi' lung-tayl'd black 'osses, an' hearses, welly as big as Grant's church, wi' a rook[2] ov 'alf-naekt black crayters stuck abeawt 'em. Eh! *dear*-a-me! whatever dun they want wi' sich mak' o' wark in *laying-by* deycent Christian foak i' th' greawnd? It's noan needed; an' dun yo' think it's o' gradely reet? Aw dunnot; for, neaw, many a poor crayter gets *into debt*, becose hoo mut do like other foak. Th' owd way wur t' best. There wur no expense, but what *mut* be, tha knows. . . .

"Yeigh! when a man dee'd, he wur shaved[3] afore he wur laid i' t' coffin. That wur al'ays done. . . . For *t' christ'nin's* we al'ays took t' childer to t' church; but if t' babby wur *ill*, tha knows, t' parson, like yo'rsel', would come to th' heawse."

"Who taught the little ones?"

"Mrs Hamer—Kitty as we co'd her. Hoo wur a fine, stout, bonny woman. Hoo"—pointing to her daughter—" wur one o' Kitty's scholars."

"What did she teach you?"

"Reading and knitting and reetways. Hoo wur al'ays knit-knit-knitting i' schoo', and just look'd or lifted her finger, and there wur silence. But there wur a dark place at t' back o' th' room to put any one in as wur *naught*."

---

[1] Lugubrious. [2] A lot, or crowd.
[3] This custom still prevails. A devoted Christian layman of our acquaintance was sent for one day, to pray with a dying man. He went as soon as he could leave his post, but was too late. The poor widow, stricken with the sorrow of a great bereavement, met him with these words—"Eh! yo'r to' lat', but—con yo' *shave* him?" This, in all her grief, she regarded as a sacred duty owed to the departed. The friend, however, who was too late to pray could not undertake the alternative function.

"What did you pay?"

"Twopence a week. It wur worth more than that," said the octogenarian mother, "to have 'em eawt o' th' road, an' they wur aluz safe wi' Kitty."

"How was the school opened and closed?"

"In t' morning we had—

> 'Now the morning's cheerful light
> Drives away the gloom of night;'

and in th' evening—

> 'And now another day has gone,
> I'll sing my Maker's praise;
> My comforts every hour make known
> His providence and grace.'

Then we said t' Lord's Prayer, and t' schoo' loased. We o' liked Mrs Hamer. Hoo wur a good woman, and John, her husband, wur a good man.[1] . . .

"Aw remember Dr Brown vera weel. He axed me to go to th' neet schoo' at Dundee. But aw towd him as aw wur freetint o' the Crowlum boggart. He told me a story abeawt a boggart where he had been. It terribly freetint o' the foak, but it turned eawt nobbut an owd lime-gell wi' th' panniers on, as squeezed into th' churchyard at neet for sake o' th' grass and shelter. T' Crowlum un freetint us o', but aw ne'er saw it. They took away th' high hedge and hollins, and after that t' boggart wur ne'er heard of. That simple job laid th' Crowlum boggart.

"Accidents? Weyn had a tothree sad uns i' t' owd place. When they wur layin' t' new engine-bed t' floorin' coom crashin' reet deawn fro' t' third storey into th' 'ole i' t' cellar. A lad and lass, brother and sister, about thirteen or fourteen, went wi' 't. Maisther Suter[2] worked like a slave that day to get t' childer out, but it wur to' lat'—to' lat'. Suter wur killed hissel' afterwards at Brox Bridge. He'd coom eawt o' th' train at Summerseat Station to walk up t' line, an' th' express caught him on t' bridge. Yeigh! An' when t' mill fire wur agait, in 1873, a gradely strong young felly,[3] as hadn't been lung married, wur

---

[1] Mrs Hamer's husband was an elder, and her son, John, was a youthful disciple of Dr Brown's at Dundee Chapel. He became a city missionary, and afterwards minister of an Independent chapel. Died, in his 80th year, June 20, 1889, and interred at St Andrew's Church.

[2] Book-keeper for the Grants.   [3] Robert Dawes.

killed. He took th' 'ose pipe threaw one o' th' upper windows, an' when he coom back, either th' ladder had been skifted or he slipped. He jerked hissel' reawnd, but he coom deawn reet on t' railing spikes yon.—Och! They carried him in, brave lad, and laid him on t' table

RUINS IN NUTTALL.

theer, an' when t' doctor opened his cloas o'er t' breast, t' blood spurted eawt i' two streams agen t' window. But he never moved. T' doctor said he wur dead. It wur Dr Smith. He wur a clever un. Aw look'd mysel', quietly, after t' doctor left, and there wur just two red spots, near th' heart, where t' spikes had gone.

"Marlocks?[1] Yeigh! there wur marlocks. One neet, Tom W—— teed a sheep-horn to Kitty Hamer cat tail. Kitty window wur *low*, an' poo'd deawn; and t' cat, fair mad, tha knows, went in, like leetnin', at t' top, an th' horn fet t' window a raddlin' slap, an' brast in t' panes. Then there wur ructions. The young monkeys abeawt wur hutchin[2] fain, but Kitty suspected *Tom*, an' went reet away an' towd his mother. But Tom wur *before* her. *Jane* feawnd him *i' bed*. It *couldn't* be *Tom!* Nawe! but Tom[3] o' th' time wur *wackerin' i' th' neest!*[4] An' Nellie Dover roasted t' cat i' th' 'oon.[5] But that wur no marlock. It happen wur a *mistake*. O' maks o' gabble went on, but Nutta foak wur o' meterly thick[6] for o', tha knows. Yeigh! An' they seyn as how Jim B—— wur freetint at th' spirits o' t' dead sheep. We *lowft*. Jim *hissel* would lowf, fro' t' yure o' t' yed to t' toe nails, if he yerd an owd crayter a-tellin' as how he e'er wackered at the ghowsts o' t' gawmless[7] sheep! Jim wur al'ays a kind, good-natured lad, never no mak' o' ill in him—no lumber, no *mischief*, tha knows, but full ov o' maks o' mirth an' marlocks. Many a time he rock'd t' *keyther*[8] for me for half-an-hour ov an ev'nin' when eawr M—— wur a babby. Aw used to ax him to *sing* for me, an' he *did*. What did he sing? Th' hymns out o' yo'r owd Dundee book—Eh! ay, *bless* him! And Jim could *contrive* aboon a bit. He could rock his mother's keyther, an' tred treddles[9] i' t' bruk wi' th' other youngsters, at t' same time. How did he do that? He got bits ov bant[10] and teed them together, an' took th' end wi' him to t' bruk, and gev it a poo neaw, an' a poo then, to keep t' keyther *gooin'!* He's a *greyt mon*[11] neaw — noan so easily freetunt noather—but he's noan preawd, an' he doesn't forget th' owd Nutta *foak*. Jim would a' sliftered some o' t' cleawds o'er th' owd place, if he'd ta'en Nutta Factory an Nutta Ho'. If *he'd* coom, we'd 'appen have marlocks agen. Marlocks! Yeigh, but Nutta were preawd as

---

[1] Frolics, pranks. [2] Fidgety or restlessly delighted.
[3] "Tom" survives, after an honourable career as an active member of one of the learned professions. [4] Trembling in the nest—bed.
[5] Oven. [6] Clannish. [7] Witless, silly. [8] Cradle.
[9] To paddle on the smoother stones in the bed of the *brook* like a weaver working the treadles of his loom. [10] Band, string.
[11] The Mayor—twice-elected—of one of our great Lancashire towns.

weel as pratty, tha knows, an' could howd up it yed wi' o' its marlockin, i' them owd days. . . . Nobry e'er wanted to lev Nutta, but like someheaw, when theyn *gone*, they dunnot care, or as it's noan so yezzy[1] for 'em to coom *back* agen."

Thus Nuttall under the Grants was evidently a pleasant and desirable place. Its memories of those times, now many years ago, are interesting and refreshing still. But the appearance of the village is sadly changed. Two of its three factories were burnt down, and have not been rebuilt. The third remains; but, for many years, only a few of the dwelling-houses have been tenanted. Yet much of the charm of the old environment remains, in the steep wooded banks of the river, from which the fields sweep up on the eastern side to Top o' th' Hoof, and in the demesne of Nuttall Hall, which comes within about two hundred yards of the village gates.

---

[1] Easy

CHAPTER V.

HOLCOMBE VILLAGE.

THE pastoral village of Holcombe is perched about half way up between the valley of the Irwell and the Hey House Level on Holcombe Hill top, on which the Peel Monument stands. It occupies the *coom* [1] at the south-east end of the Holcombe range, overlooking Ramsbottom. At its northern end a bold height juts out towards the valley. On the crest of this eminence, prominent and picturesque, stands the parish church, which, from far and near, forms a graceful and conspicuous object in the landscape.

The old chapel of Holcombe existed in 1513, and probably was built at a much earlier date. In 1645 the tithes of Tottington were given by order of Parliament to the chapels of Edenfield and Holcombe.[1] In 1706 it is stated that Eatonfield or Edenfield and Holcombe were always, within living memory, served by the same curate; that both of them were consecrated in Queen Elizabeth's reign; that in the reign of Charles I. the Bishop compelled

---

[1] See Place Names, p. 21, *supra*.

each chapelry to allow £10 per annum to the minister whom they should choose, or he should send to officiate once a month in each chapel; but that now (1706) there were only contributions of about £8 per annum to both.[1]

Edenfield Church, here

[1] Notitia Cestriensis

HOLCOMBE CHURCH AND THE RAKE.

referred to, bears on its tower the date 1614. It stands well up the slope on the opposite side of the valley from Holcombe, to the north-east, and distant from it two miles. It is interesting to find that the minister's pathway from Holcombe to Edenfield, though unused for generations, is still traceable. High up the Rake,[1] opposite the north side of Holcombe Church, may be seen built up in the roadside wall the place of the steps whereby the minister descended from the old church to cross the road. His path thence ran along below where the Haslingden highway now exists, across the *Tip o' th' Top o' th' Taper*, down by Topwood Mill and Kibboth Crew, thence along Carr Bank Meadow, through Ox-hey Wood above Stubbins, past Stubbins[2] Vale and Strongstrye, crossing the Irwell at Alderbottom, and thence along the track up the slope, right to Edenfield Church.[3] The church "was styled *Parochial* in 1738." From "having the rights of baptism and sepulture, and also the privilege of imposing a church-rate," it has been "inferred that a chapel existed here previous to the reign of Queen Elizabeth, and that either a new church was built then, or the old one for the first time consecrated."

The distinguished Puritan clergyman, the Rev. Henry Pendlebury, entered upon the incumbency of the chapelry of *Holcombe* in 1651. He was ejected by the Act of Uniformity in 1662. It is the congregation which followed him outside the National Establishment at that time whose chequered story will be told in the Second Book of this volume. But, at this point, we may conveniently put on

---

[1] See p. 26, *supra*.   [2] Notitia.
[3] The present vicar is the Rev. J. P. Yeo, admitted 1870.

record *the successors of Mr Pendlebury in Holcombe Episcopal Church*, as far as ascertainable, down to the present time.[1] There is no name recorded between 1662 and 1733.

Rev.	John Boardman was admitted in			1733.
,,	John Lowe	,,	,,	1738.
,,	William Harrison	,,	,,	1757.
,,	Richard Thickstone	,,	,,	1760.
,,	John Smith	,,	,,	1764.
,,	William Holt	,,	,,	1810.
,,	George Nightingale[2]	,,	,,	1849.
,,	Henry Dowsett	,,	,,	1875.

The old chapel of Holcombe was pulled down in 1851,[3] and the present handsome structure, erected on the grand old site, was consecrated in 1853, during the incumbency of the late Mr Nightingale. Originally, Holcombe was a

---

[1] For these particulars the author is indebted to the kindness of the present rector—the Rev. Henry Dowsett.

[2] It was, we believe, Mr Nightingale who was instrumental in suppressing the cruel practice of cock-fighting, which long prevailed in the village, where it was countenanced in person by peers sometimes, as well as by commoners.

[3] In the old church stringed instruments were used, at one time, in the service of praise. Mr John B——, well remembered as John O'Matty's—loved his bass fiddle, and played it in the church on Sundays with all his heart. On a day of special importance at Holcombe, John laid down the fiddle-stick for a moment, after tuning up, and just before the grand piece of the service began. Jim W——, as forgetful of the time and place as he was full of youthful frolic, had prepared himself for the occasion. He lifted the bow and quietly drew a piece of fat bacon along the face of it, and put it in its place again. The music began, but the bass was not audible. John, thinking the vocalists too vigorous, with a somewhat suppressed shout said, "Sing smo', sing smo'!" It was retorted, "Thy owd timber's gloppent, mon!" John, with eyes staring with amazement, steaming dewdrops forming on his brow, and the bow-arm plunging away across the unmelodious strings, replied, "Is it, hectum as like—sing *smo,' brast yo', sing smo!*" John, worthy man, discovered too late where the mischief lay.

Perpetual Curacy, under the ancient Parish of Bury, in the Diocese of Chester. But, by an Instrument under the seal of the Ecclesiastical Commissioners, dated February 1, 1866, it was declared a Rectory, under the provisions of 28 and 29 Vict., c. 42. Commodious new premises for day and

HOLCOMBE OLD CHURCH.

Sunday schools were opened in 1866, in lieu of the grim old courthouse removed in 1864.

We may also glance at that peculiar institution which strikes its roots far into the past of Holcombe—the *Rushbearing* or *Wakes*. The modern festival called the Ramsbottom Wakes, now fading towards a blank, while the well-earned holiday it brings is filling up with wise facilities for rational change and reinvigorating enjoyment, is a degenerate descendant of the old festival, which for many generations performed its yearly function at the parent village farther up the hill.[1] The long history of the latter, in its own way, furnishes a verification of the words of Goethe,—

> "That what the moment can employ,
> What it requires and can enjoy,
> The moment for itself creates."

These festivals seem to have sprung up many centuries ago in the rural districts of England, in connection with the dedication of the churches. When a church was consecrated, it was dedicated to some saint. In this fact the parishioners, no doubt glad of something to break the tedium of their life of toil, found material in many cases for two annual festivals, or parish wakes—one on the anniversary of the dedication, the other on that of the birth of the saint to whom the church was dedicated. In this case the church was strewn with rushes and flowers, while the pulpit and other parts were, as they thought, fittingly adorned with boughs, leaves, &c. Our word "wake" comes from an old Saxon word *waecan* or *waican*, which means to *excite* or *rouse*, and also to *watch*. The religious service—the wake or watch —began, like the ecclesiastical day, in the evening, just as

---

[1] The change from Holcombe to Ramsbottom was not effected by any formal resolution on the part of the people. The owner of an establishment of swinging-boats, "Dobby"-horses, &c., declined one year to climb the hill. It was a stormy day, and he located himself near the Grant Arms. The change proved a financial success. Others followed his example, and ultimately the old village was supplanted.

we still regard Christmas *eve;* and the day following was a holiday.

In anticipation of the morrow, tents and stands were erected in the churchyard, furnished with the cakes and ale of the olden time. The parishioners generally appear to have been more enamoured of the material than the spiritual festival, and so, in course of time, it came about that wakes —with the crowd of people from surrounding districts, and busy hawkers and merchants selling their varied wares, &c. —became a kind of fair or market, utterly devoid of the religious element from which they originally sprang. Unfortunately, in time they became seasons of deplorable indulgence and unruliness. So much was this the case that, even as far back as the reign of Edward I. in 1285, a law was framed forbidding the holding of fairs and markets in country churchyards. This evidently did not prove permanently effectual; for, in 1448, Henry VI., while allowing necessary victuals, prohibited the showing of goods and merchandise in connection with the great festivals of the church. Nearly a century later, in Henry VIII.'s time, Convocation, in 1536, ordered that all the dedication festivals should be held at the same time—the first Sunday in October. After this, these festivals gradually ceased, but the saint's-day festivals were not affected by the Act of Convocation. Wakes have accordingly continued to the present time.

It is said that the Rushbearing proper, *in its more interesting and ornate form*, continued in the village of Holcombe to a later date than in any other parish in the country. At the time of which we now particularly write—about fifty years ago—three gentlemen, well known in the district, had the chief management of its affairs. These were Mr Joshua

Knowles of Tottington, Mr Thomas Gorton of Hey House, and Mr John Rostron of Woodside.[1]

As the last week of August came round, a number of young men cut the requisite quantity of rushes on Holcombe Hill. These were conveyed to the appointed place in the village, and carefully piled up in the cart provided for the purpose — the Rush-cart. The rectangular mass, firmly built to a considerable height, was skilfully sloped on the top, something like the roof of a house. In its centre, duly prepared for the purpose, was planted an apple tree, with the tempting fruit freely pendent from its spreading branches, and under these, in "skin-tights," sat a boy and a girl—the representatives for the occasion of Adam and Eve. The work was executed with great precision and neatness. On its sides were securely hung teapots, brass kettles, pewter jugs, and other things bright and showy, freely lent for the purpose; and sometimes a sheet was tightly stretched across the front to act as a foil for the better display of the glittering gear, decked with gay ribbons, offered for competition at the attendant sports. When, from far and near, eager and expectant hundreds had assembled, at the hour appointed the Rush-cart, with its equipment, proud and picturesque, was drawn forth from its place of concealment; and then, up over Holcombe Hill, the welkin rang with boisterous acclamations. After being duly inspected and admired, preparation was made for its annual tour round the neighbourhood. It was drawn not by horses but by young men somewhat fantastically dressed, "like pace-eggers," firmly

---

[1] Mr Rostron died in 1845, aged 67; Mr Knowles, in 1853, aged 59; and Mr Gorton, in 1867, aged 68.

yoked with ropes prepared specially for the task. They visited not only immediately adjacent places like Ramsbottom and Holcombe Brook, but sometimes also Bury, Shuttleworth, and Edenfield, performing from time to time by the way a rude kind of dance, while a collector solicited subscriptions from the inhabitants, by whom the rush-bearers were usually received with cordiality and good-humoured interest. And, as our informant expressed it, "It was downright hard work for those fellows who drew the cart." Of this, we apprehend, there can be no doubt. The tour having been completed, the gay adornment was carefully removed, and ultimately the rushes; but, at the time to which we have been referring, they were not strewed in the church, as had been the practice at an earlier period.

There appears to run through this old village custom a fantastic representation of Edenic innocence, with an unmistakable whisper of the Fall; while the introduction of the pace- or pasch-egging element supplies also a hint of the great Recovery. There was thus woven together, in a somewhat strange and uncongenial environment, an interesting symbolic reference to primeval innocence, and the ruin and redemption of mankind. Moreover, in the hearty and hilarious character of the whole proceedings of that day we may find a vigorous though distorted and unconscious echo of jubilation, originally born of the great and gladsome hope of Paradise restored.

The sports that were associated with the Rushbearing proper were of a varied character, embracing, in the race competitions, the efforts of horses, donkeys, men, and women. In the donkey races, no man rode his own, and the last was reckoned first. The prizes given to the female athletes were clogs and similar useful articles; and the good-humoured efforts of these rustic amazons—unlike the great Homeric hero, because they never sulked, yet like him in that they were πόδας ὠκύς, fleet of foot—contributed no less than the obstinate yet *provokingly versatile* donkeys to the general hilarity of the scene.

Another source of fun and merriment was *climbing the greasy pole*, for the leg of mutton temptingly poised on its summit. The youngsters who aspired to this prize usually took, in those days, not sand but *soot* in their pockets, which from time to time they expertly applied to prevent irretrievable lapse, as the girth of the glib and glabrous shaft diminished in their arduous ascent. Before all was over, so be-greased and begrimed had the young aspirants become that sometimes it required aural as well as ocular demonstration to enable the village mothers to distinguish their own!

But the most mirth-provoking of all the proceedings was the "*grinning match*." The prize, in the form of tobacco, was awarded to the competitor who made the most effective facial contortions and grimaces, through a horse-collar provided for the occasion. It was fixed, at a convenient height, on the rising ground in front of the *White Hart*, or Higher Inn, as it was then called. Old Ralph, or, as it was pronounced, *Raiph* Fish, was the official crier of the sports, announcing each event and its conditions, as it approached, with the "O yes! o yes! o yes!"[1] of almost forgotten days. Old Ralph, on one occasion

---

[1] The old Norman legal phrase, "Oyez, oyez, oyez—listen!"

deploring the degeneracy of a younger generation, declared, to the delight of the lieges, that he would enter the lists himself, and give them a lesson worthy of the good old times. He took his place accordingly behind the collar, and forthwith inserted such a picture in the frame as set the "gazing rustics" in a roar. Poor Ralph's outfit, unfortunately, was somewhat loose and fragmentary; and the younger mischiefs, moved perhaps by older minds, began to tug this way and that at the tempting corners of one part of the faded raiment after another—Ralph meanwhile immovable at the frame, or the prize was lost—until, by the time general and uproarious laughter and acclamation declared him victor, scarce, if at all, a rag remained. Then the old man, like a startled stag, sprung right for the White Hart[1] door through the crowd, which rocked and swayed, as helplessly vanquished by their boisterous merriment as Ralph's grinning opponents had been by his peerless performance in honour of the olden times! He was soon rigged out again by kindly hands, in a much more "gradely" suit than the vanished garments had ever formed for him; and, with a mirthful twinkle in his faded eyes, and an air of high importance, as the representative and vindicator of the vanished glories of the past, he stepped forth again, like a victorious general across the field of a recent victory, and, amid the general plaudits of the sympathetic crowd, with "O yes! o yes! o yes!" louder and more imperative than before.

---

[1] This house, whose amenity has been greatly improved in recent years, and its interior elaborately enriched with antique oak, &c., is now a private residence.

In recent years we have seen a simple reference to this brave "O yes!" so spring the fountains of early and unworded memories as to fill strong men's eyes with tears, while laughter mingled at the mention of long-unthought-of scenes. But "old times were changed, old manners gone."[1] All such ongoings at the fine old bracing village high up on the side of Holcombe Hill, like most of those who formed even the last of the laughing crowds, have long since disappeared—

"Gone like the bloom upon the heather"[2]—

and, as the Rushbearing time, year by year, comes round, it but discerns the nightly glare, and catches, as it passes on, the softened murmur of the crowds of another generation, away down in the now well-peopled valley beneath.[3]

Before leaving the peaceful village, with memories so fragrant of the hoary doings of the past, let us, for a moment, turn aside to where

"The rude forefathers of the hamlet sleep,"[4]

and with them many others linked by some tender tie sufficing to determine their last resting-place. It crowns

---

[1] 'Lay of the Last Minstrel.' [2] J. B. Selkirk—'Poems.'
[3] A few miles from Holcombe, and a good many years ago, one summer day, a young clergyman, recently come to the district, in the course of a country ramble lost his way. He made for a youth whom he saw in a field not far off, and asked him the way to Bolton. In broad and somewhat picturesque vernacular, he told him. The young parson then asked, "What do you do, my lad?" "What dun aw *dew?*" "Yes, what do you *do for a livelihood?*" "Oh! aw does oddin"—odd jobs about the farm. "An' what dun *yo'* dew, maisther, if aw may be as bowd as ax?" "Oh, I'm a clergyman." "Yeigh, but what dun yo' *dew?*" "I preach the gospel—teach people the way to heaven." "Nay, maisther, awm noan so gawmless [witless]. Yo' mu'tn't tell me as how yo' can teych t' way to '*eaven*, and doesn't know t' road to *Bowton!*"
[4] Gray's Elegy.

the bold eminence, near the base of which Dundee Chapel is situated. Within its area—on the site where stood the quaint structure from which Mr Pendlebury was ejected in 1662—a modern church, substantial and elegant, now stands, and shoots its massive and stately spire towards the sky. Looking reverently about, we simply note prevailing names of the peaceful sleepers, all around—Rothwell,

HOLCOMBE CHURCH AND CHURCHYARD.

Holt, Kenyon, Hargreaves, Elton, Nuttall, Haslam, Bates, Pilkington, Whitworth, Horrocks, Greenwood, Renshaw, Rostron, Olive, Rawstron, Holt-Browne, Hollis, Brierley, Woodcock, Wild, Hamer, Wolstenholme, Ramsbottom, Markland, Haworth, Diggle, Kay, Booth, Wood, Cronkshaw, Bridge, Pickup, Fielding, Entwistle, Birtwistle, Whittaker

Knowles, Whittle, Dewhurst, Yates, Livsey, Bastow, Tattersall, Warburton, Thorp, Dearden, Forshaw, Crawshaw, Brooks, Barcroft, Sutcliffe, Crompton,[1] Spencer, and many others, whose descendants are now busy actors in the regions round about, or scattered here and there throughout the land; while others, not a few, have borne tender memories of Holcombe, fadeless and bright, across the seas to many a distant shore.

Of the numerous sepulchral rhymed and unrhymed *inscriptions*, only one now legible takes us back to the incumbency of Mr Pendlebury within the Established Church. It is inscribed on a metal plate, inserted in the horizontal tombstone, and somewhat weathered. It is dated 1656, and, as far as decipherable, runs thus—

Hic Inhu
Matur Corpus
Thoma Ainsworth
Sculptura Arithmetica
Penna ac ARTIS
Rationaria Professoris
. . . .
. . .
. .

1656

---

[1] Mr William Crompton, whose relatives are buried here, went from Ramsbottom to the United States in 1839. He introduced the "Crompton loom" for producing fancy patterns in woollen fabrics into Lowell, Mass. Subsequently the loom was improved by his son, George, who was born at Nuttall Lane in 1828. The "Crompton Woollen Loom" is, we are told, well known, not only in America but also in France, Belgium, Germany, &c. It was awarded gold medals at the Paris Expositions of 1867, 1878, and 1889, and at the Philadelphia Centennial, 1876. William Crompton died in 1891. His son predeceased him in 1886.

As noteworthy, we also select the following:—

1734
(Aged 61)
"By his own merit the greatest of Sinners,
By God's grace the least of Penitents.
May he find mercy in that day.
Ne timeat mortem repentinam
Qui timet Peccatum deliberatum."

1750
(Aged 52)
"Here lies she who in this Life
Was a tender mother and a
Virtuous Wife.
Free from malice, envy &
Sedition.
Happy are those who die
In this condition."

The Pretender—"Bonnie Prince Charlie"—had passed through the county five years before, and evidently all wives were not considered quite free from "sedition" at that stirring and eventful period.

1762
(Aged 73)
"My Anvil and my Hammer lie declin'd,
My Bellows too have lost their wind,
My Fire is extinct, and my Forge decay'd,
And in the Dust my Vice is laid,
My Coal is spent, my Iron is gone,
My last Nail driven, and my Work is done."

1846
(An Octogenarian)
"He was an affectionate Husband
A tender Parent
A true Sportsman
And a sincere Friend."

Inside the church, and now unfortunately concealed from view, an old gravestone reads quaintly, thus—

" This world's a city full of crooked streets,
Death is the market-place where all men meets.
If life were merchandise that men could buy,
The rich would live and none but poor would die."

The church tower is furnished with a goodly gas-lit clock, which, day and night, looks benignly along the village. A marble tablet, placed by the parishioners inside the church, to an honoured native, is inscribed thus—

In
LOVING MEMORY OF
WILLIAM BATES, M.D.,
Of MANCHESTER,
Whose body lies in the family vault
in the adjoining churchyard.
THE CLOCK
was placed in the Tower of
this Church, by His
WIDOW AND CHILDREN,
As a tribute of respect to His
Noble character and most useful life.
This tablet is inscribed on behalf of
The parishioners of Holcombe, in
thankful appreciation of the gift.
Henry Dowsett, Rector.
J. Meadowcroft and J. Renshaw, Wardens.
G. Thorpe and R. Bramley, Sidesmen.
Decr. 1877.

The clock forms a meet memorial; and, in its practical utility, is worthy of the widowed lady—*née* Hill—a niece of Sir Rowland Hill, who—as his statue in the heart of London records, and all the world knows—"Founded

Uniform Penny Postage, 1840." On the south side of the church, the eye catches a simple memorial window, chaste and beautiful, to Amy Beatrice Renshaw, aged 11 years.

A massive tombstone simply tells, that

> " William Plant Woodcock
> Surgeon
> Died April 26th 1884
> Aged 88 years."

Kind-hearted, genial, racily reminiscent, and devoted to his profession, his name, still familiar as a household word, is gratefully remembered in many a humble home. But perhaps the most illustrious native of the ancient chapelry was one of humble parentage, and whose name is seldom or never heard in the locality, but who became a distinguished Master of St John's College, Cambridge, and Dean of Ely—the Very Rev. James Wood, D.D. Happily a mural tablet inside the church records his name and fame (1760-1839). But another grave we must note. It is within the chapelry, although beyond

DR WOODCOCK.

the churchyard. About two miles west of Holcombe village, where, to the south of Black Moss, Stanley Rake slopes down towards the plain, is the farm of Holcombe Hey Fold. Here, about two centuries ago, in a house still pointed out, a lone preacher ministered for many years. A little farther west, in the corner of a meadow, near to Grainings old farm-house, there is, unfenced, a flat tombstone, now a good deal shattered, on which may still be read—

> " Here lies the body of
> ROGER WORTHINGTON
> who departed this life
> the 9th day of July 1709
> About the 50th year of his age.
> They that serve Christ
> In faith and love
> Shall ever reign
> With Him above."

Worthington, it is said, belonged to a family from which he suffered ostracism on account of his faith; and, in this remote retreat, in Holcombe Forest, he found ample scope for solitude, and among the scattered upland homesteads, a sphere for Christian service. A solitary sycamore grows a few yards from his grave. The track of pilgrim-feet tells that the sequestered spot is not unvisited. In sight of it, one summer day, a pilgrimage of a rather unusual kind was recited to us thus: "An owd weaver chap[1] at Howcum, when chopping sticks one day, cut off half of his fore-finger. He wrapped it up, took it to Worthington's grave, broke off a bit o' th' gravestone, and buried it under

---

[1] For more than the first half of the century there were many hand-loom weavers in Holcombe and the country round about.

it. He wur sexton and undertaker and parson o' ov a rook,[1] to a bit o' hissel! But he wanted it to be near Worthington."

We lingered one winter evening at Holcombe on the picturesque and grave-crowned crest, surrounded by the voiceless yet somehow strangely companionable village sleepers, till the deepening shadows blotted out the silent records from the stones, and frayed away the lingering line on the ancient dial-plate, still daily telling time among the silent denizens for whom time is no more. Then countless lights came out up and down the valley, and kindled along the sides of the opposite hills, like stars in the meadows beneath, instead of those, all cloud-eclipsed, in

"The infinite meadows of heaven."[2]

And the cold and gusty wind, while driving a sombre cavalcade of clouds along above the hill, like a great funereal train of the departed day, moaned round the buttressed tower of the church, and whisked and sighed with plaintive eeriness among the silent stones and lone leafless trees, as if in quest of some loved one who had fled like the vanished day, and gone to the realm of silence among the sleeping forms beneath. But, as we stood by the triple step of the darkened sun-dial, a glowing planet shone through the rifted clouds, and stars from the depths beyond; the church clock told out its tale of fleeting time, and its illumined face beamed along the upland village, as we left the impressive spot, thinking how strangely linked are the *now* and the *then*, the *here* and the *yonder*—the lowly graves of time and the glories of eternity.

---

[1] All of a heap.   [2] Longfellow.

CHAPTER VI.

CHEERYBLE BROTHERS.

WHEN William Grant, the elder of the future Cheerybles, then a lad of fourteen, and his father, also William, at the age of fifty, looked down for the first time from *Top o' th' Hoof*, where Grant's Tower now stands, to the fair middle valley of the Irwell, Messrs Peel & Yates were just beginning to build their print-works on the opposite side of the valley at Ramsbottom. It was in the year 1783. The Grants had come from a beautiful strath in the North—Strathspey, where, however, through bad harvests, desolating storms, and other causes, disaster had befallen their farming and cattle-dealing operations; and, moved by a laudable desire for the future wellbeing of a numerous family, they were now in quest of some other occupation.

Writing fifty-six years afterwards, William says: "As we passed along the old road, we stopped for a short time on the Park estate to view the valley. My father exclaimed, 'What a beautiful valley! May God Almighty bless it! It reminds me of Speyside, but the Irwell is not so large as the river Spey.'" He also wrote in the same letter—"In 1827 we purchased the Park estate, and erected a monument to commemorate my father's first visit to this valley, and *on the very spot* where he and I stood admiring the beautiful scenery below."

Ramsbottom, when thus surveyed for the first time by the Grants, was little more than a place of farms and fields and orchards, rooks and trees, an ancient tannery and an old corn mill, with numerous streams of water flowing from unfailing springs far up the mountain sides. The clear-visioned Peel & Yates were quick to detect the economic value of these pure rills, which ever since have contributed much to the industrial growth of the community, as on their continued generous flow its present and future prosperity in no small measure depends.

The Grants had a letter of introduction to Mr, afterwards Sir, Richard Arkwright, in Manchester. But he had so many applications on hand at the time that he could not engage them. They then went to the Calico Printing and Manufacturing Works of Mr Dinwiddie at Hampson Mill, near Bury. This gentleman had known the father in his earlier and more prosperous days. Mr Dinwiddie found them employment at his works. The other members of the family soon afterwards joined them. There James,[1] William, John, and Daniel served their apprenticeship; and William[2] tells us that some time after his was completed, Mr Dinwiddie offered him a partnership, which, however, he declined. Subsequently, with their father, they removed to Bury. There they commenced business on a small scale. But their united efforts

---

[1] James afterwards commenced business near Glasgow.
[2] See his letter, pp. 94-96, *infra*.

proved very successful; and, about 1800, William, John, and Daniel began calico printing in partnership, in Manchester. Their industry, promptitude, and integrity had been recognised at Bury by Sir Robert Peel, who, by affording business facilities, proved helpful to them in their steady upward endeavours.

Sir Robert found that these men, while cheerful, energetic, generous, and good-natured, could always be relied on. *That* made him their friend. And, at length, after twenty-three years of hard and honest toil, and enterprising and united industry, at Hampson Mill, at Bury, and at Manchester, William, John, Daniel, and their youngest brother, Charles— as Messrs William Grant & Brothers—purchased the print-works of Sir Robert Peel[1] at Ramsbottom in 1806.

On coming to Ramsbottom, the Grants lived in the house which had been previously occupied by Mr Henry Warren, one of the partners of Sir Robert Peel. It was originally known as *Top o' th' Brow*, but afterwards as *Grant Lodge*, and now forms the back portion of the Grant Arms Hotel.[2]

---

[1] The firm then was Messrs Peel, Yates, Warren, & Kay.

[2] Some years after it ceased to be occupied as a residence by the Grants, and when their parents had passed away, the large three-storied rectangular building, which now forms the front portion, was erected by them; and the whole, embellished with the now gas-illumined clock, bearing their initials, which still discharges its important function to the grateful lieges, was opened as a hotel in 1828. The first three tenants were William Bilsborrow, 1828-1832; Leeds Richardson, 1832-1833; and Robert Raby, 1833-1834. On the 1st of November 1834 George Goodrick became tenant. He had previously been a trusted servant of Mr John Grant at Nuttall Hall. Mr Goodrick conducted the establishment for the long period of over fifty-five years. He died, in his eighty-sixth year, on the 28th of January 1890, and on the 31st was interred at St Andrew's Church. The Volunteer Corps, whose annual dinner and distribution of prizes—for the most part under the wise and patriotic presidency of Major Grant—

The parents, at this time, were both well stricken in years—the father was seventy-four and the mother sixty-five years of age. There remained for them but the evening time of a busy and honourable life. Old Mr Grant was a genial, homely, kind-hearted man. In his latter days he was a victim of rheumatism, and very lame. Mrs Wilson—then a young employé of the firm, and afterwards Mrs Grant's maid—told us that he used to walk from Grant Lodge down to the warehouse on "the Old Ground," and sit and chat in his cheery, kindly way to herself and others. Grant Lodge, like the homes of all the sons in after years, was a very hospitable home, and a table furnished with provisions was kept by Mrs Grant for all needy comers—and they were many. "Nobody," said Mrs Wilson, "ever made a poor mouth to her and went away empty-handed." She was one of the old M'Kenzies of Tombrech,[1] in Strathspey—a woman of fine benevolence, keen natural intelligence, and great spirit and energy. While she lived, she ruled; all the family unquestioningly owned her sway. Sometimes, on a summer evening, Mr Grant, seated outside, would ask for his evening cup; and, if not just at once forthcoming, would say to Mrs Grant, whose Christian name was Grace—"O Grace, Grace, ye're Grace by name, but ye're no Grace by natur'!" The old lady, with a laugh or a smile, and a twinkle of fun in

---

had been held in the rather curiously frescoed dining-hall of the hotel for thirty years, attended the funeral in token of respect for Mr Goodrick's memory. Several large and doubtless originally costly oil-paintings, belonging to the late Messrs Grants' estate, are hung in the hotel; and its masonic assembly room is a large and elegantly appointed apartment.

[1] One of her grandnephews is a member of the Elgin County Council at the present time, and another is an office-bearer in the Presbyterian Church at Wolverhampton.

her eye, would quietly pursue her way—dropping some apt aphorism—"Ay, ay; it's lang or the stars glint." "Ye'll quaff your quaich[1] or the dews drench ye." "Nae fear o' droonin' when the stream's dry." "Patience and prudence are tittie-billie."[2] "Graces, like gangerils,[3] get their awmous."[4] "Eh, Grace, Grace, aw've seen the day." "Ay, ay, guidman, young cowts[5] kick high heels." "Nae doot, nae doot, guidwife; and snod[6] maids wad aye be dawtit."[7] "O Grace, Grace, it's makin' for mirk!"[8] "Wise weans shouldna wearie"—"Summer shadows mak' soft shelter,—the sun's still bricht a-wast the hill." Then they would laugh like two young ones, with a laughter full of heart, while in due time—*her* time—the wonted "cheerer" was supplied, and Grace graciously reinstated in marital favour. "A lucky[9] hand beats a souple tongue." "Weel, weel, it's guid gear that pleases the merchant."

MR WILLIAM GRANT OF GRANT LODGE
(Father of the Cheeryble Brothers).

Mrs Grant loved flowers and plants and trees, and they abounded, at that time, about her home. One day, when nearer fourscore than threescore and ten, she discovered

---

[1] A drinking-cup with two ears.   [2] Sister and brother.   [3] Vagrants.
[4] Alms, portion.   [5] Colts.   [6] Trim, neat.
[7] Fondled.   [8] Dark.   [9] Generous, abundant.

that a group of workmen at Topwood—some distance up the hill from Grant Lodge—were preparing to fell trees. "Cut down the trees! Na, na — they shannot do that." And, without a moment's hesitation, off she set at a surprising pace up the steep ascent, and in imperative tones ordered the workmen to desist and go back to the works. They obeyed. She returned, passing Grant Lodge, and, going right down to the Square, poured out her indignant remonstrance and absolute prohibition to her son, who promised acquiescence on the spot. That occurred over seventy years ago; and where the writer sits, he can see Topwood still adorning the mountainside.

MRS GRANT (Mother of the Cheeryble Brothers).

The life of these venerable parents of the Grants embraced something like a completed providential cycle. They began their united life with fairly happy prospects. But these were dashed by stern adversity. With a large family of young children they had to start afresh, far from the native homestead, and in unfamiliar surroundings. But they maintained their integrity; and, through many years of trustful, unremitting toil, prosperity returned; while, in the peaceful evening of their days, affluence blessed their lot. All that had been lost had then come back to them augmented manifold.

After the purchase of the estate of Messrs Peel & Yates, the firm of Messrs William Grant & Brothers rose rapidly in importance, embracing extensive foreign operations. One who had known them well in Bury in earlier times wrote in after years—"While your name has been sounded in my ears at Batavia, at Singapore, at Calcutta, in the East, it has been equally favourably mentioned to me at New Orleans, at Baltimore, and New York, in the Western World."[1]

Of the four members of the firm, the eldest, William, and the third, Daniel, were for the most part in Manchester; and the second, John, and the youngest, Charles, at Nuttall and Ramsbottom.[2]

For half a century the firm occupied a prominent place among the great houses of Manchester, and always promptly and liberally supported the ameliorative public movements and educational and charitable institutions of that important period. They were opponents of the Corn Bill in the year of Waterloo, and continued generous contributors to the agitation directed against the Corn Laws until their repeal in 1846. At their homes they were profusely hospitable, while they scattered money freely by the way to their less fortunate fellows, and were never above pulling up and

---

[1] Letter to Mr Daniel Grant from Mr John Clark, or Clerke, of Sir William Clerke's family.

[2] William never married. Daniel and Charles married sisters—daughters of Mr Worthington of Sharson, Cheshire. Daniel's wife died in her 21st year; Charles's widow married again after his death. John married Miss Dalglish of Glasgow (see Book II.) James, the eldest of the brothers, lived in Glasgow. He had a family. One of his daughters, Grace, married Mr Thomson of Batavia; and another, Elizabeth, became the first wife of Rev. Dr MacLean.

alighting from their carriage to chat with and quietly assist an old neighbour or friend whose face recalled to them the struggle of their earlier years. Of those years they were never ashamed. They had no need to be. Indeed, one of the best tributes that can be paid to their memory is just this, that there was nothing in their lives when it was their lot to be poor which caused them to be ashamed when it was their fortune to become rich. They were sound at the core.

> "The heart aye's the pairt aye
> That makes us right or wrang." [1]

A reminiscence of the late Mr John Slagg, M.P., reveals the daily experience of Mr William Grant in Manchester —" By the time of his arrival a number of poor people had gathered at the warehouse door awaiting his coming. When his carriage drew up they would divide into two lines, forming an avenue from the carriage to the warehouse door through which he passed. If he did not distribute his alms to them himself, he would send out a clerk to them, and I believe they seldom went away unrelieved."

Of the younger brother, Mr Slagg said — " I well remember how proud I was one morning when, my master having learnt they were wanting concentrated lime-juice at the works, he sent me to the warehouse to see Daniel Grant, and make him an offer of some. To my delight he ordered a hundred pounds worth. In giving the order he wasted no words, and yet did it so kindly that I have never forgotten the circumstance."

In 1824, William was made a Justice of the Peace;

---

[1] Robert Burns.

and two years later, at the head of a military force, his kindly and persuasive appeal having failed to turn the rioters from their unhappy purpose, he had to read the Riot Act at Chatterton. In 1836, he laid the foundation-stone of the Henshaw Blind Asylum at Old Trafford, and delivered an apt and sympathetic speech on the occasion.[1] The silver trowel of the function bore the Manchester Arms on one side and the Grant Arms on the other, and was thus inscribed :—

"Presented to William Grant, Esq., on his laying the first stone of a building to comprise an asylum for the blind, endowed by the late Thomas Henshaw, Esq., a school for the deaf and dumb, and a chapel for the joint benefit of both institutions, 23rd March 1836."

As the first Sir Robert Peel recognised the worth of the Grants in their early days, and proved helpful to them in their progress; so to struggling merit these brothers, in their turn, were always sympathetic, helpful friends. When young Naysmith — afterwards of steam-hammer fame — came to Manchester, and commenced business in Dale Street, with about twice as many pounds in the way of capital as he was years of age, he was introduced to the Grants, and William invited him to dine. The story of the young engineer, elicited by his host, won William's generous regard; and he told Naysmith on the spot that £500 would be at his disposal at the office, for wages, &c., any Saturday he might need it, at *three per cent, and no security!* Naysmith could only whisper thanks as he "got a kindly squeeze of the hand in return, and a kind of wink" he would "never forget — a most

---

[1] 'Manchester Courier,' March 26, 1836.

knowing wink." He discovered afterwards "that the eye was made of glass," and had a tendency to get displaced.[1] When William was a toddlin' child, a servant girl, who was very fond of him, snatched him up one day and danced round the kitchen, to his great delight, with him in her arms. But, unfortunately, she slipped, and the little fellow's face fell on the live embers on the hearth. Rescue was the work of a moment, but, unhappily, one eye was destroyed. In her old age, his mother related the incident to Mrs Wilson, as the great sorrow of her early motherhood, and, as she did so, wept again at the remembrance of the sad mishap. To the end of her days, he was as the apple of her eye.

One of William's pet maxims was, " Good masters make good workmen ; " and his favourite counsel—

> "Always be civil,
> Always be civil,
> Civility's cheap,
> Civility's cheap,
> Always be civil ! "[2]

He and Daniel, who was eleven years his junior, appear to have been each the fitting complement of the other. Daniel

---

[1] Naysmith's Autobiography, pp. 186, 187.
[2] During their shopkeeping days in Bury, the genial temper and unfailing courtesy of the Grants became proverbial. And one of a group of younger citizens on one occasion made a wager that he would demolish their " sweet civility." He went to the shop to buy cloth. Piece after piece was countered, examined, and expatiated upon, until almost the entire stock had been shown. He then fixed upon a piece. " What length ? " said William. " A pen'oth ! " answered the customer, laying down the coin. William, with unruffled temper, lifted the penny, laid it on the end of the cloth, cut its exact size from the piece, and handed it to the baffled customer with all his wonted cordiality and thanks. It was never attempted again—the sweet civility prevailed.

was endowed with commercial genius of the ampler type. William had more of the *microscopic* element in his composition, could plod unwearyingly through the minuter details of business, with an intuitive sense of their relationship to the greater end in view. Daniel's mental mould was more *telescopic*. His keen eye swept the horizon, and gauged with singular accuracy the wider and remoter possibilities of a campaign. He was the clear-visioned, hard-working statesman of the firm; William the model executive. It was, no doubt, the happy blending of these complemental endowments, and the priceless heritage of genial and generous natures, with enormous energy and unfailing brotherliness, that raised the firm of Messrs William Grant & Brothers to the position it occupied. Like qualities, in combination, have kindred results still. Of William more has generally been said than of Daniel. Of the latter, therefore, we may offer a few illustrative notes.

Quick, as he was kind-hearted and generous, with a remarkably fine eye and an admirable voice, Daniel Grant was incisive and briskly laconic in his speech. The great Chalmers described him in his prime as "a kind-hearted, rattling fellow."[1] More light in build than any of his brothers, he had too much nerve and "go" about him ever to grow stout. With a genial youthfulness of temperament, brisk and buoyant to the end of his days, he suggests, in his own way, what Dean Stanley tells us was a favourite image of Arnold's, "the eternal freshness and liveliness of the ocean." At one time William and he had each a residence in Manchester. After the

---

[1] See Book II., chap. iii., sec. 1.

former, however, purchased Springside—about two miles below Ramsbottom—he gave up his city house; and Daniel, while still retaining his, usually lived with his brother at Springside. "Their intense love for each other was manifest to all, and overflowed in affectionate words, in little tender attentions and assiduities."[1]

At Springside, an employé had for some time bothered Daniel with complaints against a subordinate, of the honest force of which he was not satisfied. At last one morning, having listened again to the grumbler, whose complaints seemed born of pique or prejudice, he characteristically settled the matter once and for all by saying, "You were first to *come;* you'll be first to *go!*" Having uttered these words with Spartan directness, and a shimmering like sheet-lightning in his full expressive eyes which betokened thunderbolts in the vicinity, he walked away. No further complaint ever reached him. Moreover, the pair, we believe, continued in their relative positions up to the death of their master, many long years afterwards.

Perhaps Daniel's sharpest rebuke, or remonstrance, uttered when he found an unsatisfactory transaction had been effected, was, "Man! man! would you give a man your front tooth?"—a sudden gust heralding no storm.

Like the homes of all the brothers, Springside was proverbially a hospitable mansion. Authors, as well as merchants, sometimes spent the evening there. On one occasion a writer of some note on the Land of the Pharaohs was with them. He was full of his book; and, after talking much and learnedly on the wonders of

---

[1] 'Memorials of Franklin Howorth.'

that ancient kingdom, he eloquently paused for his host's opinion on the theme he had been so elaborately propounding. Daniel, worthy man, was not learned in any lore, save that which centred for him in Cannon Street; and Egyptian antiquities were, then at any rate, a long way from 'Change. But he was equal to the occasion. What the Master of Pembroke Hall and Bonstetten—that mercurial Swiss, as Matthew Arnold calls him—said of the poet Gray, " He never spoke out," was never true of Daniel Grant. So, with a fine impulsive rush, like a skater clearing a bit of dangerous ice, or a batsman springing out of his ground to hit an unmanageable ball, he responded thus—" Yes! yes! Egypt! Pharaoh! Very old country! *Mummies!*" with a sharp and heavy emphasis on the embalmed ones. Egypt and the Pharaohs forthwith vanished from the scene, and were succeeded by a "rattling" time on topics nearer home.

Daniel's butler at Mosley Street—neatly named "the apoplectic butler" by Dickens—was a bit of a character in his way, and had evidently grown into his surroundings with a fine perception of the fitness of things. His name was Alfred Boot. At the time when Dickens first visited Manchester, and, as his biographer tells us, "brought away his Brothers Cheeryble" (1838-1839), Alfred had long been in command at the Mosley Street house. He was a short, thick-set, rather pudgy specimen of his kind—rotund and active, though somewhat easily "blown;" short-necked, rubicund face, head well held back, and the ample choker displaying something of a double chin. With a twinkle of humour in his eye, he was fond of a joke after his own fashion. Withal a man of much consequence in his own estimation, "he beseemed his position," as our informant, who knew both Daniel and the butler well, expressed it,—was supreme in Daniel's absence, and nobody dared to presume. Sometimes one or other of the nephews of the Grants had occasion to spend the night at Mosley Street while Daniel was out at Springside. At such times, on the following day, Daniel's fatherly interest always led him to ask Alfred at what time they got home. At the earliest opportunity, Alfred, poised and confidential, with a slight rubbing of the hands and a glimmering of humour over the rubicund face, duly gave the young men to understand that such an inquiry had been made, uniformly ending with, "Always in at ten o'clock, sir! always in at ten o'clock!" which they knew was occasionally a considerable way from the mark. But Alfred was privileged; and, with some fitting acknowledgment, they would proceed on their way, leaving the sapient butler once more proud of his penetration and sagacity.

Dickens gives "a feat of dexterity" on the part of "the apoplectic butler" in producing "a magnum of the double diamond to drink the health of Mr Linkinwater." What used frequently, as a matter of fact, to take place, was this. Daniel had what—borrowing the Indian term for the intermediate repast of the day—he called his "two o'clock tiffin" on market-days—Tuesdays, Thursdays, and Saturdays formerly; afterwards, as at present, Tuesdays and Fridays. His tiffin at two was well understood and largely patronised. On all such occasions Alfred was an important personage, but it was generally when Daniel had special friends—which was very frequently—for whom he wished to furnish the favourite "brand," that, having summoned the butler, he would say, quick as the element he mentioned zigzags a cloud, "Alfred! — Ruby! — Lightning!" and with almost incredible celerity the much-coveted vintage was placed before the guests, Alfred perhaps a little "wheasely" as the result of his fleetness and dexterity. In Daniel's will we find among "pecuniary legacies"—"To my butler, Alfred Boot, one hundred pounds, the same to be paid free of legacy duty."

Another incident, which, though occurring in very different circumstances, is equally authentic and characteristic, may here be related. It fell out one Sunday morning, in St Andrew's Church—the church built by *William* Grant for the Presbyterian congregation of which he was an elder, but which, forty years afterwards, was received and consecrated as Episcopal by the late Bishop of Manchester. Robert Burns, in his immortal "Tam o' Shanter," explains the courageous approach of the "heroic Tam" to where

> "Kirk-Alloway seemed in a bleeze;
> . . . . .
> When, wow! Tam saw an unco sight,"

by the significant lines,—

> "The swats sae reamed in Tammie's noddle,
> Fair-play, he cared na de'ils a boddle."

But "warlocks and witches" and all their kith and kin were altogether absent from the scene on this peaceful occasion, and nothing so plebeian as "swats" dreamt of. But, if not "swats," then the ancient "ruby" which Alfred so deftly decanted "reamed," *just a wee thing*, in another than "*Tammie's* noddle," that summer morning. The preacher was not the Presbyterian clergyman—Dr MacLean—but

Mr James Salmon, a theological student of the English Presbyterian Church, who had previously been an employé of the Grants. His text was the answer given by Daniel, in the den of lions, to King Darius—"O king, live for ever. My God hath sent His angel, and hath shut the lions' mouths, that they have not hurt me: forasmuch as before Him innocency was found in me; and also before thee, O king, have I done no hurt." The church has a gallery at the end opposite the pulpit, and the Grants occupied its front pews. Daniel was in his wonted place. The text had just been read when,—

"Moved with high sense of inborn powers,"—

he rose up in this front gallery pew, thrust his right hand impressively into space, and orated thus: "Yes! yes!— Daniel! Brave fellow, Daniel! Was cast into the lions' den!—the lions' den! And the lions—hurt—him—not!— hurt him not! Brave *fellow*, Daniel!—*brave* fellow!" Having thus, "his own heart eloquent," delivered himself,

"From heart to heart inspiring,"

he resumed his seat; and the young and somewhat astonished preacher, in a great silence, proceeded with his discourse. That discourse of good James Salmon's, admirable as no doubt it was, is now little if at all remembered; but the enthusiastic outburst of his old master, in admiration of his inspired and "brave" Hebrew namesake, remains. It was related to the writer, some time ago, by a lady who on that Sunday morning was in the pew with the Grants. But the incident would not have been fully characteristic of Daniel had there not been something to add. At the close of the memorable service he went to the preacher, and, with a benevolent and half-apologetic light flickering about his keen eagle eyes, slipped a sovereign into the struggling student's hand, and, in his own brusque yet heart-deep and impressive way, bid him be of good cheer.[1]

One morning Daniel, with William and John, his elder brothers, was making the round of the Square works. Passing through the block-printing department, he glanced at the work of a boy as he passed, and said to the foreman, John Roe, that it was "bad work"—"being spoiled!" John said it was all right; that he could not judge very well in its present state, but when it reached him in Manchester it would be good work. The manager passed, as was his wont, with his employers to the door of exit, and having opened it, as the Grants went out, Daniel turned and said to him, "Don't beat that boy for what I've said—don't!" John answered, "I have no occasion, sir; the boy does his work exceedingly well." "Who is he?" "He is a son of John Wardle's." This answer riveted Daniel to the spot. Old John Wardle had been a block-printer, long ago, at Hampson Mill, when Daniel was his teare-boy,[2] and had been kindly treated both by him and the motherly woman who was his wife. For a moment

"He pondered
The past, and as his heart relented,"[3]

---

[1] After completing his theological studies, James Salmon went to New Brunswick, where he closed a laborious and useful ministry some years ago. His sister Barbara, for half a century, was a loyal and devoted member of St Andrew's (Dundee) congregation. (See Bk. II., chap. iii., sec. 3.)

[2] A block-printer's assistant.

[3] Goethe.

declared profusely, "O then, he'll be a splendid man!—make a splendid workman! John Wardle's lad! sure to do well! sure to do well!" With this he thrust out his hand, and with great cordiality shook that of the manager as he walked away. This grace-act in leaving was a most unusual thing on his part. He was the most distant of all the Grants with the employés. He was like them all, however, in this, that the moment he felt he had acted unjustly—given, even though in rollicking banter, unnecessary pain, or appeared forgetful of any past kindness—he went forthwith to the other extreme of profuse and generous acknowledgment, not unfrequently quietly accompanied by some pecuniary solatium.

In Daniel's latter days, Mr Anyon, the pastor of Park Chapel, used to call upon him at Springside. He had a habit of uttering frequently a prolonged nasal *umquhm*. Daniel would jokingly say—"You must have been very fond of *treacle hum* when you were a boy, Mr Anyon." Sometimes the good pastor would seem to be a little hurt. Then Daniel relented, and slipped a sovereign, or perhaps two or three, into his hand on parting to heal the wound—

> "Let my hand
> In this firm grasp heal all the wounds I made
> With my too hasty tongue." [1]

They remained good friends to the last.

A medical practitioner of the place, who was on the most friendly terms with the Grants, asked Daniel one day to sign a testimonial, with a view to securing an appointment as factory inspector. "No! no!" said Daniel, "sign none of

---

[1] Schiller's "Maid of Orleans."

these things!" He had the kindliest feelings towards the young doctor—

> "But out
> The truth has come and leaves no doubt."[1]

"Ask me," continued Daniel, "for £500 if you want it, but I can't put my hand to anything of that sort;" and he didn't. This strong aversion to "put the hand" to any document was common to all the family to the close of their career. They would sign cheques with sometimes remarkable readiness. They knew precisely what these meant. One requires to remember that the education of these elder brothers had been very imperfect, and that an early experience of trouble and annoyance, arising from putting their hand to a document, in all probability gave rise to this lifelong aversion. Somewhat memorable, although by them unpurposed and undreamt-of troubles, after they had passed away, arose out of this peculiarity.

The following incident will show with what generous readiness cheques were sometimes signed. A member of a shipping firm in Liverpool, well known to the Grants, called at the office in Manchester, and told Daniel they were at the moment rather pressed for funds, owing to the unusual delay of vessels. "How much do you need?" asked Daniel. "From £6000 to £8000." Daniel forthwith signed a cheque for £10,000. Profusely thanking him, the gentleman proceeded to place in his hands legal securities for the amount. "No! no!" said Daniel. "Take them with you! take them with you! A thing of honour! a thing of honour! Pay when you can! pay when you can!" Remonstrance was vain. With renewed acknowledgments—conscious of an unwonted thickening about the throat and a gathering of

---
[1] Goethe.

mist over his eyes—the friend took his leave; to remember, with a twitch of emotion, to the end of his days, the prompt and generous confidence of Daniel Grant.

Kindnesses experienced by them in their early days were never forgotten. Mr Dinwiddie of Hampson Mill was their first employer. Long afterwards a grandson of his was engaged in the Square. Daniel remembered him with a legacy; and his nephew, who inherited the estates, left him a much larger sum, and made him one of his executors.

Of the parents of the Grants the father died in 1817, and the mother in 1821. At his death, the father had been in Lancashire thirty-four years, and the mother, at hers, thirty-eight. Her youngest son Charles, with all his fire and energy, was busy building the Square works when his mother died. He followed her to the grave only four years after, in 1825. The parents had been spared to participate in many years of growing prosperity in the life of their sons. And one of the most marked and beautiful features in these men was the manifest honour accorded, at all times, to their father and mother while living, and the deep and perennial reverence with which they cherished their memory—especially that of their mother—after they were gone. The genius of Dickens has seized upon this element in their character, which was clear as a sunbeam to those who knew them well, and has crystallised it in the little festive speech the one brother is supposed to address to the other at the birthday anniversary of their confidential clerk and cashier, "Tim Linkinwater"—
"Brother Charles, my dear fellow, there is another association connected with this day which must never be forgotten, and never can be forgotten, by you and me. This day, which brought into the world a most faithful and excellent and exemplary fellow, took from it the kindest and very

best of parents—the very best of parents to us both. I wish that she could have seen us in our prosperity, and shared it, and had the happiness of knowing how dearly we loved her in it, as we did when we were two poor boys—but that was not to be. My dear brother—The Memory of our Mother!"

As a matter of fact, that mother's word or wish, to the end of her days, was law to her sons. The Rev. Franklin Howorth and his wife—Sir Henry Holland's sister—"knew William and Daniel well, and retained a vivid recollection of their cheerful hospitality, their lively talk, their overflowing bountifulness, their intense mutual love. These two devoted brothers lend their witness to limit the universality of the proverb that 'still waters are deepest,' and to confute the generally received doctrine that demonstrativeness is incompatible with depth of feeling,—that truest love is shy of expression." What is stated in Mr Howorth's biography of them was true of these two brothers to the end of their days—"*They seldom passed their mother's picture without an inclination of reverence or an exclamation of gratitude.*"

Here we may conveniently insert the inscription on the weathered tomb in Bank Street, Bury, where up to this time the deceased members of the family had been laid. It is as follows:—

> Here resteth in the hope of a blessed Resurrection Mary the Daughter of William Grant of Strathspey North Britain who died the 13th day of Novemr. 1784 in the 8th year of her age.
>   Also Elizabeth the Daughter of the above William Grant now of Grant Lodge near this Town who died the 17th of November 1808 in the 35th year of her age.

Also Elizabeth the wife of Daniel
Grant of Manchester and Daughter
of Thomas Worthington Esqe. Sharson
in Cheshire who died Octr. 19th 1816
in the 21st year of her age.

Also the above-named William
Grant died June 29th 1817 in the 84th
year of his age.

Also Grace his Wife died May 16th
1821 in the 79th year of her age.

Also Charles son of the above
William and Grace Grant who died
July 9th 1825 aged 37 years.

We also give, as possessing an interest of its own, the inscription on an ornate tablet near the north end of the east wall in St Andrew's Church.

SACRED TO THE MEMORY OF
WILLIAM GRANT, ESQR.
of Elchies, Morayshire, Scotland; and Grant Lodge, Ramsbottom.
Born 1733. Died 29 July[2] 1817. Aged 84.
The effectual fervent prayer of a righteous man availeth much.
St James chap. 5 ver. 16.
Also of GRACE his Wife.
Born 1742. Died 16th May 1821. Aged 79.
Her children arise up and call her blessed. Prov. chap. 31st v. 28.
This tablet was erected in 1864 by the only
Surviving male representative of
their line and name—
WILLIAM GRANT of Carr Bank, Esqr.[1]

---

[1] Mr William Grant of Carr Bank—"the only surviving *male* representative of" the Grants—was the son of Mr John Grant of Nuttall Hall. Of his other sons, John "died at Nuttall Hall, June 12, 1851, aged 22 years;" and Robert Dalglish Grant, M.A. of Trinity College, Cambridge, and Lincoln's Inn, London, died at Bordeaux, in France, November 7, 1863, aged 33." They were buried in St Andrew's Church.

[2] Ought to be "June."

Mr William Grant—the elder "Cheeryble"—died in 1842.[1] He was an elder of St Andrew's Presbyterian Church, Ramsbottom, and the accredited representative of St Andrew's Congregation in the Presbytery of Lancashire, at the time of his death. It occurred on 28th of February; and on March 13th, Dr MacLean preached a sermon in St Andrew's Church, bearing upon the event. The text was "Remember how short my time is"—Psalm lxxxix. 47. It was "published by request," and is dedicated thus:—

To
DANIEL GRANT, ESQR.,
THIS SERMON,
Preached on the occasion of the death of his beloved
BROTHER,
IS INSCRIBED
With sentiments of the most affectionate regard
BY
ANDREW MACLEAN, A.M.

We give the following extract:—

Death has been busy within our borders. A father has fallen in Israel. A righteous man has taken his departure from among us. He, *whose pious regard erected the temple in which we worship*, now lies silent and cold within its walls. Our friend and benefactor is gone! He has "gone down to the grave, and we shall look upon his face no more!" While we bend before the stroke, and adore the deep and inscrutable ways of God, let us also meditate upon his memory, and profit by the example he has left.

Standing in *this sacred place*—which, we trust, will rear its heaven-pointing towers for ages to come, *as a monument of his piety and worth*—and before you, my brethren, it would almost seem needless for me to dwell on the life and character of the deceased. They are fully

---

[1] It was the mother of Major Grant—a visitor at the time at Springside—who closed the eyes of the illustrious Cheeryble in their last sleep.

known, and feelingly appreciated by you all. He has been known to you in public and private. He has been associated with you in the varied circumstances and connexions of human life. You have had for many years ample and unbounded experience of his benevolence and integrity. He has lived among you, and you have had converse together. Your presence in this place is a testimony of your reverence and respect. Your sympathy for his afflicted friends is a proof that your own hearts are also stricken. And the garments of mourning, which almost universally you wear, show that you honoured and loved him when living, and that you now deplore and lament him when dead.

At the south side of the east window, in St Andrew's Church, a marble tablet, surmounted by a bust, bears the following inscription:—

SACRED
to
The Memory
of
WILLIAM GRANT OF SPRINGSIDE, ESQUIRE,
THE FOUNDER OF THIS CHURCH.
Born at Elchies, Morayshire, Scotland, on 15th of April 1769.
Died at Springside on 28th February 1842.
Distinguished by vigour of understanding,
Spotless integrity of character, and true benevolence of heart.
He lived a benefactor to his species,
And died universally lamented.

A rhymed tribute to Mr Grant's memory, by a member of the warehouse staff in Manchester, was published after his death. It is surmounted by a silhouette of Mr Grant, and followed by the accompanying note:—

This generous, good, and affectionate master died on the 28th day of February, about a quarter past seven o'clock A.M., 1842, aged 73 years, and was interred on the 5th of March, attended by a numerous procession of gentlemen from Manchester, Liverpool, and the neighbouring country. In passing their family monument, the funeral was joined by many hundreds of their workpeople and friends. The country and the village of Ramsbottom appeared one general scene of mourning from his hall to the church, where he was laid in a vault, inside his own temple, which he had built and dedicated to the Lord. See the Rev. A. MacLean's Funeral Sermon.

EDWARD KAY.

A framed copy still hangs in the vestry, at the east end of St Andrew's Church (now Episcopal), not many feet from where he was laid to rest. How this Presbyterian church became an Episcopal place of worship will be hereafter fully explained.

Here we may appropriately insert *in extenso* the letter of Mr William Grant, written in answer to one by a relative of the Rev. Sir W. H. Clerke, who was rector of Bury from 1778 to 1818, and whose wife was the Lady Clerke who, in 1798, on a memorable occasion, presented colours to the Bury Loyal Volunteers. In this letter, *for the first time, we have the venerable Cheeryble's own account* of the advent of the Grants to the valley of the Irwell, and their subsequent remarkable career.

SPRINGSIDE, *May* 17, 1839.

DEAR SIR,—Allow me to acknowledge the receipt of your esteemed favour of the 10th. My father was a dealer in cattle, and lost his property in the year 1783. He got a letter of introduction to Mr Arkwright (the late Sir Richard), and came by the way of Skipton to Manchester, accompanied by me. As we passed along the old road, we stopped for a short time on the Park estate to view the valley. My father exclaimed, "What a beautiful valley! May God Almighty bless it! It reminds me of Speyside, but the Irwell is not so large as the river Spey.

I recollect Messrs Peel & Yates were then laying the foundation of their print works at Ramsbottom. We went forward to Manchester and called upon Mr Arkwright; but he had so many applications at the time that he could not employ him. There were then only Arkwright's mill, on a small scale, and Thacary's mill in Manchester. There was a mill on the Irwell belonging to Mr Douglas, two belonging to Messrs Peel & Yates, the one at Radcliffe Bridge, the other at Hinds; and these were the only mills then in Lancashire. My father then applied to a Mr Dinwiddie, a Scotch gentleman, who knew him in his prosperity, and who was a printer and manufacturer at Hampson Mill, near Bury. He agreed to give my father employment, and placed my brother James and me in situations, where we had an opportunity of acquiring a knowledge both of manufacturing and printing; and offered me a partnership when I had completed my apprenticeship. I declined his offer, and commenced business for myself on a small scale, assisted by my brothers John, Daniel, and Charles, and removed to Bury,[1] where I was very successful; and in the course of a few years [in 1800?] I removed to Manchester and commenced printing in partnership with my brothers. My brother Daniel commenced travelling through the north of England and almost to every market town in Scotland. In 1806 we purchased the print works belonging to Sir Robert Peel, etc., situated at Ramsbottom. In 1812 we purchased Nuttal factory. In consequence of the death of Mr Alsop, the workpeople had been long short of employment, and were very destitute. We ordered the manager to get new machinery, of the first-rate construction, and greatly extended the building; and before we began to spin or manufacture, we clothed the whole of the hands at our own expense; prepared an entertainment for them, and observed that the interests of masters and servants are bound up together; that there are reciprocal duties to perform, that no general or admiral could be brave unless he was supported by his men; that we knew how to reward merit, and would give constant employment and liberal wages to all our faithful servants; and I am happy to say that they, as well as those at our printing establishment, with very few exceptions, have conducted themselves with great propriety.

In 1818 we purchased Springside, and in 1827 we purchased the Park estate, and erected a monument to commemorate my father's first visit to this valley, and on the very spot where he and I stood admiring the beautiful scenery below. There is a fine view from the top of the tower in a clear day, and the Welsh mountains can be descried in the distance.

---

[1] While at Bury, old Mr Grant used on special occasions to regale the lieges near the shop with music from a hand-organ, which must have been a costly instrument in its time. This ancient organ since Springside sale has been in the possession of Mrs Bentley of Lodge View, Ramsbottom.

We attribute much of our prosperity, under divine Providence, to the good example and good counsel of our worthy parents. They expressed a wish that I would build a Sunday school, and erect a church to worship God in, according to the ritual of the Church of Scotland, as a tribute of gratitude to Him for His great kindness to the family. I cheerfully complied with their request, and both have been finished years ago. We have done business, on a large scale, at all the places you have named, exporting our goods and receiving the productions of those countries in return ; but trade for some years has been very unproductive—profits being so small, and the risk great, that we have been very much inclined to retire on the moderate fortune we have acquired with great industry, were it not to give employment to our work-people ; but we feel unwilling to throw our servants out of employment at a time when many are only being worked three days in the week.

Widely and sincerely William's death was mourned; but to Daniel it was a supreme bereavement. The irrepressible sprightliness indeed still scintillated about the lithe and agile form, but the very genuineness of the man, the moral transparency — the εἰλικρίνεια, as the Greeks called it — made it impossible altogether to conceal the consciousness of how much had gone from him. A mellowing sense of solitude, with its deep "deciphering oracle within,"[1] henceforth went with him through the busy haunts of men. And as the larks spring from the valley up through the mountain shadow to greet the coming day, so now his deepest thoughts sought yonderside the "bourne," until the mortal "mure" was rent, and he pursued them to the realm of day. The ruptured fellowship was then restored. Thirteen years after William's death, Daniel himself—*the second of the immortal "Cheerybles"—passed away.*

---

[1] De Quincey.

On the south wall of the church, overlooking the passage in front of the communion table, another tablet bears these words :—

>   This monument is erected
>   To the Memory of
>   DANIEL GRANT, Esquire,
>   of Manchester,
>   Who died 12th March 1855. Aged 75 years.
>   READER,
> If you are in poverty, grieve for the loss of so good a friend ;
>   If born to wealth and influence,
> Think of the importance of such a trust ; and earn in like manner,
>   By a life of charitable exertion,
>   The respect and love of all who know you,
>   The prayers and blessings of the poor.
> Is it not to deal thy bread to the hungry, and that thou bring the poor that are cast out to thy house? when thou seest the naked, that thou cover him ; and that thou hide not thyself from thine own flesh?
> Then shall thy light break forth as the morning, and thine health shall spring forth speedily ; and thy righteousness shall go before thee ; the glory of the Lord shall be thy rereward.
> Then shalt thou call, and the Lord shall answer ; thou shalt cry, and he shall say, Here I am.
>   Isaiah, 58 Chap. ; 7, 8, and 9 verses.

And, less than two months after the death of Daniel, the last of the brothers, John, went to his rest.

From the sermon on John xiv. 1, 2, preached by Dr MacLean on "the morning of Sabbath, May 13, 1855, on the occasion of the death of John Grant, Esq., of Nuttall Hall," we extract the following :—

I have chosen this passage of sacred Scripture as my text on this occasion, because it is—as far as my memory serves—among the latest, if not the very last passage, which it was my privilege to repeat to the venerable Christian whose death we now deplore. The doctrines I have now preached from it were the doctrines deeply impressed upon his heart; they were the principles of his firm and unfaltering belief; they were the source of his trust in life, and the spring of his comfort and peace in death.

I have now earnestly to solicit your kind indulgence, brethren, while I attempt to discharge my present melancholy duty. It is not an easy thing to speak when the heart is full, over the fresh grave, as it were, of one with whom, but as yesterday, you held kind and Christian converse, and whom you have long honoured and loved. I cannot but feel, too, at this trying moment, the painful remembrance, that only a few weeks have elapsed since, from this sacred place, I gave expression to our united grief and regret over the death of one whose name we shall not soon or easily forget. And now, before our hearts are recovered from the stroke, another, and he the last of his generation, has passed away. Alas! all the stately trees have now fallen! The Three Brothers have gone to their graves! The men once so united in heart and hand—the men whom we have so long honoured and esteemed—who so dearly loved this valley—who have contributed so largely to its prosperity and beauty—and whose names have been associated, far and wide, with industry, enterprise, and benevolence—all of them have now run their busy race: they have passed away like shadows from the stage of time, and the place that once knew them "now knows them no more"! *Their silent tombs are now before us; beneath this sacred roof their ashes are mingling:* together they are sleeping "the sleep that knows no waking," till, loud over heaven, and earth, and sea, shall be heard the "voice of the archangel and the trump of God." . . . Unlooked for and unexpected has this second visitation come—at a time when the heart was full of hope—when dark and dreary winter, with all its dangers, had passed away—when spring had come with its promises of health and gladness—and when many a heart rejoiced to see our venerable friend reappearing in the sunshine, glad and grateful to his God for being permitted to breathe the sweet reviving breeze along the fields and lanes he had loved so long,—at such a moment he sickens and dies, leaving upon our hearts the melancholy lesson of the deceitfulness of all human hopes, and of the frailty and vanity of man.

But not unlooked-for to himself did his summons come; long had he lived in earnest and faithful preparation for the world to come; long had "his loins been girt, and his lamp burning," and he himself waiting and watching for the coming of the Lord.

Before the year 1855 closed, Jane Dalglish, the widow of Mr John Grant, also died. On the morning of January 6, 1856, Dr MacLean preached a sermon on the occasion of her death from Revelation xiv. 13. We give its concluding paragraphs:—

It appears as if almost unnecessary for me, in this sacred place, and before you, dear brethren, who are all witnesses of her worth, to speak of the life and character of the deceased. Long has she proved herself a blessing indeed to this valley! Warmly alive to all the best interests of the people. Ever anxious to do good. Abounding in gentle charity. Liberally upholding all Christian churches and schools. Encouraging the old and the young in wisdom's ways. Furnishing a continued stream of books and tracts, oftentimes prepared by her own hands, for the edification and instruction of the people. Giving bread to the hungry, clothing to the aged and poor; comforts, in their day of need, to the sick and the dying, and goodwill and kindness to all. Verily of her it may be said, "The blessing of him that was ready to perish came upon her; and she caused the widow's heart to sing for joy. She was eyes to the blind, and feet was she to the lame. She was a mother to the poor."

It has always appeared to me a most tender and touching scene, and presenting, perhaps, one of the most precious and affecting remembrances that the living could render to the dead, when we read, in Holy Writ, how the apostle Peter—in obeying the call of the disciples to come to the house of Dorcas, who had died—entered into an upper chamber where the dead lay, and found all the widows standing and "weeping, and showing the coats and garments which Dorcas had made for them, while she was still with them." How many of the poor, of the infirm and aged, who have passed away from the stage of time; and how many still around us, whom she has fed, and comforted, and clothed, would, weeping, bear the same warm and grateful tribute to the kind heart that is now at rest! May these, her works of gentle charity, follow her into heaven—not, indeed, as any ground of her acceptance and admission there, but as proofs of her love,—as done in the name and for the sake of Him "who loved us, and gave Himself for us;" and who has promised that even a cup of cold water given to a disciple, for His sake, shall in no wise lose its reward; and that, inasmuch as it has been done unto the least of His children, He holds it as done unto Himself.

I presume not to speak of the departed in the more private relations of life. I know full well how tenderly she loved, how faithfully she discharged her duties to her family, and how devotedly her love was returned; and I know that for many a day their hearts will melt in sorrow over the loss of one who was to them a mother—faithful, tender, and true. One consolation, at least, and that not a small one, in the goodness of God, has been allotted to them. They were permitted, one and all, to watch her troubled couch, to minister to her wants, and to stand around her when her eyes closed upon this world; and when, with the gentleness of an infant's slumber, she fell asleep, we trust, in Jesus.

"Blessed are the dead which die in the Lord from henceforth: Yea, saith the Spirit, that they may rest from their labours; and their works do follow them."

On the north wall of the church, over against that of Daniel, is placed the monumental tablet of John and his wife. It is inscribed thus:—

IN MEMORY OF
JOHN GRANT OF NUTTALL HALL, ESQR.,
Who died May 6th 1855. Aged 80 Years.
And of JANE his Wife,
Who died December 28th 1855. Aged 56 Years.
This Monument is Erected by
THEIR SURVIVING CHILDREN.

Not alone as a memorial of sorrow at the irreparable loss they have sustained in the death of their parents, and to perpetuate the remembrance of the many virtues of these beloved ones for ever departed, but that succeeding generations may read, and, reading, fondly share the affectionate admiration of those so gentle and so good.

"And I heard a voice from heaven saying unto me, Write, Blessed are the dead which die in the Lord, from henceforth; Yea, saith the

Mr John Grant of Nuttall Hall.

Spirit, that they may rest from their labours; and their works do follow them."—Rev. xiv. 13th verse.

"And God shall wipe away all tears from their eyes; and there shall be no more death, neither sorrow, nor crying, neither shall there be any more pain; for the former things are passed away."—Rev. xxi. 4th verse.

"And they shall see His face; and His name shall be in their foreheads."—Rev. xxii. 4th verse.

> Calm on the bosom of your God,
> Dear spirits, rest you now;
> E'en while on earth your footsteps trod,
> His seal was on your brow.
>
> Dust to its narrow house beneath,
> Souls to their place on high;
> They who have seen you when in death,
> No more need fear to die.

The benefactions of Mrs John Grant, in the form of clothing, &c., have been enjoyed, year by year, by old villagers almost to the present time.

Yet another monumental tablet ought to find a place in this record. It is on the north wall in St Andrew's Church. The inscription runs thus:—

> IN MEMORY
> of
> ELIZABETH GRANT,
> The beloved wife of
> The REV. ANDREW MACLEAN, A.M.,
> Who died on the 16th April 1848.
> Aged 39 Years.
> Upright in mind, and warm and tender in
> heart, it was her earnest desire to walk in the
> steps of the meek and lowly Jesus, and to
> abound in the fruits of His love.

"Son of man, behold I take away from thee the desire of thine eyes with a stroke."

One more tablet, recently erected on the south wall of the church, records the decease of "the last surviving child" of Mr and Mrs John Grant—Mrs Lawson of Aldborough Manor. It bears the following inscription :—

SACRED
To the Memory of
ANDREW SHERLOCK LAWSON
of Aldborough Manor,
in the County of York, Esquire,
Who died May 22nd, 1872.
Also of ISABELLA, his wife,
Who died June 10th, 1890.
The last surviving child
of JOHN GRANT
of Nuttall Hall, Esquire.
This monument is erected
By their Children.

The Ramsbottom and Nuttall estates are now the property of Mrs Lawson's second son — Mr John Grant Lawson, M.P. for Thirsk and Malton, Yorks.

RAMSBOTTOM IN 1893.—THE "SQUARE" IN THE FOREGROUND.

CHAPTER VII.

RAMSBOTTOM [1] (INDUSTRIAL).

THE history of the textile manufactures of England is full of interest. It is rich in examples of that ingenuity, skill, and steadfast persistency in industrial effort, of which any people may be proud, and which, when allied with integrity and honour, are the surest precursors of progress and success. But whatever may be said of other departments, such as woollen, silk, lace, &c.—and much might be said of any one of them—yet we venture to affirm that neither this nor any other country, in either ancient or modern times, can furnish any parallel to the cotton industry of Lancashire. While gathering its raw material from points on the earth's surface as wide asunder as the poles, and sending it back in vast quantities, transformed

---

[1] The Ramsbottom Local Board, after two previous ineffectual efforts, was ultimately formed in 1864. Its area, then, embraced only the present *central* ward. The other three wards were added in 1883. The following is a list of the successive Chairmen, and the years of their respective presidencies: Mr William Grant, 1864-1867; Mr Lawrence Stead, 1867-1884; Mr Henry Heys, J.P., 1884-1885; Mr Edmund Rothwell, 1885-1886; Mr Edward Wild, 1886-1887; Mr Edward Cunliffe, J.P., C.C., 1887-1892; Mr H. L. Sladin, 1892. Its four wards embrace 6327 acres, and an assessable value of about £70,000. A small directory of the Local Board District was prepared and issued by the late Mr James Markland, who was long an active member of the Board.

into goodly fabrics, to compete, even in the face of hostile tariffs, with the kindred products of those who grow the cotton at their doors, yet its progress and results have been truly wonderful. It has clothed and fed millions; it has built splendid cities; it has equipped fleets of

> "Argosies with portly sail,
> Like signiors and rich burghers on the flood,"[1]

frequenting many seas; and it has touched the fringe of heathenism, with no unkindly hand, on many a distant shore. True to the great Christian heritage of England, it has reared many sanctuaries, provided many schools, and never been unmindful of the claims of charity. It has, moreover, produced a race of men whose broad common-sense, and ready perception and appreciation of integrity and fairness, have not only helped to elevate the standard of commercial honour, but also affected beneficially the legislative history of our time. Yet it cannot be called old. A century and a half ago it could scarcely be said to exist. True, we are told the cotton trade was introduced into Spain by the Mahommedans about the tenth century, and slowly found its way in the succeeding centuries to other European countries. Up to the middle of last century, however, it was only a small thing; indeed, purely cotton goods were never then produced. The fabrics up to that time were mixed with linen or wool, cotton supplying only the *weft*. Arkwright's spinning-throstle was the first machine that produced a thread of cotton sufficiently slender and strong for *warp*. The

---

[1] "Merchant of Venice," Act i. sc. 1.

rise of the cotton industry proper is coeval with a series of inventions extending over a period of fifty years, and ending just about a century ago. These are associated with the names of men, some of whom endured much hardship and not a little wrong, but who have proved benefactors to mankind. There was Wyatt, with his spinning by rollers, and John Kay, with his fly-shuttle, in 1738; Arkwright, with his "throstle,"[1] in 1769; Hargreaves, with his carding-machine and spinning-jenny, in 1770; Samuel Crompton, with his marvellous "mule," in 1779; and the ingenious clergyman, Edmund Cartwright, who with his power-loom, in 1785, may be said to have brought in the jubilee of that rare inventive genius out of which were destined to spring results so beneficent to millions unborn. And to all these must be added James Watt, with his new motive force — the steam — harnessed and handy just in the nick of time.

On the heels of this advance in spinning and weaving came calico-printing. In this Messrs Peel & Yates were among the earliest and most successful. They began their works on the "Old Ground" at Bury in 1770, and on the "Old Ground" at Ramsbottom in 1783. The firm of Messrs William Grant & Brothers purchased the works at Ramsbottom in 1806 and began operations on 1st January 1807. William Grant tells us that, before this time, his brother Daniel had commenced travelling through the north of

---

[1] His spinning-frame moved by water-power was popularly known as the "Throstle," from the sound it emitted in working, being supposed to resemble the singing of a throstle or thrush. It was called the "Water-frame," from being driven at first by water-wheels. It has since been, for the most part, superseded by the "Mule" of Crompton, invented ten years later at Bolton.

England, and to almost every market town in Scotland.[1] And for fifteen years, until the famous *Square* was built, the

RAMSBOTTOM IN BEGINNING OF CENTURY (SHOWING GRANT LODGE).

new firm successfully prosecuted their work on "*the old ground*," in the premises they had purchased from the Peels.

---

[1] See Letter, p. 95. A characteristic incident is furnished by an early experience of Daniel's in Glasgow. He had been seeking, perhaps somewhat persistently, to exhibit his patterns to the head of a firm there, when the worthy citizen, suddenly irate, seized them and pitched them out into the muddy street. Daniel followed and picked them up. Extracting only humour from the graceless act, he returned, undaunted, wiping the mud-stains from his samples, and, his fine keen face and eyes aglow with fresh assurance, said, "Now, sir, I'm sure you'll give me an order,—there's a fortune in these—a fortune—just look at them!" That day was begun a lasting friendship between the pair, and a business connection both long and lucrative between the two firms.

These premises were, for the most part, scattered about on or near what is still known as the Old Ground, in the centre of Ramsbottom. It extended across what is now Bolton Street on the *west*, to Silver Street on the *east*, to Bridge Street on the *north*, and to Smithy Brow on the *south*.[1]

The *Bridge Street* of to-day was then mainly the bed of a brook, and, at first, very appropriately, it was called *Water Street*. There were stepping-stones across from the works on the Old Ground side, to a row of old cottages, which occupied part of the north side of the brook, above where the Primitive Methodist Chapel[2] was afterwards built. Mr and Mrs Samuel Wilson occupied one of these cottages in 1824. The stepping-stones were about opposite the present Post Office, or the Royal Oak, as pointed out by Mrs Wilson (in September 1891). Farther up, a house stood by itself, not far from the old Post Office, and near to the ground afterwards covered with the premises occupied by Mr Samuel Wilson till his death in 1879, and now tenanted by Mr Schofield and Mr Sutcliffe.

In the region of what is now St Paul's, from Messrs Ashton's works to Bridge Street, extended the Crowtrees farm. It was long occupied by Mr Richard Schofield and his son. The farm-house, with a cottage at its east end, occupied the more western portion of the area now covered by St Paul's Church. To the north, and extending nearly half way down the lane, was a

---

[1] Beyond this there was then a long drying-house at Scotland Place. When transformed into dwelling-houses in after years, Dr MacLean lived in it for some time before going to Barwood House.
[2] Now Mr Holmes' Furniture Warehouse and *Ramsbottom Observer* Office.

well-remembered rookery—"the crow trees"[1]—from which the name of the present street—Crow Lane—as well as that of the old farm itself was derived.[2]

From a point eight or ten yards beyond the north-east corner of the cottage, eastwards, the orchard wall went right to Bridge Street, and the orchard extended round the south front of the house to Crow Lane; from which, about opposite the entrance of the present vicarage, the front door of the farm-house was reached by a flagged approach about eight yards in length. From the orchard wall on the east, the Crowtrees Meadow extended down to the old toll-house, and from that point was bounded by the goyt[3] extending round to Messrs Ashton's factory. The farm itself was bounded on the *east* mainly by that goyt, on the *south* by the line of Bridge Street, on the

---

[1] When the crow trees in Crow Lane were removed, the crows went to the trees which long ago grew near the cricket-ground and the paper-mill; and when these also disappeared, the dusky denizens migrated to their present home between Barwoodlea and the Square.

[2] A tenant of this property, whose name is still kindly remembered by older people, had a vein of originality in his character. Before taking the Crowtrees farm, he lived some distance farther up the valley; and near his house grew a favourite tree. He resolved that its timber should enclose him, when

"In his narrow bed for ever laid."

The tree was felled, and the admonitory receptacle duly made. For years, in the first instance, he utilised it as a clothes chest; and, when the end came, it enshrined the aged tabernacle as it was laid in its last resting-place. The Athenian hero had cedar, the Roman, marble or stone, but the worthy tenant of Crowtrees farm chose his home-grown sycamore or elm, which answered the final purpose equally well, while it paid "a double debt," like Goldsmith's

"box, contrived a double debt to pay—
A bed by night, a chest of drawers by day."

[3] Water-channel or mill-race.

St Paul's Church, Ramsbottom.

north by Messrs Ashton's factory, and on the *west* by Crow Lane wall. That wall was about five feet high, and finished with triangular coping-stones, familiarly known as "cock'd hats." It extended from Bridge Street past the orchard, the farm-house, and the "crow trees," right down to Messrs Ashton's. On the *opposite* side of the farm, between the old toll-house and the present constabulary premises, may still be seen part of an old boundary wall also covered with "cock'd hats." Where the wall abuts on the pavement, a chiselled upright stone bears on one side W G & B, and on the other S & T A—that is, William Grant & Brothers; Samuel & Thomas Ashton. Mr Richard Schofield the younger, still a vigorous citizen, remembers well ploughing this meadow, and leaning occasionally over this boundary wall at the end of his furrow, and chatting with "old John Grime," whose son still occupies the old toll-house.

Forty-seven years ago, the railway struck through the Crowtrees meadow, some twenty or thirty yards from this point; and since then the farm has been occupied by well-built streets and factories, with a commodious sanctuary for the living, and a sleeping-place—God's acre[1]—for the departed sons and daughters of toil. The Church—St Paul's—was built in 1850, and enlarged in 1866. Its first incumbent was the Rev. James Hornby Butcher. In 1870

---

[1] This resting-place of the dead, now so closely surrounded by the habitations of the living, ought, we think, for obvious sanitary reasons, to be reverently closed. It might in time be transformed into a comely garden of flowers and shrubs. More than a generation ago there were many well-tended little garden allotments within the old farm area. But they have only transmitted to us their memory in such names as *Garden* Street and *Garden* Mill.

he was appointed to Audenshaw. The Rev. W. H. Corbould—the present vicar—succeeded him in 1871. During Mr Corbould's incumbency much educational work has been effected in the large and well-appointed day-schools; and the amenity of St Paul's has been greatly enhanced by the erection of an admirable palisaded boundary wall, the seemly addition of trees and shrubs, and the building of a goodly vicarage.[1] In all this the vicar has been loyally supported by Mr Henry Heys, J.P., who has been churchwarden and treasurer of St Paul's for more than thirty years. Travelling towards the river from Crowtrees farm-house, there was no building till the toll-house was reached. It still remains, lessened in height, like a portion of Carr Street, by the raising of the road; and the grey slating

REV. W. H. CORBOULD.

---

[1] Alas! since these lines were written, Mr Corbould has passed away. He had been failing in health for some time, and a sudden seizure

stones on its roof, with other features, indicate its age. Beyond this, Peel Bridge had been erected and Peel Brow Road made about the time of the French Revolution, fully thirty years before the building of the Square. The Act of Parliament, under which these works were effected, is dated 1789. They were paid for by the Peels. Across the bridge, on the *east side* of the river, there were no houses in the *Old Ground* days. Some time afterwards the farm-house at the south end of Kenyon Street was reared. It is now occupied by Mr John Kenyon, the long connection of whose family with the place has furnished a name for the street. There would also belong to about the same period the row of grey-slated cottages running northwards from the foot of Peel Brow—nearly opposite Patmos Chapel of the U. M. Free Church.[1] Considerably farther south, "*the old engine*," now converted into dwelling-houses, was once a busy carding-mill, run at one time by the paternal grandfather of the late Messrs W. Wild & Brothers, of Shuttleworth.

Returning to the upper end of Bridge Street, the accompanying plan will show the Old Ground works of Messrs Peel, as they were transferred to the Grants on 1st January 1807. With the exception of 21 and 22,[2] which were removed early,[3] these buildings remained till after the

---

resulted, in a few days, in his death, on the 18th of May 1893, at the age of sixty years. One of his last messages to the writer was this,—" I want to see that book." Alas! alas!

[1] Founded, 1836; rebuilt, 1874.

[2] These figures refer to the numbers on the accompanying plan.

[3] These must have been removed by 1814 or 1815, when Bolton Street was made. It was made under an Act passed in the 49th year of George III., for constructing a turnpike from Edenfield to Little Bolton. The Grants probably contracted for this section of the work.

building of the Square in 1821-22. The varied operations were then gradually transferred to the new works, while the buildings on the old ground were demolished, and the materials, in part at least, sold.

In Callender Yard, at the foot of Carr Street, there was a water-wheel[1] of considerable height, which turned the callenders, &c. (16). The water power came from Carr Street, or Devil Hole, Mill. The stream now goes underground to "John Gray's Lodge." A long building (17), still existing as cottages between the yard and Carr Street, was occupied by those engaged as pinners—*i.e.*, in putting pins in blocks and rollers. Thence the old name of the spot at the entrance from Carr Street to Callender Yard—"Pin-roller Nook" (18). At Carr Street Mill[2] the Yorkshire-men were engaged on woollen fabrics, and at Topwood Mill wool-combing was carried on by them.

The blacksmith's shop was at the upper end of the Pin-roller building in Carr Street. There John Hamer did the ironwork for the Old Ground, and shoed the horses, &c. At Barwoodlea, where the stables, &c., are now, were bleach-works in the Old Ground days.

The crofters had only small wages, about 13s. a week; they had also annually, from the firm, a coat and waistcoat each; and the lads had each a full suit. Not the least appreciated boon, however, was the holiday when they got their new clothes. It was deemed a great occasion. They

---

[1] A son of John Cunliffe, who was designer for the Grants, lost his life by falling into this wheel. It was some time after he was missed ere the little fellow's body was found. It was got at length in the mill-race, which still exists, deep under one of the houses between Callender Yard and Bolton Street.

[2] The newer part is now occupied by Messrs James Brooks & Son.

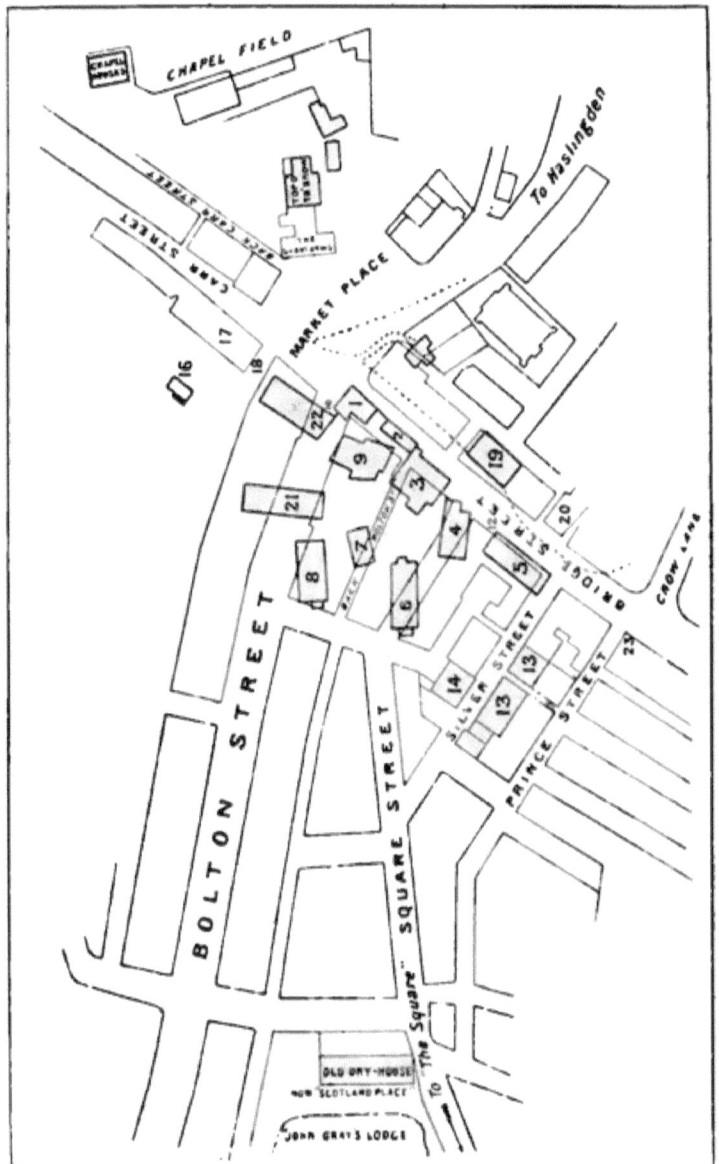

"Old Ground," Ramsbottom.

assembled at Grant Lodge, had, old and young, as much as they could eat and drink, and, afterwards, they " fiddled and danced and sang " to their hearts' content. "The old maister was alive then"—the father of the members of the firm. He died in 1817. The custom, however, continued after his decease.

The *gates* of the *principal entrance* to the Old Ground works stood in the line of the present Bolton Street, not far from its junction with Bridge Street (10). On entering the gates, the buildings on the left stretched out into about the middle of the present Bridge Street, and downwards, in succession, with short fenced intervals, to about the middle of Silver Street. The building at the junction of Bolton Street and Bridge Street (1) was used for drawing, engraving, printing, &c., and a little farther down was the old colour shop (2), used in early days for Sunday School purposes. Here the cradle of the Sunday Schools of Ramsbottom was rocked, under the same roof and at the same time, by Presbyterians and Methodists, during the second decade of this century.[1] Farther down, and still extending into Bridge Street, the stabling, joiner's shop, &c. (3), covered most of the ground between Back Bolton Street and Square Street. It was afterwards built on by Mr Arthur Lowe. The centre of the block is inscribed

A and A
L
1834.

The barn, hay-mow, &c. (4), shot diagonally across Square Street, where it joins Bridge Street, touching the site of

---

[1] Sunday Schools were begun in Manchester in 1784.

the present shops on either side. Starting a little farther down, a long rectangular building (5)—print-shop below and drying-house above—from about Mr Butterworth's shop, covered the sites of the saddler's shop, the Post Office, and Mr Renshaw's, and extended into Silver Street, within a few yards of Mr Richard Barlow's establishment. The old houses, still existing in Silver Street, formed the eastern boundary of the works (13). Up towards Smithy Brow, a large block-printing shop (6) shot N.W. and S.E. across Square Street, and farther up (8) was another large building lying in the same direction, and stretching from Smithy Brow across the site of the Clarence Hotel, &c., to Mr Sladin's shops in Bolton Street.

Near the centre of the Old Ground stood an old farm-house (7), at the upper end of which was the milk-house, where milk was sold. The farm-house itself was swallowed up by the works. The principal warehouse, counting-house, &c. (9), right in front on entering the gates, stretched from Bolton Street nearly to Back Bolton Street, and touched the present line of Bridge Street, a little above Back Bolton Street.

About the lower end of the present block of buildings extending from Silver Street to Prince Street, flanked at either extremity by the premises of Mr Barlow, in the corner of a field, all alone, stood the dungeon [1] (23). Its site was just about opposite Crow Lane. When, in after years,

---

[1] Near the upper end of Union Street and not far from the dungeon stood a solitary cottage. In it lived an old woman well known as Ailsa Thorrocks—that is, Ailse or Alice o' th' Horrocks, or Alice Horrocks. She had a peculiar fondness for cats, which she dressed up in caps and pinafores, like children. By a sad mishap, her bed caught fire, and the frail body was found "burnt to a cinder."

Ramsbottom Cricket Field and Players.

it disappeared, and the Messrs Ashton built the houses extending from Prince Street to Palatine Street—the row then opposite Crowtrees Orchard and Meadow, and now in the main opposite St Paul's Burying-Ground—they were commonly called *Dungeon Row*. From the dungeon right down to the place where now have long stood the buildings on the south side of Bridge Street, the railway hotel, railway station, paper-mill, &c., all the way round by the cricket-ground to the site of the Square, there were only fields and trees with an old orchard—no doubt the orchard of Cawdaw Mill—a memorial of which is happily preserved to us in *Orchard* Mill. On the site now occupied by the Square were a number of substantial Peel-erected buildings for callendering, dyeing, drying, washing, &c. These were demolished by the Grants to make room for the new works. When the Peels in 1783 began operations in Ramsbottom, there existed, near the site of the Square, an old corn-mill called the *Cawdaw Mill*.[1] This they removed. It, with its appurtenances, occupied the space—now mostly road and lodges—extending from about the Square Street end of Orchard Mill to about the north-east corner of the Square.

On the *higher side* of Ramsbottom, in the Old Ground days, there were the old grey-slated houses on both sides of Carr Street, in Back Carr Street, and Chapel Field,[2]

---

[1] There was no doubt a rookery near the spot then, as there happens to be not far off still; and the *cawing* of its sable occupants, the jack*daws*, manifestly suggested the name *Cawdaw* for the mill.

[2] The field which extends from Carr Bank to Grant Lodge and Back Carr Street was called Chapelfield. Chapel Houses and Peel Street were built near its lower margin, overlooking Back Carr Street, &c. The only

the Carr Street or Devil Hole Mill, Carr Fold, The Gutter, the fulling mill at Kibboth Crew,[1] Carr Barn,[2] Topwood Mill, Tanners, and Foot o' th' Rake. From a little decayed gable window in one of the old houses here, which belonged originally to the De Willoughbys, a small coloured diamond pane was rescued, some years ago, by Mr Samuel Wilson. It bears initials and date, and is in the possession of Mrs Rostron of Turton Bottoms, Turton. There were also Dundee Chapel and Manse, the farm on the opposite side of the lane (held by the Unitarian congregation at Bury), the lower three of the seven cottages a little below the manse garden, with a few which still remain on the same side about a hundred yards still farther down. The Old Dun Horse also existed as at

"FOOT O' TH' RAKE" PANE.

---

explanation we have found of the name Chapel Field is that in the upper part of the block called Chapel Houses, above Carr Street Mill, preaching was carried on at one time.

[1] In 1795 Mr Richard Wallwork, and afterwards his son, Mr Thomas Wallwork, occupied it.

[2] Now Carr Bank. It is beautifully situated on the crest of one of the lower slopes of the Holcombe range, just where it begins to sweep gradually down to the south-east, towards the Carr and Grant Lodge. The present house, with which is preserved a portion of its predecessor, was built and its grounds admirably laid out and planted in 1850. It was

present. But from that inn to Pin-Roller Nook,[1] on the *west* side of Bolton Street, not a house existed at that time; nor, indeed, were there any on the *east* side, until the Old Ground was reached. Crow Lumb was then the only house between Nuttall Lane farm and Nuttall farm, down at the old village.

The *flower-garden of Grant Lodge* occupied what is now the Market Place. It was laid out "in the shape of a heart," whose lines curved round right and left from the front of the house towards the gates, which, with stone pillars and rounded capitals, stood just opposite the top of Bridge Street. Round the outer fence of the garden ran a row of goodly trees, which was continued along in front of what is now the Conservative club and Dr Deans' surgery, and past the site on which the old Wesleyan Chapel was built in 1825, and where the handsome and commodious modern structure, its successor since 1874, now stands. The trees extended northwards towards the point where the New Jerusalem Church was afterwards erected[2] and the Rev. S. Pilkington unostentatiously laboured for twenty years. He passed away on 23d May 1889, in his 55th year. The only well for spring water in the centre of the village in those early Old Ground

---

prepared for Mr John Grant, the younger, of Nuttall Hall, who, however, did not live to occupy it. It was occupied for a time by his brother, the late Mr William Grant, and subsequently, for some years, by the late Mr William Stead. Afterwards, till his death it was the residence of the late Mr Henry Stead, J.P. The view from Carr Bank is very fine—whether up the valley or down towards the distant plain, or across to the range of hills linking Top o' th' Hoof with Cribden, Whittle Pike occupying the mid distance between.

[1] Now the confectioner's shop at the foot of Carr Street, and close to Callender Yard.
[2] The first meeting-place was built in 1831, the present church and School in 1876.

days was at the lower end of the north side of Carr Street.[1] No. 6 or 8 Carr Street covers the spot. The water came from Chapel Field, and was very hard. It was much prized, but *not* very abundant in its flow, and persons and pitchers were to be found sometimes not only during the day but during a good part of the night, waiting for their turn for a supply. On one memorable occasion, a too protracted wait by that weary well resulted in the birth of a young citizen on the spot. From the well a grove of trees extended right up into the field beside Grant Lodge. At a later period this water was taken forward to what is now the Market Place, nearly opposite Mr Whittaker's[2] then, and the New Market Inn at the present time. It continued there for many years, and is well remembered still by people in middle life. For washing purposes the brook furnished an abundant supply. And there was not only the Bridge Street brook, which is

REV. SAMUEL PILKINGTON.

---

[1] "Judy's Spout" existed near Springwood. It is so called from Judy or Judith Kenyon, who lived in a cottage near by.
[2] "Where Jack Butcher used to go to sharpen his knife on t' stone"—that is, Mr John Whittaker, butcher.

now conveyed in a conduit[1] to beyond the old toll-house, but two streams, a few yards apart, at a higher and lower level, flowed through the Callender Yard[2] along the site of the houses on the west side of what is now Bolton Street. At a point about Dr Macleod's surgery, in Markland Street, they shot diagonally across the line of Bolton Street to the lower end of the Co-operative premises; thence behind the site of the Baptist Chapel and Lodge View;[3] the higher to Barwood Bleach Croft, and the lower to a lodge between Barwoodlea and the Square. After the Square was built these streams went to supply "John Gray's Lodge," which the Grants formed on what was previously a green field.

Rev. Robert Maden.

[1] As described to the writer by one who saw it made—"a big soof."
[2] Off Central Street, behind the old library at the foot of Carr Street.
[3] The higher of these streams was under the present roadway between Lodge View and the Lodge.

In the Baptist Chapel, which we have just had occasion to mention, the late Rev. Robert Maden long and earnestly ministered. It was built in 1862, but the Baptist interest had taken form in the town about 1844.[1] The congregation for thirty years enjoyed the ministry of Mr Maden. Born of godly parents a few miles farther up the valley, at Cloughfold, in Rossendale, on 1st March 1831, and trained at Horton Baptist College, he began his ministry at Ramsbottom in 1858. It continued till a short time before his death on 3d December 1888.[2]

Reverting to the topography of old Ramsbottom, we may note that the road *southwards* from the centre of the village was a very rough one in those days. It ran from the foot of Carr Street, opposite Grant Lodge, past the Callender Yard, along somewhere about what is now called Central Street, and nearly parallel with the line of Bolton Street. It struck across the high ground near the foot of Callender Street to beyond the upper end of Lodge View, and then traversed the front part of the site of the Roman Catholic Chapel. Proceeding right up, within the line of the present buildings, it passed where the front of St Andrew's Presbyterian Church now is, and went on by Rosehill, across the site of the new Primitive Methodist Chapel[3] and Hope House; and from about the front of Dr Crawshaw's house in Barwood Mount its trend was slightly to the right or southwest, till it reached Dundee Lane. A part of this old track

---

[1] The first meeting-house of the Baptists in Lancashire was founded at Bacup in 1691. See 'Life of Oliver Heywood,' p. 281; and Halley's 'Lancashire Puritanism,' vol. ii. p. 326.
[2] His successor is the Rev. James M'Cleery.
[3] The first built in Bridge Street, in 1833, was replaced by this in 1889.

is still traceable. It runs from near the top of Kay Brow,[1] by the well, along the upper side of the lodge to Rosehill, whose houses have long blocked its progress. Fortunately, it has for a long period been superseded by the admirable Bolton Street and Bolton Road of modern times. The line of the old road is very interestingly determined at this point by the existence still of the original arched conduit for the stream which flowed under it, on its way then to the lodge and the bleach croft below at Barwoodlea, but now to the Square.

Rev. B. G. De Mullewie.

We interpolate a sentence at this point, while these sheets are passing through the press, to record the death of the Rev. B. G. De Mullewie, of the Roman Catholic Chapel, to which we have just had occasion incidentally to refer. A gentle-natured and unostentatious Belgian, he ministered to his people in Ramsbottom and the neighbourhood for nearly a quarter of a century, and was cut off after a brief illness, on 27th February 1893, in his 57th year.

The growing prosperity that had attended the efforts of the Grants led them, about 1820, to resolve upon the erection of a calico-printing establishment of such magnitude

---

[1] So called from Mr Edward Kay, a partner of the Peels, who owned and occupied Barwoodlea, before it was purchased by the Grants. He died in 1819, in the 61st year of his age, and was interred at Holcombe.

as would enable them to concentrate their varied operations within its single area. The Square was the result. It was built in 1821-22. The external measurement of each of its four sides is 241 feet, and it is three stories high. How did the new works come to be constructed in this form? Where did the idea come from? An incident in the life of Mr Charles Grant, related to the writer one day by Mrs Wilson, reveals the *genesis* of the *square*—the Square at Ramsbottom and the Square of Charles Dickens.[1] One Monday morning Charles called for his horse "Wellington," mounted, and set off without saying anything to "Robert," —the groom—or any one in the house as to where he was going. Days and nights passed and nothing was heard of him, and the family had begun to feel great anxiety, when, about midnight on the following Saturday, he returned, horse and rider alike wearied with their journey. His aged mother, relieved and rejoicing, hurried off her granddaughter Grace, and Eliza,[2] midnight though it was, half-dressed, to Nuttall Hall, to apprise Mr John of his return. Grace threw up small stones at her uncle's bedroom window to awake him, and then called out that "Uncle Charles" had come. When Charles was asked "where he had been, and whatever had taken him so unexpectedly away," he told them he had been to Hull or Nottingham—Mrs Wilson is not sure which, but thinks it was one or other of these towns—where he had seen an establishment in which confections were made which greatly interested him. It was, he said, constructed in the form of a square, and surrounded with water. The raw materials

---

[1] 'Nicholas Nickleby,' chap. xxxvii.   [2] Mrs Wilson.

went in at one side of the entrance, and the manufactured articles were turned out at the other, ready for the market. *That*, he said, he was resolved, was the form in which their own new works should be built. The "Square" on the verge of the Irwell at Ramsbottom stands to-day exactly as here described—the river and the adjacent lodges leaving only *terra firma* for the necessary approach. We asked, "Who was the architect of the Square?" "They had none." "Who made the plans for the builder?" "John Cunliffe, the drawer,"[1]—that is, the designer at the print-works. "They set Adam Brooks and other masons to work, and superintended it themselves." Charles was the soul of this enterprise. The building was up at the first of its three stories when the ox was roasted in its centre for the coronation celebration of George IV.—July 19, 1821.

On that coronation day there was a great and memorable demonstration at Ramsbottom. The morning presented a very animated scene. From far and near, up the valley and down, from isolated homes and busy hamlets and villages that flecked the sides of the neighbouring hills, were seen trooping the goodly company of hand-loom weavers employed by the Grants. They gathered, we are told, to the number of eighteen hundred at the appointed rendezvous in Ramsbottom, and were there joined by those employed in the

---

[1] Perfectly in harmony with this statement is the inscription on his tombstone at Old Dundee Chapel—

SACRED
To the Memory of
JOHN CUNLIFFE, OF RAMSBOTTOM,
Designer and Architect,
Who departed this life April 23, 1824,
Aged 50 years.

works. All were decked in their gayest attire—the girls in white jean dresses and pink sashes. At the appointed hour the great procession was formed, and marched to Bury. At its head, on horseback, rode the Grants—William, John, Daniel, and Charles—and a numerous company of gentlemen friends. Mr John Grant of Nuttall Hall occupied the place of honour, bearing some impressive symbol, which Mrs Wilson described as "a grand thing, like what you see on the pennies, with a crown on it." Bury was duly reached, and it was admitted that the procession of the Grants fairly eclipsed all others on the great occasion. One leaf, however, July though it was, fell from the stately tree —one home, amidst the rejoicings, was filled with sorrow. It was "a broiling day," and one of the girls drank freely at a wayside well on the route, became suddenly ill, and died.

The processionists, having returned to Ramsbottom, were entertained at a grand banquet provided by the firm. The tables were placed across the field[1] lying between Grant Lodge and Carr Bank. A bullock and many sheep had been roasted inside the Square works, which were being built at the time. "There was such bringing and borrowing of knives and forks, and many dozens were bought." "They were brewing for weeks and weeks before; and the puddings —what numbers!—great round 'uns in cloths, boiled in the boilers!" To Mrs Wilson, who was in the merry midst of what she described, we are indebted for these and many other particulars embodied in these pages. Those were palmy days —"Daniel Grant used to come from Manchester on Sunday

---

[1] Chapel Field.

mornings in a carriage and four with postilions. He generally

MRS WILSON AND HER MINISTER.[1]

brought merchants with him—mostly foreigners. They always went together in the forenoon to worship at 'Dundee.'"

Some time before the coronation festival an event occurred at Grant Lodge which Eliza was not likely ever to forget. She and

---

[1] "Snapped" by the photographer when the full page picture was taken, and inserted in deference to many friends, because it had caught the ordinary happy expression of Mrs Wilson's face.

another occupied a bedroom in the older part of the house, and one night, during a terrific storm, while asleep, the roof above them suddenly gave way, and the brick chimney-stalk came thundering down among the broken timbers. Thus rudely roused, they found themselves helplessly, yet, in the circumstances, mercifully wedged in by the fallen beams. The crash of the roof, louder for the moment than the howling of the storm, startled the other inmates of the house. But the doorway was blocked with the fallen roof and masonry, and approach to the imprisoned damsels was found to be impossible. In the terror and commotion caused by the collapse, Charles—always the man of action—was soon at the point of danger, and, with characteristic impetuosity and heroism, never rested till he dug his way right through door and brick and densely-packed *debris* to the corner where the imprisoned pair were lying. The rain and wind had checked the choking dust, and, fortunately, they were little or none the worse for the alarming mishap. Mrs Wilson had nothing but kind, and sometimes pathetic, words for "Mr Charles." What was true of his brothers was pre-eminently true of him—he would have done *anything* for his mother. And Mrs Wilson never forgot how much she owed to the prompt and skilful rescue he effected during that awful night of storm.

Another incident connected with the building of the Square works, related to the writer many years ago by one who long occupied an important place in them, is somewhat illustrative of those times. One day—it *might* be soon after the coronation festival—the masons, complaining greatly of thirst, marched off towards Holcombe Hill; not, however, to any of the limpid springs there to have it quenched! They halted at the old inn in the village of Holcombe, and tried another beverage. By-and-by Charles, finding the works deserted, set out in quest of the delinquents. He found them, and requested them to resume their work. They would return, of course, as he wished, but meanwhile he must, they urged, partake with them. He yielded. There, unhappily, lurked his greatest peril. The hours flew fleetly past—

> " As bees flee hame wi' lades o' treasure,
> The minutes winged their way wi' pleasure ;
> Kings may be blest, but Tam was glorious,
> O'er a' the ills o' life victorious ! "[1]

Mr John Grant next missed the errant builders; and, having set out in pursuit of the lost tribe, somewhat to their dismay he found them and their young master alike absorbed in other occupations than building the Square! The elder brother, justly irritated, gave expression to his indignation by pushing the foreman off his chair. Charles, impetuous, seeing this, made a rush at his brother, who fled precipitately, hotly pursued; but being clearer-headed, he was also surer-footed, and so escaped unscathed. By next morning, not before, the thirst was allayed, and the work resumed.

Charles Dickens, in 'Nicholas Nickleby,' uses the name of *Charles*—" Brother Charles and Brother Ned"— though, without doubt, the personalities of William and Daniel are in his eye. Charles's name, however, was the one specially identified with the building of the Square. But for him, it may be said without fear of challenge,

---

[1] Robert Burns, " Tam o' Shanter."

"The Square" would never have existed. The youngest —born in Lancashire—and best educated, he was also the most forceful, resolute, and commanding of all the Grants. Poor Charles! He died, in 1825, at the age of thirty-seven. How true it is

> "That souls are dangerous things to carry straight,
> Through all the spilt saltpetre of the world!"[1]

Three brothers remained. Of these, William was the eldest and Daniel the youngest. Mr John Grant, always more of a yeoman than a merchant or manufacturer, admirably managed the landed property acquired by the firm; while, being resident at Nuttall Hall, about an equal distance from the Square and Nuttall village, he also took some oversight of the works at these places, especially the latter. The great enterprises of the firm, however, were mainly in the hands of William and Daniel. While controlling the works at Ramsbottom, their headquarters were in Manchester.

In those days a foot-bridge over the Irwell, on the south side of the Square, connected the works with the path across the holm to Nuttall Hall. One year that part of the holm opposite this foot-bridge was growing turnips, and Mr John Grant one morning caught a young man carrying one of the tempting esculents into the works. By way of punishment, he ordered the offender to eat it on the spot. He began, but by-and-by the wheels drave very heavily, and once and again he wished to be excused. But no, the master was inexorable. He stood over him with his walking-stick until root, bulb, tops, and all had

---

[1] E. B. Browning, "Aurora Leigh."

been consumed. Then, with an admonition, he sent him to his work. It was a somewhat drastic chastisement, and never forgotten. For years after, even the *sight* of a turnip was, if possible, avoided. So one would readily suppose!

Another incident, at an earlier date, will show the rough-and-ready way in which offenders were sometimes handled in those times. Bleaching was then carried on by the Grants, and one dark night the watchman on his rounds observed that one of the pieces stretched on the bleach-field was gradually receding from its original position. He suspected the cause, and adroitly succeeded in capturing the delinquent in possession of his booty. He was locked up, and, next morning, marched off to Bolton to appear before the magistrates. But, before starting to face the august tribunal, the piece which he had stolen, still wet, was wrapped round his body and firmly secured; and, thus swathed, he had to march to his trial—seven miles— at a quick pace. "He wur welly [wellnigh] melted, and fairly at t' fur end when he got to Bowton." No wonder! The magistrates, it was presumed, duly considered the punitive value of this unique and melting march to justice, and imposed a correspondingly mitigated penalty.

At the time of its erection and equipment by the Grants, the Square was considered one of the most perfect works of its kind — a model calico-printing establishment.[1] It

---

[1] In vol. i. of the second edition of 'Chemical Essays,' principally relating to the Arts and Manufactures of the British Dominions, by Samuel Parkes, F.L.S., M.R.I., F.S.A.Ed., Member of the Royal Asiatic Society of Great Britain and Ireland, Fellow of the Geological and Astronomical Societies of London, &c., published in 1823, we find the following reference to the "New works on a larger scale of Messrs William Grant & Brothers, of Ramsbottom"—that is, to the Square. The author says:

embraced machine-printing from the first, but at that time the *machine* occupied a subordinate position to the *block* printing. Afterwards, however, the machine-printing became supreme, although it never *entirely* supplanted the other at the Square. These works ran their course, under the Grants, in about forty-five years—1821-1866.[1]

Since 1867 the Square has been occupied as bleach-works[2] by Messrs Hepburn & Co., who have been wont to employ from 300 to 400 people.

"This establishment I have lately seen; and having been surprised, not only at the greatness of the concern, but also at the judgment which has been displayed in the arrangement of the building and the adaptation of one part to the other throughout the whole of this extensive manufactory, I obtained leave to make drawings and take measures of the machinery—for the purpose not only of correcting what was said of the Ramsbottom print-works in the former edition of these essays, but also to direct the attention of the public to an establishment which does honour to the country, and reflects the utmost credit on the talents and enterprise of the proprietors. . . . In erecting this establishment, the proprietors have evidently studied neatness and elegance as well as usefulness; and in the whole of their machinery they seem to have availed themselves of every new invention that can be considered an improvement in calico-printing. . . . It is the opinion of good judges that these print-works will be capable of beginning and finishing one thousand pieces per day throughout the year; and that, when completed, they will be the largest and most convenient works of any in Europe."

[1] The following were successively managers of the Grants' works:—

Mr Joshua Knowles, who afterwards established the well-known print-works at Tottington, was manager on the Old Ground, but left before the opening of the Square.

Mr Charles Grant, at first, practically managed the Square.

Mr Thomas Greig, who went to Rosebank in 1831.

Mr Charles Guest, *Mr Richard Crossley*, and *Mr R. D. Whittenbury* followed. From 1852 to the present time the management of the estate of the Grants has been practically in the hands of Mr J. S. W.—now Major—Grant.

[2] Messrs Hepburn, by their chief engineer, Mr James Sadler, have equipped these works with the most approved mechanical appliances, including some admirable patents, the fruit of Mr Sadler's ingenuity and skill.

About five years after the erection of the Square, and a mile and a half farther up the valley, the Chatterton Riot took place at the factory, now in ruins, at the village of Chatterton. On the 23d of April 1826, and three following

SCENE OF CHATTERTON RIOT (STUBBINS CHURCH IN THE DISTANCE).

days, a resolute crowd of both men and women, maddened by hard times — the pressure of heavy taxation,[1] dear

---

[1] The National Debt in 1688 was only £664,263. 105 years afterwards – at the *beginning* of the French Revolutionary War—in 1793, it amounted to £239,350,248. That war *added* £601,500,343. Thus, on the 1st of February 1817, it reached the enormous sum of £840,850,591, with an *annual* charge of £32,014,851. By 1820 the debt was reduced to £794,980,481, with an annual charge of £29,789,658. *At the time of the riot*, Great Britain and Ireland, with a population *less* by about *fifteen millions* of people than in 1891, and with greatly depressed industries, was

bread,[1] little employment, and a dread of the power-looms depriving them of what little they had—swept like a whirlwind through the Rossendale and Ramsbottom Valley, and destroyed the obnoxious machinery. They—to the number of about 5000—were met on the 26th by a detachment of soldiers at Messrs Aitken & Lord's mill at Chatterton, while they were fearlessly effecting their fell purpose. The soldiers —Queen's Bays and Riflemen—had been held in readiness at the works of Messrs Ashton. As a Justice of the Peace for the County Palatine, Mr William Grant rode at the head of the detachment, and, after making a frank and kindly but fruitless appeal, read the Riot Act. The soldiers, it is said, acted with great forbearance; but, after some of them had been injured with missiles thrown by the rioters, they were ordered to fire. Five men and one woman were killed, and a large number wounded. One old man was busy at the destructive work in the mill when the firing began. But he went doggedly on, simply remarking—" Ne'er mind 'em, lads; we may as well be shot as *clemmed* for want of meyt." Another, near him, was shot through the arm, but, notwithstanding, went on cutting out the warps in the looms. A woman, nearly half-a-mile away was hit by a stray-bullet and bled to death on the spot; a fine fellow — a blacksmith named Lund, from

---

paying annually as *interest* on the National Debt *alone*, about £29,000,000. We have often, long ago, heard the older people refer to these times as *the dear years*, when the four-pound loaf was three shillings, and oatmeal sixpence a pound ! With a population in 1891 of over *thirty-eight millions*, instead of about *twenty-three* millions, as in 1826, the National Debt was £684,070,959, and the annual charge on the nation was about *twenty-five millions* of pounds. In 1893 it is £671,042,842.

[1] The Corn Laws enriched the landed interest, but impoverished the people, by raising the price of bread, &c.

Haslingden — was shot in the abdomen. He struggled across the river, reached the bank, and died, a piteous sight; while, not far from him, another victim writhed in hopeless agony. The large tale of wounded were borne from the scene as speedily and secretly as possible. The dragoons, in dispersing the crowd, acted mercifully, or the slaughter would have been much greater. They used the *flat* of their swords, telling the imperilled rioters as they overtook them to get out of *sight* in the goyt among the bushes, &c. In those days the extreme penalty of the law was dealt out freely to offenders against it, and forty-two of the rioters, including seven women, were, for this riot, sentenced to death. The recommendation to mercy by the jury, however, saved them from capital punishment. To repair the damage done by the rioters cost the county about £20,000. Only a few years ago one of the last survivors of the wounded—James Riley—died at Nuttall Lane. Any successor of Charlotte Brontë may find rich material in the fierce outburst of a brave and industrious and much-enduring people, which culminated in the sad and ghastly scene at Chatterton.

This district suffered from three riotous periods in the earlier part of the present century—viz :

The *Luddite* Riots in 1812.[1] They originated in Nottingham, and spread rapidly. Here, they were known as the *Shuttle-gathering* Riots, because the actors took forcible possession of premises and seized the *shuttles* of those who would not "come out." They thus stopped the works.

---

[1] So called from Ned Ludd, who broke some stocking-frames at Nottingham, in 1782.

The rioters mistakenly thought that by this action they would compel the masters to pay higher wages. It had the opposite effect. It increased the people's hardships, and these were already severe enough. The half-starved hand-loom weavers, poor fellows, might be seen, at that time, searching the fields for herbs and roots to eke out their meagre household fare. May such an era *never* come again! It was the time of the French War. *That* brought enormous taxes, dear bread, and bad trade. Next came—

The *Power-loom* Riots, above referred to, in 1826; and then—

The *Chartist* or *Plug-drawing* Riots, in 1842. In the last case the rioters knocked out the *boiler-plugs* in the mills assailed, opened the sluices, &c., and thus again stopped the works. The Chartist leaders, unhappily, held that a six weeks' cessation of work would compel the Government to concede their *six points*. Hence the riots. These, like the previous riots, caused much excitement throughout the country—special constables were sworn in, the military called out, &c. Ramsbottom had, amongst its people, some ardent Chartists. It is supposed that the leaden bullets dug up some years ago at 72 Bolton Street had been concealed by one of these of the advanced type. Between the ceiling and the floor of an old house in Ramsbottom Lane a *pike-head* was found quite recently. Its blade is 11 inches, by 2 at its widest part. This weapon was probably concealed at an earlier period. It is in the possession of Major Grant. The six points of the "People's Charter" do not, nowadays, look so very alarming. They were embodied in a Bill, prepared in 1838 by six M.P.'s and six working men, and asked—I. Manhood suffrage—a vote at 21 to every man being of sound mind and unconvicted of crime. II. The Ballot. III. Equal electoral districts. IV. Annual Parliaments. V. No Property qualification of M.P.'s. VI. Payment of Members of Parliament.

In 1839 a leader among the Chartists lived at 72 Bolton Street. He was well known, and is still remembered. At a great Chartist demonstration in the year named, he headed the forces; and, no less ardent, his wife, who, like Charlotte Corday, "never lacked energy," took her place beside him, bearing conspicuously *the cap of liberty*. There were imposing illuminations on the occasion, and at one point in the proceedings a "Noah's dove" emerged from the distant darkness, hovered over the assembly, and then disappeared again. It returned, however, but unfortunately, before it reached its designed terminus, the wire apparatus failed, and the messenger of peace was turned upside down! Our Registrar, Mr James Spencer, was present, as a lad, on the occasion. Pike-heads in those days were forged from old files, &c., with great avidity. One form of weapon embraced three parts—viz.: a *hook* on one side, an *axe* on the other, and the *pointed pike* between —the hook intended to unhorse the dragoon with, the battle-axe to brain him, and the pike to deal the *coup de grace*.

Behind *all* these unhappy occurrences there were manifestly one or other or both of two elements—First, and mainly, the pressure of want; second, the conviction that, in some way, it was caused by misgovernment and greed. The remedy sought by the operatives was twofold —reform of Parliament and better wages—a fairer share of the financial fruits of their hard industrial toil. In this purpose, by *constitutional* methods of action, happily, they have at length marvellously succeeded. But "there remaineth yet very much land to be possessed."

Many years ago, an old residenter who had lived through these trying and exciting times, and knew especially well about the Chatterton Riot — speaking in his last days of the riotous proclivities of his fellow-operatives, said to the writer — "*They're slow o' gaitin', but oh, they're bad to lay!*" — loth to begin, but, once started, exceedingly difficult to stop.

SAMUEL BAMFORD.

Among local leaders in those old stirring times, the name of Dr Macdougall, who also lived in Bolton Street, is often mentioned: and Samuel Bamford, of Middleton, is still affectionately remembered by old people who had evidently been loyal disciples long ago. Looking at a portrait of Bamford one day recently, one of these, with the fire of earlier days kindling in his eyes, and a spice of scorn in his tone, said, pointing to the likeness—"We've noan sich English blood neaw as when that owd chap wur amung us! He wur a good un, wur Sam. He wanted no mischief—no mak' o' lumber, nawe! but what wur straight and jannock[1] o' reawnd; an' we'd ned on it then, and we want it neaw. He wur one o' th' best on 'em, noan o' yo're kankert sort, an' no 'atchet ov his own to grind. Sam wer'n't thinkin' o' hissel'—*not* 'im, but o' *them as wur clemmin'*, an' there wur rooks ov 'em i' them days, an' we've some yet. Its noan to' lat' to give th' owd cause a push up th' hill. An' they put 'im i' gaol—go' lad! —for tryin' to mak' things reet. Many a good un's been put i' t' cage, maisther—what seyn *yo?*"

"Yes, indeed, you're quite right there."

"Yeigh! aw'm reet. A gradely rook o' them owd martyrs were amung it, wer'n't they? An' them Kovynanthurs yon, as aw used to read abeawt, when aw wur a lad, in an owd book o' mi gronfeyther's co'ed 'Nafthaly' ('Naphtali'), or summat like that, when t' king mut thrut bishops an' prayer-books deawn their throats willynilly. Aw think they seyn as how o' *their* parsons wur bishops to start wi', an'

---

[1] Jannock means originally the old Lancashire oatmeal bread. It was good and wholesome, and, indeed, many if not most of the men of finest physique of past generations in this locality had benefited by its virtues. It is referred to in the following lines:—

"And brave ale of Halton I have,
And what meat I had to my hire,
A pudding may no man deprave,
And a *jannock* of Lancaster-shire."

They occur in the "Shepherds Play," which was acted at Chester in 1577 in honour of the visit of the Earl of Derby to the city.—(Note in 'Bury Times,' May 24, 1893.) Secondarily, it means genuine, upright, fair, trustworthy.

they'd rayther mak' t' prayers for theirsels like t' first bishops, as they ned 'em. Aw used to be sum an feyn to read that owd book, an' aw al'ays thowt as how they wur reet. Sich mak' o' wark as prayin' tha knows, is like t' Ramsbottom loaves—*whoam-made 's best eytin'*. If Sam 'ad been yon, he'd ha' been a Kovynanthur—dunnot yo' think so?"

"It's very likely he would."

"He wur as good a Christian, mind yo', as here an' there a one; an' so wur his wife—a brave Middleton lass, an' a rare good wife for Sam. They made *their* own prayers, an' could sing their own hymns too, yon. When Sam wurn't a-whoam, hoo did it' wi' th' little un 'ersel'. They wur a good sort. Hoo marched to Peterloo, i' 1819, as weel as Sam! They owt to ha' g'en *him* a pension i'sted o' th' jail. At th' time o' th' Chatterton Riot, but for Sam, aw'l tek mi 'davy [affidavit], th' rougher end would a' smashed th' looms i' Rochda and Middleton and Heywood too, as weel as Rossenda. 'Twur so. Its a gradely pictur o' th' owd cock, as how. Awm sum an feyn to see thy honest face agen, owd mon, even on papper—good—owd—lad!"

We may interpolate another snatch or two in the vernacular by the way.

"Limiteds? There wur no sich Limiteds i' them days. Better bout, some met say; but that's to' mich. Wi' gradely gaffers o' th' reet mak', they'd do weel enoof. But, by gum, we 'n bin lick'd lat'ly, wi' er own brass. An' they do get t' cream fro' th' big keaw someheaw. Them Limiteds meon sometimes *hun*limited haxegrindin."

"What 's that?"

"Haxe-grindin', yo meon?"

"Yes."

"Weel, maister, sin yo' ax, aw'l try to enleeten yo'."

"Good!"

"It's summat like this—yo' pay th' bills, an' t' sarvint teks o' th' cream, an' 'appen levs yo' nobbut a sup o' blue milk. That's abeawt t' size on it. Them gaffer-chaps can sumtimes get howd o' theawsands o' peawnds for thersels, whol t' poor share'olders finger next to nowt. Aw knows. There's deycent owd foak who'd saved a hundred or teaw i' their younger days, an' they're half-clemmin' to-neet, whol sumbry else's axe is on their grindlestone. That's what aw co' *hunlimited haxe-grindin'*. An' there's lots on it.

"That's hard on the gaffer-chaps, isn't it?"

"Ne'er fear—yo'll find 'em creawse an' peort as pynots [brisk and pert as magpies]. Awm noan larn'd, yo' can guess, as t' Yankees say, an' appen a bit rouf i' th' maeth, but aw like what's square an reet. No haxe-grindin' for me, bi' th' mon! [by *the* Man.] Nawe! Never whol aw'm wick! A fair field an' no favver, but noan o' them 'angment 'atchets!

"Some maisthers when theyn getten a bit rich, lev us, an' t' capital goes wi' 'em. That's bad for us. But weyn some o' th' reet sort left—gradely good uns fro' Brox to Bacup—such as t' Hardmans, and Hoyles, and Porritts, and Aitkens, and Madens. Like th' owd Grants, they live i' th' valley and keep th' brass a-whoam for use. We want moar o' that sort. They don't lev us when they'n made a bit ov a pile. An' we owt to stick to that mak' o' maisthers—noan o' yo'r idle glob-trottin' Mounty Kerlo fellys, maishin' thersels up like foo's, and makin' ducks and drakes o' th' brass.

"Mind yo', th' maisthers have had a bad time of it lat'ly, an' weyn had enoof o' fightin'. We should be i' t' same boat wi' 'em neaw, pooin' gradely t'one wi' t'other, for t' best o' reawnd. They're killed wi' taxes, and tariffs, and o' mak' ov expenses. T' saddle's clapt on th' wrong nag. They owt to tax *far heavier* them as do little or nowt for t' country, either wi' hond or brain, an' yet get millions ov good money every year that's been work'd for by other foak. Th' hard workers—maisthers and men—get to' little and are burdened to' mich, an' th' idle uns get to' mich, and arn't burden'd enoof. That looks as plain as t' nose on one's face, or t' sken ov owd Bassett the bellman. What thinken yo'?"

BASSETT THE BELLMAN.

"Owd Bassett" here referred to was long the public bellman. He had a great voice—could be heard as far off as Holcombe and Shuttleworth—a kindly heart, and a striking *sken* or squint. In his rounds, at stated points, he expected to see certain well-known faces, and, in their absence, would prelude his announcement, *ore rotundo*, with some such request as, "Tell Peggy Pilkington as Bassett is 'ere wi' himportant pooblic hinformation!" When Peggy appeared, the lieges were forthwith enlightened. After his death, others tried to assume his tintinabulant function, but failed. One of the old "apprentices," he formed a link with a vanished era, and had no successor—"Owd Bassett the Bellman."

Some fifty or sixty years ago, three well-known employés of the Grants, on pleasure bent, were climbing one day towards Ashworth Moor. All the three, as it happened, had very pronounced *squints*. While marching, Indian file, some ten or twelve yards apart, they met a "fureigner" (a stranger to the valley). When abreast of the third, suddenly pulling up, and feigning some alarm, he asked—" Dun they o' *sken* where yo' come fro"?' "Yeigh! bi th' mon!" "Eh! What fur?" Stepping towards him with a facial contortion worthy of Ralph Fish at the "grinning match," he answered—" To gloppen [frighten] great gawbies like thee," as the stranger took to precipitate flight down the hillside!

In 1830 the founder of the cotton industry at Ramsbottom, the first Sir Robert Peel, passed away. Nearly *sixty* years before, a little farther down the valley, and within sight of the bold hill on which for now over forty years has towered a massive and enduring memorial of their illustrious son, Robert Peel used to take little Nellie Yates on his knee, in *her* father's and *his* partner's house, and say, " Nellie, thou bonnie little brid, will ta be my wife?—wilt ta, Nellie?" And Nellie winsomely was wont to say, as she nestled on the knee of the genial lodger and kinsman, "Yes, Robut." "Then I'll wait for thee, Nellie — that I will; and I'll wed thee and none elze, my bonnie little lass," was Robert's frank and cheery but characteristically earnest reply. He did wait— ten years, and he did wed the winsome girl, in 1783, the year in which he founded his works at Ramsbottom. And the keen-visioned glance which detected so unerringly the undreamt-of possibilities of the cotton industry, was equalled by this early recognition in little Nellie of those inestimable qualities which, in after years, so eminently adorned the first Lady Peel. Those sixty years, however, had now told their tale—

SIR ROBERT PEEL.

no ordinary one in the busy life of the Peel family—and Lady Peel, many years before, amid deep and widespread sorrow, had gone to an honoured grave, when, on the 3d of May

1830, the long and distinguished career of her husband—the first Sir Robert—then the squire of Drayton Manor, Tamworth, came to a close, in the eighty-first year of his age.

LADY PEEL (neé NELLIE YATES).

Four years after his death, what he had predicted of his son Robert, while yet a youth, was verified—Nellie Yates's eldest son became Prime Minister of England in 1834.

But Ramsbottom, since these opening decades of the century, has made steady progress in every respect. In 1802 Messrs Ashton built a mill a short distance above Peel Bridge, and for more than seventy years the spinning and manufacturing firm which they founded contributed much towards the advancement of the village. Messrs James and John Ashton, who had previously carried on hand-loom weaving at Middleton, built the mill in 1802. It was replaced by modern structures more than sixty years afterwards. Their three sons —Samuel, Thomas, and Richard — succeeded them, as Messrs S. & T. Ashton. Thomas, who lived at Middleton, was not an active partner. Both Samuel and Richard were. Mr Samuel lived near Bury, and Mr Richard, who was a Justice of the Peace, lived at Limefield. His son, Mr Edward Ashton, was connected with the works till 1877.

MR RICHARD ASHTON, J.P.

In 1812 the Messrs Grant purchased the factory at Nuttall village. And, altogether, for nearly sixty years, on the Old Ground, at Nuttall, and in the Square, embracing for a considerable period hundreds of hand-loom weavers employed at their homes dispersed over a wide country district, the firm of Messrs William Grant & Brothers was the main factor, alongside the firm of Messrs Ashton, in the industrial development of Ramsbottom. Where, in population, the Grants and the Ashtons found hundreds, they left thousands.

Besides the works of the Grants and the Ashtons, there also existed, in the early part of the century, the works of Mr Sandiford, at Stubbins. These, greatly enlarged since, now form the extensive and progressive establishment of Messrs Wm. Rumney & Company, for engraving and calico printing. Some years ago this firm purchased the works — spinning and manufacturing—of the above Messrs Ashton, in Ramsbottom. At the Stubbins works, quite recently, a new and promising branch has been added to industrial art. With artistic skill and mechanical ingenuity, Messrs James and Alexander Young (the latter managing partner in the firm) have devised, and the Rossendale Glass Decorating Company have patented, a method of printing *glass* with enduring colours. Indeed, by this happy device, wood, leather, glass, or any kindred substance, can be effectively printed or ornamented with any design, and with a

MR WILLIAM RUMNEY.

K

facility akin to that familiar in printing calico. The possibilities of this ingenious achievement are obviously important and manifold. Ramsbottom will wish it a great and prosperous future.

Mr Wm. Rumney, of the above firm, began his career at Stubbins, in partnership with Mr Greenhalgh, in 1855. The partnership was dissolved in 1861. With extraordinary energy and success, as sole partner, Mr Rumney conducted and extended the business till 1882, when, on the 11th of August, after a brief illness, he passed away in the sixtieth year of his age.

There was also, early in the century, the spinning and manufacturing establishment, now a ruin, at Chatterton, long in the hands of Messrs Aitken & Lord, in whose possession it was at the time of the riot in 1826.

In 1831 Mr Thomas Greig went from the Square to form, with his brother Mr Bennett Greig and Mr Watson, the firm of Messrs Greig, Watson, & Greig, at Rosebank Print Works. These works have, ever since, been steadily and successfully carried on. They were for many years worked by one of the nephews of the Messrs Greig—Mr Thomas Greig Stark, J.P., and since his sudden death at Cairo, in December 1891, by his son, Mr John Stark.

On the west side of the valley, opposite the Chatterton estate, lies that of Stubbins Vale, where, during the past forty years, Mr James Porritt, J.P., and during the latter portion of that period, his sons—Mr Richard and Mr John Austin Porritt—have done so much by their model works, elegant residences, and judicious planting of trees, not only to advance the industrial prosperity, but also to enhance the amenity and beauty, of this portion of the valley.

The brothers Porritt—Joseph, James, and Samuel—began their woollen-manufacturing career at Dearden Clough Mill

MR JAMES PORRITT, J.P.

in 1838, and took Springwood Mill, Ramsbottom, in 1845.

The former factory was nearly wrecked by the memorable "Cowpe Flood." Subsequently Mr John Austin joined the partnership, and the firm became Messrs Porritt Brothers & Austin. This firm began to build the splendid works at Stubbins Vale in 1851. In 1857 Mr Joseph retired from the partnership and established the firm of Messrs Joseph Porritt & Sons at Sunnybank, Helmshore; and, similarly, in 1866, Mr Samuel founded the firm of Messrs Samuel Porritt & Sons at Bamford. Of these brothers, Mr James, the venerable head of the firm at Stubbins Vale, still survives.

Opposite Stubbins Vale, on a prominent plateau above Chatterton, stands Stubbins Congregational Church, a graceful structure erected mainly by the generosity of Mr James Porritt and his family. The church, equipped with a costly organ and stained-glass window, the schools with caretaker's house, and the burying-ground, with boundary walls, &c., have cost altogether about £10,000. Of this sum, Mr James Porritt, in one form or another, has contributed about £5000, and his eldest son, Mr Richard Porritt, about £2000. The late Mr William Rumney furnished £500, and the late Mr Samuel Porritt £300. The pastor is the Rev. Thomas Cain.

In 1846 the Lancashire and Yorkshire Railway from Manchester to Rossendale was opened. It furnished fresh facilities for commerce, and tended to develop local enterprise.

In 1854 the cotton manufacturing firm of Messrs Laurence Stead & Brother was formed. Their business expanded with marked rapidity. Their mills were kept going all through the terrible time of the cotton famine. And, for many years, when fully occupied, their factories found employment for the greater part of a thousand people. The senior partner died

STUBBINS VALE.

in 1891, aged sixty-seven; and the junior, Mr Henry Stead, after a long illness, twelve months later, in June 1892, aged sixty-six. Born within a stone's throw of old Dundee Chapel, they were trained under the Grants at the Square. And since the works of the Grants were closed, thirty years ago, no firm has done so much for Ramsbottom as that of Messrs Stead; while, since Daniel Grant died in 1855, no individual man has accomplished so much for the good of the community as the late Mr Henry Stead. The large place which the firm occupied in the industrial wellbeing of the town may be estimated by the distress which has been experienced since, unhappily, their factories were closed, a few months after the surviving partner had passed away.

MR LAURENCE STEAD.

Of the Steads there were five brothers, one of whom, Thomas, died in early manhood. Joseph and William are referred to subsequently. They were all men of exceptionally fine physique, strong, genial-natured, and sympathetic. They were leaders in opposing political camps, and with unflinching

Mr Henry Stead, J.P.

fidelity fought out their respective contentions on the public platform in years gone by. Yet what was true of the Grants was also true of the Steads — their brotherly regard for one another was something refreshing to witness. Their father, James Stead, came from a vigorous Yorkshire stock; and their mother, Catherine Kirk, daughter of Thomas and Catherine Kirk—interred at Dundee Chapel—from an equally vigorous race farther north.

The Ramsbottom Paper Mill Company, Limited, have greatly extended and improved their premises during recent years, and their works, which give employment to about 250 people, now constitute an important factor in the material wellbeing of the town.

In addition to the foregoing, there are also the large and well-appointed co-operative works at Stubbins, embracing both spinning and manufacturing; Victoria Mills, with which the name of Mr Henry Heys has long been associated; the Palatine Mill of Messrs J. & E. Rothwell; the mills of Messrs William Ashworth & Company, and Mr Barnes, in Railway Street; Messrs Rostron, Old Ground; the Rose Mill, recently extended and equipped at great expense, by Mr E. Cunliffe; and the modern and extensive premises known as the Star Mill.

On the east side of the river, abutting on Kenyon Street, beyond Peel Bridge Mill, there is the manufacturing establishment of Mr Samuel Harrison;[1] and, farther up, that of Messrs Schofield & Ashworth. In the same locality, the soap and chemical industries have long been worthily represented by the works of Mr Edward Cunliffe and those of Mr Alcimus Isherwood and Mr John Barnes. Across the

---

[1] Closed since 1892—About to be opened by Messrs Hargreaves.

valley, in the dell, at the foot of Deep Clough, are Carr Works, the refining works of Mr Samuel Porritt—Messrs W. W. Burtwistle & Co.—while, farther down, Springwood Mill is occupied by Messrs Hitchon & Shepherd. The first machinist's shop in Ramsbottom was that of Mr James Robinson, where Messrs Rostron's mill now stands on the Old Ground. Mr Gabriel Lund's Foundry appeared towards the close of the first half of the century; and about the same time the foundry and machinist's works of the late Mr Arthur Bentley were established in the premises now occupied by Mr John Wood. Some ten years later were begun the founding and engineering works of Mr William Sharples, Irwell Street Foundry, and some years afterwards the kindred works of Mr Joseph Strang, Prince's Foundry—both of which have expanded into important establishments. There are also the Irwell Tin Works, long associated with the name of their founder—the late Mr Richard Mason. Heald-making and reed-making have been carried on successfully in Square Street by Mr Thomas Sharples and his sons, Mr Robert and Mr William Sharples, since about 1860.

On the Shuttleworth side of the valley, the following establishments have also long materially contributed to the prosperity of the neighbourhood — viz., Edenwood Mill, under the late Mr Charles Ratcliffe, and now his son, Mr Fred. Ratcliffe; Dearden Clough Mill, under Mr George Clegg; and farther up the Clough, Bridge Mills, formerly Mr Rostron's, now in the hands of Mr Alexander Barlow and his sons; Turn Mill, under Mr Richard Nuttall; and Lodge Mill, under the Messrs Ramsbottom.

In the village of Shuttleworth, for a long period, employment was afforded by the mills of Messrs William Wild &

Brothers. Their works have been sadly missed since they were closed some twelve or thirteen years ago, after the death of the last surviving partner. Fortunately, the Bleach Croft of Messrs William Rumney & Co., of Stubbins, still holds vigorously on its way; and one of the mills—the Lower Mill—built by Messrs Wild in the dell below the village, is now worked by Mr Hitchon Hitchon. For nearly half a century the paper-making industry was represented in Shuttleworth by the works of the late Mr James B. Ingham and his son, Mr Harold Ingham, who, to the loss of the old village, and the regret of many friends, transferred his energies to Nottingham in 1889.

REV. EDWIN DYSON.

While referring to Shuttleworth, we deem it deserving of note that it has always been the practice of the present vicar of the parish—the Rev. Edwin Dyson—to ask his Nonconformist brethren, at the interment of any of their people, to unite with him in conducting the funeral service. Had a course so seemly and reasonable been adopted by others, there would have been little demand for Burials Acts, and many unseemly scenes, and much unhappy bitterness throughout the land, would have been prevented. St John's, Shuttleworth, was consecrated in 1848. The Rev. H. P. Hughes was incumbent from 1845 to 1875. Mr Dyson succeeded in 1875.

Glancing from the north-east to the south-west extremity of the district, Holcombe Brook Factory, successively under Mr Boothman, Mr Hutchinson, and others, and the Reddisher Wood Works, have also furnished their quota towards our industrial advancement. And there are other names, some almost forgotten, which claim a place in connection with the industrial progress of the town, such as Alsop, Wallwork, Wolstenholme, Proctor, Horne, Hutchinson, Wallace, Parkinson, Hamer, and others. There should also be mentioned the late Mr Christopher Geldard, who for many years occupied Rose Mill, and Mr William Stead, who, like the Nuttall Manufacturing Company since, did something to revive the vanished vitality of the manufacturing establishment at the old village of Nuttall. For the Company recently formed there, and for the Star Mill[1] Company—for whom the extensive Cobden Mill premises have been enlarged, readjusted, and fully equipped—the community at large will wish a long and prosperous career, in company with their elder brethren, who have long borne the burden and heat of the day, striving loyally, through many trying years, to maintain and advance the wellbeing of Ramsbottom.

---

[1] Now the property of Ramsbottom Industrial and Provident Society, Limited.

About half-a-mile south of Nuttall village, at Brooksbottom, are the extensive and well-built spinning and manufacturing mills of Messrs Joshua Hoyle & Sons. The original mills of the firm, long established, are at Bacup. One of the partners of this firm—Mr Isaac Hoyle—represented the Heywood and Ramsbottom division in Parliament

BROOKSBOTTOM MILLS[1] (ROWLANDS CHAPEL IN THE DISTANCE).

from 1885 to 1892. His retirement from parliamentary life occasioned deep and widespread regret.

Engraving for calico-printers has been carried on for a long period at the Hazlehurst Works, by Messrs John Spencer & Sons; Messrs Wood & McRae at one time had a large

---

[1] The narrowness of the ravine prevented the artist from getting a good picture of the fine main frontage of the mills.

engraving shop—now the front part of Hope Mill in Nuttall Lane—and Messrs William Rumney & Company, along with their print works at Stubbins, maintain also a large and well-equipped engraving department.

We should also note, in connection with the trade of Ramsbottom, the extensive quarrying operations carried on in the immediate vicinity—at Scout Moor, by Messrs Whittaker; at Fletcher Bank, for a long period by the late Mr Richard Wild, and now by his successor, Mr Joseph Ellerbeck; and on the Holcombe range, by Mr Jeoffrey Grime Wild.

The Ramsbottom Industrial and Provident Society, Limited, was established in 1858. It has proved, in many respects, an important institution. Its aggregate sales for the past twenty years amount to more than a million and a half sterling—the annual average being over £75,400. The average dividend paid during these years has been 2s. 8d. in the pound. The Society has long maintained a library and reading-room, and in other ways has accomplished valuable educational work, on which it has spent over £5000. The original Co-operative premises in Ramsbottom bore "Cussons, Castle, Warburton, & Compy."

As representative of the local building industry, we select the names of the late Mr Thomas Heap, who built the Co-operative Company's premises; and the late Mr James Garnet and his son Robert, the latter of whom, unfortunately, was crushed to death by the fall of an arch, from which the supports had been prematurely removed. Some of the best edifices in the neighbourhood came from the Garnets — Park School, the Wesleyan Chapel, and St Andrew's (Dundee) Presbyterian Church may be taken as specimens. Messrs Platt & Castle, with others, have succeeded them.

For upwards of thirty years Ramsbottom has maintained a vigorous and efficient corps of Volunteers. Its captain for the first year, 1860-61, was the late Mr T. Greig Stark of Rosebank; and the late Capt. John Aitken of Elton Bank, Edenfield, held the command for the next ten years. He was succeeded by Mr J. S. W.—now Major — Grant, who has commanded the corps up to 1893. His was the first name enrolled, and it is amidst universal regret that he now retires. That retirement has come about by neither diminished interest in the corps nor abatement of physical vigour, but simply by the operation of inflexible military rules, in the resistless glide of time. The genial and generous Major has been the soul and mainstay of the corps, and his name will always be honourably associated with its formation and history, and gratefully remembered by his comrades and all loyal and patriotic citizens. It has been a gratification, not only to the Volunteers, but to the community at large, to learn that an officer so likely to maintain the prestige of the corps as Lieut. Hoyle of Bass Field succeeds Major Grant.

MAJOR GRANT.

The writer cannot close this chapter without a special reference to the venerable nonagenarian friend, Mrs Wilson, whose clear and accurate memory has so often assisted him during recent years in his quest for reliable information about the Ramsbottom of the early part of this century. Mrs Wilson was the daughter of Mr Peter Macfarlane, who served his apprenticeship with the Peels, and afterwards went to the north of Ireland, where, at Carrickfergus, he married a Miss Stirling; and there Eliza was born in 1802. Owing to the unsettled state of Ireland, the father returned to Lancashire, and sometime afterwards he was rejoined at Ramsbottom by his wife and their two daughters. At first they were employed at Messrs Ashton's, but afterwards went to Manchester. There, soon after, Mr William Grant met the father, and induced him to come with his family to Messrs Grant's works at Ramsbottom. Eliza, in the first instance, was engaged in the warehouse, on the Old Ground. There, one day, a young man was brought to her by Mr Grant to be instructed in the craft of "hooking on." She "showed him how to hook on his very first piece." In after years he became manager of the Square works, then in their glory; subsequently he went as a partner to Rosebank Print Works, then became a well-known figure on Manchester Exchange, and eventually purchased an estate under the shadow of the Grampians, where he spent his latter days, and where his son, a few years ago, succeeded him. The youth whom Eliza Macfarlane initiated into the mysteries of "hooking on," about three-quarters of a century ago, was Mr Thomas Greig.

Eliza was taken from the warehouse into the service of Mrs Grant at Grant Lodge, and subsequently became the wife of Mr Samuel Wilson, who, at the time of his marriage, was an employé of Messrs Grant, but afterwards, for more than half a century, a well-known shopkeeper in Ramsbottom till his death, in 1879, at the age of ninety-three years. During the time Mr and Mrs Wilson were in business, many a family, in the town and neighbourhood, did the venerable pair materially help to rear. Of few, at such an advanced age, could it be said so truly as of Mrs Wilson that "her eye was not dim, nor her natural force abated." With quite youthful facility, till near the close, she threaded needles without the aid of glasses, which, indeed, she had never needed. And, as the years glided round, she still, unaided, climbed the steep ascent of Holcombe Hill with the succeeding generations. Twice, during 1890, she picnicked on its summit, having ascended by the most direct and steepest path—that which is reached by way of Hillend meadow. Her minister called to see her on the day after her second ascent, and on asking if she felt tired, she said she did not feel much different from usual. Before leaving, they had their wonted season of prayer together. The little group embraced four generations. As on these occasions she almost invariably did, she concluded with a brief prayer herself. Soft-voiced, reverential, and impressive, it was this—"The Lord bless you and your family, and keep you from all evil, for Christ's sake, Amen. The Lord bless me, and keep me from all sin, for Christ's sake, Amen."

Faith, after all, is the true tonic of life. Mrs Wilson had not come thus far on her long pilgrimage without knowing something of the trials incident to the human lot. But, with the well-thumbed New Testament in her hand, and trusting that love which, having sacrificed for us,

"Is as the very centre of the earth
Drawing all things to it,"

and, moreover, never complaining of such things as

"The weary weight
Of all this unintelligible world,"[1]

our worthy mother, "content and cant," in gentle cheerfulness meekly lived what, six hundred years ago, Dante's peerless genius wrote, *In la sua volontade e nostra pace*—in the will of her Saviour and Lord she found unfailing peace. "Even to your old age I am He, and to hoar hairs will I carry you."

Mrs Wilson passed away, ten days after entering her 92d year, on the 27th of March 1893. Her last brief prayers with us, near the close, were these—"May the Lord bless and keep us every night and morning, and accept of us for Jesus Christ's sake. Amen." "May the love of God which passeth all understanding be upon us all for ever and ever. Amen and amen!" This, the last, was repeated while the writer held the frail and chilly hand to say for the last time, "Good-bye." And, softly as a wearied child falls asleep on its mother's breast, our venerable friend passed to her eternal rest. The sunset, like the long life, was calm and peaceful.

---

[1] Wordsworth.

BOOK II.

THE CHURCH OF THE CHEERYBLE BROTHERS.

THE CHURCH OF THE
CHEERYBLE BROTHERS.

CHAPTER I.

GENERAL HISTORICAL INTRODUCTION.

THE spiritual forces which produced the Reformation, and ultimately in the main re-fashioned the face of Europe, had been at work in England for several hundred years before the middle of the seventeenth century. Emanating from the contact of human souls through Holy Writ with the Eternal, such forces are not to be put down by the hostile agencies and instruments of time. Forfeitures and imprisonments, exile and slaughter, mutilations and martyrdoms, grappled with them in their representatives, and sought to bar their progress, but in vain. Once experimentally known, they cannot be permanently proscribed. They shed benign light, unleash human liberty, promote human progress, beget human happiness. There were, unhappily, nations which faced the terrible task of their suppression or extirpation—Spain with its pitiless Inquisition and inhuman *autos da fe;* France with its black Bartholomew slaughter of 70,000 Protestants,[1] its dragonades, &c. But not less terrible has been the penalty. It is possible by such drastic doings practically to kill out the enlightened conscience of a kingdom, and thus leave it like a rudderless vessel, the sport of the billows and the victim of the storm. Nations cannot escape from the law embodied in the inspired words, "They sow the wind, and they shall reap the whirlwind." The Reformation forces dominate the civilized world to-day. In the sixteenth century the unsaintly hand of Henry VIII. had struck the Pope from the apex of the ecclesiastical pyramid in England, and elevated his own portly person to the sacred altitude instead. But, while he thus arbitrarily gave to England a new Pope, and despoiled the pampered and polluted monasteries, he neither sought to change the doctrines of the Church nor to reform her government. He was, indeed, as ready as any of his predecessors, princely or papal, had been to burn or behead those who ventured, for instance, to deny the doctrine of transubstantiation, or to challenge his own absolute supremacy. Archbishop Cranmer—learned and cultured, inconstant and vacillating, endowed with a marvellous genius for compromise—whose fame was lit into lasting lustre by his hard martyr fate, did, and did well, what was possible to unite ecclesiastically the reform which, like the king's, was political, not doctrinal, with that which was distinctly doctrinal and scriptural,—what had recently declared itself *at Court*, with what for many generations had been making its way *throughout the kingdom.*

---

[1] Perefixe, Archbishop of Paris, says 100,000; Sully, a Protestant, 70,000; De Thou, a Roman Catholic, 30,000; Lapopilinière, a Protestant who returned to the Roman Church, 29,000 ('Memoirs of Admiral Colligny').

The one sprang out of the assumption of a new function by the monarch, the other from a vitalizing faith that possessed the people. The one, acting from a potent and despotic will, downward, meant simply a transference of ecclesiastical allegiance; the other, pulsating from the hearts of the people, outward and upward, meant the moral and spiritual transformation of character and life. The *former* was what we may pretty accurately call Anglican Popery or Anglicized Romanism, which has borne ever since, and is bearing now, abundant fruit "after its kind"; the *latter* was English Puritanism, which, though for the most part outside the National Church, has extended the limits, and deepened and broadened the citizen rights and liberties, of the British Empire, and greatly enlarged the spiritual dominion of Christ.

This Puritanism—the simply Protestant element at that time within the Church of England—made rapid strides during the brief reign of Henry's son and successor, Edward VI. Images were removed from the churches; the Latin language was discarded, and the services conducted in the English tongue; auricular confession was discontinued; the sacramental cup was given to lay communicants; the "Bloody Statute" of the late king was repealed,—its first article enacted that whoever denied the doctrine of transubstantiation should be declared a heretic, and burned without opportunity of abjuration; a new service-book was prepared by Cranmer, Ridley, and others, and ordered to be used,— the "First Prayer-book of Edward VI."; and the clergy were allowed to marry. The prelatic polity of the Church, however, remained intact; and the mass of the clergy accepted the changes, and continued within her pale. If the papal head had been struck from the English hierarchy, the trunk remained. Although, therefore, very imperfectly reformed—the least reformed, indeed, of all the Reformation Churches—yet it was at this period that the English Establishment first took rank amongst the Reformed and Protestant Churches of Europe. But Edward was followed by Mary. The old *regime* was re-established. Her reign, with such prelatic agents as Gardiner and Bonner, proved as dark and desolating, cruel and blood-stained, as Edward's had been bright and hopeful, Protestant and progressive.

Mary died in 1558. Elizabeth succeeded, and with her accession Protestantism regained the supremacy. By Elizabeth's first Parliament the Book of Common Prayer was ordered to be read in all the churches; the Thirty-nine Articles were fixed as embodying the national faith; and the queen was declared to be the head of the Church. It is a striking proof of the ecclesiastical demoralisation of that period, that of the 9000 clergymen who ministered in English parishes under Mary, only about 200 resigned rather than adopt the altered order of things under Elizabeth. They appear to have been willing to accept Popery or Protestantism at the bidding of the monarch, provided they were allowed to hold their livings. It was a singularly baneful and humiliating condition of things.

After an illustrious reign of nearly forty-five years, Elizabeth was succeeded by James I. in 1603. Coming to the English throne from the Northern Kingdom, which was both Puritan and Presbyterian, and whose Church even he declared to be "the purest Kirk under the sun,"[1] the English Puritans hoped, very reasonably, for countenance and aid from the

---

[1] See M'Crie's 'Story of the Scottish Church,' p. 82.

king in their desire to complete, or at least advance, the work of reformation in the yet very imperfectly reformed National Church. . They humbly and hopefully approached him. Confident in his own learning and wisdom, and professedly with a view to unite Prelatists and Puritans in a comprehensive Church, James held a great conference at Hampton Court. The astute bishops, however, had accurately gauged the pedantic monarch. Whitgift did not hesitate to say to him " that the king spake by the special assistance of God's spirit ; " while Bancroft, kneeling, " protested his heart melted with joy that almighty God had given them such a king as since Christ's time had not been ! " The noble Puritan representatives, while strong and unshaken in argument, could not compete with this method of persuasion. The flattery prevailed. The Prelates triumphed—not, however, by the force of their arguments, but by the fulsomeness of their adulation.

In England the faith of the Church, the form of her government, and the order of her services continued to be manipulated, and with awful sanctions, arbitrarily imposed for the most part by kings and courtiers, without any formal reference whatever to the advancing intelligence and just rights of the Christian people themselves. Yet the highest interests of every individual citizen were involved, and the Church was called " Protestant " and " Reformed." With advancing Biblical knowledge, this state of things caused growing dissatisfaction. The Puritans believed they had a remedy : its worth had been proved by the other Reformed Churches. They simply sought to bring the English Church, as such, openly and avowedly to the rock of Scripture, to find safe and common standing-ground there. *That*, their

Bibles had taught them, was the right foundation. *There*, they wished their Church to rest. In this, however much circumstances might be against them, they were unquestionably right. It clashed, however, with the cherished notions of the Stuarts. *They* would be supreme. Charles I., as a man, was of a higher type than his father. But unfortunately, he had inherited an enhanced conception of even his father's doctrine of absolute monarchic rule by right divine. He accordingly disliked both Parliaments and Puritans. At that time, fortunately for the nation, they were closely akin, and interlaced one with the other. Both impinged on the current notions of regal absolutism. Parliaments had the bounden charge, at all hazards, to maintain the native civil rights and liberties of England, without. The Puritans stood also for the native rights and liberties of the sacred realm of conscience, within. Both were imperilled. Wentworth[1] with his drastic and despotic policy of "thorough"—the despot's sword ruthlessly supreme in the State—and Archbishop Laud, with his relentless "thorough and thorough"— the despot's cruel mutilations and chains on the fair form of the Church—by the agency of the odious Star Chamber, aimed at the destruction of both. Fines, imprisonments, whippings, ear-cropping, nose-slitting, face-branding, death itself, were their most potent arguments. Liberty, civil and religious alike, north and south, was being crushed and broken. It was the Puritanism of England and Scotland that saved the liberties of the two kingdoms in that evil hour.

Quem deus vult perdere prius dementat. Laud, not satisfied

---

[1] Earl of Strafford.

with ecclesiastical supremacy in England, madly persisted in thrusting upon the Northern Church the prelatic episcopacy of the Southern establishment, to supplant in that region the presbyterian episcopacy[1] of the New Testament. In company with King James, who had long been an irritating dabbler in the senseless work, Laud had made an attempt in this direction, in 1617, which did not succeed. Presbytery, in the north, was pre-eminently the intelligent faith of an earnest, Scripture-loving people, and therefore not a thing which either prince or prelate might chop and change at will. Prelacy, in the south, was dictated mainly by the will of the autocratic court—the ecclesiastical analogue and handmaid, then and since, of feudalism in the State. With characteristic pertinacity, under Charles I., Laud tried again. A liturgy and prelatic bishops were thrust, *nolens volens*, upon the Presbyterians of Scotland. In 1637, the mine of suppressed wrath was simply and suddenly sprung. They rose in indignation, signed, a few months after, their famous Covenant—many of them with blood drawn from their veins—cast off the unscriptural and despotic imposition, and re-established the Presbyterian worship and polity throughout the land. The quaint and striking incident within the walls of St Giles's Cathedral, in Edinburgh, proved eventually fatal to Prelacy in Scotland, simply because it acted like the torch that explodes the mine.

It was not the north, be it remembered, that had interfered with the south, but the purblind prelatic leaders of the south that persistently invaded the most cherished rights and liberties of the north—*these*, not the generous-minded English

---

[1] See Appendix A, 'New Testament Episcopacy.'

people, nor the English Parliament, nor the "inferior clergy," but *the prelates and the prince.* Why couldn't they let Scotland alone? They ought to have known by this time that there was something more than printers' ink or leaf of gold in her *"Nemo me impune lacessit."* Yet Charles assembled an army, and in 1639 marched northwards to enforce subjection to his will.[1]

The Covenanters only *now,* and as a *dernier ressort,* armed and met Charles on the Borders, at Dunse Law. He very prudently made concessions, and, like his royal father and Laud two and twenty years before, wisely journeyed homewards. But the bane that blighted his life and reign evinced itself. He acted perfidiously. While using words of peace and amity to the Covenanters, he had, months before, instructed his official representative so to treat them as to disarm suspicion until he was ready, and then he would settle their "damnable covenant"[2] for them. It was easier said than done. They stood for liberty, he and the bishops for oppression. However, yielding to the solicitations of his prelatical counsellors, and having obtained funds from them for renewing the war, Charles set out again with

---

[1] "As *the parliament of England,* with whom Charles had also quarrelled, *refused to grant him supplies* for this outrageous undertaking, *the bishops,* by the advice of Laud, *came forward with large contributions. The inferior clergy of the English Church declined all interference in the quarrel,* but the papists, who expected everything from the triumph of the King's party, and acted under the private directions of the Queen, were not slow in contributing to the object." (Clarendon's 'State Papers,' vol. ii.; Hardwick's 'State Papers,' vol. ii. pp. 118-124, &c.; Prynne's 'Hidden Works of Darkness,' p. 177, &c.) "The war thus commenced, having been instigated by the advice and supported by the money of the prelates, and being moreover *mainly designed to support their episcopal pretensions,* was commonly called by the English people *the bishops' war,* and Charles was termed in ridicule—'*Canterbury's knight.*' —Principal M'Crie's 'Story of the Scottish Church,' p. 170.

[2] Bishop Burnet's 'Memoirs of the Dukes of Hamilton.' Folio; 1677.

an army in the following year. The Covenanters met him at Newburn-on-Tyne, and, to the joy of his oppressed[1] subjects in England, his army suffered a disastrous defeat. Not the "Covenant," but the infatuated and misguided prince, was in a fair way of being settled. Yet more loyal subjects than these Covenanters did not breathe within his dominions.

The Reformation, in the north, had been a free, Scripture-nurtured growth among the people—not, in any measure, the arbitrary dictate of a monarch; and, rendering to Cæsar the things that were Cæsar's and to God the things that were God's, these people, with intelligent loyalty, honoured a distinction which did not, to a like extent, emerge into practical clearness in the south. They recognised two sovereignties, distinct yet related—one over matters spiritual, belonging to man's Redeemer and Lord; the other over all civil concerns, accorded to the earthly prince. Charles was king of the country, but Christ was the Lord of the conscience. Along the frontier line between these now well-distinguished kingdoms, the Covenanters took their stand in defence of the ennobling realm of spiritual freedom. Time has

---

[1] The *English people* had no heart in the doings of Charles. He himself wrote to the Marquis of Hamilton "that he was now fully satisfied of what that nobleman had told him in the gallery at Whitehall—viz., ' That the nobility and gentry of England would never incline to invade Scotland, and thereby *begin an offensive war.*'" (Memoirs of D. of Hamilton, p. 139; Nalson, vol. i., p. 231). M'Crie, p. 173. Again, "Nothing could alter the opinion of the English officers and soldiers, who said *they would not fight to maintain the pride and power of the bishops.*" "They had been impressed into the service against their will."—M'Crie, p. 173. Once more the blame lay with the prelatic bishops—the representatives of that non-scriptural and post-apostolic institution which Dr Benson, the present Archbishop of Canterbury, calls "*the historic episcopate.*" Its responsibility, in connection with the Stuarts, for oppression and bloodshed in the seventeenth century, is simply appalling.

amply vindicated both their insight and their heroism—for, with whatever lingering lineaments of less enlightened times, the British Empire to-day maintains their great contention. But, at the time referred to, the king, urged on, unhappily, by the arrogant and ambitious bishops, had usurped the dominion that was *not* his. The sacred realm of *conscience* did not own his sway: its sanctions issued from a loftier source, and pointed to a more august tribunal. The only sovereignty the people could acknowledge *there* was that of the King of kings.[1] This was their birthright, and no earthly sovereign should filch it from them. Come weal, come woe, they would worship God as truth-illumined conscience urged; and although, in the face of hostile princes and prelates, the practical maintenance of that inalienable right might—as indeed it proved—sadly lengthen out their martyr-roll, and steep the precious heritage once more in tears, yet even so, thus consecrated afresh, they would transmit it to their children, unsullied and unimpaired. They did not fail. Such men do not fail. They may suffer, but they succeed.

> "Freedom's battle once begun—
> Bequeathed from bleeding sire to son,
> Though baffled oft, is ever won."

Their history verifies the poet's words. Such were the men whom Charles I., in such unprincely fashion, sought to deceive and to destroy; but by whom instead, as we have

---

[1] "The motto on their banners, 'For Christ's Crown and Covenant'—that is, for the royal headship of Christ over His Church, and for the covenant in support of it, was meant to vindicate their appearance in arms, by proclaiming to the world that it was *solely in behalf of the rights of conscience and religion*."—Dr M'Crie's 'Story of the Scottish Church.'

already seen, his army was overthrown, in 1640, at Newburn-on-Tyne. That defeat had far-reaching consequences in English history. It necessitated, on the part of Charles, the assembling of the great historic Parliament which met on the 3d of November 1640—the Long Parliament; and rallied the long-suffering Puritanism of England, as it had never been before, to rescue the nation at once from the pitiless persecution of the bishops and the ill-starred despotism of the unhappy prince. Lords and Commons alike were sick of the barbarous and high-handed doings of Strafford and Laud.[1] They were impeached and condemned.

Notable for much with which, in this brief sketch, we are not specially concerned, one of the earlier and most memorable Acts of that Parliament was—

"An ordinance of the Lords and Commons assembled in Parliament, for the calling of an Assembly of learned and godly divines and others, to be consulted with and by the Parliament, for the settlement of the government and liturgy of the Church of England, and for vindicating and clearing of the doctrine of the said Church from false aspersions and interpretations. June 12, 1643."

Here is the preamble of the celebrated Act calling the great Assembly:—

"Whereas, amongst the infinite blessings of Almighty God upon this nation, none is nor can be more dear unto us than the purity of our religion; and for that, as yet, many things remain in the liturgy, discipline, and government of the Church which do necessarily require a further and more perfect reformation than, as yet, hath been attained; and, whereas it hath been declared and resolved by the Lords and Commons assembled in Parliament, that the present Church government by Arch-

---

[1] See Note, 177, *infra*.

bishops, their chancellors, commissars, deans, and chapters, archdeacons, and other ecclesiastical officers depending upon the hierarchy, is evil and justly offensive and burdensome to the kingdom, a great impediment to reformation and growth in religion, and very prejudicial to the state and government of this kingdom; and, therefore, they are resolved that the same shall be taken away, and that such a government shall be settled on the Church as may be most agreeable to God's holy Word, and most apt to procure and preserve the peace of the Church at home, and nearer agreement with the Church of Scotland, and other Reformed Churches abroad; and for the better effecting hereof, and for the vindicating and clearing of the doctrine of the Church of England from all false calumnies and aspersions, it is thought fit and necessary to call an Assembly of learned, godly, and judicious divines, who, together with some members of the Houses of Parliament, are to consult and advise of such matters and things, touching the premises, as shall be proposed unto them by both or either of the Houses of Parliament, and to give their advice and counsel therein to both or either of the said Houses, when, and as often as, they shall be thereunto required: Be it, therefore, ordained by the Lords and Commons in this present Parliament assembled, that all and every the persons hereafter in this ordnance named, that is to say," &c.

Thus the *Westminster Assembly of Divines* was convened by the Lords and Commons of England. Every English county was represented by one or more of its most distinguished clergymen. Scotland was represented by only five of her clergymen and three ruling elders. The Assembly met for the first time on the 1st of July 1643, and continued to sit till the 22d of February 1649. During that period it met *eleven hundred and sixty-three* times. The results of its distinguished labours were the following:—

1. The *Directory of Public Worship*, presented to Parliament in 1644;

2. The Form of Presbyterial Church Government and of the Ordination of Ministers, 1645.

3. The *Confession of Faith*, in 1646;

4. The *Shorter Catechism*, in 1647 ; and

5. The *Larger Catechism*, in 1648.

These documents constitute England's answer, by *her one great national and representative assembly of divines*, to the question which at length she had fairly faced—What, according to the Holy Scriptures, ought to be the doctrine, worship, and government of the Church of Christ ? That answer is clear and unmistakable. England as a whole, however, was not ready for its practical adoption. Where ripe or ripening, ere long, fiery persecution dashed the fruit, and where rich of promise, it blighted the bloom. The great Englishmen of the illustrious assembly were before their time.

Nearly two centuries and a half have now elapsed since they accomplished their great task. The Scriptural doctrines and polity which they formulated unite the Presbyterian family of Churches throughout the world, at the present time. Moreover, ecclesiastical England to-day feels her need of something which, like these documents, combines righteous and well adjusted order with popular representation and democratic freedom. Feudalism in the Church, as in the State, will be remedied by democratic representation. But neglecting such subsidiary matters as traces of temporal environment and polemic reference, the Westminster standards, in their great cardinal elements[1]—Scriptural, penetrative, benign, and withal capable of vast and varied adaptation—are *an enduring possession*, one of England's great gifts to the world. And as Thucydides said of his history that it was composed for the instruction of posterity rather than the gratification of his contemporaries—κτῆμα τε ἐς ἀεὶ μᾶλλον, ἢ

---

[1] See Articles of Faith, &c., Presbyterian Church of England, 1890.

ἀγώνισμα ἐς τὸ παραχρῆμα ἀκούειν ξυγκεῖται[1]—so in effect it may prove of these documents as a whole in this kingdom, that they were destined to benefit later generations rather than the troubled era that gave them birth. Meantime, while increasingly operative in many ways at home, their influence, like a beneficent river, deep-channeled, pure, and fertilising, flows on in ever-augmenting volume through many other lands.

The Word of God liveth and abideth for ever. These Westminster *formulæ* spring from that living source, and, as informed by its vitality, they were not for an age, but for all time. Their practical bearing on human life—including "all sorts and conditions of men"—is expressed in the peerless answer to the first question of the *Shorter Catechism*—"What is the chief end of man?" *Man's chief end is to glorify God, and to enjoy Him for ever.* We remember the impressive words of Thomas Carlyle, towards the end of his days, "The older I grow—and I now stand on the brink of eternity—the more comes back to me the first sentence in the Catechism which I learned when a child, and the fuller and deeper its meaning becomes—' Man's chief end is to glorify God, and to enjoy Him for ever.'" Let England, as becomes her greatness, keep an open mind, and, in those ecclesiastical changes which soon may come, be mindful of the rich heritage, which is peculiarly hers, in the fruits of her great Assembly's labours at Westminster.

Of the *personnel* of the Parliament above referred to, in its earlier years, Clarendon himself was constrained to write thus: "As to religion, they were all members of the

---

[1] Book I., cap. 22.

Established Church, and almost to a man for Episcopal government. Though they were undevoted enough to the Court, they had all imaginable duty to the King, and affection for the government established by law or ancient custom; and without doubt the majority of that body were persons of gravity and wisdom, who, being possessed of great and plentiful fortunes, had no mind to break the peace of the kingdom, or to make any considerable alterations of the government of the Church or State."—History, vol. i. p. 184.

How then came this Parliament, so composed, to overthrow so soon the English hierarchy—the prelatic episcopacy of the Church of England—and to substitute for it the presbyterian episcopacy of the New Testament and the Reformed Churches, &c.? We may note the following contributive causes :—

1. The conviction that the hierarchy was inimical to both Church and State, and that the liturgy, &c., needed reform. —See Preamble of Act of 1643, pp. 173-174 *supra*.

2. The adoption of the Protestant principle of direct appeal to the Holy Scriptures.

3. The great body of English Puritans, including many clergymen of the Established Church, were, by this time, Presbyterian in sentiment.

4. The arrogance and oppressive tactics of the bishops.

5. The sad disclosures [1] made at the trial of Archbishop Laud.

---

[1] "As a specimen of the cruelties exercised by the Star-Chamber, we may notice their treatment of Dr Alexander Leighton, father of the celebrated Archbishop of that name. This worthy man, who was a professor of divinity in St Andrews, was apprehended in London, at the instigation of Laud, and on the charge of having published a book entitled 'Zion's Plea against the Prelacy,' was thrown into prison. There he lay

London and Lancashire were deemed the most Puritan portions of the realm. The former at once adopted the Presbyterian polity and form of worship, while the County Palatine, with characteristic ardour, early presented to Parliament a petition, largely signed, asking for the establishment of the Presbyterian system. It was granted. An "Ordinance of Parliament" dated 2d October 1646, grouped the parishes of Lancashire into nine Presbyteries, and formed of them a Provincial Synod, whose meeting place was Preston.[1] The *first* Presbytery of Lancashire met in

in a filthy hole, infested with vermin, for fifteen weeks; and when served with his libel, he was reduced to such a state of distress that his hair and skin had come off his body, and he was unable to appear at the bar. In this wretched condition he was condemned unheard to suffer the following sentence in November 1630. On hearing it pronounced, we are told that Laud 'pulled off his cap and gave God thanks,' but the bare recital of it, in the petition of Dr Leighton, some years afterwards, at the trial of the Archbishop, sent such a thrill of horror through the Parliament that the clerk was repeatedly ordered to stop till the members had recovered themselves. 'This horrid sentence was to be inflicted with knife, fire, and whip, at and upon the pillory, with £10,000 fine; which some of the lords of court conceived could never be inflicted, but only that it was imposed on a dying man to terrify others. But Laud and his creatures caused the sentence to be executed with a witness; for the hangman was animated with strong drink all the night before in the prison, and with threatening words, to do it cruelly. Your petitioner's hands being tied to a stake, besides all other torments, he received thirty-six stripes with a treble cord; after which he stood almost two hours in the pillory, in cold, frost, and snow, and then suffered the rest, as cutting off the ear, firing the face, and slitting up the nose. He was made a spectacle of misery to men and angels. And on that day sevennight, the sores upon his back, ears, and face not being cured, he was again whipped at the pillory in Cheapside, and there had the remainder of the sentence executed, by cutting off the other ear, slitting up the other nostril, and branding the other cheek!'"—(Neal's 'History of the Puritans,' vol. ii. p. 385; Ludlow's Tracts, p. 23; Dr M'Crie's 'Story of the Scottish Church,' p. 187.)

[1] The influence of Presbyterianism in Lancashire, during its establishment in the county, is thus estimated by Dr Halley in his 'Lancashire Puritanism': "Public worship was observed with more order and solem-

Manchester. A copy of its minutes, 1647 to 1660, is to be found there in the Chetham Library.[1] The *second* Presbytery embraced the parishes of Bolton, Middleton, Bury, Rochdale, Dean, and Radcliffe. Its stated meeting-place was Bury. Its minutes are preserved in the Bodleian Library at Oxford.[2] The Chapelry of Holcombe, being in the parish of Bury, belonged to this Presbytery, as did also that at Turton, where Mr Pendlebury was ordained.

THE REV. HENRY PENDLEBURY, M.A., OF CHRIST CHURCH, CAMBRIDGE, 1651-1695.

About a mile and a half north of the town of Heywood, and just on the hill-top above Bamford Hall, stands the old farm-house of Jokin, or Jowkin. The original part of the building

---

nity than had been previously known in the county. *The salutary influence of religious principles was observed diffusing itself among all grades of social life, and elevating the morals of the people. . . It secured a general respect for the clerical character, a becoming regard for the solemnities of religion,* and a regular administration of its ordinances such as had never been enforced in the county under Episcopal authority."—Vol. i. p. 464. "It has been said that, 'while to no religious party of that time is England so much indebted as to the Presbyterians, to no Presbyterian family is it more indebted than to the Booths of Dunham Massey.' Their descendant bears now the title of Earl of Stamford and Warrington. Other old families of kindred spirit, devoted to Presbyterian principles, were the Asshetons, Hultons, Ashurts, the Hydes, and Hollands of Denton (represented now by the Earl of Wilton), and the Hoghtons of Hoghton Tower. These last were the hospitable entertainers of King James on his famous Lancashire 'progress'; and though at one time Hoghton Tower had been a noted rendezvous for Jesuits and seminary priests, it continued for long after the Restoration a welcome retreat for godly Presbyterians like Newcome, Ambrose, and Oliver Heywood, with John Howe and many more."—Drysdale's 'History of the Presbyterians in England,' pp. 324, 325.

[1] Recently published by the Cheetham Society.

[2] About to be published by the Cheetham Society. In the Public Library, Bolton, there is a copy presented by the Rev. T. Boston Johnstone of that town.

is easily detected by the old mullioned window at the back, now filled up with solid masonry instead of glass. Looking southward, from the front, across the Bamford Hall demesne, the busy town of Heywood is seen in the open plain beneath, while, about a hundred yards to the west of the house, a wooded steep of considerable height dips abruptly down to the bed of the Norden, whose narrow winding dell and sylvan banks, with the breezy uplands on either hand beyond, have much to charm the eye and yield bracing exhilaration to the spectator.

On the crest of the slope on the opposite side of the Norden, and distant from Jowkin about half a mile to the north-west, stands the well-known Ashworth Chapel,[1] with memories fragrant of old Puritan days.

Back in those memorable times, in 1626, the year after Charles I. ascended the throne, and on the 6th of May, a boy was born at Jowkin destined to live through seventy

---

[1] A worthy and very homely parson of this church, who passed away not many years ago, used to persist in wearing what Sir William Gull called "the Lancashire wooden shoe." He regularly visited Bury in his clogs. On such occasions the neighbours used to honour him with the execution of small commissions,—"Eh, passon, good mornin'; art beawn' for Bury?" "Just starting." "Wilto fotch me a tothree smo' things fro' t' badger's" [that is, the provision merchant's]? "Surely, surely," &c. And it was no uncommon thing to see the kindly and accommodating parson returning leisurely in the evening, with his ample pockets distended to their utmost capacity by "loads o' treasure," both varied and burdensome, for his expectant and complacent parishioners. There was, in his parish, an estimable son of St Crispin, whom he was wont "to camp"—*i.e.*, chat or gossip—with. One evening when the parson called, he observed a goodly array of jobs that had been executed during the day. After finding out what the day's financial result would be, and multiplying it by six, he said, "Why, you can earn more in a week than my income is!" "Yeigh, passon, for *six* days, mind yo; but yo fotch me a dule of a clinker on t' Sunday!" The venerable parson used to tell this story with great glee to the end of his days.

of the most eventful years of England's history, bearing irreproachably a worthy part in the sacred office to which he was called, and leaving behind him a record of learned and devoted Christian labour, with a loved and honoured name. It was *Henry Pendlebury*. Grave and thoughtful from childhood, apt, loving learning and pursuing it with alacrity and unwearying diligence, the boy was early marked out as a promising aspirant to the Christian ministry. After attending such schools as were available in his early years, he became a pupil at the Bury Grammar School.[1] There he received the scholastic drill necessary for matriculation at the University of Cambridge, where, in Christ Church College, he passed through the required curriculum of study, and graduated M.A. in 1648.[2] Having returned to his native county, he preached on the 16th of August 1648[3] his first sermon in Ashworth Chapel, within sight of his birthplace, and to the people who had known him and watched his progress from his childhood. There, we are told, he officiated for some time as a probationer. He was ordained, along with a fellow-candidate, Mr James Livesey, at Turton Chapel, in the parish of Bolton, by the second *classis* or presbytery of Lancashire, on the 3d of October 1650. The clergymen who officiated on the occasion were—

---

[1] Bury Grammar School was founded in 1625 by the Rev. Henry Bury of Bury, who endowed it with £300. After some hitch or lapse, difficult now to explain, it was resuscitated or reinvigorated by a new endowment from the Rev. Roger Kay in 1726. Since that time it has held an unbroken course; and never, perhaps, during its long history, has it done more effective service to the community than under its present head-master, the Rev. W. H. Howlett.

[2] "Brief Account of the Life of Pendlebury" prefixed to 'Invisible Realities' (1696), by the Rev. John Chorlton, of Manchester.

[3] 'Noncon. Memorials,' vol. ii. p. 96.

The Rev. John Tilsley, vicar of the famous parish of Dean, from which he had the honour of being ejected three times; the Rev. Thomas Pike, of Radcliffe; the Rev. Jonathan Schofield, afterwards ejected from Dowglas; the Rev. Tobias Furniss, Rector of Bury; and the Rev. Robert Bath, vicar of Rochdale. The wife of the last named was a niece of Archbishop Laud, who sent him to Lancashire, and was greatly disappointed when he proved a Puritan.

After his ordination, Mr Pendlebury preached for nearly twelve months at Horwich Chapel, in the parish of Dean. At this time, after years of bitter strife and bloodshed, Cromwell had prevailed. The second Charles was a fugitive. James, the seventh Earl of Derby—a prisoner of Cromwell's, taken after the battle of Worcester—had just been executed across the Affetside ridge at Bolton, on the previous day, when, on the 16th of October 1651, Mr Pendlebury was inducted by the second Presbytery of Lancashire to the ancient chapelry of Holcombe. It was a memorable event in the picturesque village, perched high up on the side of the hill. And from the old church then, as from its more stately successor, the prospect up and across the Ramsbottom valley, or southward over the forest-flecked but now myriad-peopled plain, or along the ample amphitheatre of hills guarding then, as now, the picturesque middle valley of the Irwell, must have been highly impressive. Stretches of primeval forest still clothed the neighbouring heights, and shadowed the numerous dells so deftly graven down their varying slopes by rills and brooks, acting through countless ages with deepening force and widening sweep as they neared the ample vale beneath.

The forest laws, happily, had disappeared more than a

century before, and the disforested domain had ever since, with increasing population, been coming under the sway of aggressive graziers and agriculturists. And, cotemporaneously—instead of grunting boars and bellowing bulls, or even bounding stags, as in days of yore—in growing hamlets and remote sequestered homes might now be heard the homely sound of the weaver's loom and the lively whirr of the spinning-wheel.

The raw material, then, was native wool—not cotton; yet, notwithstanding, we see in these humble doings the origin or archetype of the great staple industry of the district at the present time: that the acorn, this the oak; yonder the fountain, here the broad fertilising stream; for dusky forests we now have smiling fields and ample factories; for solitary huts and booths, substantial farmsteads, elegant mansions, and goodly towns; for forest trails and pack-horse tracks, macadamised or well-paved roads and railways; and for the forest chase the no less eager but more beneficent pursuits of industry and commerce. And, if we have not now the billmen and bowmen, who in days of yore stood for Lancashire in many a well-fought field, yet representatives of the old royal forest have not been wanting in the great campaigns of modern times; and in no part of the realm will be found more loyal and devoted corps of efficient Volunteers.

The world had to wait till the *eighteenth* century for the impetus given to the great industry of Lancashire by the united genius of Wyatt, Arkwright, Hargreaves, Crompton, Cartwright, and James Watt. But it was only the middle of the *seventeenth* when Mr Pendlebury entered upon his sacred duties at Holcombe. He was at the time in his twenty-sixth year. Still an ardent student, sedulously acquiring the theological and patristic lore for which he was afterwards distinguished, a man of much prayer and meditation, weighty and impressive rather than facile and voluble as a preacher, yet homely and helpful as a pastor, his influence as a gifted and devoted minister of Christ's evangel was soon felt over his own wide and needy district and far beyond its limits. Neighbouring clergymen as well as their people held him in high estimation. But while one of the most distinguished of the brethren, he esteemed himself the least; was "most eminent for humility, meekness, and self-denial, wherein he shone above his fellows." A call was addressed to him from Ringley, but the warm appreciation of his own people led to its declinature. He preached twice every Lord's day at Holcombe, and much to other congregations, far and near. His sermons were all fully written out, and delivered with little variation without the use of notes, notwithstanding the variety of matter and the number of Scripture quotations they contained. He was indeed a model parish parson—accompanying the saving light of cultured Gospel preaching with the kindly warmth of Christian comfort and consolation, while leading the people to a higher moral plane by a pure and peaceful, humble and unselfish life, lived in earnest toil for them before their eyes. For eleven years all went well. But suddenly the gathering momentum of this happy and pervasive pastorate was rudely arrested within the Established Church. In 1662 came the despotic and prelatic Act of Uniformity which still blots the Statute Book of England. Its ruthless enforcement, with a refinement of cruelty, drove some two thousand of the most learned and laborious, loyal and conscientious ministers of the Church of England out of their pulpits and their homes. One of these was the eminent Presbyterian clergyman of Holcombe, the Rev. Henry Pendlebury.[1]

He preached his farewell discourse on Revelation iii. 11 —" Behold, I come quickly : hold that fast which thou hast, that no man take thy crown." With seemliness and Christian dignity avoiding any reference to the harsh measures by the Government of the recently restored but faithless and ungrateful[2] prince—Charles II.—he earnestly

---

[1] As a specimen of its kind we give a copy of the document by which the Bishop of Chester removed the amiable and gifted Isaac Ambrose from his church at Garstang :—

"Whereas in a late Act of Parliament for Uniformitie, it is enacted that every parson, vicar, curate, lecturer or other ecclesiastical person neglecting or refusing, before the Feast Day of St Bartholomew, 1662, to declare openly before their congregations his assent and consent to all things contained in the Book of Common Prayer, established by the said Act, *ipso facto*, be deposed, and that every person not being in holy orders by episcopal ordination, and every parson, vicar, curate, lecturer, or other ecclesiastical person failing in his subscription to a declaration mentioned in the said Act to be subscribed before the Feast Day of St Bartholomew, 1662, shall be utterly disabled, and, *ipso facto*, deprived and his place be void, as if the person so failing be naturally dead. And whereas Isaac Ambrose, late vicar of Garstang, in the county of Lancaster, hath neglected to declare and subscribe according to the tenor of the said Act, I do therefore declare the church of Garstang to be now void, and do strictly charge the said Isaac Ambrose, late vicar of the said church, to forbear preaching, lecturing, or officiating in the said church or elsewhere in the diocese of Chester. And the churchwardens of the said parish of Garstang are hereby required (as by duty they are bound) to secure and preserve the said parish church of Garstang from any invasion or intrusion of the said Isaac Ambrose, disabled and deprived as above said by the said Act, and the churchwardens are also required upon sight hereof to show this order to the said Isaac Ambrose, and cause the same to be published next Sunday after in the parish church of Garstang before the congregation, as they will answer the contrary. Given under my hand this 29th day of August 1662.—GEO. CESTRIENS.

"*To the churchwardens of Garstang, in the county Palatine of Lancaster.*"

[2] The Presbyterians, always loyal, had taken a decisive part in bringing about his restoration to the throne of England, and he had engaged to

exhorted his people to hold fast "their profession and practice of religion, the Gospel and Gospel truths, their Christian graces — the effects of the Father's special distinguishing and separating mercy, the fruits of the Son's blood, and the work of the Holy Spirit; to hold fast their religious duties in the heart, in the house, and in the life — their detestation of sin, their love and esteem of the Word of God, their communion with Him and their own hearts — their fellowship with the saints — their serious care for eternity, and whatsoever is in itself good." He concluded thus — "As for you who are making it your care and study to hold fast that you have, I have this word of comfort to leave with you — Christ is keeping grace, life, and glory for you, and is keeping *you* by His power unto salvation, and you shall never perish; only watch, and hold fast; let no man take thy crown; and behold, He will come quickly!"

After his removal from Holcombe, he went across the valley and found a home at Bass Lane, in Walmersley, within sight of the old one — distant from it about a mile

---

maintain toleration and liberty of conscience. (See Macaulay, vol. i. p. 149. Also, Drysdale's 'History of the Presbyterians in England,' pp. 371, 373.) He said — "We do declare a liberty to tender consciences; and that no man shall be disquieted or called in question for differences of opinion in matters of religion, which do not disturb the peace of the kingdom." (See Declaration of Charles II. from Bredà; Clarendon's History, vol. vi. pp. 232-234, in 'English Puritanism' — Documents, i. Also Worcester House Declaration — Reliquiæ Baxterianæ, pp. 259-264, in Documents, ix.; and Drysdale, p. 376.) Moreover, when previously crowned, at Scone, in Scotland, in taking the oath to defend and support the Church of that realm, "kneeling and holding up his right hand, he used these awfully solemn words: 'By the Eternal and Almighty God, who liveth and reigneth for ever, I shall observe and keep all that is contained in this oath.'" — Dr M'Crie's 'Story of the Scottish Church,' p. 236. Yet, notwithstanding, after ascending the English throne, counselled by the bishops and supported by a despotic Parliament, he meted out, north and south, ruthless oppression and persecution.

and a half, and two miles and a half north of Bury. Here, as opportunity offered, he continued to minister to his people. For, as Mr Chorlton tells us—" He was ever mindful of his ordination vow, and could not think that any power upon earth could null his commission, which he had received from Christ to preach the gospel." His services continued to be greatly sought after by the people of neighbouring parishes, and "he was free to spend and be spent for their souls' good." But the *Conventicle Act*[1] came into force on the 1st of July 1664. With his people, he appears in the main to have successfully braved the terrors of that Act, until the execrable *Five Mile Act*,[2] in 1665, banished him from his home and his people. A friend, however, was not wanting in that dark day. Mr Tong—father of the Rev. William Tong, the biographer of Matthew Henry—furnished, in his own house, near Bolton, a hospitable retreat for the exiled minister. Moreover, this generous host gladdened the grate-

---

[1] If, in addition to the members of a household, *five* persons of sixteen years or upwards met "under colour or pretence of any exercise of religion in any other manner than is allowed by the liturgy or practice of the Church of England," each such person was liable to the following punishment—1st offence, 3 months in gaol, or fine of £5; 2d offence, 6 months in gaol, or fine of £10; 3d offence, 7 years transportation, and seizure of property, or fine of £100. If neither the property nor the friends of the victim furnished a sum sufficient for transportation charges, he could be detained in practical slavery by the transporting contractor for the first five years, &c. "Any house or other place" could be entered by force, saving that "of any peer of the realm, whilst he or his wife shall be there resident." In such a case his Majesty's sign manual was indispensable. Freeholders beyond a certain value and other propertied people *were exempted*.

[2] That nonconforming "parsons, vicars, curates, lecturers," and such persons as "take upon them to preach, unless only in passing upon the road," *shall not come* or be *within five miles* of any city or town corporate, or parliamentary borough, or *parish or town wherein they had ministered or taken upon them to preach*—upon forfeiture for every such offence of £40. The fines to be divided thus—one-third each to the king, the poor, and the informer.

ful guest by greeting him as his spiritual father, and telling him that a sermon he had preached in Leigh Church was the means of his conversion.

Two years later, in 1667, notwithstanding the Conventicle Act, we find him preaching near Bury with the heroic Oliver Heywood.[1] Indeed, in prosecuting his ministry after the ejectment, and in the face of oppressive penal laws, Mr Pendlebury appears to have enjoyed a happy immunity from some of the outward sufferings to which others of the brethren were cruelly subjected.

In 1672[2] Charles II. published his famous *Indulgence*.

---

[1] "*September* 19.—Set out on my journey towards Lancashire, where I preached with Mr Pendlebury at Cockey Chapel."—Life of Oliver Heywood.

[2] The following is a copy of the interesting licence granted to the Rev. Oliver Heywood:—

[SEAL.]   CHARLES R.

Charles by the Grace of God, King of England, Scotland, France, and Ireland, Defender of the Faith, &c. To all Mayors, Bayliffs, Constables, and other our Officers and Ministers, Civil and Military, whom it may concern, Greeting. In pursuance of our Declaration of the 15th of March 1672, We do hereby permit and licence Oliver Heywood of ye Presbyterien Perswation to be a teacher of the Congregation allowed by Us in a Roome or Roomes in the house of John Butterworth, in ye parish of Halifax, in ye County of Yorke, for the Use of such as do not conform to the Church of England, who are of the Perswasion commonly called Presbyterien—With further license and permission to him, the said Oliver Heywood, to teach in any other place licensed and allowed by Us, according to Our said Declaration. Given at Our Court at Whitehall, the 25th day of July, in the 24th year of Our Reign, 1672.

By His Majesties Command,

                                              ARLINGTON.

These licences were recalled in 1675. "At the close of 1674, the King called *the bishops together* to consider what should be done to serve the cause of religion; and, after various consultations also with the Ministers of State, *he was advised to recall the licenses, and put the laws against the Nonconformists in execution*. This was soon after done by proclamation, and it was not long before Mr Heywood felt its effects."—'Life and Works of O. Heywood,' vol. i. pp. 181, 182, 200, 201.

Under it, persons as well as places were licensed, and we find, in the Rolls Court Record, that the following houses in this district were licensed for Presbyterian services:—

The house of James Grime, Tottington, Lancs., Presbyterian, Sept. 5/72.
,, ,, James Unsworth of Bury, Lancs., Pr., Sept. 5/72.
,, ,, James Chorleton of Holcombe in Lancsh., Sept. 5, 1672, Presbyn.

There can be no doubt that these were places in which, at this time, Mr Pendlebury prosecuted his ministry. Towards the close of this year, we learn from the autobiography of his cotemporary and friend, Henry Newcome of Manchester, that he was injured by a fall, from the effects of which, happily, he recovered. Through all the difficulties and dangers involved in fidelity to his Gospel ministry, he continued a student. He was familiar with most of the ancient fathers, and had fully studied the Protestant controversy. Archbishop Tillotson caused his 'Treatise on Transubstantiation' to be printed in 1687. He was one of the Hulton Lecturers, at Bolton, his coadjutors being Messrs Newcome of Manchester, Baldwin of Eccles, and Walker of Newton Heath—as required by the foundation deed, "four of the most eminent ministers in the county."

At a date we fear not now precisely determinable, a *temporary* place of worship was provided for him at Bass Lane. With this as his centre, preaching twice every Lord's Day, and dispensing the Lord's Supper monthly, he pursued unremittingly, for many years, his pastoral and evangelistic work. "He lived as he preached, and preached as he lived"—the doctrine scriptural, the life a transcript of the teaching. And we are told that the Lord crowned his ministerial labours with great success—that he had seals to his ministry all along from the beginning to the close. That awe-inspiring period was now approaching. He was present for the last time at the meetings of the United Brethren,[1] on September 4, 1694. His last illness was somewhat protracted. He welcomed it with deep submission to the will of God—content if the Lord, whom he served by His Spirit in the Gospel, had more work for him to do in the Church below; but, if not, to depart for the blessedness of the saints above, and to be with Christ, which was far better. "I am free," he said, "to go to my rest. I have had enough of living, and am filled and satisfied with this life on earth."

Many friends, hearing of his illness, came from distant places where he had preached to visit him. To each he dropped some word of fitting counsel—telling those who had been converted under his ministry to give God the glory, and to walk worthy of their high vocation; and exhorting such as had been built up in grace by his labours to go on their way rejoicing, though they should see his face no more. Towards the close of his sickness his sufferings were great; but under them all, with great patience, he glorified God, declaring his hope of future blessedness, and saying—"I am not sick unto death, but unto eternal life. In a little while all will be well." Secure and calm, the feet on earth, the heart and hope in heaven—

> "As some tall cliff that lifts its awful form,
> Swells from the vale, and midway leaves the storm;
> Though round its breast the rolling clouds are spread,
> Eternal sunshine settles on its head."

---

[1] A post-Revolution Association of Presbyterian and Independent Ministers. It ceased about 1700. Minutes in Cheetham Library, Manchester.

To some friends,[1] near the end, he said—"I can now look back upon my way and work in the ministry and say, 'I have been faithful;' and I can look within and say, 'I have peace;' but, after all, the foundation I would fix on is Christ and His righteousness: I would make Him all in all."

And *He* was enough. In Him, completeness, complacency, conquest, were by grace the portion of this lowly and loyal minister of His holy Gospel. And the time of his departure was now at hand—he had fought a good fight, he had kept the faith; and, henceforth, there was laid up for him a crown of righteousness, which the Lord, the righteous judge, would give him at that day.

His pious soul, which, through the whole course of his life, had been bent towards God, showed its longing and preparedness for the full and eternal fruition by sweet and ardent breathings after Him—breathings which, during his last night and morning, were often expressed in these words: "Father, come and take me home to Thyself." The prayer was heard and answered. He *came;* the day dawned, the shadows slipt away, and the wistful, toil-worn pilgrim was

---

[1] Among other brethren in the ministry who visited him during his last illness, and, at his request, prayed with him, was the Rev. Oliver Heywood, in whose ordination by the Second Presbytery of Lancashire Mr Pendlebury had taken part at Bury forty-four years before. With some other questions, Mr Heywood asked—"What are your thoughts now as to your Nonconformity? Do you repent of it?" The dying pastor answered—"I bless God I am abundantly satisfied with it, and if I were to make my choice over again, and if it were possible for me to see all the sufferings which I have undergone for it (which are nothing to what many of the precious servants of God have suffered), and if they were all laid together, I would make the same choice which I have made, and take my Nonconformity with them; and I bless God that I never so much as tampered with them." "What legacies have you to leave?" "I am unfit to give

at home. He died at Bass Lane on the 18th of June, 1695,[1] about eight o'clock in the morning, in the seventieth year of his age, and the forty-fifth of his ministry. His death was deeply felt and widely mourned.

"Mr Pendlebury dead! A great loss," said Henry Newcome. "Mr Henry Pendlebury, . . . a man of great learning and strict godliness, and every ministerial qualification, entered upon his rest," wrote Matthew Henry (1695).

His body was interred in Bury churchyard, close by the chancel wall on the south side, on the 20th June 1695. A vast concourse of people came to the funeral, and made great lamentation over him. The Rev. Robert Seddon, of Bolton, preached the funeral sermon in Mr Pendlebury's chapel, at Bass Lane, on Daniel xii. 13—"But go thou thy way till the end be; for thou shalt rest, and stand in thy lot at the end of the days."

The sermon has not been preserved. But Mr Seddon tells us, in his prefatory epistle to "The Books Opened" (by Mr Pendlebury), that he was a skilful workman, not needing to be ashamed, rightly dividing the word of truth, and giving to every one his portion; that he did not put the two-edged

---

counsel to you, my brother, but the words of the Apostle I leave with you —'Be not weary of well-doing, and you shall reap in due time if you faint not.'"

[1] In Dr Evans's list (see p. 204, *infra*) "William Pendlebury" appears as minister of Leeds. This, we apprehend, was Mr Pendlebury's son. He died in 1729. The Northowram Register says that "Widow Pendlebury, near Turton, in Lancashire, mother to Mr Pendlebury, of Leeds, died November 18th" (1713). This, no doubt, was the "virtuous spouse" on whom, Mr Chorlton tells us, Mr Henry Pendlebury devolved all his secular cares. Tradition says that Mr and Mrs Pendlebury occupied a small farm at Bass Lane, and that *he*, when asked, could not tell its stock. Mrs Pendlebury proved a helpmeet indeed. All honour to her memory!

sword of the Spirit into a silken scabbard and flourish it in the air, but dexterously wielded it that it might reach the consciences of men ; and, moreover, that those who had been blessed by the sermons when preached, craved their publication that others might receive similar blessing.

Mr Chorlton's closing sentence in his brief sketch is substantially this—Mr Pendlebury was beloved of all, and reverenced especially by his brethren in the ministry ; while his people, for whom he laboured nearly forty-four years, would be ready to say of his worth, what the Queen of Sheba said of the wisdom of Solomon—" The half was not told." As he loved his Lord, so he lived for the people—

> " In his duty prompt at every call,
> He watched and wept, he prayed and felt for all
> And, as a bird each fond endearment tries,
> To tempt its new-fledged offspring to the skies,
> He tried each art, reproved each dull delay,
> Allured to brighter worlds, and led the way."

With that happy thought of Goldsmith's we should have been glad to close our brief sketch of this venerable and saintly man of God. That, however, cannot be. Something incumbent, though uninviting, remains. Mr Pendlebury was buried " close by the chancel wall on the south side " of Bury Parish Church. His grave no longer exists. It was violated some twenty years ago by the ecclesiastical authorities when the new church was built. The remains, after a peaceful repose of 175 years, were removed and thrown into a common receptacle.[1] A fitting memorial, we hope, may yet be reared near the spot where he was laid to rest.

---

[1] The late Rev. W. R. Thorburn, M.A., of Bury, in his " valedictory discourse " published in 1874, says : " I have stood on his grave, remem-

Some one has beautifully said that "sacrifice to heroes is reserved until after sunset." And, with the dust of death settling on the sealed lips of Henry Pendlebury, one remembers, amongst many others, such kindred spirits as John Angier,[1] Isaac Ambrose,[2] John Tilsley,[3] and Nathaniel Heywood,[4] who already slept like him within "the shut of

---

bered his character, and prayed God that many like him might be raised up to preach the Gospel in this neighbourhood. And it is also true that the grave has been desecrated on the occasion of the building of the New Parish Church. I find no fault with the ecclesiastical authorities, but I grieved in my heart to see it. I spoke to some, and they said it was of no use. Henry Pendlebury's bones, about 170 [175] years after burial, were removed from the place where they lay so long, and cast into a common receptacle. . . . I believe we should get into a little quarrel or difficulty if it were proposed to put up a tombstone to our proto-Nonconformist, instead of the original; but I mention it, and if it were possible to put up a stone, I would do it and get the means from others. The name of a good man will be held in everlasting remembrance." Mr Thorburn's honourable interest in this matter has proved not quite unavailing. Since his decease, with the consent of the late Canon Hornby, a small memorial brass has been inserted in the floor of the church as near as possible to the spot where the grave of Mr Pendlebury had been. It is 16 in. by 6½, and is placed in the tiled passage on the south side of the chancel. It is inscribed thus—

"HENRY PENDLEBURY,
A Faithful Minister of the Gospel,
Who died 18th June 1695,
Was interred in this place."

Born the year after Bury Grammar School was instituted, he left its benches for Cambridge nearly two centuries and a half ago; and few, if any, of the *alumni* of the venerable local *alma mater* ever proved more learned and worthy, or bequeathed a memory more stainless and exemplary to the pupils of succeeding generations.

[1] Of Emmanuel College, Cambridge; minister of Denton. Died September 1, 1677, in the 72d year of his age and 49th of his ministry.

[2] Isaac Ambrose of Garstang, B.A., of Brasenose College, Oxford. Died 1664, aged 72.

[3] Of Dean. Died 1684, aged 60. He was M.A. of Glasgow University.

[4] Of Trinity College, Cambridge; minister of Ormskirk. After his ejectment from that parish a poor man came to him, and said—"We would gladly have you preaching again in the church." "Yes," said Mr Heywood, "I would as gladly preach there if I could do it with a safe

even;" but one also thinks, and not, we hope, without inspiring emotion, of such men as Henry Newcome, Oliver Heywood, and Thomas Jollie, in whose eyes the light was still shining, but whose feet were already chilled by the mountain shadow, so soon to deepen into night.[1] "The day is Thine: the night also is Thine!" "They that be wise shall shine as the brightness of the firmament, and they that turn many to righteousness as the stars for ever and ever."[2]

The published works of Mr Pendlebury are the following:—

(1) A Plain Representation of Transubstantiation. 1687.

(2) Sacrificium Missaticum, Mysterium Iniquitatis: or, A Treatise concerning the Sacrifice of the Mass. 1768.

(3) An Exposition of the Shorter Catechism.

(4) The Barren Fig Tree. A practical exposition of Luke xiii. 6-9.

(5) Invisible Realities the Real Christian's Great Concernment. In several sermons on 2 Cor. iv. 18. And, The Books Opened. Being Several Discourses on Rev. xx. 14. By Henry Pendlebury, A.M., late Minister of the Gospel at *Rochdale* in Lancashire; author of the Plain Representation of Transubstantiation. London: Printed by J. D. for Ann Unsworth, of Manchester; and sold by Jonathan Robinson at the Golden Lion in St Paul's Churchyard. 1696.

(6) Slate, in his 'Select Nonconformists' Remains,' publishes three Sermons of Mr Pendlebury—two on "The Design of Christ's Ascension," John xiv. 2; and one on "Light in Darkness," Psalm xcvii. 11.

The volume, published in 1696, represents Mr Pendlebury as "late Minister of the Gospel at *Rochdale*." This has long

---

conscience." The man replied—"Oh, sir, *many a man nowadays makes a great gash in his conscience; couldn't you make a little nick in yours?*"—Life, in his brother O. Heywood's Works, vol. i. p. 461. Nathaniel died in 1677, aged 45.

[1] Henry Newcome died in September 1695; Oliver Heywood in 1702; and Thomas Jollie in 1703.

[2] "Mr Baldwin, Mr Pendlebury, Mr Newcome, Mr Seddon—all ancient, eminent ministers—dead in one year's time, which made a great breach in that Salford hundred."—Oliver Heywood, Works, vol. i. p. 441.

been a puzzle. He was never *statedly* a minister at Rochdale. But, "in connection with the rise of dissent in Rochdale, it may be stated that a Presbyterian Chapel existed in the town previous to the erection of the chapel in Blackwater Street, but its situation is not known. The Revs. Oliver Heywood and Henry Pendlebury preached in Rochdale occasionally, soon after the Restoration in 1660."—(Baines, vol. i. p. 489.) Rochdale is six or seven miles from Bass Lane; Bury about two and a half. Is it possible that *Bass Lane*, badly written, and not known to the London printer, became *Rochdale*, a place "*in Lancashire*" more likely to be known to him?

THE REV. EDWARD ROTHWELL, 1695-1731.

Mr Pendlebury was succeeded by the Rev. Edward Rothwell. The name of the former appears for the *last* time at the meetings of the United Brethren on 4th September 1694, and that of Mr Rothwell for the *first* time on 6th August 1695, just seven weeks after Mr Pendlebury's death.

Mr Rothwell had been trained for the ministry by the Rev. Richard Frankland, at Rathmell, in Yorkshire.[1] He

---

[1] Calamy says that "Bishop Cozens solicited Mr Frankland to conform, promising him not only his living, but greater preferment. Mr Frankland told him that his unwillingness to renounce his ordination by Presbyters made him incapable of enjoying the benefit of this favour." In the Nonconformist Memorial we are also told that after Mr Frankland was "silenced, he lived at Rathmel, which was his own estate, where he was persuaded to set up a private academy. Sir Thomas Liddell sent his son George to be educated under him, and many others followed his example, so that in the space of a few years he had to the number of three hundred under his tuition, and many of them were worthy and useful ministers of the Gospel."—'Nonconformist Memorials,' vol. i. pp. 489, 490. One of these was the Rev. Edward Rothwell. Mr Frank-

was ordained at Rathmell on 7th June 1693, and ministered for some years at the Presbyterian Chapel, Tunley, near Wigan. In the Deed of Surrender, in 1713, of "Little Edmunds," in Nuttall Lane, Holcombe—the ground on which Dundee Chapel, Ramsbottom, was built—he is still designated "Edward Rothwell, of Tunley, in the County of Lancaster, Clerk." The Trust Deed of Tunley Chapel represents Mr Rothwell as minister there in 1703, and he is said to have left for Holcombe or Dundee Chapel about 1706. It is difficult to determine the precise date at which he took formal charge of Mr Pendlebury's congregation. A baptismal register, now in Somerset House, helps us. It is the oldest we have been able to discover connected with the congregation. It is in the handwriting of Mr Rothwell, extends from 1699 to 1730 inclusive, and has the following inscription:—

"A Register of Baptisms Solemnized with water in the Name of the Father, and of the Son, and of the Holy Ghost, by Ministers of a Congregation of Dissenting Protestants at Dundee, near Holcome, in the Parish of Bury and County of Lancaster."

Prefixed to the Register is the following note: "The Congregation formerly assembled near Bass Lane, in Walmersley, where the Rev. Henry Pendlebury officiated after his ejectment from Holcome Chapel for Nonconformity in 1662. He died in 1696 [ought to be 1695], and Mr Rothwell appears to have succeeded him about the year 1699.— George Brown, M.A., V.D.M." = *Verbi Dei Minister*, Minister of the Word of God.

While at Tunley, Mr Rothwell educated several young men for the ministry. One of these, in all likelihood, was

---

land died in 1698. His funeral sermon was preached by Mr Chorlton of Manchester, who, two years before, had written the sketch of Mr Pendlebury's life.

Mr Braddock, who afterwards became his colleague at Dundee Chapel, and another was the Rev. John Pilkington, who became minister at Walton and Preston. This fact may furnish a satisfactory explanation of the foregoing statements, which represent Mr Rothwell as minister of Tunley and Holcombe or Dundee Chapel[1] at the same time. Aided by his students, we apprehend that for a number of years he had charge simultaneously of both congregations. A few years after the opening of Dundee Chapel, his congregation, as we shall see presently, built another, some four miles distant, in which he ministered conjointly with Dundee.

In a brief historic sketch by Dr Brown prefixed to the "Minutes of the Session of the Presbyterian Congregation assembling at Dundee Chapel, Holcombe, in the Parish of Bury, Lancashire," he tells us that "the Manuscript Volume," which we have not been able to discover, but from which he made extracts, "contains also sermons by Heywood of Stand, Burns [Bourne] of Bolton, Jolly of Pendlehill, Milne Whittaker, Mather, Wilkinson, Griffis [Griffiths], &c., which were preached at Walmersley, Buckden, and *Holcombe Lower Chapel*"—*i.e.*, Dundee Chapel.

On 30th April 1710, Mr Waring preached a funeral sermon in Walmersley[2] for Mr James Kay of Sheephey, and another for Mr Jeremy Kay of Lowe from Phil. i. 20, on 21st May 1710. On the 8th May 1710, Mr Burgess[3] preached a

---

[1] The congregation worshipped at Bass Lane, on the other side of the Irwell, till Dundee Chapel was built, in 1712. At Dundee, as at Tunley, Mr Rothwell engaged in tutorial work.

[2] Bass Lane, Walmersley, Mr Pendlebury's Chapel.

[3] The Rev. James Burgess of Darwen. His son, of the same name, was Minister of Whitworth, and author of the celebrated sermon on Mark v. 42, which bore the title, "Beelzebub driving and drowning his hogs." This

funeral sermon for Henry Moorcroft of Bircle from Heb. iv. 9. On 22d April 1711, Mr Mills preached a funeral sermon for Ann, the daughter of William Holt in Holcombe, from Matt. xxiv. 44, and on the 22d May 1711, Mr Rothwell preached a funeral sermon for the aunt of the writer of these manuscripts, whom he styles his "near and dear relation." " These particulars," adds Dr Brown, are here mentioned for the purpose of preserving the names of some of Mr Rothwell's contemporaries, the memory of whom seems almost forgotten. Messrs Griffiths and Turner were also contemporaries ; the former, as it appears, besides being a correspondent, preaching for Mr Rothwell in February 1715, and the latter in March 1715." And further, he writes: "As everything connected with the former history of a place which has been occupied so long as a place of worship must be interesting, the following documents taken from papers in the Rev. Edward Rothwell's handwriting may be here inserted." They are *three* in number, and refer to—

I. The Building of Dundee Chapel, thus :—

"May 27th, 1711. This is to certify all whom it may concern that in order to the building of a New House in Nuttall Lane, I nominate and appoint Edw. Hamer, Rich. Rothwell, James Rothwell, Edward Hamer, William Holt, John Ramsbottom, Lawrence Duerden, Lawrence Buckley, Richd. Bridge, Thomas Rothwell, Abraham Wood, John Barnes, by my order to bargain, contract, and agree with the workmen that shall be employed in the building aforesaid, which contracts and agreements I

---

sermon, which produced some stir when its eccentric but gifted author published it, deals with these three points—viz. :

I. *The Devil will play at small game rather than none at all*—"All the devils besought him, saying, Send us into the swine that we may enter them."

II. *They run fast whom the Devil drives*—"The whole herd ran violently."

III. *The Devil brings his hogs to a fine market*—" Behold the whole herd ran down a steep place into the sea and were choked."

shall stand to fulfil and see performed, and what money the persons aforesaid lay down on this occasion shall be repaid. Witness my hand.
(Signed) EDWARD ROTHWELL."

Dr Brown says—" He [Mr Pendlebury] was succeeded by the Rev. Edward Rothwell, a person of some property in the neighbourhood, who gave a piece of ground on which a chapel was built and a burial-yard laid out in 1712. This ground being contiguous to a farm called Dundee, the chapel is often called 'Dundee Chapel,'[1] and, from its local situation, 'Holcome Lower Chapel.'"

II. The Application for its Registration under the Act of Toleration. Clause XIX. of that Act runs thus :—

"Provided always that no congregation or assembly for religious worship shall be permitted or allowed by this Act, until the place of such meeting shall be certified to *the bishop of the diocese*, or to the *archdeacon of that archdeaconry*, or to the *justices of the peace* at the general or quarter sessions of the peace for the county, city, or place in which such meetings shall be held, and registered in the said bishop's or archdeacon's court respectively, or recorded at the said general or quarter sessions: the register or clerk of the peace whereof respectively is hereby required to register the same, and to give certificate thereof to such person as shall demand the same, for which there shall be no greater fee nor reward taken than the sum of sixpence."

Of the three alternative methods of registration offered by this clause, Mr Rothwell chose the second, and applied to the Archdeacon, but it was of the Archdeaconry of Chester, Manchester, in those days, having no thoughts of diocesan honours.[2]

---

[1] It was the other way about—the farm gets its name from the chapel, not the chapel from the farm.

[2] Its population, indeed, was less than that of Ramsbottom at the present time. In 1710 it was about 8000. Seven years later, in 1717, the population is said to have been the same. In 1756 the first attempt was made to enumerate the population of Manchester and

To this quarter accordingly went the following application from the Rev. Edward Rothwell, worthy man, for *a certificate of toleration to preach the gospel* in the chapel " lately erected and builded " in Holcom by him :—

"Whereas the Congregation of Protestant Dissenters in and about Holcom has ever since the Toleration resorted to a Meeting House in Walmersley, *now gone to ruin and decay;* and whereas the people of the said Meeting House apply'd themselves to me to give them leave to Erect and Build a New one upon my Land in Nutal Lane, in Holcom, to which I have consented, These Are to Certify to the Archdeacon of the Archdeaconry of Chester, that the said House is lately Erected and builded in Holcom aforesaid, for the use and purpose of Religious Worship, according to the Intent, Direction, and Appointment of an Act of Parliament, Intituled an Act for exempting Their Majesties Protestant subjects Dissenting from the Church of England from the Penalties of Certain Laws; and also of a late Act now made in the tenth year of Her Majesty Queen Anne, Intituled an Act for Preserving the Protestant Religion, &c., whereby the former Act is ratified and confirmed, and 'tis required at All Times inviolably to be observed. Whereof I hope, and humbly request, that the Archdeacon will now take Notice, and the Register insert the same in the Register of the Archdeacon's Court, and give me a certificate thereof, that the said ——"

Dr Brown adds " cætera desunt." The concluding words of the documents are wanting. Any one interested, however, and reading intelligently what has survived, will have little difficulty in supplying the substance of what is missing.

The date, too, is gone. This may, however, be determined with sufficient accuracy. The application tells us that " the

---

Salford. At that time it was estimated that the *two* towns contained 19,839 persons. Not till 1847, when the inhabitants within its parliamentary borough numbered upwards of 300,000, and it had become the commercial centre of some two millions of people, was the new diocese constituted; and Dr James Prince Lee entered upon his labours as the first Bishop of Manchester in 1848. Up to that time we formed part of the ample Diocese of Chester.

said house *is lately erected* and builded." Now, the authority to proceed with the building, given above, is dated March 27, 1711, and, as will appear presently, the new place of worship was formally opened on the 5th August 1712. It would not be opened before it was registered, nor be allowed to stand long unoccupied after it was built, for the old one across the Irwell, at Bass Lane, was "now gone to ruin and decay," and it was completed when the application was made. We may, therefore, fix the date of registration in the summer of 1712, a short time before the opening—most likely it was in July.[1]

The Opening of Dundee Chapel is thus recorded in Dr Brown's Sketch :—

"This chapel was opened on Tuesday the 5th August, 1712, when sermons were preached by the Rev. Mr Rothwell and the Rev. Mr Gilliburn [Gellibrand] of St. Helens. Mr Rothwell chose for his text Exodus xx. 24—"In all places where I record my name I will come unto thee and bless thee," and he commenced his sermon as follows: 'My beloved friends, the neighbours of my native county who have built here a place both decent and convenient *for the service of the Eternal God;* and though you have met with many oppositions in carrying the work thus far, yet be not discouraged if I tell you that the greatest work is still behind. I do not mean a vestry or an organ loft: No, not a material but a spiritual building. God's temple should be holy, whose temple ye are. Lest I should be tedious in my preface, I will return to the words of my text.

---

[1] But why not determine this small question absolutely by procuring an extract from the Register of the Archdeaconry? This we endeavoured to do; but the result of the effort leads us to state that the thing seems utterly hopeless. Any one who has prosecuted a like quest, in the same quarter, will readily sympathise with this statement. The chaotic mass of decayed and decaying documents still existing, of which there appears to be no official register extant, is simply appalling. But more have been destroyed. And notwithstanding something like even heroic devotion on the part of certain officials, in recent years, in respect of what remains, the mischief, however regrettable, is we fear practically *beyond remede*.

And in this chapter we have the promulgation of the ten commandments; and though as *legal* they are abolished, yet as *moral* they are binding for ever. Here is also the prohibition from idols in the text, and also a very gracious promise which appears to be truly evangelical.

I. There is the promise.
II. The place where the promise is made.
III. God's blessing them who meet to remember His name.

Mr Gilliburn on that occasion preached from Matt. xviii. 20—"Where two or three are gathered together in my name, there am I in the midst of them;" and the following is the commencement of his sermon: "By referring to these words I would not be thought to touch upon doubtful disputations; for it is not the place we meet in, nor the congregation we assemble with, nor the ministry we sit under, that will do us any good, except God be with us and bless us. Alas! what will ordinances do, if the God of ordinances be not with us? Though the Ark be not with us, yet if the God of the Ark be with us it is enough. Again, if the place we met in be ever so mean, if God there meet with us it is good and comfortable.

I. Here is a promise made by the God of heaven.
II. Here are those to whom the promise is made—"Who meet together."
III. Here is something of the number. Suppose they be but few, yea, very few—two or three—though they be but poor and mean in the world, yet if they meet in My name, I will meet with them and bless them."

Dundee Chapel, therefore, was built after the spring of 1711, and before the autumn of 1712; was registered in the Archdeaconry of Chester most likely in July, and opened by Mr Rothwell and Mr Gellibrand on the 5th of August 1712. "In a memorandum book still in existence," says Dr Brown, "Mr Rothwell records his intention of attending a provincial meeting at Preston, in May 1715, at which Mr Heywood of Stand was to preach."

III. The third document copied by Dr Brown refers to *A Survey of the Congregation*. In the famous library founded in

London by Dr Daniel Williams, there is an original manuscript relating to the time we are now approaching in our narrative. It was prepared by Dr John Evans, the colleague and successor of Dr Daniel Williams, the Presbyterian Minister of the Church in Hand Alley, Bishopgate Street, London, and contains a record of the Presbyterian and Independent Churches existing in England between 1717 and 1729. It furnishes the names of the ministers, the number of hearers, county voters, borough voters, esquires, gentlemen, tradesmen, farmers, yeomen, labourers, &c., connected with the several congregations, and also the amount received by them from the Presbyterian Fund. The immediate object of this laborious undertaking appears to have been to convince the Government of that time—the time of George I.—of the position and influence of the Churches referred to, with a view to the repeal of the Schism[1] Act. We have said the *immediate* object of Dr Evans, because it is stated that he contemplated writing a history of the English Nonconformist Churches, and that Neale made use of the valuable materials he had collected in writing his well-known 'History of the Puritans.'

In this list of Dr Evans there stand, in the section of Lancashire, and district of Bolton, under their appropriate headings, the following—" Holcomb, near Bury, 5. 4. Edward

---

[1] That Act passed in 1713, in the reign of Queen Anne, meant this—That any Nonconformist who acted as a tutor or teacher of any kind should be imprisoned without bail. It has, not unjustly, been described as " One of the worst Acts that ever defiled the Statute Book of England." It was repealed in 1719. Green thus accounts for the heartless enactment: " The Ministry, in their anxiety to *strengthen themselves by binding the Church to their side*, pushed through the Houses a Schism Act which forbade Dissenters to act as schoolmasters and tutors."—' English People,' p. 703.

Rothwell, 570, 23." The "5" and "4" indicate the grants from the Presbyterian Fund—most likely two half-yearly payments of £5 and £4 respectively. The other figures will be explained by Dr Brown's extract, which is in these words:—

"Decr. 16, 1717. On a survey of his Congregation by Mr Rothwell, it appeared that there were in it 120 heads of families, 23 of whom had votes in the election of M.P., and the Congregation consisted of about 570 persons. The freeholders were Samuel Waring, Robert Waring, Richard Kay, John Kay, James Kay, *Goosford*, James Kay, *Bass Lane*, James Hardman, Robert Hardman, Wm. Kay, *Dutch Road*, James Holt, *Spout Bank*, Ed. Hamer, *Summerseat*, John Wild, John Hill, Edward Hamer, *Buckden*, Richard Rothwell, James Rothwell."

These facts evidently formed the substance of the return to Dr Evans from Dundee or Holcom, which thus, no doubt, contributed its part in effecting the repeal of the Act above referred to, as well as of another of a kindred spirit—the Act against occasional Conformity—in the same year, 1719. They would also, we may fairly assume, furnish the ground for one part of the following statement by Dr Halley in his 'Lancashire Puritanism;'—" The only other meeting-houses in the county which in the early part of last century were frequented by more than five hundred persons were that at Monton, under the ministry of Jeremiah Aldred; that at Rainford, under Ronald Tetlow; that at *Holcom, under Edward Rothwell;* that at Darwen, under George Griffiths; and that at Walmsley, under James Milne. " The *last two* "—Darwen and Walmsley—" were congregational."—Vol. ii. p. 325. " Holcom" or Dundee was Presbyterian.

In the year 1719 an event occurred in connection with Dundee which had no inconsiderable influence upon its after-history—the congregation erected a Presbyterian Chapel at Bury. Dr Brown's sketch thus states it:—

"The town of Bury being more central for many of the Congregation, a Chapel was erected there in 1719, and from that time Mr Rothwell and Mr Braddock (who had been chosen his assistant) preached at Bury and Holcombe alternately, till the death of the former, after which Mr Braddock confined his services to Bury, and laboured there till 1770—a period of more than fifty years. A traditional account exists of the distinguishing excellencies of these two venerable men—'Rothwell for preaching, but Braddock for praying.'"

These worthy men laboured in cordial harmony in the dual charge till the standard dropped from the elder colleague's hand in 1731.

After Mr Rothwell's death in 1731, Mr Braddock confined his ministrations to what by that time no doubt had become the more important of the two congregations—that at Bury. His ministry continued till 1770. He was "considered for many years as at the head of the Lancashire Provincial Meeting, having probably delivered more charges than almost any minister among the dissenters."[1] He was buried[2] in the graveyard adjoining the Chapel at Bury.

Mr Braddock was succeeded in the Bury Chapel by the Rev. John Hughes, whose ministry was continued there till his death occurred in 1803.[3] He also was buried in the Bank Street Burying Ground.

Mr Hughes in his youth enjoyed the ministry and

---

[1] Addition to Dr Raffles' MSS. Signed J. W. (Joshua Wilson).

[2] The inscription on his tombstone is as follows:—

"Here lies the remains of the Rev. Thomas Braddock who was fifty years Minister of a dissenting congregation in this place. His faithful services are still remembered by his beloved people, and by them tho' dead he still speaketh. He dyed Novr. 13th, 1770. Aged 75."

[3] His tombstone bears the following inscription:—

"Underneath this tomb resteth the body of the Rev. John Hughes, upwards of 32 years Minister of the Society of Protestant Dissenters assembling at this place; who died Sept. 23rd, 1803. Aged 55."

friendship[1] of the Rev. Job Orton.[2] In Orton's letters there is one written to Mr Hughes which contains the following interesting words:—

"I could wish to see revived something of that spirit which appeared so eminently in your predecessors Pendlebury, Rothwell, and Braddock. I hope you will never give any of your aged hearers reasons to complain that it is not with them as it was in years past; but will support the high credit which the ministry at Bury hath long been in for seriousness, zeal, and usefulness. . . . I can hardly wish for you anything better than that you may resemble your excellent predecessor, who had few equals in every part of his office and character. Such an amiable mixture of cheerfulness and gravity; such a deep seriousness in speaking of religion; his discourses so plain and so judicious, so rational and yet so evangelical."

These were eminently seasonable words, as time proved; but, unhappily, not permanently influential. Mr Hughes continued Trinitarian, as all his predecessors had been, for nearly twenty years; but in 1789-1790, six years after his aged friend and counsellor had passed away, he declared himself Arian in doctrine. His congregation adhered to him. The father of the late Sir John Holker, however, left at this time, and as no other Nonconformist place of worship existed then in Bury, he joined the Established Church. The New Road[3] Independent Church was formed in 1792, and Bethel in 1806. The successor of Mr Hughes began his ministry in Bury in the year of his predecessor's death, and continued till 1831. Doctrinally, he was at first Arian, but afterwards became Humanitarian.

---

[1] The old Baptismal Register of Silver Street, Bury, now in Somerset House, has the following: "Job Orton, son of the Rev. John Hughes by Bridget, his wife. (Baptd.) by Mr Holland."

[2] Author of 'An Exposition of the Old Testament,' 'Memoirs of Dr Doddridge,' &c.

[3] This congregation was formed by Seceders from the Established

The next minister—inducted in 1831—was the Rev. Franklin Howorth. He advanced to the orthodox faith, and was constrained to resign in 1853. Subsequently, he and his adherents built the Christian Church, Rochdale Road. Cultured and consecrated, his saintly and memorable ministry in the pulpit, and in the street and homes of Bury, extended over half a century.

In the Bury Cemetery, under a spreading chestnut tree, in a spot selected by himself, rest his mortal remains, awaiting the resurrection; and, on a slab of Norway granite, grateful souls will long continue to read the simple but sufficient inscription—

> "IN LOVING MEMORY OF
> FRANKLIN HOWORTH,
> For fifty years Minister of the Gospel in this town.
> Born November 24, 1804,
> Died June 12, 1882.
> CHRIST IS ALL AND IN ALL."

Bank Street, though it still bears the name "Presbyterian Chapel," continues, as its present minister frankly expressed it, "downright Unitarian."[1]

In 1719, as we have seen, the chapel at Bury was built, and Mr Rothwell and his youthful assistant, Mr Braddock, ministered at both places. Three years later, in 1722, a

---

Church. Mr Winder, a clergyman's son, was one of the leaders, a Mr Woodcock was another, and the third prominent leader was Mr William Burford, a well-known workman of the Peels. Its *genesis* is found in this fact—viz.: A group of devout and spiritually-minded Episcopalians incurred the displeasure of the Episcopal authorities of the time by holding prayer-meetings, and, in consequence, left the church. Happily, they continued their good work, and became the founders of New Road Chapel, which was opened in 1793. John Wesley had preached in Bury in 1788.

[1] 'Bury Guardian,' 27th February 1886.

Trust Deed was executed, for the benefit of the minister of Dundee, a copy of which is now in our possession. Not a little historic interest attaches to it, and it will at this point fittingly find a chronological place. It is headed as follows :—

> "Copy of an Indenture, the original of which is in the possession of Mr Rothwell at Temple, near Manchester," and endorsed "Money belonging to the New Chapel, settled on Feoffees, 1722."

The deed, *verbatim et literatim*, runs thus :—

> "This Indenture made Anno Domini 1722, May the first, and in the eighth year of the reign of our most gracious Sovereign Lord, George, by the grace of God over Great Britain, France, and Ireland, King, Defender of the Faith, &c., Between William Holt, of Holcom, Tanner; John Ramsbotham, of Redishes, and Thomas Rothwell, of Strongstie, Yeoman, on the one part; and Andrew Holt, of Holcom, Thomas Rothwell, of Holcom, John Holt, Millhouse, Tanners; Samuel Hamer, of Summerseat, Tradesman; James Rothwell, of Chatterton; John Ramsbottom, of Redishes, junior; and Richard Rothwell, of Strongstie, Yeoman; Trustees for the purposes herein hereafter mentioned, Witnesseth, that the said William Holt, John Ramsbotham, and Thomas Rothwell, for divers good causes and considerations them hereunto moving, have transferred, and do by these presents transfer the trust they have of several Sums of Money, hereafter to be mentioned for the ends and intents ensuing, to the said Andrew Holt, Thomas Rothwell, John Holt, Samuel Hamer, James Rothwell, John Ramsbotham, and Richard Rothwell. To Wit, Five pounds deposited by John Sale in the hands of Joseph Whitworth, Clerk, for the propagating religion according to the way practised by Dissenting Protestants as may appear by an Indenture bearing date the 20th day of March, 1716. And also Six pounds, being part of the Ten pounds given by Margaret Finch, of Shevington, to the *Congregation formerly called by the name of Mr Pendlebury's*, as may appear from an Indenture under the hand and seal of Peter Finch, of Shevington, bearing date September 17th, 1708, now in the hands of Richard Kay, of Chesham, with the partition or division of the said sum of Ten

pounds on the backside endorsed; Likewise the sum of Five pounds given by the wills of Arthur Bromily, of Pallet, and Margaret his wife, to the Congregation convening at the New Chapel lately erected in Nuttal Lane, in Holcom, and for the use of Protestant Dissenters there. Now it is hereby declared and agreed by and between all the said parties to these presents, and these presents are upon Trust and Confidence that they the said Andrew Holt, Thomas Rothwell, John Holt, Samuel Hamer, James Rothwell, John Ramsbottom, and Richard Rothwell, their Executors, Administrators, and Assigns do at all times hereafter faithfully Employ and Improve the said several sums, amounting in the total to Sixteen pounds, to the best yearly or other profit they can, and as shall be most convenient for ever hereafter (so long as the Lords of this Realm will tolerate or indulge the same) towards *the supporting or maintaining of an able Protestant Minister of the Gospel*, and particularly Edward Rothwell, Clerk, or his successors for the time being, who shall preach the word of God purely and administer the Sacraments of the New Testament sincerely, *being of the Presbyterian persuasion*, officiating at the New Chapel, Oratory, or Meeting Place lately built and erected in Nuttal Lane, in Holcom, by the congregation convening there, and who shall be sound in the faith of a sober and Christian conversation, Professing so many of the Doctrinal Articles of the Church of England as are required to be subscribed by the Act of Indulgence or Toleration entituled an Act of Parliament made in the first year of the reign of King William and Queen Mary for the exempting of their Majesties' subjects dissenting from the Church of England from the penalties of certain laws. But supposing there should happen a Repeal of the said Act of Exemption and Toleration, so that the said Minister cannot officiate in the said Chapel or Oratory, nor the said moneys or the profit thereof annually coming in cannot be disposed of for the use of the said Minister as before expressed, that then and in such case they the said Andrew Holt, Thomas Rothwell, John Holt, Samuel Hamer, James Rothwell, John Ramsbotham, and Richard Rothwell, do covenant and agree for themselves, their Heirs, Executors, Administrators, and Assignees, that the said sum of Sixteen Pounds with the said Interest, Increase, and Improvement thereof, be laid out and disbursed for the benefit and advantage of such poor Widows and Children within the Manor of Tottington, and not elsewhere, as have no relief from the officers of the said town or manor at the sole discretion and direction of the aforesaid Feoffees and Trustees. And lastly it is agreed and concluded by the aforesaid Trustees that the yearly profit or product of the said moneys shall on every first day of May yearly ensuing be paid unto the said Edward Rothwell, now Minister of the said Chapel, or to his successor for the time being, or in case of the Repeal of the Act of Toleration to and for the uses and purposes, designs and ends before herein mentioned and no other whatsoever. Provided always, and it is hereby declared and agreed that when there shall be only three of the foresaid Trustees surviving and remaining, they shall have full power, liberty and authority, to fill up and supply the within number of Trustees, that by so doing the good intents and pious purposes of the within-named Donors and Benefactors may not by any failure of this nature be frustrated or eluded. In witness whereof the parties aforesaid have hereunto put their hands and seals the day and year first above written. Sealed, signed and delivered (with the stamps on the paper according to Act of Parliament in that case provided) in the presence of us—JOSEPH HAMER, ROBERT HOLTE, WILL HOULT (L.S.), John x (his mark) (L.S.) RAMSBOTHAM, THOMAS x (his mark) (L.S.) ROTHWELL, ANDREW (L.S.) HOULT, THOMAS ROTHWELL (L.S.), JOHN HOULT (L.S.), SAMUEL HAMER (L.S.), JAMES ROTHWELL (L.S.), JOHN RAMSBOTHAM (L.S.)."

This appears a long document for the slender sums to which it relates, but these amounts, in the opening decades of the eighteenth century, would be the equivalents of much larger in the closing one of the nineteenth.

And now, if, strictly for the purposes of this narrative, we might be permitted to follow at beseeming distance our distinguished Puritan predecessor of the seventeenth century, we should say, looking at this "Indenture," and proceeding interrogatively, we may consider it (1) Doctrinally; (2) Ecclesiastically; (3) Historically; (4) Partitively; and (5) Administratively!

As to *doctrine?* The ministers of Dundee must be orthodox " Protestants"—holding certain statutory articles of the Church of England, which means—say, 35½ of the famous 39, the *first* being " Of Faith in the Holy Trinity." The excepted articles we may call the Traditional—Article XXXIV.; the Homiletical—XXXV.; the Episcopal or Prelatical—XXXVI; and the Ceremonial—the first part of XX.

As to *ecclesiastical polity?* The ministers of Dundee must be " of the Presbyterian persuasion."

As to *historic continuity?* This was " the congregation formerly called by the name of Mr Pendlebury's."

As to *apportionment of funds?* The " six pounds " here secured to the minister of Dundee was " part of the ten pounds given by Margaret Finch to the congregation." What became of the other four ? The gift of ten pounds was in 1708. The congregation was then undivided. But the chapel at Bury had now been built some three years; and, no doubt, the " Partition or Division " referred to apportioned the minor sum to the promising daughter at Bury, and the major, to the worthy parent at Dundee.

As to the *Executive* Department? Until this deed came into our hands some little while ago, it was not known by the Dundee people that the above trust had ever existed. How the sums of money in the Indenture were ultimately administered will appear in another interesting document of a totally different kind, for which, however, it will be necessary to wait in this narrative till the opening decade of the next century. Having thus accentuated in the above deed some salient points which are specially germane to our purpose, we leave it for the present.

From 1719 to 1731 Mr Rothwell and Mr Braddock prosecuted their united ministry, devoted and drawing together. On the 31st of January 1731, in the Bank Street Chapel at Bury, Mr Rothwell preached his last sermon. He died on the Monday week following—the 8th of February—and was buried in Dundee Chapel, Holcom, on the 10th of February 1731. In the Register at Northowram, near Halifax, there is the following entry in 1731 : " Mr Edward Rothwell preacht at Bury, Jan. 31 ; died, Feb. 8 ; buried in his own chapel in Holcombe, Feb. 10."

Thus, " Edward Rothwell, clerk," " sound in the faith and of a sober and Christian conversation," having "preached the word of God purely, and administered the Sacraments of the New Testament sincerely, being of the Presbyterian persuasion, officiating at the New Chapel, Oratory, or Meeting Place in Nuttal Lane in Holcom," was laid to rest within its walls, after a ministry of nearly forty years, thirty-two of which were spent in connection with Dundee congregation—"the congregation formerly called by the name of ' Mr Pendlebury's.' "

Mr Pendlebury, his predecessor, was inducted to the chapelry of Holcombe in 1651. Thus, the united period covered by the ministry to this congregation of these two clergymen extended to about eighty years. During the next eighty years there were *fifteen* ministers, of some of whom little is known.

As enquiries are sometimes addressed to the writer, it may be of importance, at this point, to give, as the result of an exhaustive search in Somerset House, the following list of Baptismal Registers :—

Bass Lane and *Dundee*, kept by the Rev. Edward Rothwell, 1699-1730.

Silver Street, Bury (now Bank Street Unitarian), kept by Revs. Braddock, Hughes, Allard, and Howorth, 1730-1837.

Dundee and *Hol. Brook*, by Rev. P. Ramsay and others, 1802-1817.

Dundee, by Rev. Drs Brown and MacLean, 1817-1837.

It will thus be seen that, for the first eleven years of its existence, Silver Street or Bank Street Congregation, Bury, had its Baptismal Register kept at Dundee Chapel, Ramsbottom, by the senior minister of the united charge, the Rev. Edward Rothwell. After his death the Register for both places appears to have been kept at Bank Street by Mr Braddock and his successor, Mr Hughes, up to 1802, the year before Mr Hughes's death. By that time the doctrinal change at Bank Street had become unmistakably manifest, and Dundee Chapel adhering to the old Presbyterian faith, resumed at that date a register of its own. From 1719 to 1730 there is no separate register for Bank Street, and from 1730 to 1801 there is no separate register for Dundee.

CHAPTER II.

1731-1811.

AT this point, having closed a period of eighty years from the induction of Mr Pendlebury to the Chapelry of Holcombe, we begin a second well-marked period of the same length, terminating in 1811.

Dr Brown, writing seventy years ago, says: "From the death of Mr Rothwell the history of this congregation is involved in obscurity. The bulk of the congregation appears to have attended Mr Braddock's ministry in Bury." To these words Dr Brown adds an interesting statement respecting local Presbyterian endowments, and their relationship to Dundee Chapel and Bank Street, Bury. He also, happily, tells us that "The following are mentioned as having been ministers at Dundee Chapel, but the chronological order has not been ascertained, except in a few instances where the dates are inserted—Griffiths, Turner, Walkden, Halliday, Aspinall, Valentine, Taylor, Entwistle, Grindrod (about 1782), Simpson (about 1784), Main (from about 1786 to 1795), Holmes (1797), Hacking, Ramsay (1806 to 8th December 1811), Nelson, Brown (ordained 27th August 1818, resigned 10th July 1829).

We shall do what we can to clear up the "obscurity"

attaching to Dundee Chapel. It is greatest during the half century or so immediately succeeding the death of Mr Rothwell.

The first name we meet with after Mr Rothwell's time is that of a *Rev. Mr Griffiths*. About him we have not obtained any information. Among those trained, as Mr Rothwell had been, at Rathmell, under the Rev. Richard Frankland, there was a Rev. Peter Griffiths; and, in him, Mr Frankland *may* have supplied a second minister to Dundee.

The next name is that of a *Rev. Mr Turner*. In Dr Evans's list, 1717-1729, there is a Rev. John Turner at Walton, and another of the same name at Northwich in 1724. We find no trace of any other preacher of the name in this region at the time except the worthy Baptist apothecary, also a Mr John Turner of Manchester, who became pastor of the little chapel in Byrom Street in 1730, and of whom Dr Halley tells us that " he was sometimes called from the pulpit to attend his patients, when he left the good people to sing and pray until his return."

Of the next minister, however, the *Rev. Peter Walkden*, we fortunately have some knowledge. He was trained in Manchester, by the Rev. James Conningham, M.A., of Edinburgh University. Mr Conningham in 1700 became the colleague of Mr Chorlton, the successor of Henry Newcome, in Cross Street Chapel, and, at the time of his death in 1716, was Presbyterian Minister of Haberdashers' Hall, London.

At this time, and for a century and a half afterwards, the lack of University training, from which the Nonconformists were so long unrighteously excluded in England, was supplied, as far as practicable, by scholarly and well-trained ministers guiding and assisting young men in their studies.

Thus Peter Walkden, who was born in the neighbourhood of Manchester in 1684, became a student under Mr Conningham in 1706. He began his ministry at Garsdale, near Sedberg, in the East Riding of Yorkshire, on the 1st of May 1709. In 1711 he removed to a farm in the hamlet of Thornley, near Chipping Clitheroe, where he took charge of preaching stations at Hesketh Lane and Newton in Bolland.[1] At this place he wrote a diary which has been found of much interest, since its publication in 1866, by the late Mr Dodson, of Preston.[2]

Mr Walkden became minister of Dundee in 1738, and continued there till 1744, when he went to the Old Tabernacle at Stockport, where he laboured till his death, on Sunday the 5th of November 1769. Beneath the wooden floor of the old chapel there, a tombstone, bearing a long Latin inscription, covers the dust of the godly minister, homely pastor, and quaint diarist, gentle Peter Walkden. His son, who succeeded him at Hesketh Lane, is said to have composed the Latin inscription.

Following Mr Walkden we have a *Rev. Mr Halliday*. Respecting him we are unable to furnish any information. We have not found any trace of a minister of the name about this period, save that of the Rev. Thomas Halliday,

---

[1] In Dr Evans's list, as it appears in James's 'History of Legislation on Presbyterian Chapels,' there stands—"Chippen and Holland in Yorkshire, Peter Walkden." It ought to be Chipping and Bolland or Bowland—the Borderland between Lancashire and Yorkshire. Thornley, where Mr Walkden lived, is near Chipping, and, like Hesketh Lane, is in Lancashire. Newton, where he also preached, lies in Bolland in Yorkshire.

[2] 'Extracts from the Diary of the Rev. Peter Walkden, Nonconformist Minister, for the years 1725, 1729, and 1730, with notes by William Dodson, Preston.' W. & J. Dodson, London; Simpkin, Marshall, & Co., 1866.

who was minister at Milford in Derbyshire, and tutor at the Academy at Daventry.

Next on the list at Dundee Chapel comes the name of a *Rev. Mr Aspinall*. This is probably the same as the Mr Aspinall who stands seventh in the long list of ministers at Risley, near Warrington. He had, we believe, been minister at Walmsley before going to Risley; and he may have found his way to Dundee afterwards.

In 1755,[1] a Trust Deed helps us to the name of another minister—the *Rev. John Helme*. After discovering, in 1883, the Dundee Chapel trust deed of 1811, it was not difficult to find its predecessors in the muniment room at Clitheroe Castle. One of these—a surrender to new trustees, of date 18th Oct. 1755—has the following words—"All that one building . . . consisting of four bays adjoining to Nuttall Lane, formerly called Little Edmunds, . . . now in the possession or occupation of John Helme, Clerk, or his Assigns." Mr Helme had been educated under Dr Caleb Rotheram of Kendal, and is referred to by Dr Halley as "of Walmsley."[2] He was however, according to the before-mentioned deed, minister of Dundee Chapel in 1755. But in the 'History of Blackley Chapel'[3] we find it stated that "for the next two years [1755-1757] the resident minister [at Blackley] was the Rev. John Helme of Holcomb." The words, "or his assigns," where they occur in the deed of 1755, are unusual, and have no similar place in any of the other surrenders excepting that

---

[1] In 1752, during the Ministry of the Rev. John Stanley in Bury, the first organ was built in its Parish Church.
[2] Halley, vol. ii. p. 394.
[3] 'A History of the Ancient Chapel of Blackley,' by the Rev. John Booker, B.A., of Magdalene College, Cambridge, Curate of Prestwich, Manchester. George Sims, St Ann's Square: 1854.

of 1713, and there Mr Rothwell is still spoken of as "of Tunley." Blackley, as the crow flies, is some ten miles distant from Dundee Chapel, and Mr Helme, aided by "his assigns," may have been minister concurrently of both chapels.

We next come to a *Rev. Mr Valentine*. In the list given by Dr Halley of ministers settled in Lancashire who had been educated by Dr Rotheram at the Academy at Kendal, up to its close in 1752, we find the Rev. "Joseph Valentine of Wharton," near Bolton. It might be he who became minister of Dundee at this time. There was also a Rev. Thomas Valentine. But as he was minister at Blackley from 1731 to 1755, when he died on the 10th of May, it could not be he who at this time came to Holcom.

Following Mr Valentine we have a *Rev. Mr Taylor*. A Rev. John Taylor went to Walmsley, near Bolton, about 1783, and he may at an earlier date have ministered at Dundee. We have found no trace of any other likely Taylor.

One name more, and again we shall touch solid chronological ground. It is a *Rev. Mr Entwistle*. At a later date, 1788, a Rev. W. Entwistle began what proved, in the first instance, a popular ministry at Ilkeston, in Derbyshire. Afterwards, however, he appears to have been deserted by the greater part of his people, mainly because he was courageous enough to be the first to preach the Gospel in the playhouse at Belper. Whether he is the gentleman symbolised by "Entwistle" at Dundee Chapel we cannot tell.

This name brings us to the close of five somewhat dreary decades at Holcombe; perhaps not so dreary there, however, as over much wider areas, north and south, throughout the land.

The following incident may probably belong to the period

we have now reached or are approaching. While service was going on one Sunday in Dundee Chapel—conducted that day by a non-clerical preacher—distant shouting began to disturb the devotions of the worshippers. It grew every moment in vigour and volume, and very soon culminated in one grand exultant shout near the chapel. The people were startled; but the preacher, who, perhaps, from the pulpit could see better than his hearers what was happening in the immediate vicinity of the building, was equal to the occasion. His oratory, indeed, was extinguished for the moment by the unhallowed tumult, but, quickly recovering himself, he said with an unwonted look and gesture—"We'll close the sarvice; *aw think they'n t'en her!*" When the story was told to us by one who had heard it, and especially from an old and well-known residenter who, as he said, had "a printed book" with an account of the day's proceedings, we very naturally asked "Whom, or what, had they taken?" "Why," he replied, "they were hunting a hotter or a foumart [an otter or a polecat], or something of that sort, and they killed it just by the chapel!"

At this point, once more a Dundee Chapel trust deed assists us to a name—the Rev. William Grindrod. In a surrender to new trustees, dated 14th August 1782, we find Dundee "now in possession of William Grindrod, clerk, and Abraham Hamer." A manse had now been provided. It appears for the first time in this deed, which runs thus: "One building of four bays, . . . now used as a Dissenting Chapel, *and an house* for the use and benefit of the minister thereof for the time being." Mr Abraham Hamer subsequently was ordained to the eldership. He was from his youth a well-known and devoted member of the congregation, lived to be a very old man, and will need to be referred to again. The Rev. William Grindrod is probably the gentleman who kept an academy in Manchester for many years, and was also minister at the Independent Chapel, Partington, near Middlewich, in Cheshire.

Mr Grindrod's successor at Dundee was the Rev. David Simpson. He had passed through the usual curriculum at St Andrews and Edinburgh, and became minister at Eastwood, near Todmorden, in 1770. "It is said he was 'compelled to retire,' because 'he was supposed to be an Arian.'"[1] He came to Holcome in 1783, and remained about three years. He afterwards went to Low Row, near Richmond, in Yorkshire, where he died on the 22d of March 1808, in the 70th year of his age.

An exceedingly interesting and rare little book,[2] recording a survey of our township in 1794, contains the following record:—

"Chapel Houses belonging to *Dissenting Meeting* at Holcome—

One Cottage, William Maine, 1.10 ⎫
One do., Abraham Hamer, 1.15   4.10."
One do., Richard Hall, 1.5 ⎭

The figures indicate the rateable value—£4, 10s. The "William Maine" occupying "One Cottage" is the Rev. William Maine, who succeeded Mr Simpson in 1786, and

---

[1] 'Old Dissenting Chapels,' by Rev. B. Nightingale.
[2] 'A new and Actual Survey of the Township of Tottington, Lower End, in the Parish of Bury *and County of Lancaster*, taken in the year 1794, by Robert Smith, John Kay, and John Brandwood, wherein is shown the yearly value of every Farm, Building, Cottage, and Field, together with the *Owners' and Occupiers' Names*, to which is added an Appendix shewing at one view the total value of every estate.' 1795.

continued at Dundee till 1795. Like his predecessor, he had previously been minister at Eastwood, in Yorkshire.

The *three* "Chapel Houses" recorded in the above "survey" furnished a puzzle which baffled us in our quest for many a day. In the trust deed of 1782 "*an house* for the use and benefit of the minister" first appears; twelve years later, in 1794, there were, as above, *three* houses; but, in the memory of Mrs Wilson already referred to, whose recollection went back distinctly to 1814, and who lived for some time in the manse a few years later, — there was at that time, 1814, only *one* house, the manse, substantially as it exists to-day. It is a strong, well-built structure[1] of two storeys and a gabled attic, of squared and finely dressed millstone grit from one of the quarries in the neighbouring hills, and placed right against the east end of Dundee Chapel. Moreover, although the time to which the matter relates is not very remote, yet, to the present hour, not a spark of light on the difficulty has been found anywhere, excepting what has come most opportunely from a single time-tarnished leaf, received some time ago, inside an old minute-book, from Mr George Brown, of St Michael's Hamlet, Liverpool, who was born in Dundee Manse, and had found the humble but helpful document among the papers of his late revered father, Dr Brown. This lucky leaf not only enables us to read the riddle

---

[1] The Peels' firm had, since 1783, works at Ramsbottom, and one of the partners—Mr Warren—took an interest in Dundee. This may account for the superior style of the old manse building for its time. Mr Job Wilson, who afterwards for many years was pastor of an Independent congregation at Northwich, was a trusted employé of the firm, and enjoyed, in connection with Dundee Chapel, the friendship and kindly interest of Mr Warren.

of the premises, but, strangely enough, also incidentally tells the tale of the trust funds of 1722. Fortunately, its date is preserved, and it will most conveniently appear in its chronological place in 1808.

After Mr Maine came the Rev. Benjamin Holmes, in 1796. He continued at Dundee till 1798, when he went across the valley to the Independent Chapel, then newly erected at Park,[1] whose first minister he became.

Dr Brown, in his historic sketch, thus refers to the event and a sequent circumstance of some interest:—

" During the incumbency of Mr Holmes, the Independent Chapel at Park in Walmersley was erected. Mr Holmes was translated to that charge in 1798, and *an attempt was made to shut up Dundee Chapel and appropriate the property* to the benefit of Park, but *the result of a lawsuit prevented* this from being carried into effect."

---

[1] The building and opening of Park Chapel are described by our Independent friends, in the 'Evangelical Magazine' of the time, thus: "On Sunday, July 1st [1798], a very neat place of worship called Park Chapel, about four miles on the road from Bury to Blackburn, was opened for religious uses. In the morning Mr Blackburn of Delph began the service with prayer and reading suitable portions of Scripture, and Mr Roby of Manchester preached from Matthew xviii. 20, 'Where two or three are gathered together in my name, there am I in the midst of them.' In the afternoon Mr Roby preached from Job xxv. 4, and Mr Blackburn from 1 Cor. iii. 11. Before the erection of this building a small handful of people had assembled at Holcombe Chapel, about a mile and a half distant from the present. The chapel was in a ruinous condition, and, what was worse, the Gospel was either not faithfully preached in it or but little blest, till it pleased God, a year or two ago, to send Mr Holmes among them: his activity and diligence has been very acceptable and successful. In consequence of this, some respectable Dissenters in the neighbourhood proposed to unite with the old congregation, and by their liberality and influence principally the present commodious chapel is erected in the centre of a populous neighbourhood, destitute of any other place of worship. On the morning of the day on which it was opened, the chapel was much crowded, and in the afternoon one half of the congregation could not press in. The service was therefore conducted with much seriousness in the open air."

Mr Holmes remained at Park Chapel till 1809, when he removed. After this, Park, we are told, passed through "peculiar trials," and was vacant till July 1816, when the *Rev. George Partington* became its minister. The change, since 1798, must unhappily have been very marked, for, four months after he began his pastoral duties, only "five persons were united in Church fellowship." He resigned in 1826. In 1828 he was succeeded by the *Rev. John Williams*, who resigned on November 3, 1830. He was followed by the *Rev. Benjamin Nightingale* in 1832. But trouble having arisen, he resigned in 1835. Mr Nightingale appears to have been a man of resolution and energy. He did not leave the neighbourhood. Deeming himself wronged, and believing that he still had service to render in the locality, he set resolutely to work, and succeeded in raising funds and erecting a commodious chapel. It was planted about three-quarters of a mile along the road from Park, in the village of Bank Lane or Shuttleworth. It was, in the circumstances, a laborious undertaking, and is supposed to have impaired the heroic worker's health. He toiled on bravely, however, in his ministerial duties till 1847. On the 11th of April of that year he passed away to a serener sphere, in the 64th year of his age.[1] He had no successor, and the building was purchased from the trustees by the Messrs Wild of Shuttleworth, who transformed it into cottages. A graveyard also was formed, and some bodies were interred. They were, however, subsequently removed.[2]

---

[1] Mr Nightingale was a native of Tockholes, near Blackburn, was ordained at Newton in 1820, and had charge of the churches at Newton and Wymondhouses before coming to Park.

[2] The late Mrs Leonard Wild used to tell how Mr Leonard, then her

In Slate's 'History of the Lancashire Congregational Union,' &c., under the year 1838, we find the following record :—

"*Park Chapel*, between Bury and Haslingden, being in

PARK CHAPEL (BUILT, 1798).

a low state, received a grant to enable the friends there to procure and support a minister among them;

---

fiancé, on his way home from her father's at Nuttall Lane, found on one occasion near midnight an eager and awestruck group engaged in removing one of these bodies to another resting-place.

but no one has yet been found willing to undertake it."—(P. 87.)

On the 2d of March 1840, however, the church was re-formed, and consisted of six communicants. In the following year, the congregation had another pastor settled amongst them—the *Rev. Edwin Robinson*. His ministry covered about three years. He resigned in 1844. He was followed by one whose name is still well and worthily remembered in the district—the *Rev. John Anyon*. He proved a devoted pastor to the people for twenty-two years. He died in 1867. His name is still fragrant of humble-minded, faithful toil and kindly pastoral care. His successor was the *Rev. R. C. Lumsden*. Mr Lumsden's ministry at Park continued about four years, from 1868 to 1872, when he resigned. After him came the *Rev. John Robinson*, who proved a faithful, sympathetic, and devoted pastor. He came in 1874, and considerations of health led him to seek a change of sphere, which he found in 1880 at Elswick in the Fylde country. He was succeeded in 1881 by the *Rev. Henry Banks*, who resigned in 1890. His successor is the Rev. William Gibson, who was translated from Brampton in 1891.

Recrossing the valley from the parish of Walmersley to that of Holcombe, we find that the successor of Mr Holmes at Dundee was a *Rev. Mr Hacking*. Of him we have no trustworthy information. Slate refers to "Mr Hacking, a young man of promising abilities," who was about this period in the neighbourhood of Ormskirk, and, it is said, afterwards for several years at Ebenezer Chapel, Darwen. But whether he was the Mr Hacking who officiated at Dundee we cannot tell. Nor have we been able to determine precisely either when the Dundee Mr Hacking came or when he went away.

About his successor—the *Rev. Peter Ramsay*—we have no such difficulties. His connection with Dundee began in 1806.

Mr Ramsay was born on the 27th December 1772, and hailed from the parish of Strathmartine, near the town of Dundee, in Forfarshire. Not favoured with any University course, he was kindly aided in his preparatory work by an Independent minister at the Northern Dundee—the Rev. William Innes; and he afterwards received such training for the ministry as was practicable under that good and devoted man, to whom Manchester Independency owed so much in the beginning of the present century—the Rev. William Roby. Every one who knows anything of the work he did, in conjunction with a devoted Christian merchant, Mr Robert Spear (1803-1809), as Dr Halley puts it, "by training pious young men for the ministry, and directing the labours of itinerant preachers over a wide extent of country round Manchester," will revere Mr Roby's name.

In Slate's History we find the following interesting paragraph relating to the Lancashire Congregational Union[1] and Dundee Chapel—"The first meeting of the Committee was held in Manchester, October 22d, 1806, when the Rev. P. S. Charrier of Lancaster, Rev. John Adamson of Patricroft, Rev. D. Edwards of Elswick, and Rev. Peter Ramsay of Holcombe, with their churches, were admitted into the Union."

Mr Ramsay had just come from Mr Roby's tutorial class, and it was very natural that he should wish to join the Union, of which Mr Roby was an ardent advocate, and whose rules he had helped to frame. But, while it is not a

---

[1] It was formed "in the Vestry of Mosley Street Chapel, Manchester, September 23d, 1806."

matter of any importance, it would be interesting to know how far, and in what way, the trustees and the congregation were made cognisant of Mr Ramsay's action. One thing we do know—viz., that the Grants came to Ramsbottom just at this time, and from the first occupied an influential position

DUNDEE CHAPEL AND MANSE (BUILT, 1712; RENEWED, 1809).

at Dundee Chapel. And they, from first to last, were staunchly and persistently Presbyterian. The appeal for funds by Mr Ramsay himself and others, in 1808, bears the fact that Dundee "was erected by a Presbyterian minister of the name of Rothwell . . . nearly a century ago."

At that date (1808) the old chapel had weathered the storms between the closing years of Queen Anne and the decadent period of George III. And with the youthful years of a new century and the generous impulse of a fresh pastorate it was, doubtless, felt to be seemly, as well as necessary, to do something to renew the youth of the venerable fabric in which the Gospel had been preached for close upon a hundred years. We find, accordingly, that it was resolved to make an effort to deal with the building. This we learn from the faded leaf to which we have already referred (p. 222), and which throws so much light on the past of Dundee Chapel. It comes to us in the form of a "petition" or appeal for funds to effect the desired improvements. We now give it, *verbatim et literatim* :—

To the several and respective members of the Congregation of *Dundee* dissenting chapel, in the parish of Bury and County of Lancaster, in particular, and to the opulent and benevolent members of other congretions in the said county dissenting from the Established Church of England, in general.

The Petition of the Minister and Trustees of the said Chapel humbly sheweth,—

That nearly a century ago, a Presbyterian minister of the name of Rothwell erected the chapel now called Dundee Chapel, consisting of three bays, erected on his own ground, but left it unendowed;

That in process of time a few small presents and legacies were given by persons composing, or who had composed, a part of the congregation there ; to be put out at annual interest, and such interest applied towards the support of a Minister of said Chapel, *pro tempore;*

That about 27 years ago, the congregation being much decreased, from a variety of causes and circumstances, it was thought expedient to call in the greater part of such monies as were not then already lost ; and with the aid of subscriptions, to be obtained from Dissenters or Presbyterians in its vicinity, to convert the most north-westerly bay into a dwelling-house, and about ten years after to call in remainder of such monies, with the view to erect another house at the south-east end of the said chapel (within the yard) for the perpetual melioration of a minister's maintenance, which alterations and improvements were actually soon after made; but—

That, now the Congregation being upon the increase, and the roof of the old chapel in a decayed and ruinous condition, your petitioners think that it is necessary and expedient, not only to re-convert the house at the north-west end into its primitive form—a part of the chapel—but also to raise the whole chapel to the same elevation as the house at the south-east end of the chapel is, for the sake of uniformity and preservation of both roofs, if money can be procured to effect those purposes; and,

That, therefore, your petitioners humbly solicit your generous and voluntary contributions, to enable us to make the above-mentioned desirable alterations and improvements; and they will, as in duty bound, ever pray, &c.

May 13, 1808.

This appeal has an eye to the past, with a view to the future. As to the *past*, it *explains the puzzle of the premises*. It tells us that about 1780[1] "the most north-westerly bay" of the chapel was converted into a dwelling-house. The old chapel had *four* bays.[2] Thus about one fourth part of the building, at the upper or Holcombe end, was appropriated for this purpose; and this, no doubt, is the "house for the use and benefit of the minister" referred to in the deed of 1782. Then, "about ten years after" (1790) "another house" was erected, "at the south-east end of the chapel (within the yard)." This evidently refers to *the present manse*. Its front entrance was at one time on the south side, between the window and the chapel, at which place, from Dundee Lane,

---

[1] "About 27 years" before 1808—the date of the appeal.
[2] In the deeds of 1713, 1755, and 1782, the chapel is said to be of "four bays." In the deed of 1811 the number is not stated. The present structure had then, no doubt, just been reared. It has *three*, not "four bays," like the original building, and is 48 ft. 6 in. long.

the door lintel may still be seen in the wall. This door was built up before Dr Brown took possession in 1819. There were, therefore, *two* houses—one at either end of the chapel. But the "survey" records *three*. The explanation may be this: the premises at the upper or north-west end may, in 1794, at the survey, as in 1782,[1] have been occupied by *two* tenants, and for each tenant there may have been recorded a house. It will be seen presently how and when the three again became one.

But the document also *reveals the ultimate destination of the trust funds* of 1722. By 1780, a portion of these had evidently, in some unexplained way, been lost. For at that time they called in "the greater part of such monies as were *not then already lost*," to transform part of the chapel into a dwelling-house. About 1790 the "remainder of such monies" was called in to erect another house—the present manse— "for the perpetual melioration of a minister's maintenance," &c. These "monies" were in trust "towards the supporting or maintaining of an able Protestant minister, . . . being of the Presbyterian persuasion." While some part of them appears to have been lost, the benefits of the remaining portion have, since about 1780, been enjoyed by successive ministers, in the form of a manse.

But, *next*, the "petition" looked to the *future*. Its object is clearly expressed—"not only to re-convert the house at the north-west end into its primitive form—a part of the chapel —but also to raise the whole chapel to the same elevation as the house at the south-east end[2] of the chapel is, for the sake

---

[1] See Trust Deed, Appendix B.
[2] The present Dundee house or old manse.

of uniformity and preservation of both roofs, if money can be procured to effect those purposes."

The Grants—Messrs William Grant & Brothers—purchased the Print Works of Messrs Peel & Yates situated at Ramsbottom, in 1806, and began to run them on the 1st of January 1807. Of this family more will fall to be said by-and-by. Meanwhile it is necessary to know that at this period their connection with Dundee congregation began. Its subsequent history, as will appear, was very materially affected by their influence.

The "petition," as printed above, was, no doubt, duly issued. How did it fare with it as to procuring funds? So far as we have been able to ascertain, no record of any kind exists to tell the actual financial result of the appeal. Fortunately, however, we have obtained testimony that may be trusted which explains substantially what transpired at this juncture in the history of Dundee. In the latter days of Mr John Grant of Nuttall Hall, while talking one day to Mr J. S. W.—now Major—Grant, of the early experiences of the family in Ramsbottom, he referred to their connection with Dundee Chapel. Speaking of some appeal that was made for funds to repair the chapel, he said they were greatly disappointed with the result. They themselves had always, according to their means, willingly and promptly contributed for kindred purposes, and they expected from others a like prompt and liberal response. It proved, however, in this case, neither prompt nor liberal. In consequence of this, feeling somewhat chagrined and impatient, they resolved to prosecute the appeal no further, and determined to undertake the necessary work themselves. And accordingly they did so. But what did they eventually deem the work that was necessary? The "petition" aimed at restoring the north-western "bay" to the chapel, and raising the chapel walls to the level of the manse. But something more than this, and different, was undoubtedly done. We know, from the testimony of Mrs Wilson, who lived till after 1891, that chapel and manse alike stand at present substantially as they were within five or six years after the time referred to. But the chapel is now considerably *higher* than the manse, and the walls have *not* been raised. They are homogeneous throughout, from foundation to roof. The conclusion, therefore, seems clear—that the Dundee Chapel of 1712 was demolished, and the present structure of *three* instead of "four bays" reared on its site, soon after the issue of the petition in 1808, and that the expense was borne mainly, if not almost exclusively, by the Grants.

From that time the old manse has been the only residential portion of the Dundee premises. It has sometimes been occupied by the minister, but for the most part, as at present, let to a tenant.[1] In the year 1808 therefore, or soon after, the chapel of 1712 was no doubt taken down and the present structure reared on its site. In 1811 *a new deed was executed*, "renewing and extending the trust."

Of the four surviving trustees at this time of the deed of 1782, none was resident in the immediate neighbourhood. In 1811, of the four new trustees appointed, three were locally resident—viz.: " William Woodcock[2] of Holcombe,

---

[1] This further simple fact we have gleaned about Dundee Chapel, that the first undertaking of Mr John Wild—father of the late Mr Edward Wild —as a young joiner and builder, was putting the roof on it at this time.
[2] Father of the late Dr Woodcock. See p. 67, *supra*.

gentleman," "William Grant of Grant Lodge, merchant," and "Charles Grant of the same place, merchant."[1] The *fourth*, who proved the last survivor of the group, was "Edward Rothwell of Bolton, painter."

In the Appendix (B) will be found an important group of trust deeds—the most interesting and remarkable being the first one given, the deed of 1811. It was the rather remarkable and singularly timely discovery of *this* document in 1883, which shaped the course of much that is memorable in connection with the recent history of Dundee Chapel property. Looking carefully over this group of deeds, we ask our readers to note briefly three points of interest:—

First, as to dates. The meeting-house provided for Mr Pendlebury at Bass Lane, Walmersley, on the opposite side of the Irwell from Holcombe, and at a date not precisely determined, but subsequent to 1662, was still in use in 1710, for "on the 30th April 1710, Mr Waring preached a funeral sermon, in Walmersley, for Mr James Kay, of Sheephey." But, in 1712, Mr Rothwell—Mr Pendlebury's successor—says it was "now gone to ruin and decay." In the same year, 1712, Dundee Chapel was opened. The above four Dundee deeds stretch from that time to 1883—the earliest covering the years 1713-1755; the second, 1755-1782; the third, 1782-1811; the last, and long lost, 1811-1883. In 1883 the Dundee congregation appointed new trustees, under the Morton Peto Act, in St Andrew's (Dundee) Presbyterian Church.

Second, as to an extinct local industry. A well-known part of the west or Holcombe side of Ramsbottom is called

---

[1] The elder Cheeryble and his brother.

"Tanners." But no one remembers the existence of any tannery in the locality. Beyond doubt, however, one existed there in the course of last century. In the deed of 1755, we learn that the sole surviving trustee in 1754 of the group of nine appointed in 1713 was "Thomas Rothwell, of Holcombe, in the parish of Bury and county of Lancaster, Tanner." Moreover, years ago, in excavating at Tanners, the remains of an old tan-pit were discovered, and one result of the disclosure was unfortunately the permanent pollution of what had previously been a useful well.

Third, as to the terms of the trust. The deed of 1713 is a simple surrender and admittance, and contains no declaration of trust. In that of 1755 it is expressed thus: "As ffeofees in trust of the above-mentioned premises to such uses as the same is now set apart, and to be continued for the service of divine worship, and to no other use or service whatsoever." In 1782 the actual use of the four-bayed building is stated thus: "Now used as a Dissenting chapel;" and the trust thus: "As ffeofees in trust to and for such uses as the same is now set apart, and to be continued for the worship of God, the interment of the dead, and the emolument and benefit of a Dissenting minister for the time being for ever, according to the custom of the said manor." In 1811 we find a further development or dilution of the original terms of the trust, for we now read: "As ffeofees or trustees in trust according to the custom of the said manor, to and for such uses, ends, intents, and purposes as the same is now set apart, and to be continued for the service and worship of God, the interment of the dead, and the emolument and benefit of a pious, preaching, dissenting minister for the time being for ever of the said chapel, being the original intent thereof, and to and for no other use, trust, intent, or purpose whatsoever."[1]

Thus, from the simple words "for the service of divine worship,"[2] well known, with other kindred phrases, in Presbyterian deeds of the post-Revolution period, were evolved somehow the terms of the deed of 1811. The *how* presents an interesting question. Can we trace the process? We may, at least, group a few facts.

(1) The deed of 1755 came into existence during the ministry of the Rev. John Helme, who had been trained at Kendal in the academy of Dr Caleb Rotheram. In his time we have the first formal declaration of the trust, clear and characteristic, "for the service of divine worship."

(2) The deed of 1782 emerged during the ministry of the Rev. William Grindrod, who, at another time, was, it is believed, minister of the Independent Chapel at Partington, near Middlewich. In his time we have introduced "the emolument and benefit of *a Dissenting minister*," &c.

---

[1] When, in 1885, the trial for the ejectment of those persons who, in 1883, had forcibly seized Dundee Chapel property, came on, their counsel contended, and with unquestionable effect on the mind of the learned judge, that the words "pious, preaching, Dissenting minister" constituted the above (1811) an Independent deed, and Dundee, therefore, Independent property. The earlier deeds referred to above, be it remembered, were not before his lordship. Nor had the bequest deed of 1722, with its "Presbyterian persuasion" clause, come into our hands at the time of the trial. We had, indeed, to establish our case, not only without aid from the deed of 1811, but in direct opposition to the interpretation of it, which, for the time being, prevailed. Happily we had no difficulty in doing this; and what alone, at present, it seems necessary to point out is the fact, that the words "pious, preaching, Dissenting minister" on which so much might have depended are not found in the original declaration of trust at all. Its terms are simply, "for the service of divine worship."

[2] The Rev. Edward Rothwell, the founder, in his sermon at the opening of Dundee Chapel, said it was "for the service of the Eternal God." See p. 202, *supra*.

(3) The deed of 1811 appeared during the ministry of the Rev. Peter Ramsay, who came to Dundee in 1806, from the tutorial class of Mr Roby of Manchester. In that year he joined the Lancashire Congregational Union, which had just been formed, and, subsequently, several subscriptions were sent by him from Dundee to the Union.[1] In Mr Ramsay's time the terms of the Dundee deed became—"for the emolument and benefit of *a pious, preaching, Dissenting minister,* . . . being *the original intent thereof,* and to and for no other use, trust, intent, or purpose whatsoever." Thus the process of evolution culminated.[2]

Here, before passing on, we may refer, briefly, to the subscriptions to the Lancashire Congregational Union, which really are generous as well as "interesting," as Mr Nightingale puts it.

The Grants were ready givers. As all, or nearly all, the Dundee congregation were people employed at their works, the masters to the end of their days, very unwisely in some

---

[1] "It is interesting to note that, in the Second Report of the Lancashire Congregational Union (December 31st, 1808, to December 31st, 1809), 'Holcombe,' with Mr Ramsay as minister, contributes to the Union Funds £2, 12s. 6d., and 'Park,' with Mr Holmes, £1, 5s. In the next report 'Dundee,' with Mr Ramsay, contributes £2, 15s. 6d., and 'Park' is not named. For two or three years afterwards Dundee sent £2, 2s. annually to the Union funds."—'Old Dissenting Chapels,' by the Rev. B. Nightingale, Congregational Minister, Preston.

[2] Mr Nightingale, in his 'Dundee Chapel' sketch, calls it a "*free Independent Church,*" and tells us that Dundee Chapel, with Mr Ramsay's ejection, drops out of the Union Reports, ceases to be Independent, and becomes Presbyterian *in the modern sense of the word!*"—('Bury Times,' 'Preston Herald,' and other newspapers in which the sketch appeared, August 31st, 1889.) It would have been interesting to know from our brother whether, in his estimation, Dundee had been "*Independent*" in the ancient or "in the modern sense of the word." But he does not inform us.

respects, generally paid "the charities" or "benevolences," as they were called, instead of the office-bearers taking congregational collections. And there can, we think, be little or no doubt that the two-guinea and two-guinea-and-a-half subscriptions were given by them. But as their representative, who knew them well, said to the writer, they would never for a moment dream that, in aiding a recently formed and struggling Union of Nonconformist Churches in its much needed evangelistic work, they could be supposed by anybody to surrender either their own Presbyterianism or, had it been possible, that of the old foundation at Dundee. When wanting a minister, Presbyterian Theological Halls were far off, but Manchester was near; and Mr Roby, a prime promoter of the Union, had furnished them with a minister for the old Presbyterian chapel. The new minister supported the Union. *That* would be enough. *His* word would readily secure the subscriptions.

While the Grants had little acquaintance with rival ecclesiastical systems, they had a great and honourable love for the church of their fathers, the Church of Scotland, which is, of course, Presbyterian. But with the kindred Presbyterian foundation, humble, yet time-honoured, which they found on English soil at Ramsbottom—the place, from that time, of their memorable industrial efforts, and the centre of their splendid commercial success—they and their parents at once became identified. Moreover, from the first, with whatever mingling of human infirmity, they took a personal interest in all its concerns, which proved deep, warm, generous, and lifelong.

We shall now, for the present, leave the trust deeds, the latest of which is dated 30th of April 1811. At that time,

> "All seemed as peaceful and as still
> As the mist slumbering on yon hill."

But, before the year quite died away, the proverbial "bolt from the blue" suddenly descended, and Mr Ramsay's ministry at Dundee came abruptly to a close. This brings us to a *second ejectment* in the history of this congregation. It occurred in the 150th year of its existence outside the national establishment. Unhappily, it is not the last to be recorded in its annals.

The facts of the extrusion of the Rev. Peter Ramsay, with their graceless glimpse of vulgar wit, are these: On the morning of Sunday, December 8, 1811, the service in Dundee Chapel proceeded as usual until the text was announced. It happened to be taken from the 1st Epistle of Peter. Immediately on its announcement some one shouted—"Nay, lad, it's th' last Epistle of Peter here!" Whereupon a number of young fellows of the rougher sort, evidently acting in concert, proceeded to remove the minister. He appears, very naturally, to have resisted their astounding interference, when the leader of the group—the youngest of the Grants, at this time twenty-three years of age—with a warlike spring "punst [kicked] in the panel of the pulpit door." Mr Ramsay was then extruded from the building. The event naturally caused much talk and commotion in the locality, with the rupture of some friendly bonds, while the actors in the affair were never forgotten.

By more than one aged member of the congregation, whose years reached back to the closing decades of the last or the opening years of the present century, we have been told with awe of the fate, in after years, of most of those reckless and misguided men. As if pursued—such was the view—by an avenging Providence, they came to mournful and untimely ends. One of them was crushed to death by the sudden fall of a block of stone in a neighbouring quarry; another, under the influence of drink, fell in the street and was taken up dead; one informant remembered old Mrs Grant, who died in 1821, speaking to her of, and she herself personally knew about, the distressful end of a third; while the youthful leader, gifted with endowments which, rightly wielded, meant far higher things, passed away, in mournful circumstances, some fourteen years after the expulsion. The Rev. Peter Ramsay was still preaching the Gospel long after these youthful assailants had crumbled into dust.

But what was it that brought about this ejectment? *Why was the deed done?* The story, as briefly and usually told, is simply this: By some utterance or utterances in the pulpit the minister had offended the mother of the Grants, and this offence was avenged in the drastic way we have described. More fully ascertained, the facts are something as follows:—

The Grants, from the time that prosperity began to flow upon them, were generously, even profusely, hospitable. Even at the date of this Dundee transaction they had a wide business connection, embracing a considerable and constantly augmenting foreign element; and it was a well-known custom of theirs to invite business friends, especially those from foreign parts, to spend the Sunday with them at Ramsbottom. They themselves, and invariably their guests with them, attended the service at Dundee Chapel on Sunday morning. In the after part of the day the servants were allowed to attend, while " the company " enjoyed at home what might sometimes prove a tolerably prolonged sederunt at dessert. The ecclesiastical half-time system—which, by the way, the eighty intervening years have by no means cast into desuetude—was evidently disapproved of by Mr Ramsay, who, if he ever tried, did not, it seems, confine himself to private remonstrance. Instead of that he launched out in pulpit philippics against those guilty of feasting and fuddling or " fuddling and drinking " instead of attending the house of God. In the circumstances, of course, every hearer would know where the oratoric bomb was meant to light and lacerate. And, however well-intentioned the preacher might be, his method of reproof was certainly unwise, proved grievously offensive, and unhappily was sternly resented. The preacher in the present case need *not* have been less faithful. He might have been more judicious.

There is, however, another side to this story, that has never reached the lip of popular rumour, but which, notwithstanding, we feel bound to state. In 1879, a lady who had reached the venerable age of threescore and ten, and who had journeyed from a distant town on the coast of Lancashire, called upon us. Her father was Mr John Rothwell, and her mother a daughter of Mr and Mrs Abraham Hamer. Mr and Mrs Rothwell for some years occupied the manse at Dundee, where their daughter was born in 1809, and where Mr Ramsay lived with the Rothwell family when in 1811 his ejectment took place. Interesting and intelligent, she said she was descended from " Parson Rothwell "[1] who founded Dundee Chapel. She had visited us, moved as she said by a

---

[1] Her father, John Rothwell, became an elder in Dundee Church in 1828 (see Minutes, p. 263, *infra*), removed to Northwich in 1838, and died about 1848. He was, she said, a son of Mr Thomas Rothwell of Holcombe, who died in 1781 (see p. 235). This was the gentleman already referred to above in 1755 as "Thomas Rothwell the younger of Holcome, aforesaid tanner," whose father was the last surviving trustee of those appointed by

strong desire to make known to the present minister of the congregation the real cause of Mr Ramsay's expulsion from Dundee, which had never been popularly known. It was this. A fair member of the Grant family, afterwards well known, had, it appears, looked with tender eyes on the preacher; but, unlike the gay actors in the historic scene in Belgium's capital a few years later, of whom Byron wrote that

"Eyes looked love to eyes that spake again,"

Mr Ramsay's did not speak again, or at least not in the orthodox lover-like fashion. This non-requital of the fair damsel's affections becoming known at Grant Lodge, stung the family pride—always a highly sensitive element throughout their history—and prompted the expulsion.

This may, in the circumstances, be fairly regarded as the view Mr Ramsay himself took, and expressed to his inner circle of friends, of the occurrence; but its acceptance, as even in the main not inaccurate, cannot be held to supersede the other and popular view. It is just possible there was a mingling of both. For if this tender element happened, in the first instance, to give abnormal tension to the relations between the Grants and the minister, any hard-mouthed and ill-advised pulpit utterances on his part would all the more readily quicken resentment, and precipitate a catastrophe.

After his extrusion from Dundee, Mr Ramsay removed to Holcombe Brook, a hamlet lying about a mile south of the old chapel, and from that centre ministered at a number

---

Parson Rothwell in 1713, and he *may* have been the parson's grandson. Thus the line of descent would be established, and the lady—Mrs Gandy of Lytham—would be the great-great-granddaughter of the Rev. Edward Rothwell who succeeded Pendlebury about 1699 and built Dundee in 1712.

of neighbouring places—Summerseat, Boardmans, Affetside, Four Lane Ends, &c., for about two years and a half. During that time he received for his work from the Lancashire Congregational Union, which he had loyally served, the sum of ten pounds. In the Union report of 1814 there is an elaborate account of his labours. We cordially agree with the words of our brother, Mr Nightingale of Preston, when he says, in his 'Old Dissenting Chapels,' that "unless Mr Ramsay's people contributed very liberally he was not burdened with much filthy lucre." He certainly cannot have been very greatly exposed to the infirmity and offence of Jeshurun, who, we are told, "waxed fat and kicked." At this time, like Goldsmith's godly vicar, we doubt not he would have reckoned himself

"Passing rich on forty pounds a year."

He had, however, a unanimous invitation to labour at Tintwistle, in Cheshire; and Bethel Chapel, Bury, would have received his ministrations. He preferred Deardengate Independent Chapel, Haslingden, about four miles north of Ramsbottom. There he prosecuted his ministry for thirty-two years, and, after eight years of well-earned retirement, died on Sunday, July 2, 1854, nearly forty-five years after his ejectment, at the patriarchal age of fourscore and two.

Mr Ramsay's individuality was well marked, and is still remembered. Many stories respecting him are to be found floating about in the locality. They relate, for the most part, to a *brusque* and breezy kind of banter, which appears from time to time to have cropped up during service in the chapel.

Mr Keith Johnston, in his great Gazetteer, tells us that Haslingden " stands in a wild alpine region, abounding in stone and coal;" and we know that its inhabitants—estimable and enterprising—claim for it the distinction of being the highest market town in England. The effect of the exhilarating air of alpine slopes is wont to make delighted pilgrims almost dance. At Deardengate, however, it, or something else, seems to have made Mr Ramsay's people doze. Against this dozing during divine service he appears to have waged a willing, well-intentioned warfare. Take the following as characteristic specimens of his method of attack —"Heigh! heigh!! See, S—— is asleep again! Look at her!" The fair sleeper, startled into consciousness, promptly retorted—"Well, yo' should preych so as to keep us wekken!"

On another occasion, making, what old Weller, in a very different discourse, called "rather a sudden pull up," he shouted "Fire! fire! fire!" The alarmed people asked, "Where? where, Mr Ramsay? where?" With statuesque, Dantean grimness, he replied, "In hell, for sleepy sinners!"[1] Much has happened in this district, as elsewhere, since those days, and such *outré* proceedings do not now occur. It does not appear, however, that because of them the people loved their aged pastor less, and perhaps they caused him to be remembered all the more.

We may now leave this subject, with the reference made to it by Dr Brown in his sketch. It is in these words:

---

[1] It was not at Haslingden, however, but in a church elsewhere of another denomination, where the atmosphere had been rather close, and the sermon, perhaps, somewhat soporific, one Sunday morning, that after service one worshipper said to another forming part of a group going homeward, "Eh, Dick, did ta yer Ned snoring i' t' sermon?" "Yer him? Did aw yer t' thunder i' Friday neet? Ned's a coshun—he fairly wekken'd us o'!"

"A disagreement having taken place between the Rev. Peter Ramsay and the principal landed proprietors in the neighbourhood, Mr Ramsay found it necessary to leave on 8th December 1811, and afterwards accepted the charge of the Independent Congregation at Deardengate, Haslingden."

The "principal landed proprietors" were, of course, the Grants. But is there any *proof* that all or any of the elder brothers actually approved of what the youngest had done? The following incident will show that it was so. James Bennet, after being many years in America, revisited Ramsbottom, and gave a lecture on his reminiscences in connection with Dundee Chapel. He, then a young man, and his wife, were present when Mr Ramsay was ejected from the chapel, and the latter intimated, outside, that he would preach in the graveyard in the afternoon. He did so, and James and his wife were present. Next day, at the works, Mr William Grant came to him and asked if he had heard Mr Ramsay in the afternoon. He said he had; whereupon Mr Grant said, "You go down and work in the croft!" Bennet, who was not quite out of his apprenticeship, was a block printer, and accustomed to work in a dry and very warm room; and to go down to the cold damp croft was as great a punishment as the master could well inflict. He went, as ordered, but he said he never forgot it. This incident shows, clearly enough, that more than Mr Charles Grant approved of the expulsion of Mr Ramsay. That event of 1811 closes the *second* period of our history. Like the first, it covers eighty years.

CHAPTER III.

1811-1891.

AT this point we begin the third period of eighty years, and this will bring us down to the time of writing. It falls conveniently into three minor periods of unequal length—viz.:

I. From 1811 to 1829; embracing the ministry of the Rev. Thomas Nelson, and that pre-eminently of the Rev. Dr George Brown, with the prominent and memorable part taken by Mr William Grant as elder and trustee; official documents, minutes, &c.

II. From 1830 to 1869; embracing the ministry of the Rev. Dr Andrew MacLean; the building of St Andrew's Church by Mr William Grant; its forcible seizure; reception and consecration by the Bishop of Manchester; death of Dr MacLean, correspondence, claim, &c.

III. From 1869 to 1891; embracing the ministry of the Rev. J. Kerr Craig, with the building of *New* St Andrew's; and that of the present minister, including the liquidation of church debt, the forcible seizure of Dundee property and its recovery by trustees appointed by St Andrew's (Dundee) congregation, memorial notes, Presbytery and Parliament.

Section I.—1811-1830.

Some time after the ejectment of Mr Ramsay, the Rev. Thomas Nelson, a licentiate of the Presbytery of Edinburgh, came to Dundee Chapel. Mr Nelson was a native of the parish of Auchtergaven, in Perthshire—a parish which suggests the name of Lord Nairne, who in 1745 left his estates and the splendid baronial mansion, whose restoration after a destructive fire he had all but completed, to follow the fortunes of the young Pretender, and never saw loved Auchtergaven again. On his attainder his title was forfeited and his estates sold. These were purchased by the Duke of Atholl, who razed the stately mansion to the ground. Mr Nelson, though licensed, was not ordained. He remained, however, at Dundee Chapel for about three years. In 1890, we discovered a volume of the 'Evangelical Magazine' for the year 1814, which, strangely enough, has bound up with it a sermon bearing the following title :—

A sermon preached in the Presbyterian Chapel, Holcombe, on the 7th day of July 1814, being the day appointed for a general thanksgiving for the return of peace. *Deus nobis hæc otia fecit.*—Virgil. By Thomas Nelson, licentiate of the Presbytery of Edinburgh. Bury: Printed by B. Crompton, Fleet Street. 1814.

The text is Psalm cxvi. 12, "What shall I render unto the Lord for all His benefits toward me?" We extract the following portions from the closing section of the discourse :—

"It becomes us to show our gratitude to God for His benefits by the deep devotion of our hearts, and the active endeavours of our lives to perform the duties enjoined by the authority of His commandments. . . . If thou rejectest the counsel of God against thyself, and, because thy deeds are evil, despisest the light which He has sent into the world, revealing mercy and pardon and eternal life; then thou hast nothing to do to declare the statutes of the Lord, or to take His covenant in thy mouth. But if, on the contrary, . . . when thou framest thy lips to utter His praise thou feelest devotion actuate thy heart; if thou turnest not away thy foot from the house of prayer on the day which He has commanded thee to worship Him in the public assemblies of His people, 'but callest the Sabbath a delight, the holy of the Lord, honourable, and dost honour it; not speaking thine own words, nor finding thine own pleasure;' if with the conviction of faith, and the sentiment of hope, thou thankest Him for His unspeakable gift, that of sending His Son to redeem the world from the dominion and the punishment of sin, to bring in a perfect righteousness, and life and immortality to light; thou shalt enjoy the peace which has been proclaimed for thee on earth, and be raised to the glory that is reserved for thee in heaven.

"Come then, my brethren, and let us learn righteousness from the judgments of the Lord, which have been abroad in the earth. Let each of us, in his own place, walking in his uprightness, at once maintain the greatness of our country and show our gratitude to God for His benefits towards us. 'For righteousness exalteth a nation, but sin is a reproach to any people.'"

The peace whose thanksgiving celebration at Dundee Chapel has furnished us with this sermon was that which resulted from the overthrow of Napoleon, followed by the treaty between him and the allied European Powers, in which he renounced the empire of France and the kingdom of Italy for himself and his descendants. The treaty was signed by him at Fontainebleau, on the 11th of April 1814. That peace, however, did not last long. He chose the isle of Elba for his residence, and it was constituted a principality for him. But he landed again in France, and his martial magic soon placed him once more at the head of a splendid army, which, however, was finally shattered to pieces at Waterloo. Wellington did in the field what Nelson had done on the sea, and Europe had peace. After Waterloo, very wisely, the fallen Emperor was sent to a safer distance, where—at Longwood, in the interior of the rocky isle of St Helena, in the South Atlantic—he died on the 5th of May 1821.

Looking behind and beyond the stern impulse and environment of Napoleon's powerful and pitiless career to a truer Heart and a wiser Hand, unfolding, amidst the distractions and distresses of the nations, the purposes of wisdom and beneficence, one can hear, in this Emperor's overthrow, an echo of the words wrung from another,[1] who bit the dust nearly fifteen centuries before, "The Nazarene hath conquered."

We now touch an important epoch in the history of Dundee Congregation—the ministry of the Rev. George Brown, M.A. Mr Brown was born in Aberdeen on the 15th November 1789, studied at Marischal College, where he took his M.A. degree in 1808, took divinity under Dr Lawson of Selkirk, was licensed to preach by the Presbytery of Aberdeen on the 18th January 1815, and ordained at Ramsbottom on the 27th August 1818. He left Ramsbottom in July 1829. In January 1844, the University of Aberdeen conferred upon him the degree of LL.D. On June 16, 1844,

---

[1] The Roman Emperor Julian, commonly called the Apostate.

he was inducted to the Presbyterian Church at Brampton, which charge he resigned in February 1851. He then retired to Liverpool, where he died on 15th March 1869, and was interred in the necropolis of that city.

In Dr Brown's sketch prefixed to the Minutes of Dundee Session we find the following:—

"At a meeting of the late Associate Synod, held at Edinburgh in April 1817, application was made for a regular supply of sermon, and the following were sent by the Presbytery in succession: the Rev. Andrew Scott of Cambusnethan, Mr John Robb, the Rev. William Proudfoot, and Messrs William Nichol, William Fraser, and George Brown, M.A."

Mr Brown began his services in Dundee Chapel on the first Sabbath in June 1818, and soon after the persons attending the chapel petitioned the Presbytery to appoint one of their number to preside in the election of a minister. "The Presbytery, however, were of opinion that the congregation was not in such a condition as to warrant their going all this length at the time, but for the accommodation of the people they agreed to ordain Mr Brown in the meantime to the work of the ministry at large, and to continue his labours at Holcombe Presbyterian Chapel for an indefinite period. The ordination accordingly took place in Dundee Chapel on Thursday, the 27th day of August 1818. The Rev. George Lawson of Bolton [soon after translated to Kilmarnock, and thereafter to Selkirk] preached from 2d Cor., ii. 16. The Rev. Dr Jack of Manchester gave an account of the proceedings of the Presbytery in reference to this business, received from Mr Brown the confession of his faith, and offered up the ordination prayer, by which, and the laying on of the hands of the Presbytery, Mr Brown was solemnly set apart to the work of the ministry. The Rev. Dr Stewart of Liverpool concluded with a charge to the minister founded on 1st Timothy, iv. 16, and a short address to the people."

Three months afterwards, on the 22d November 1818, the following were declared to be the members in full communion, as given in a list of the original members :—

> HENRY DUNCAN.
> ISABELLA DUNCAN.
> ABRAHAM HAMER.[3]
> MARY HAMER.[4]
> SARAH HAMER (afterwards WILKINSON).
> JOHN LAWSON.
> MRS GRACE GRANT.[5]
> MRS HELEN CUNLIFFE.
> WM. GRANT,[1] ESQ.
> THOS. VICARS.[2]
> MARGARET VICARS.
> MARY CHADWICK.
> JOHN HAMER.
> MARY HAMER.
> NANCY CORNWALL.
> JOHN CARNSON.
> MRS HANNAH WHITTAKER.

On the 20th December 1818, Mr Brown presided in the election of elders, when Messrs Abraham Hamer and William Grant [the future Cheeryble] were unanimously elected. After 'regularly serving their edict,' or making public proclamation to allow any to state objections against them, and none being urged, he ordained them in the presence of the congregation to the office of the eldership on 17th January 1819.

On the 2d February 1819, the Associate Presbytery of Edinburgh was again petitioned to appoint a day for the

---

[1] The elder Cheeryble.
[2] Thomas, who was a mason, chiselled *the stone eagles* still to be seen on a wooded bank immediately to the north of the stables, &c., at Nuttall Hall.
[3] Abraham's name appears as tenant of the Dundee House in 1782.
[4] See funeral sermon by Dr. Brown, p. 258, *infra*.
[5] Mother of the Cheerybles. See p. 75, *supra*.

election of a minister, and the petition was granted, and the Rev. Dr Jack[1] appointed to preside on Thursday, the 25th February 1819.

"On Sabbath, 14th February, the Lord's Supper was administered for the first time. Thomas Ker and John Barr, ruling elders from Manchester, were present, and assisted. The Rev. George Brown presided, and twelve members besides the elders communicated." On 25th February 1819, the Rev. Dr Jack, agreeably to the Presbytery's appointment, preached and presided in the election of a minister, when the Rev. George Brown, M.A., was unanimously chosen; and the call was signed by 12 members and 21 adherents. As this call and paper of adherence connected with Dr Brown's settlement at Dundee have some local interest attaching to them, they are here given. They are the forms that were, at the time, used by the Secession Churches.

Copy of the Call to Rev. G. Brown.

We, the elders and members of the Associate Congregation of Holcombe, being destitute of a fixed pastor, and being assured by good information, and our own, of the ministerial abilities, piety, literature, and prudence, as also of the suitableness to our capacities of the gifts of you the Rev. George Brown, have agreed to invite, call and intreat: likewise, we, by these presents, do heartily invite, call and intreat you the said Rev. George Brown to undertake the office of a pastor among us, and the charge of our souls. And further, upon your accepting of this our call, we promise you all dutiful respect, maintenance, encouragement, and obedience in the Lord. In testimony whereof these presents written on stamped paper by Thomas Richardson, clerk, are subscribed by us at Dundee Chapel this twenty-fifth day of February, one thousand eight

---

[1] Dr M'Kerrow's predecessor in Manchester. On 7th September 1827, Mr Brown officiated as Presbytery Clerk *pro tem.* at the ordination of Dr M'Kerrow. (M'Kerrow's Life, p. 23.)

hundred and nineteen years, before these witnesses, John Killer, warehouseman, and Thomas Greig, colourmaker. And we intreat the very Rev. the Associate Presbytery of Edinburgh to sustain this our call to the said Rev. George Brown, and to take the ordinary steps towards his settlement among us as our pastor.

> (Signed) William Grant, Elder ; Abraham Hamer, Elder ; John Lawson, John Hamer, Alexander Smith, Sarah Hamer, Mary Chadwick, Mary Hamer, Jane Smith, Mary Hamer, Thomas Richardson, Helen Cunliffe.

That the above names to the number of twelve were subscribed by the persons themselves or by me at their desire is attested by

> John Killer, witness.
> Thomas Greig, witness. } (Signed) ROBERT JACK, Moderator.

Thomas Richardson, whose name occurs twice in the above "call," was long the highly valued bookkeeper and confidential clerk of the Grants, and may have been the prototype of the immortal "Tim Linkinwater" in 'Nicholas Nickleby.' Mrs Wilson, who knew him well, often referred in her latter years to the estimable character of "Thomas Richardson." With Tim for Thomas, Dickens also gives in the name "Tim Linkinwater," numerically, the precise syllabic equivalent of the prototype's name.

COPY OF PAPER OF ADHERENCE TO THE ABOVE CALL.

We, the seatholders in this chapel, do hereby signify our hearty concurrence in the call given to the Rev. George Brown and our willingness to receive him as our minister. In testimony of which we have subscribed our names before these witnesses, John Killer, warehouseman, and Thomas Greig, colourmaker, at Dundee Chapel this twenty-fifth day of February, one thousand eight hundred and nineteen years.

> (Signed) James Cunliffe, Archibald Watt, William Kay, William Officer, George Fletcher, George Whittingham, John Farrar, Thomas Knowles, John Carnson, William Holt, James Thornton, Thomas Wild, Hannah Killer, Henry Warburton,

Peter M'Farlane, Rachel Woodcock, Alice Rostron, Rachel Rostron, Betsy Rostron, Joseph Morris, Henry Whittaker. That the above names to the number of twenty-one were subscribed either by the persons themselves or by me at their desire is attested by

John Killer, *witness*.
Thomas Greig, *witness*. } *(Signed)* ROBERT JACK, *Moderator*.

The Petition for Moderation in a call above referred to is as follows:—

Unto the Rev. the Moderator and other members of the Associate Presbytery of Edinburgh, to meet at Edinburgh or Leith on the 2d day of February next, the petition of the Associate Congregation of Ramsbottom (Holcombe) sheweth,—

That your petitioners, in compliance with your appointment, and under the superintendence of the Rev. George Brown, have taken the necessary measures for organising the congregation by the admission of members and the election of elders. Being desirous that the remaining forms prescribed for the admission of the Rev. George Brown to the pastoral charge of this congregation may be gone through without delay, they hereby request that you will adopt the necessary steps for this purpose by appointing a Moderation to take place as soon as possible.

Praying that the Spirit of God may assist and direct you in all your deliberations, your petitioners have directed this petition to be subscribed, on the 27th day of January 1819, in their name by

(Signed) WM. GRANT, *Chairman*.

P.S.—The stipend will consist of a house and garden, rent free; fifty pounds per year to be paid by the Messrs Grant for their and families' seats, and the income arising from the remainder of the pews, as well as from Lady Hewley's legacy—should all which not make one hundred pounds per year, the deficiency to be made up by Mr William Grant.

To the Rev. P. Comrie, care of the Rev. Dr Peddie, Edinburgh.

The formal induction of Dr Brown to the pastoral charge is thus recorded:—

On the 25th March 1819, the Rev. Dr Jack preached by appointment of the Presbytery at Dundee Chapel, and admitted the Rev. George Brown to the pastoral charge of this congregation. His name, together with that of Mr William Grant[1] as ruling elder, was subsequently enrolled in the list of members of the Associate Presbytery of Edinburgh; and upon the happy union of the Associate and General Associate Synods in 1820, and the formation of the United Associate Presbytery of London, under the inspection of the United Associate Synod of the Secession Church of Scotland, his name was annexed to the roll of the Presbytery of London. (A list of its members is added.)

The full title of the Dundee Chapel Minute Book is as follows:—

Minutes of the Session of the Presbyterian Congregation assembling at Dundee Chapel, Holcombe, in the Parish of Bury, Lancashire. Under the inspection of the Associate Synod and of the Associate Presbytery of Edinburgh; and afterwards on the Union of the two great branches of the Secession Church, under the United Associate Presbytery of London, in connection with the United Associate Synod of the Secession Church of Scotland.[2]

The elaborate title of this Minute Book may, for the sake of some readers, be the better for a brief explanation.

The Associate Synod, with which Dundee Chapel became ecclesiastically connected in 1818, was one of the two Synods of the Secession Church of Scotland which, happily joined in 1820, became the United Secession Church. To this union there is a reference in the first of the following Dundee Minutes. This—the Church of the Erskines—was

---

[1] The senior Cheeryble.
[2] We may copy two small receipts found between the leaves of the old Dundee Minute Book:—
"Received from the Session of Ramsbottom, the Synod Clerk's fee for the meeting of Synod in April 1819, amounting to the sum of 2/6.
"LEITH, 27th April 1819.   THOMAS AITCHISON, Collector."
"EDINBURGH, 25th April 1820. Received from the Session of Ramsbottom, 8/- due for year's Clerk's fees.   PAT. COMRIE."

united in 1847 with the Relief—the Church of Gillespie and the younger Boston—and formed the United Presbyterian Church. The English branch of this Church coalesced with the Presbyterian Church in England in 1876, and thus was constituted the Presbyterian Church of England, of which Dundee congregation forms a part.

It may be interesting to note at this point the successive ecclesiastical relations of Holcombe or Dundee congregation, Ramsbottom. The Rev. Henry Pendlebury, who became its first minister outside the national establishment, was inducted to the pastorate of Holcombe in 1651. After a period of more than forty years from his induction, more than thirty from his ejectment—and on the nether side of eight-and-twenty years of Episcopal oppression, during which 60,000 persons suffered in England alone for conscience and Christ's sake, of whom 5000 perished in prison [1]—Mr Pendlebury is found representing his congregation at the *Meeting of the United Brethren* in Manchester in 1694. In 1695 the name of his successor, the Rev. Edward Rothwell, appears in the list.

In subsequent years, of one of which we have a note—1715—the congregation was connected with the Lancashire Provincial Meetings.[2] After the death of Mr Rothwell, in 1731, it held on its lonesome way, strangely chequered with vicissitude—sometimes "almost extinct," "in perils oft," but evidently bravely resisting the prevalent solicitations to Arianism, which ensnared so many in all the Churches of

---

[1] In Scotland during the same period 18,000 perished in resisting the foolish attempt to thrust Prelatic Episcopacy on the Scottish people, who much preferred the Presbyterian Episcopacy of the Apostles and the New Testament. [2] See p. 169, *supra*.

last century—until the application to the Associate Presbytery of Edinburgh in 1817 linked it ecclesiastically with the Secession Church. After the Union of 1820 it was transferred from the Roll of the Presbytery of Edinburgh to that of the Presbytery of London. Its connection with the United Secession Church ceased on the resignation of Dr Brown in 1829, and under his successor Dr MacLean, it was in 1833 one of the congregations that formed the Presbytery of Lancashire, and in 1836, the Synod of the Presbyterian Church in England. Since the Union in 1876, it has been a constituent part of the Presbyterian Church of England.

Lancashire, in the middle of the seventeenth century, had nine presbyteries and eighty ministers. " Holcom " belonged to the second presbytery. The Presbyterian Church of England has now two presbyteries in Lancashire—Liverpool and Manchester—with sixty-six ministers.

In the fifty-five towns and parishes embraced by the " Ordinance of Parliament" constituting the Lancashire classical presbyteries in 1646, Liverpool, like Lord John Russell on an important parliamentary occasion, is "conspicuous by its absence." Manchester in those days was the seat of the premier presbytery. Now, however, presbyterially, Liverpool in importance holds the first place, Manchester the second. Holcome or Dundee Congregation, Ramsbottom, therefore, as a constituent unit of the Presbytery of Manchester, belongs to-day, as it did nearly two centuries and a half ago, to the second *classis* or presbytery of Lancashire. In this, as in some other respects, we apprehend the Congregation of St Andrew's (Dundee) Presbyterian Church stands unique. Moreover, all the diversified ecclesiastical relations embraced between the two extremes, linked together in this coincidence, are just so many intra-family arrangements, found necessary, from time to time, by the exigencies of hard and adverse circumstances. They are clear and intelligible enough within the family circle itself, as well as to all beyond its limits who take an intelligent interest in its concerns. As to intra-congregational equipment, no local records, excepting the extracts embraced in Dr Brown's sketch, have come to us from last century, to tell us how much or how little organisation existed within the congregation itself. Indeed, up till 1818 we have no record of the election or ordination of either ministers, elders, or deacons. Whatever oversight was exercised by laymen would, no doubt, be taken by those whose character and influence naturally assigned to them the task—such men as Abraham Hamer, who at a great age died in the eldership at Dundee in 1825. His wife predeceased him in 1824, in her 76th year. Abraham and his godly wife took, all their lives, a deep interest in Dundee Chapel. Dr Brown in Mrs Hamer's funeral sermon, published in 1824, says: "It was her happiness to have been early dedicated by her parents to God, and brought up by them in the nurture and admonition of the Lord. Her heart's desire and prayer to God was that religion might prosper in her neighbourhood, and that the ordinances of the Gospel might be administered in their purity in the place where we are now assembled, and which she had been accustomed to attend from her earliest childhood. As the mother of a numerous family, she was conscientious in bringing them up in the ways of godliness; and she possessed the happy art of making religion appear engaging, and not overshadowed with gloom. Her acquaintance with the doctrines of the Gospel was accurate and extensive, and more attention seems to have been paid in her younger days to systematic views of divine truth than unhappily is done by the present generation."

Mrs Hamer's life stretched back to 1749, within eighteen years of the death of Mr Rothwell; her husband's perhaps further. The parents of this venerable pair were cotemporaries of the Rev. Edward Rothwell "of the Presbyterian persuasion,"[1] while they themselves were still devoted members of Dundee Congregation, the husband—Mr Abraham Hamer—an elder, during the ministry of Dr Brown. They and their parents therefore unite the ministry of the Rev. Edward Rothwell—1699-1731—with that of the Rev. G. Brown—1818-1829.

Poor, wronged—poor, perhaps, because wronged—isolated, placed in what was then a thinly populated and little frequented locality, Dundee had passed through the frosts of a long winter, evidently appropriating such fit nutriment as came within its reach—biding its time. And, as a stunted and frostbitten stem, still quick, deep down at the germinating centre within, needs but the genial sunshine and refreshing rains to unfold its pristine leafage and display its specific bloom, so this hardy survivor of a rudely ravished vine, that had weathered so many storms, only needed the fitting opportunity to display its radical type and bear its appropriate fruit. That fitting season came, when, having applied to the Associate Presbytery of Edinburgh, the congregation received from the Secession Church the Rev. George Brown, M.A., as its minister.

The time in the history of Dundee when, according

---

[1] Trust deed of 1722. Appendix B.

to the record of our Independent brethren, it evidently was most nearly "extinct," was in 1798, when Park Chapel was built. At that time, they tell us, the Old Chapel at Dundee "was in a ruinous condition;" that "some respectable Dissenters in the neighbourhood proposed to unite with the old congregation, and by their influence and liberality, principally, Park was erected;" and to crown all, the Minister of Dundee went across the valley and became the first minister at Park. These statements, in the 'Evangelical Magazine' of the time, might lead us to suppose that Dundee was not only almost but altogether "extinct." But was it really so? What happened? The worthy authorities at Park, no doubt for some good purpose, next proceeded to take possession of Dundee property. This evidently proved too much. The limit of endurance had been passed. The venerable form of Old Dundee, suddenly revivified, confronted them in the law courts, proved its ancient Presbyterian lineage, and preserved its time-honoured heritage. Dundee was evidently still worth a good many dead ones! Under the ministry of Dr Brown, begun nearly twenty years afterwards, it quickly unfolded into a fully organised ecclesiastical unit, and the influence of his ministry is traceable down to the present hour. Every survivor from his time in the congregation has stood by it, with distinguished loyalty, in the trials through which it has passed; and to one[1]—now gone to her rest—who gratefully remembered it, and described vividly an ordination of elders which she then witnessed for the first time, the recovery of the Dundee property from the

---

[1] Mrs Murray of Nuttall Lane, whose children to the third generation are amongst us.

Independents, in 1885, proved literally like life from the dead.

A few extracts from the Session Records during Dr Brown's incumbency will, with other matters, bring before us some subjects of interest and persons of influence in the neighbourhood of Ramsbottom at that time.

"DUNDEE CHAPEL."

April 16th, 1820.—The session met in the minister's house and was constituted. Adjourned to the chapel, gave the right hand of fellowship to Henry Duncan and John Hamer [1] immediately after they had been set apart by prayer to the office of the eldership.

Agreed to continue Mr Grant as the representative of the session in the superior courts—the moderator to transmit his name to be inserted in the roll of the Associate Synod, prior to its meeting on the 25th current.

Approved of the sentiments expressed in a letter from the moderator to a member of Synod, to be communicated, respecting the agreeable prospect of a union taking place between the two great bodies of the Scottish Secession, in which this session heartily concurs; and also of the expressions of condolence on the loss the Synod has lately sustained by the decease of several of its members, particularly its late venerable Professor of Divinity, the Rev. Dr Lawson of Selkirk (under whom Dr Brown had studied theology). Agreed to celebrate the ordinance of the Lord's Supper on the first Sabbath of next month.

August 12th, 1821.—It having been stated to be the desire of the majority of the session and congregation that the Lord's Supper should not be celebrated in the public manner in which it has hitherto be done, as it has given occasion to the scoffs of the profane, and has kept back a few who might otherwise have come forward to the ordinance; the moderator consented that on the ensuing occasion he would dismiss the congregation before administering the ordinance, at the same time giving liberty to any to remain to witness its celebration.

August 19th, 1822.—Had occasion to notice the death of Mrs Isabella Duncan since last communion, and desired that the dispensation might be

---

[1] See Note, p. 47, *supra*.

improved for quickening the zeal of survivors, and that others may be raised up to fill the places of departed members, that the heritage of God may be enlarged in our border. Delivered communion tickets, &c.

October 26th, 1823.—A number of plans were suggested and approved of for promoting a revival of religion in the congregation and a better attendance on public worship. Among other means it was proposed to institute a Sunday-school in the chapel, as the Sunday-school in Ramsbottom and Nuttall failed in one object for which they were designed—the distance from the chapel preventing the regular attendance of scholars at public worship. The elders were appointed to converse with Mr Grant, who was absent from this meeting, and to endeavour to procure his concurence and co-operation in carrying this plan into effect. Pastoral visitation of the minister, accompanied by an elder, at the houses of persons attending the chapel and others on Sabbath evenings, was another means proposed, and resolved on. On week days it had been found impracticable here in many cases, from the nature of the avocations of the people, which left them no leisure for this purpose, and therefore the Sabbath evening was recommended, when families could be regularly convened. Agreed that the visitation should commence next Sabbath evening, and that John Hamer should accompany the pastor. Spent the rest of the meeting in prayer by the members in rotation, with singing[1] in the intervals, the moderator concluding the meeting.

January 25th, 1824.—Pastoral visitation had been performed on Sabbath evenings. On three evenings the pastor, accompanied by John Hamer, visited 17 families in Nuttall, Bank Lane, Higher and Lower Shipperbottom, &c. On two other evenings 9 families in Nuttall Lane were visited in company with Abraham Hamer. The visits seemed to be well received, and it is hoped will be ultimately useful. The state of the pastor's health has obliged him to discontinue his visits for some weeks past, but he hopes soon to be in a condition to resume them. It was reported that Mr William Grant has given his sanction to the establishment of a new school in connection with the chapel, and has kindly engaged to defray the expense ; and in order to relieve the minister from

---

[1] The praise, in Dundee Chapel, was led by a flute. An agitation sprang up in Dr Brown's time for an organ. In deference to his wishes, however, that instrument was not introduced.

the burden of superintending the secular affairs of the chapel, which have been hitherto left solely to his care, he has also sanctioned the formation of a committee of which the elders are to be members *ex officiis*, to judge in all matters relating to the external affairs of the congregation and school, and authorises them to draw on him for what pecuniary assistance they should find requisite. The moderator reported that he had had some conversation with Mr and Mrs Wild,[1] of Bank Lane, in reference to their intention of becoming church members, and that his interviews with them were very satisfactory. Agreed to spend the remainder of this meeting in prayer by the members in rotation, with a particular reference to the revival of religion in this congregation and neighbourhood, and for direction as to the best means of encouraging the labours of the pastor and promoting the cause of Christ. At this part of the meeting several church members and others were present, and the devotional services were conducted by Messrs John Hamer, Nuttall; Henry Duncan, James Sagar, and Abraham Hamer; and the moderator concluded with prayer and pronouncing the blessing.

DUNDEE.

April 20th, 1827.—A member proposed that a collection for pious purposes should be made at every communion, which was unanimously agreed to, and John Wolstenholme engaged to consult Mr Grant on the subject.

October 28th.—Met for the celebration of the Lord's Supper. Collected £2. 2s. 7d. for pious and charitable purposes, including a donation from Mr Daniel Grant[2] after the dismission.

January 15th, 1828.—Proceeded to the election of three elders, when John Rothwell,[3] John Hamer, sen., and Ralph Manuel were unanimously chosen. The devotional exercises of this meeting were conducted by Mr Greig, John Hamer, sen., and the moderator.

February 3d, 1828.—The elders-elect were ordained in due form. A charge was afterwards given to the elders, and exhortation addressed to the members and congregation at large, and, after the dismission of the

---

[1] Their son, Mr William Wild, was long an elder in St Andrew's (Dundee) congregation, and for many years its treasurer. He died in 1879. Mrs William Wild was one of the nieces of Dr MacLean.

[2] The younger Cheeryble.

[3] With whom Mr Ramsay lived, in 1811, in Dundee Manse.

congregation, the session was constituted—present, with the moderator, Mr Grant and the elders ordained.

March 16th, 1828.—Read draught of a petition to be presented at next meeting of Synod, praying to be disjoined from the Presbytery of London, and, along with the other congregations in this county and the congregation in Kendal, to be formed into a distinct presbytery.

April 15th, 1828.—The minister, elders, and members met for prayer and conversation. The meeting was opened by John Rothwell, after which part of Ezekiel xviii. was read and commented on. Mr Manuel next engaged in prayer. The meeting then chose, on the recommendation of the session, Messrs Greig, Wolstenholme, and Harwood, to form, along with the elders, a committee of management of secular affairs belonging to the chapel and Sabbath-school. A member laid before the meeting the draft of a letter to Messrs Wm. Grant & Brothers, requesting them to allow a public annual collection for the school, and the payment of seat-rents, which might be applied to the erection of a gallery, enlarging the minister's house, or any other purpose that might be thought expedient. It was unanimously approved of, and Messrs Rothwell, Hamer, sen., and Wolstenholme were appointed as a deputation to wait on Messrs Grant, to present the letter and receive a reply.

May 27th, 1828.—Met with the members of the church for consideration and prayer. The devotional exercises of the meeting were conducted by Michael Harwood and R. Manuel, and concluded by the pastor. Hebrews, 12th chapter, formed the subject of conversation, and Isaiah xlii. 16 was proposed for consideration at next meeting.

Sebastian Duncan is no longer a member of the church, having removed to the United States of America, with the cordial recommendation of this session for his exemplary, zealous, and pious deportment, and for his active exertions as a Sabbath-school superintendent.

As a member of presbytery has since communicated with Messrs Grant on some of the topics adverted to at the meeting on 15th April, it was thought proper for the present to take no further steps in the business.

July 5th, 1828.—Proceeded to examine the Sabbath-school accounts, which were passed. Appointed Mr Greig treasurer. Agreed to incorporate the fund for general purposes, along with that for the school. As Mr Grant intimates his desire (communicated to the moderator in a letter from Dr Stewart, which was read) that the seats in the chapel should be let, appointed the elders to wait on Mr Grant, to consult with him about the best means for carrying his wishes into effect.

July 15.—The session met along with the church members for prayer and conference. There was laid before the meeting and read the draft of a letter in the name of the minister, elders, and members of the church, to the individuals proposing themselves as members of the church about to be organised at Mount Street, Blackburn, expressive of their goodwill and their desire to cultivate a friendly intercourse with them, as part of the same church. The letter was unanimously approved, and Mr Manuel was authorised to sign it in the name of the meeting, and to forward it by the first opportunity.

July 24th.—The session and committee met after sermon by the Rev. Andrew Tod—Mr Grant absent. It appeared that various proceedings of late had been offensive to Mr Grant, and, particularly, it was alleged that the minister had been personal in his preaching and in the hymns given out in the chapel. After a good deal of conversation and explanations, it was found that Mr Grant was labouring under mistakes, and must have been misinformed about some of our proceedings; and it was agreed that a deputation should wait upon him, and endeavour to have matters sufficiently explained, that such unpleasant understandings should no longer exist.

Springside, 28th July 1828.—A deputation, consisting of the minister, Messrs Greig, Rothwell, and Manuel, waited on Mr Grant, and happily succeeded in convincing him that he had been misinformed or mistaken in those points which had been the subject of the late unpleasant misunderstandings. Concluded with prayer.

November 1st, 1828.—The elders and deacons met after a meeting of the committee of the Missionary and Bible Association. Took into consideration the propriety of building a new school at the back of the chapel, by means of subscriptions and the funds that may be raised by seat-rents. Agreed as to the necessity of the measure, and appointed Mr Manuel to consult with Mr Grant on the subject.

December 9th, 1828.—Met with the members of the church for prayer and consideration. The pastor read some interesting intelligence in reference to the revival of religion in different parts of America. It was unanimously agreed that a revival was much to be desired in this place and neighbourhood, and it was judged expedient to have a meeting for special prayer for the outpouring of the influences of the Holy Spirit. Appointed for this purpose the evening of 1st January next.

January 13th, 1829.—The session met with the members of the church. Admitted to church fellowship Joseph Morris and Mary Harwood. Read part of James's 'Church Member's Guide.' After the church members were dismissed a message from Mr Grant was delivered, requiring the pastor to leave his charge for alleged personality in his preaching the preceding Sabbath forenoon. Deliberated on the subject—found that the pastor had not been guilty of any ecclesiastical offence, and recommended conciliatory measures as far as practicable.

January 25th, 1829.—Met with the members of the church at the conclusion of public worship. Introduced the new members, and delivered tickets of admission to the Lord's Table to intending communicants. Adjourned.

Afternoon.—Celebrated the ordinance of the supper in the usual form. Twenty-seven communicated. Absent—Thomas Vicar, Mrs Kay, Mary Haworth, and Mr Grant, who has withdrawn from the church, and is no longer to be considered a member.

January 26th, 1829.—The eldership and deacons met. Mr Manuel commenced with prayer. Took into consideration the case of the pastor. Agreed that the session bring the business before the next meeting of Synod, by way of reference, and engaged to attest the character of the pastor, whom they consider persecuted for his endeavours to be faithful to his charge. The moderator concluded with prayer.

The last minute, simple and pathetic, is as follows :—

June 30th, 1829.—Met with the members of the church for prayer and conference. Certificates were granted, in prospect of removal from the neighbourhood, to Mrs Elizabeth Brown, Miss Hall, Mary Haworth, and Simpson Tod.

Agreed to observe the ordinance of the Lord's Supper on 12th July next, on which day the pastor is expected to take a final leave of the congregation. Read Acts xx., on which the pastor made some remarks suitable to his present prospects with his people. The devotional exercises were conducted by Messrs Manuel, Michael Harwood, Simpson Todd, and the pastor.

In leaving these extracts, we may briefly refer to a few points:—

1. The position occupied in them by Mr William Grant is somewhat extraordinary. To understand it at all, one needs to remember that not only was he an elder, and the acting local trustee of Dundee property, but that most likely he had himself rebuilt Dundee Chapel for the congregation, twenty years before; while at the time referred to he was paying the principal part of the minister's stipend, was the employer of nearly all the people connected with the chapel, and that his displeasure in this case might mean to them dismissal from the works. Let it be noted, to the honour of the elders and deacons, that in these circumstances they resolved to stand by their minister, should he determine to resist the action which, most unhappily, Mr Grant was led to take.

2. It is interesting to find that Sabbath-schools must have engaged Dr Brown's attention immediately after he came. Nuttall was then, and for long after, a very busy and populous village; and Ramsbottom was growing up round the works of the Grants and the Ashtons. At each of these centres a school was established; and, subsequently, there is reference in these minutes to forming one at the chapel, and to the chapel and school accounts being incorporated.

3. The gallery referred to was not put in till after Dr Brown's time, and the new school at the back of the chapel was never built.

4. It gives a painful idea of the condition of a portion of the people in those days, and shows what need there was for such work as Dr Brown was doing, to find that the sacred

solemnity of the sacrament could "give occasion to the scoffs of the profane." "Nowhere," said Dr Arnold of Rugby, in speaking of bad behaviour at prayers—"nowhere is Satan's work more evidently manifest than in turning holy things to ridicule." Thorough, deep-running foundation work was evidently needed, alike in the hearts and the intellects of the people. That both had due attention, is proved by the fact that several of the youths who passed through Dr Brown's classes were enabled to devote themselves, in after years, to the Gospel ministry; while, all through the minutes, it is manifest that he was yearning after and working towards a much-needed revival of spiritual life among the people. What we may call his *prayer and consideration* meetings may have a hint for our own times.

Yet—and sadly enough one says it—this good, scholarly, and devoted man was compelled to leave his charge at a time in the history of a growing industrial community when his example and labours were most needed, and most likely to tell with beneficent effect on the future character and higher wellbeing of the people. We shall leave the minutes to tell their own simple tale to all interested and impartial readers, adding only this—that even the most fair and charitable view of all the circumstances connected with this regrettable event makes it difficult to acquit Mr Grant—genial, generous, and benevolent as his life proved him in the main to be—of harsh and unwarrantable treatment of Dr George Brown. Our early ideal of the "Brothers Cheeryble," both of whose names—William and Daniel—appear in the foregoing minutes, led us to endeavour to ascertain, as far as was practicable, how Mr Grant's unhappy attitude towards his minister had been brought about. The result of these inquiries, prosecuted in the most likely and trustworthy quarters available in recent years, is simply this—and it accords perfectly with what stands on the face of the minutes themselves—that most probably Mr Grant was the victim of idle, persistent, and unscrupulous tittle-tattle. The same element may have had something to do with what occurred eighteen years before, in Mr Ramsay's time, and may not have been altogether absent from the still more lamentable events in the following generation, some forty years afterwards, in the time of Dr MacLean.

The office-bearers of Dr Brown were loyal, and he might have resisted. But he knew that Mr William Grant was supreme in the district. Those who knew the family well say substantially this—their word was law, as if they had been kings. And so the lowlier vine stooped before the statelier palm. Dr Brown and his estimable wife—or, as a lingering lineament of the courtesy of a now vanished era led him sometimes to write it, his "consort," "the Pastor's consort"—and three boys born in Dundee manse, left a grateful and sorrowing people, for Liverpool, in July 1829. There he opened an academy, over which he successfully presided for a number of years. During these years another son and a daughter were added to the family group. Of this family, Alexander, the eldest, took his M.A. degree at Marischal College, Aberdeen. Afterwards he became a sharebroker, and died young. Robert *Grant*, the third son, studied at Glasgow University and the Edinburgh Free Church Theological Hall, and was ordained by the Presbytery of Duns as missionary of the "Scottish Society for the Conversion of Israel." He was several years in Alexandria, and afterwards in Aleppo. While on a visit of inspection to the Saleeby schools in Lebanon, he had a sunstroke, from the effects of which he suffered for several years. On his recovery he became minister of the Presbyterian Church at Guernsey for a few years, then at New John Street, Birmingham, after which he returned to his old interests in the Jews, and became secretary to the "British" Jewish Society in London. Unhappily, while on deputation work, in their service, he met with an accident, from which he died on December 13, 1879, leaving a widow and three sons and three daughters. Mr Grant Brown, whose good work was thus suddenly closed, and whose name is still affectionately remembered in the Presbyterian Church, and far beyond its pale, was an accomplished linguist. He spoke no fewer than ten languages, and, of these, Hebrew and Arabic with special fluency. The two surviving sons of Dr Brown are well-known merchants in Liverpool, and respected elders in the Presbyterian Church of England. Miss Brown resides with her eldest brother, Mr George Brown, at St Michael's Hamlet, where their revered father peacefully spent the closing years of his long life. Such is the family record; and, borrowing the words of Elizabeth Barrett Browning, it may be added—

"The vines that bear such fruit are proud to stoop with it,
The palm stands upright in a realm of sand."

But the gifted poet's words will not cause us to forget that it *is* a palm "all the same." The venerable member of the congregation to whose testimony we have already had occasion to refer, was present in Dundee House on the evening when Dr Brown, in 1819, brought his bride home. She had been sent to the manse by old Mrs Grant of Grant Lodge—the mother of the Cheerybles—with whom she was

MRS WILSON, IN HER 99TH YEAR.

living at the time. Mrs Brown had some difficulty in understanding the vernacular of the district ; she had none, however, with the speech of Eliza Macfarlane (afterwards Mrs Wilson). Mrs Brown, therefore, asked Mrs Grant to allow Eliza to transfer her duties to the manse. This the old lady kindly did, and so Mrs Wilson for some time was the maid of the manse. She had many interesting memories of that period, and that happy home, over seventy years ago. One of her duties, as she used to tell with gentle glee, was to take the pulpit Bible and psalm-book to their place in the chapel on Sunday mornings, which was duly attended to with becoming reverence week by week.

One morning, in the summer of 1819, a handloom-weaver from the weaving shop farther down the lane, long since transformed into cottages, called out to her that news had come of the birth of a princess, who might some day become the Queen of England. She did, and is to-day " Britain's Empress Queen."

Dr Thomas Chalmers with the Cheerybles at Dundee Chapel.

In the year 1823 an interesting event occurred in connection with Dundee Chapel, of which, so far as we know, there exists no record. It was made known to us by the worthy lady to whose testimony we had occasion to refer in endeavouring to explain the ejectment of Mr Ramsay. She informed us, in 1879, that Dr Thomas Chalmers, during the ministry of Dr Brown, to whom he was personally known, on one occasion preached in Dundee Chapel. Associated with the visit in her memory was the following incident. Mr Woodcock of Holcombe—the father of the late Dr Woodcock—had vowed, it seems, that he would never enter Dundee again, because of the extrusion of Mr Ramsay. He was, however, very anxious to hear the illustrious preacher, and fell upon the following device. He prevailed upon Mr John Rothwell to open a movable pane in the window near which he sat, and outside this he stood all the time of the service in a drenching rain. At one point the rain came splashing in, and the pane was closed by some one near. Mr Rothwell, however, pretending to be perspiring, wiped his brow and re-opened the pane, and so Mr Woodcock was enabled to hear to the end. Such was the story. We remembered no reference to such a visit by Dr Chalmers in Dr Hanna's Memoirs of the great leader of the Free Church of Scotland. On a fresh glance over the Memoirs, however, we found in the journal of Chalmers two distinct records of visits to the family of the Grants—the first clearly referring to his preaching at Dundee Chapel; the second supplying some interesting references to a gentleman well known in Manchester at the time and for more than thirty years afterwards. As to the first visit: in his tour through England in search of information on the state of the Poor Law Administration, Dr Chalmers reached Manchester on Saturday, September 9, 1822. He writes:—

"I reached Mr Daniel Grant's, of Manchester, about seven, and found Mr Dalglish[1] there with a letter from you. . . . I was not long at Manchester before I smelt a design against me to preach; and as I had to go to Nuttle and preach there on the morrow, the first suggestion was that I should preach in Manchester on the Tuesday. But I had so decidedly resolved against all week-day sermons in England,

---

[1] Of Messrs Dalglish & Falconer, Glasgow. He was the father of Mrs John Grant, of Nuttall Hall, Ramsbottom.

that, rather than this very obnoxious arrangement, I forfeited my prospect of a quiet domestic Sabbath in the country, and consented to take Manchester on the Sabbath evening."

Dr Chalmers accordingly on the Sunday was a guest at Nuttall Hall, the residence of Mr John Grant, preached at Dundee or " Nuttle " (see p. 19, *supra*) on Sunday morning, and returned to Manchester and preached at Mr Roby's chapel in the evening.

The occasion of the second visit of Dr Chalmers is referred to by Dr Hanna thus :—

In the midst of his Glasgow labours, a call had been made upon Dr Chalmers to preach for the Sabbath-school at Stockport. So early as the year 1805, a few zealous and liberal inhabitants of that town, at a cost of upwards of £4000, had raised an edifice capable of accommodating, with every convenience for instruction, upwards of 4000 children. Large as this building was, it was soon filled to overflow. To raise the funds necessary to liquidate a debt still remaining upon it, and to meet the current annual expenditure, the managers had established an anniversary celebration, at which many eminent clergymen officiated.

Dr Chalmers posted, at the rate of 1s. 3d. a mile, by Hawick and Carlisle, to Manchester, which he reached on Saturday, 9th October 1824.

"Wrote Mr Grant of my arrival. This was followed up by the appearance of Mr Robert Dalglish, our young St Andrean,[1] who came, it seems, from Liverpool to-day for the purpose of seeing me. I *went over with him to Mr Grant's*, where I was *most kindly received*. . . . Mr Grant is very peremptory on the subject of my spending some days, but I must be off on Monday night, or very early on Tuesday morning.

"*Sunday*.— . . . About twelve Mr and Mrs Grant came in their carriage, and the former accompanied me in a chaise to Stockport. I was to visit the school at one, and the sermon was to begin at half-past five.

---

[1] See p. 276, *infra*.

My other friends from Manchester were to come in the evening in two carriages, and one of them a chaise-and-four. . . . The number of my hearers was 3500.

"*Monday.*— . . . Found a company in David Grant's, and he kept me up till two in the morning. A kind-hearted, rattling fellow.—*N.B.* The collection [at Stockport] is now £401."

Here is the point of special interest. Who was it that Dr Chalmers here describes as "a kind-hearted, rattling fellow," who kept up the peerless practical prophet of his age "till two o'clock in the morning"? The Memoirs answer *David* Grant, and the interest becomes eclipsed. It ought to be *Daniel* Grant, the younger of the two "Brothers Cheeryble," who had also entertained the illustrious divine two years before. He was, without any question, a kind-hearted, rattling fellow. These words of Dr Chalmers describe the real Daniel more concisely than anything in 'Nicholas Nickleby.' In that book, all the world for fifty years has been in possession of a representation of this remarkable man, limned by the greatest English novelist of his time. Inimitable and imperishable, it was yet executed at second hand. The artist and his subject never met.[1] By the correction of the above mistake, in a Christian

---

[1] Referring, on 12th May, 1884, to Stocks House, Chetham, the residence of the late Mr James Crossley, F.S.A., president of the Chetham Society, the 'Manchester Guardian' says: "Here it was, in the cosy dining-room at the back of the house, that Dickens first made the acquaintance of the subsequently celebrated originals of the Cheeryble Brothers in 'Nicholas Nickleby,' in the persons of Daniel and William Grant." "By *report*—by many characteristic stories told with graphic glee to the distinguished literary group, which included Charles Dickens and Harrison Ainsworth, 1838-1839—Dickens no doubt learned much of the character and career of the Grants. His genius supplied the rest. There is no evidence that he ever met them in person, either at Stocks House, Mosley Street, Springside, or anywhere else. Indeed, his own declaration

name, we come into possession of a miniature of the same interesting character, by the greatest pulpit orator and ecclesiastical leader of his age. Moreover, this was done direct from the living subject.

It was on the occasion of the visit to Stockport referred to above that Dr Chalmers, to his consternation, found an orchestra of over 100 members—professional singers, male and female; instrumentalists with "brass drums, trumpets, bassoon, organ, serpents, violins without number, violoncelloes, bass viols, flutes, and hautboys"—was to share with him the sacred service of the day, his "prayers and sermon to be mixed up with their music." The Doctor objected to this mingling of prayer and preaching with orchestral performance, and having observed that one person advertised to take a prominent vocal part was named "Cheese," he reinforced his argument by humorously "telling them that in his country the cheese was never served till the solid part of the entertainment was over!" He reversed the order, however, on this occasion. He stayed in the vestry till the "tremendous fury" of the platform had subsided, and then electrified the great congregation from the pulpit. But he quietly adds that before he left his "private room they fell to again!"

Thinking of the caligraphy of Dr Chalmers, the writer remembered that, some twenty years ago, he received from a venerable relative, who was a great admirer of Dr Chalmers, an autograph letter of his. With a view to assure himself as to how easily Dr Hanna might read "David" for "Daniel," he

---

ought to be conclusive—'The Cheeryble Brothers, with whom I never interchanged any communication in my life.'" (Preface to 'Nicholas Nickleby,' dated "Devonshire Terrace, May 1848.")

searched for and found the sheet, and was confirmed in his conclusion. But, to his surprise, he found that the letter was addressed to " Patrick Falconer, Esq., Dalglish & Falconer, Glasgow." Written two years before the first, and four years before the second, visit to Manchester above referred to, it was indited to the partner of, and contained a message of remembrance to, Mr Robert Dalglish, who was the father of Mrs John Grant, of Nuttall Hall, and the "young St Andrean"—Mr Robert Dalglish, jun., at that time sixteen years of age—who was afterwards (1858-1874) Member of Parliament for Glasgow, and died at the Cottage, Lennoxtown, in June 1880.

The letter refers to procuring a preacher for the following Sunday afternoon, while Dr Chalmers was to be in Fife. "A hasty visit," says Dr Hanna, "was paid to Kirkcaldy *in the end of July* [1820]. In passing through Edinburgh on his return to Glasgow, Dr Chalmers spent a night at Merchiston Castle, where Dr George Bell was residing. 'He assures me,' says Dr Chalmers, 'that had I declared myself a candidate, I would have obtained the Moral Philosophy Chair,'" &c. Dr Chalmers was at this time full of what he called his "parochial operations." We give here the concluding portion of his letter to Mr Falconer:—

It is very gratifying to observe the demand for our schooling in the Parish. Should it become much more intense, a second fabric will be called for.

I am always glad to hear from you, and will be thankful for a letter. There is a depth of experimental feeling in all you write and say about Christianity which to me is very exciting. I have generally expended all the little strength I have on my professional studies ere I proceed to letter writing, so that I cannot promise you a return in kind for your communications. Give my best compliments to Mrs Falconer. Remember me also to Mr Dalglish. And we have need of one another's prayers. Do give me a place in yours.—Believe me, my dear sir, yours very truly,

THOMAS CHALMERS.

The letter is dated "Trackboat, July 17, 1820." Before the time of railways, he was evidently going by the Canal to Edinburgh, to cross the Forth for Kirkcaldy.

SECTION II.—1830-1869.

Dr George Brown left Dundee in July 1829, and was succeeded by the *Rev. Andrew MacLean, M.A.*, a licentiate of the Church of Scotland. Dr MacLean, born in 1799, was a native of Glasgow, studied in the University of that city, took his M.A. degree in 1818, and, after his theological curriculum, was licensed by the Presbytery of Glasgow. He was known to the Dalglish family, and, in this way, came into contact with the Grants, and subsequently received a call to Dundee Chapel. He was ordained in Glasgow, and entered upon his pastorate at Dundee, Ramsbottom, in the beginning of 1830.

No session records during the incumbency of Dr Mac-Lean, before troubles arose in 1869, have been discovered. The communion rolls, however, during his entire ministry have been found, and are in our possession. From the latter we learn that the number of communicants "at the time of the acceptance of the charge by the Rev. Andrew MacLean, A.M., January 1830," was twenty-nine, including office-bearers. These were: *Elders*—William Grant, John Rothwell, Ralph Manuel. *Deacons*—John Wolstenholme, Thomas Greig, Michael Harwood.

The call was signed altogether by 143 members and adherents. Under the ministry of Dr MacLean the congregation gradually increased, and Mr William Grant, in the summer of 1832, took practical steps to carry out a long-cherished purpose of his to erect a new Presbyterian church for the Dundee congregation. That purpose was of a very sacred character. One of the most marked characteristics of Mr William Grant and his brothers, as has already been observed, was the honour in which they held their father and mother while they lived, and the impressive and perennial reverence with which they cherished their memory after their decease.

Now these parents had a deep and sacred wish, made known to William during their lifetime, and left with him as a sacred commission at their death. It was this—that "he should build a Sunday-school, and erect a church to worship God in, according to the ritual of the Church of Scotland, as a tribute of gratitude to Him for His great kindness to the family." That is, that he should erect a Presbyterian church and Sunday-school. We have inserted (pp. 94-96, *supra*) the letter written by Mr William Grant himself more than half-a-century ago, from which the above words are taken. It will, happily, make this and some other matters *once and for ever plain*. We may add that "the ritual of the Church of Scotland," from which Dr MacLean had just come, was, and is, just the ritual of the Presbyterian Church of England, and the ritual of the new church—St Andrew's—was precisely the ritual of old Dundee Chapel.

In 1832 Mr Grant evidently felt himself in a position to give effect to this sacred wish of his parents. Accordingly, the foundation stone of the new church was laid by himself in that year, on the 14th of June. In 1884 we discovered a hymn-paper of great interest. It is the hymn that was sung by Dundee congregation at the laying of the foundation stone *of their new church* in 1832. It is framed in a piece of solid timber, scooped out to a depth sufficient to admit of the insertion of the printed sheet and a sheet of glass. The glass is secured by small tacks at the corners and a little putty. *This* hymn-paper, in its unique frame, was received from a venerable member as something so trifling that, while other things had been readily produced as of more apparent value, this was not deemed worthy of even a passing notice. Persistency prevailed, and was unexpectedly rewarded. The hymn, printed by "Crompton, printer, Bury," is, with its significant heading, surrounded by an ornate border. The heading is as follows:—

HYMN
to be sung by the
CONGREGATION ASSEMBLING AT DUNDEE CHAPEL,
on the
LAYING OF THE FOUNDATION STONE
of their
NEW CHURCH,
On THURSDAY the 14th of JUNE 1832.

On this great occasion the people assembled at Dundee Chapel. The Freemasons of the district, in their well-known insignia, with a numerous company of gentlemen friends, joined the Grants at Nuttall Hall. Thence, headed by a band of music, they also proceeded to Dundee. There, all having been formed into processional order, with the Grants and the minister at their head, they marched down to the site "of their new church," where the hymn was sung. The 'Manchester Guardian,' of June 16, 1832, thus records the event:—

"On Thursday last the foundation stone of a new chapel, in connection with the Established Church of Scotland, was laid between Nuttall and Ramsbottom, by William Grant, Esq., assisted by his brothers. A numerous procession, consisting of gentlemen from the neighbourhood and from a distance, together with a lengthened array of the "brethren of the mystic tie," and attended by an excellent band of music, set out from Nuttall Hall, the residence of John Grant, Esq., and on reaching the ground the ceremony was performed in their presence and that of a large assemblage of people from the surrounding district. The Rev. Andrew MacLean, minister of the congregation, conducted the religious services, and delivered an appropriate address, which was followed by one of warm and right feeling by the benevolent founder. Along with other mementoes, a plate was deposited in the stone, describing the intended erection as a tribute of gratitude to Almighty God, on the part of Mr Grant, for the many blessings He had been pleased to send him, and as a token of the interest he feels in the welfare of the people in this part of the country. After the ceremony, about one hundred and fifty gentlemen sat down to dinner in the Grant Arms Inn, and above four hundred children connected with the schools of the place were regaled with a plentiful entertainment. The chapel is to consist of a handsome and commodious structure of stone, with a tower, executed in Gothic style, after designs by Mr Welsh of Birmingham. Though the whole of the expenses (which will not be small) are to be defrayed by Mr Grant, yet we need hardly say that this is only *one* of the many instances of that gentleman's princely and well directed munificence.

The church is picturesquely situated, just opposite Nuttall Hall, at the top of a high wooded bank of the Irwell, in a field abutting on Bolton Street on the west and Nuttall Lane on the south. Northwards it looks across the town, and away up the valley to Cribden and the Rossendale hills; while near the base of the plateau on which it stands are Barwood House, long the residence of Dr MacLean, and, not far from it, the immortal Square. Eastwards, across the river, on the crest of the hill, on the Park estate, above Nuttall

Hall, is seen the Memorial Tower of the Grants. The church is planted near the lane which runs between Dundee Chapel and the old village of Nuttall, and with its square tower and graceful pinnacles is a conspicuous and interesting object in the landscape. It cost upwards of £5000. The clock in the church tower was made by Mr John Buchanan, the engineer at the Square—a man of mechanical genius. He was engaged for several years on the task, and as every wheel had first to have its pattern fashioned in wood before it was cast in brass, and manifold experimentings and readjustings were necessarily incident to such an undertaking in an isolated case, it may be said that the clock, while it is a remarkable specimen of its kind, must have cost, all things considered, perhaps as much as, or more than, the clock of any other church tower in the county. The ingenious engineer and clockmaker died on the 5th December 1865, and was interred at St Andrew's Church.[1]

The church was opened on the 15th June 1834. The 'Manchester Guardian,' of June 21, 1834, thus chronicles the opening:—

NEW CHURCH.—"On Sunday last the new church at Ramsbottom, near Bury, was opened for divine service, when the Rev. Andrew MacLean delivered two sermons to a very numerous and respectable congregation. The church was built at the sole expense of William Grant, Esq., and is in connection with the Established Church of Scotland."

---

[1] A glance round this graveyard supplies many well-known names—MacLean, Greigs, Sutor, Buchanans, Whittenbury, Steads, Bentley, Hamers, Grays, Wright, Murrays, Rothwells, MacLachlan, Wilds, M'Raes, Kays, Strangs, Nightingales, Smiths, and many others.

After the event a lithograph picture of the church was published, bearing the following inscription :—

ST ANDREW'S CHURCH, RAMSBOTTOM,
IN CONNECTION WITH THE ESTABLISHED CHURCH OF SCOTLAND.
Erected in the Year of our Lord 1832, by WILLIAM GRANT, Esq. of Springside, one of Her Majesty's Justices of the Peace for the County Palatine of Lancaster,
Son of William Grant of Elchies, Morayshire, Scotland,
As a memorial of his gratitude to God for many mercies, and as a testimony of his anxious desire for the promotion of the best interests of a rapidly increasing population.
ANDREW MACLEAN, M.A., Minister.
Hansom & Welsh, Architects.
H. Harris's Lithography, New Street, Birmingham.

Thus William Grant honoured the wishes of his departed father and mother. It would, however, be a mistake to forget that both John and Daniel were heart and soul with him in the good work. William was the eldest of the three surviving brothers at Ramsbottom, and a deference akin to that paid to the mother by her sons while she lived was, after her death, accorded to him by his brothers while he lived. It may also be stated here, once for all, as a matter lying entirely outside the realm of question or doubt, that these men and their parents were all their days ardently and loyally attached to the principles and worship of the Church of their fathers—the Presbyterian Church—as distinguished from Episcopacy on the one hand and Independency on the other.

We shall now furnish a few extracts from the Presbytery and Synod minutes, to show the active interest Mr William Grant took, not merely in the congregation at Ramsbottom, but in the proceedings of the Presbytery of Lancashire and

the Synod of the English Presbyterian Church. He and
his minister occupied no inconspicuous place during, what
we may call, the formative period of reviving organic life in
the Presbyterianism of England.

On the 19th of April 1833, an important and historic
meeting of Lancashire presbyters was held in the church in
St Peter's Square, Manchester. "According to previous
arrangement," ministers and elders from various congregations
met for the purpose of forming a Presbytery. "There were
present the following ministers and elders as commissioners
from the several congregations." Here amongst others
stand—as commissioners from St Andrew's Church, Ramsbottom—the names of the Rev. Andrew MacLean, minister, and
Mr William Grant, elder. Dr MacLean was appointed
moderator. The first and principal motion was the resolution
to form a presbytery. Its terms were these: "That a
presbytery be formed under the name of the Lancashire
Scottish Church Presbytery, and that it comprise the
following ministers, with their elders and congregations."
This was moved by the Rev. Dr Hugh Ralph, of Liverpool,
seconded by Mr William Grant, the representative elder
from Ramsbottom, and unanimously agreed to. Among the
names constituting the presbytery thus formed were, of
course, those of the minister and elder of St Andrew's,
Ramsbottom. Thus constitutionally formed, the presbytery
next passed a series of articles of agreement. The eighth of
these runs thus: "That the several congregations shall be
considered as connected with this presbytery until their
respective sessions shall, in consequence of an act of their
own, give in a written instrument stating their resolution of
withdrawing from connection with the presbytery." The

congregation of St Andrew's (Dundee) Church, Ramsbottom, has continued a constituent and integral portion of the presbytery thus formed, duly represented by its successive ministers and elders, down to the present hour.

On the 2d of July 1834, this presbytery, of which Mr Grant and his minister were members, passed the following resolution relative to St Andrew's Church, which Mr Grant had just built for Dundee congregation : " A statement having been laid before the presbytery that a new church had been recently opened at Ramsbottom, in connection with the Church of Scotland, for the purposes of public worship in accordance with her discipline and doctrines ; and that William Grant, Esq. of Springside, magistrate for the county of Lancaster, had, out of his Christian liberality, and using for the glory of the Great Giver the abundance with which Almighty God has blessed him, founded, built, and adorned that sacred edifice, the presbytery did pass a unanimous vote of thanks, and further directed their clerk to transmit to the said William Grant, Esq., an extract of their minute, bearing their recorded thanks for this his work of beneficence and piety, accompanied with their earnest prayers to the Author of all mercies that he may long be spared to live in health and happiness, and that after death an abundant entrance may be administered to him into the kingdom of Heaven." This was of course formally put into Mr Grant's hands, and subsequently we find him in his wonted place as a member of presbytery. A similar minute, a few years later, records the thanks of the same Presbytery to the late Mr Robert Barbour for Ancoats Church, Manchester.

In 1836 another historic step was taken. The Presbytery

of Lancashire and that of the north-west of England were constituted a synod. St Andrew's, Ramsbottom, stands among the rest as an integral synodic unit.

In 1841 the Synod—augmented by that time by the incorporation of the Presbyteries of London, Newcastle-on-Tyne, and Berwick-on-Tweed—appointed " Dr MacLean " and three other ministers, and "Mr William Grant," with two other elders, to represent the English Synod at the meeting of "the General Assembly of the Church of Scotland."

On the 18th October 1836, in St Andrew's Church, the communicants numbered 122, and the elders were William Grant, John Rothwell, and John Wolstenholme. On the 27th February 1840, the number was 120, and the elders were— William Grant and John Wolstenholme. Mr William Grant died in 1842; his brothers Daniel and John in 1855.[1] In 1856 the communicants numbered 133. The elders were Robert Kay and Robert Haworth.

A pew-rent book covering about 12 years, 1845-1857, is in our possession. On one of its pages near the end is a statement, dated "Barwood, 23d November 1852," signed by Dr MacLean, to the effect that all the seat-rents were to "be regularly paid to him as part of his stipend." Receipts for a number of years are engrossed in the book. We copy one :—

Received this day from Mr Robert Kay, elder of St Andrew's Church, the sum of £42, 10s., being the amount of seat-rents collected by him up to March 1857.—ANDREW MACLEAN.

22d June 1857.

In July 1858, Dr MacLean was elected to the moderator-

[1] See pp. 92, 96, 97, supra.

ship of the Presbytery of Lancashire. In 1863 he attained the highest honour the Church has to confer, being chosen moderator of the Presbyterian Church in England, and duly presided over the meeting of its Synod held that year in the city of Manchester.

St Andrew's Church was "beautified" in 1866, and reopened on November 30th of that year. The deacons or managers were, as in many Presbyterian congregations, elected annually. The following circular for 1867, issued by the deacons, will not be devoid of interest :—

A meeting of the seatholders will be held in this church on the evening of Wednesday the 4th December, for the purpose of electing two deacons for the ensuing year. A Statement of Accounts for the past year will be found on the other side. [Two deacons retired annually.]

St Andrew's Church, Ramsbottom, *Nov. 26, 1867.*

The statement of accounts appended embraces sums for all the usual congregational expenses; for a " duplicate key for the church; " a joiner and builder's bill " for work done, £4, 16s. ; " also for " painting and whitewashing Dundee School, £4; " and " troughing Dundee School, £1, 3s. " The statement is "audited and found correct by Wm. Markland and Wm. Stead, auditors." The annexed circular has also some value attaching to it :—

Bye-laws for the government of St Andrew's Church, Ramsbottom :

1. The temporal affairs of the church shall be under the control of four deacons, to be chosen annually by the seatholders on the feast of St Andrew.

2. That the seat-rents be paid quarterly in advance.

3. That any seatholder allowing his or her seat-rent to be more than six months in arrears, the deacons have the power to re-let the pew without any notice being given to the holder.

4. The deacons recommend the seatholders to take proper care of

their pews, and not to deface them by writing on them, or in any other way.

5. No person will be allowed to have the keys of the church without the church-keeper being in attendance.

6. Any seatholder having complaint to make about the state of the pews, or any other cause, the deacons will have pleasure in taking the complaint into consideration.

7. The door-keepers, church-keeper, and other officials connected with this church are hereby charged not to execute any order without the same having been submitted to the deacons and received their sanction.

St Andrew's Church, Ramsbottom, *May* 1867.

The charges for marriages and funerals are duly tabulated on the fly-leaf of the circular.

While these pages were passing through the press (Oct. 1893), the writer came into possession of the minutes of the deacons' court of St Andrew's Church, from January to October 1867. Among other minutes of interest is found the following: "April 22d, 1867—Mr Henry Stead in the chair. Resolved, 2d, That no person be allowed to have the keys of the church without the church-keeper being in attendance." The deacons for the year were Messrs " Leonard Wild, Henry Stead, Arthur Bentley, and James Duckworth."

In the year 1869, the Rev. Dr MacLean entered the 40th year of his ministry at Ramsbottom. Although threescore and ten, yet the testimony of the one[1] who knew best is that "he was a hale, strong man" until those troubles arose with which we must now deal. We are too near the time of the occurrences not to feel the delicacy and difficulty of the task. Moreover, the consequences, or at any rate sequent events, nearer and more remote, have such a tragic semblance about

---

[1] Mrs MacLean, who still survives, and resides at Fallowfield, Manchester.

them, as greatly to enhance the difficulty. We shall endeavour fairly and impartially to state the facts.

Mr John Grant of Nuttall Hall was the last survivor of the four brothers Grant at Ramsbottom. Mr William Grant of Carr Bank—afterwards, like his father, of Nuttall Hall—was in 1869 his only surviving son, and the only surviving *nephew* of the " Brothers Cheeryble." The united estates of all the Grants were, therefore, in his possession. He was educated at Eton, and, with episcopal surroundings there, like many another in similar circumstances, had acquired a liking for the liturgical service. The lady who became his wife was also an Episcopalian, with a decided leaning to what we may call the more ornate order of the Anglican service. This element, *ab initio*, formed an important factor in the case.

This Mr William Grant, the younger, had latterly attended St Paul's Episcopal, not, as previously, St Andrew's Presbyterian Church. Let it also be remembered that, prior to this year, Dr MacLean had experienced treatment he deeply felt, in being required, somewhat summarily, by Mr William Grant, to leave Barwood House, where he had resided for upwards of a quarter of a century. With no suitable house available, it necessitated the breaking up of his natural history museum, and much else fitted to occasion pain. Since the Rev. Dr Brown left in 1829, the Messrs Grant had let, and received the rent of, the manse and garden at Dundee Chapel, and the Minister—by the goodwill of William Grant (the elder Cheeryble), the founder of the church, and his successors, Daniel and John, had occupied Barwood House, a much ampler mansion, which his venerable friend had told him he was to occupy for his lifetime.

Nor should it be forgotten that Dr MacLean's first wife was a niece of the Grants, who had, prior to her marriage, lived with her uncle, William Grant, at Springside.

"Hale and strong" though Dr MacLean was for his years, it was not to be wondered at that occasionally he needed a substitute, especially after his removal from Barwood House in 1862. The only residence he could secure, for a time, was a small and damp house at the gable end of a mill, distant from the church nearly two miles by road. Afterwards, Dr MacLean rented a house at Barwood Mount, not far from the old home. He was residing there during this eventful year, 1869. Prior to the events we have now to narrate, Mr William Grant the younger had entertained the thought of building a new Episcopal church. To one of his most trusted friends one day, he said, pointing to an admirable site in Ramsbottom—"I could like to see a fine church planted on that hill-top."[1] The gentleman replied—"Put the money for the purpose in the bank, and it can be done." "That hill-top," however, was within St Paul's parish, and the vicar of that time proved averse to any reduction of his parochial territory.

Sometime subsequent to this Mr Grant suggested that Dr MacLean, seeing he was not so vigorous as he had been, should resign, and declared his readiness to "grant him a retiring pension of £200 per annum." An offer apparently so generous and seasonable—so Grant-like withal—would usually be accepted *simpliciter*, and the resignation tendered to the Presbytery in due form. Dr MacLean might have taken this course. In that case, he would have secured the stipend

---

[1] Precisely the site now of the new St Andrew's Presbyterian Church.

for his lifetime, and left the Presbytery to deal with whatever difficulty might afterwards arise. To his honour, however, it must be recorded that he chose a different course. He was quite willing to resign on the £200 a-year, but he stipulated a simple condition—viz., that the congregation should have the choice of his successor. In ordinary cases, such a condition would never be stated, and, if it were, it would be forthwith conceded; for it is the inalienable right of a Presbyterian congregation to choose its own minister. But this was evidently felt by Dr MacLean to be not an ordinary case. He was cognisant of what had been going on, and evidently feared that his congregation would, in the event of an unconditional resignation, have the free exercise of this constitutional right, in St Andrew's Church, imperilled. With the imminent risk of losing the income, he held by the condition. Mr William Grant, who, cost what it might, was not a man to be thwarted, would not yield what the stipulation required. The office-bearers approached him on the point in vain. Thus matters stood, when Dr MacLean received the following communication:—

To the Rev. ANDREW MACLEAN.

BOLTON STREET, RAMSBOTTOM.

I, the undersigned John Domett, as agent for and acting on behalf of William Grant, Esq., the owner of St Andrew's Church, Ramsbottom, hereby give you notice that it is the intention of the said William Grant to terminate your employment by him as pastor of the said church at the expiration of three calendar months from the service on you of this notice, and that from and after the expiration of the said period of three calendar months the stipend of £200 per annum heretofore paid you by the said William Grant, in respect of the said employment, will cease to become payable or to be paid.—Dated this 29th day of June 1869.

(*Signed*) JOHN DOMETT.

Steel and flint have grazed, and the latent element is revealed. This notice, ecclesiastically considered, is simply nonsense. But financially, the position, so far as the £200 per annum went, was in Mr Grant's hands.[1] The £4000 formally set apart by his uncle (the elder Cheeryble) for the endowment of St Andrew's Presbyterian Church, from which the £200 per annum came, was practically under his control; while he also claimed to be "the owner of St Andrew's Church!" And, clearly enough, he was prepared to press both these points, rather than allow the congregation to exercise their undoubted right in that church. Early in July, Dr MacLean and his people appeared before the Presbytery in Manchester. The Presbytery, soon after, conferred with the office-bearers and congregation in St Andrew's, and made such arrangements as would enable the people to call a colleague and successor[2] to their minister. A month later the following document was printed and published:—

RAMSBOTTOM, *14th August* 1869.

To the Congregation of St Andrew's Church, Ramsbottom.

St Andrew's Church, Ramsbottom, was built in 1832, and was intended (as the founder, by the inscription inserted in the foundation stone, declared) to be held in connection with the Established Church of Scotland. This intention has, however, not been carried into effect;

---

[1] As in the case of the church, no deed had been handed over, but, *without any doubt*, the money had been solemnly set apart for the endowment of St Andrew's Presbyterian Church.

[2] At that time the writer was asked officially to preach at St Andrew's; but circumstances led him meanwhile elsewhere. Strangely enough, however, five years later, and then after twice writing a declinature within a few months, he was constrained to visit Ramsbottom, and ultimately to leave the matter of translation in the Presbytery's hands. He became minister of the congregation in 1874, and thus inherited the tangled ecclesiastical skein which he has since tried to unravel.

St Andrew's is not in connection with the Established Church of Scotland, and the minister has pronounced for the Presbyterian Church of England.

St Andrew's has hitherto remained in the hands of my predecessors and myself, and is now (as I am advised by Sir Roundell Palmer and other eminent counsel) my absolute private property, subject to no charitable trust.

Although I have for some time past been dissatisfied with the existing state of things—considering the incessant change of preachers, and continual uncertainty as to who would conduct the services, prejudicial to the best interests of the people—still I have been disinclined to take active steps to terminate it. When, however, Dr MacLean intimated to me his ill health, and the "great expense" of finding "supplies," I was led to suppose that he would be glad to be relieved of his charge. Hence my intimation to him that I would be ready (as I still am) to grant him a retiring pension of £200 per annum.

I may cause the church to be placed in connection with the Established Church of Scotland—if agreeable to that body—in which case the services would have to be conducted strictly in accordance with her form of worship.

With regard to Dundee Chapel, which I believe to be held in trust, I shall be ready to convey such interest as I may have in it to trustees, to be approved by the Charity Commissioners, to be held upon such trusts as the Commissioners may declare to be subsisting with regard to it.

I do not desire anything except what belongs to me, but what is my own I mean to dispose of as I think proper.

I have a high regard for those who attend the present services, and have always endeavoured to evince this feeling, and I trust that the steps which I intend to take will meet with the approbation of many of them—I will hope of all; but should there be, as very possibly there may be, some dissentients, I can but ask them that they will give me credit for doing what I conscientiously believe to be right.—I remain, yours truly,

WILLIAM GRANT.

It is necessary to refer very carefully to some of the statements made in this circular. First, as to the words, "in connection with the Church of Scotland." William Grant, the founder of St Andrew's Church, took a leading part in the formation of the Lancashire Presbytery of the English Presbyterian Church, in 1833—that is, just while he was building St Andrew's Church (see p. 279). At that time, and for years afterwards, this Presbytery, and others in England, wished and hoped, and year after year by their representatives pleaded at the bar of the Assembly of the Church of Scotland, for the establishment of some connection—incorporative, or at least representative—between it and themselves. In 1835 that Assembly promised some fitting recognition. Thus encouraged, in 1836 the English Synod was formed. In 1839 the name, used loosely in common parlance before, was formally determined by the Synod—"The Synod of the Presbyterian Church in England, in connection with the Church of Scotland." Later, however, in the same year, the General Assembly in Scotland came to the conclusion that it could not grant the "connection" asked, because the English Synod existed within the territorial limits of a sister establishment. This decision was formally communicated to the English Synod of 1840, and explained at length by Dr Candlish and Alexander Murray Dunlop, Esq., advocate, the duly accredited deputies of "the Church of Scotland," whereupon the Synod did "resolve to act in perfect accordance with the same." The result of this was, what some English Presbyterians all along had wished—viz., the establishment of separate and independent jurisdiction by the English Synod; and accordingly the words "in connection with the Church of Scotland" were struck out of the title, and the designation became simply "The Presbyterian Church in England." Now, William

Grant, as already stated, was building St Andrew's Church when the Presbytery was formed in 1833, and in 1840, he was still the representative elder of St Andrew's, Ramsbottom, in the Synod of that year, which resolved as above. Moreover, that "Synod," in support of the Church of Scotland in her great contention for the constitutional liberties of her people, which issued, in 1843, in the Disruption and the Free Church, unanimously resolved to "petition the Legislature that no minister be intruded into a congregation or parish against the will of the Christian people." And, subsequently, Mr William Grant had the honour, along with his minister, of being appointed by the English Synod one of its deputies to the General Assembly of the Church of Scotland, at its meeting in the following month of the same year—1840. The man, therefore, who "pronounced for the Presbyterian Church in England" was William Grant, the venerable founder of St Andrew's Church; and his minister, all along, was with him. About this time, Mr Grant declared that he would "stand by the Church of Scotland." But that was during her "ten years' conflict" with the civil power, for the restoration of those rights of which she and her people had been long deprived, in violation of the provisions of the Revolution Settlement, as well as the Treaty of Union between the two kingdoms. And when he was appointed a representative deputy from England to her venerable Assembly, it was with the sympathetic report in his hands of the English Synod's non-intrusion petitions to the two Houses of Parliament. He died in 1842, but the facts stated will indicate on which side of the frontier line between intrusion and non-intrusion, oppression and liberty, coercion and constitutional right, he had taken his stand. There was grit and steel as well as benevolence in William Grant ; and on such an issue, having taken his stand, he was not the man to budge. Nor did his brothers after him. The last—the father of Mr William Grant, jun.—died in 1855. He was a member of the Presbyterian Church in England, and a regular communicant at St Andrew's Church (p. 285). He, too, like his predecessors—the immortal Cheerybles—" pronounced for the Presbyterian Church of England" to the end of his days.

In view of the above facts, is there any valid force—moral, ecclesiastical, or legal—in the first paragraph of this circular, as a ground for the course which Mr William Grant, the younger, pursued? We think not. But, further, if Mr Grant himself believed there was force in what he wrote, why did he not take steps to hand over St Andrew's to the Church of Scotland? He says, in this very circular, " I may cause the church to be placed in connection with the Established Church of Scotland." Well, why did he not? The Rev. J. Kerr Craig, then only recently ordained, in order to facilitate a solution of the difficulties in this direction, offered to resign his charge, and make way for a minister from the Northern Church. Here is his account of what took place. We extract it from a letter in 'The Manchester Examiner and Times,' of date May 22, 1875 :—

> It may interest your readers if I state that while Mr Grant was negotiating with me, by proxy, regarding the old "Dundee Chapel," I stated that if St Andrew's did not legally belong to the English Presbyterian Church, if Mr Grant was prepared to hand over the title deeds to the Church of Scotland, I would willingly resign my charge, with the consent of my Presbytery, and allow the congregation to have a minister from the Church of Scotland to be my successor. It is scarcely necessary to add that I never heard anything more of the offer.

That was surely a seasonable and generous offer. Why was it ignored? Assuming, as we wish to do, the element of sincerity in the circular, why was this happy solution not effected? As we shall learn on Episcopal authority presently, new Episcopalian friends were on the scene, and, apparently forgetful of the golden rule, a totally different *dénoûment* was in contemplation.

As to the second paragraph of the letter, it must be said that Sir Roundell Palmer's opinion was based on a purely *ex parte* statement. Much of what we have stated and some more was not before him.

With regard to what is stated in the third paragraph, it is sufficient to say that Mr William Grant did not attend St Andrew's Church at the time, and, therefore, had no direct personal acquaintance with "the services." His deep sense of what was "prejudicial to the best interests of the people" may thus fairly be taken *cum grano salis*.

Then Mr Grant hinted that he might "cause the church to be placed in connection with the Church of Scotland, in which case the services would have to be conducted strictly in accordance with her form of worship;" but this he never showed any intention of doing. Moreover, the services of St Andrew's Presbyterian Church *then*, and of the congregation before and *since*, have always been "conducted strictly in accordance with the form of worship" to which he refers.

As to Dundee Chapel. He may not have known it,[1]

---

[1] In the first instance, we understand, he considered Dundee property part of the Grants' estate. Indeed, in the official map, 1833, of the Ramsbottom Estate of Messrs William Grant and Brothers, *the Dundee Chapel, manse, and garden, all appear as their property*. Before writing the above circular, however, *he was informed* of the probable existence of *a trust*. Hence the reference in the circular.

but, with all deference, Mr Grant really had no more right to put its key or that of the manse in his pocket, than he had to put that of Manchester Exchange or Windsor Castle.

As to *the rest* of the circular, the facts will furnish the most impartial testimony.

On Sunday, the 26th November 1869, it was intimated from the pulpit that the Presbytery would meet with the congregation in St Andrew's Church on the following Tuesday evening, to consider the position of affairs. On the Saturday evening previous, Mr Grant's agent had procured the keys from the church officer. On Sunday, strange-looking men, who held down their heads as the worshippers retired, were in the church, and the keys remained in the agent's hands. The three months' notice sent to Dr MacLean would run out on the 29th. On Monday, the following notice was issued :—

RAMSBOTTOM, *September* 27, 1869.
To the Congregation of St Andrew's Church, Ramsbottom.

I am informed that an intimation was given to the congregation of this church on Sunday last that a meeting would be held in the church on Tuesday evening, at seven o'clock, for the purpose of considering what course should be adopted by the congregation in defending what are alleged to be their spiritual rights.

However willing I might have been under any other circumstances to have permitted the use of the church for any purpose of religious discussion, I cannot, having regard to the present state of things, allow any such meeting to be held; and I therefore give you notice that I have given direction that the church and churchyard are to be kept closed on Tuesday evening next, and any persons attempting to hold such meeting will be treated as trespassers.

Not being desirous of preventing free discussion on the part of the congregation, I shall have no objection to a meeting being held at Dundee Chapel, if such place be thought convenient.—I remain, yours truly,

WILLIAM GRANT.

On Tuesday evening a vast crowd assembled. At the time appointed the office-bearers and members of Presbytery in procession reached the gate. Between the ex-detective in charge of the mercenary force within, and Mr Sudlow, solicitor, who accompanied the Presbytery and office-bearers, the following colloquy took place :—

Mr SUDLOW—Who are you acting for ?

Ex-D.—Mr Grant.

Mr SUDLOW—Well, we demand admission to the church.

Ex-D.—My instructions are not to allow you entrance.

Mr SUDLOW—Are you instructed to use force if we do get in ?

Ex-D.—That will have to be another consideration.

Mr SUDLOW—You refuse to open this gate to the elders and congregation of the church ?

Ex-D.—I do.

Mr SUDLOW— By whose instructions ? Are they in writing ?

Ex-D.—I have instructions in writing. I have received verbal instructions from Mr Grant, and written instructions from Mr Domett. My written instructions are to take charge of the church, and to let no one in. I refuse to admit the congregation.

The Rev. J. C. Paterson, of Manchester, then turned to the assemblage in the road and the avenue to the gate, and, in a voice ringing clearly through the still air, and which could not fail to be heard by every one present in the breathless silence which prevailed, said : " Friends, they have forcibly shut out the elders and congregation from the church. A formal demand has been made for admittance, and it has been emphatically refused. There is no use making a riot :

we will go now to our old chapel where the congregation formerly worshipped, and will there consider what steps should be taken."

Writing with a knowledge of the constituent elements of that crowd, and the spirit and purpose which animated the

St Andrew's Church (now Episcopal).

more aggressive portion of it—embracing muscular and fearless delphmen from the neighbouring hills, with stern implements at hand—we feel bound to state that, but for the clear and emphatic, yet not hope-excluding, words of Mr Paterson, the church, with whatever consequences, would have been stormed and taken in a few minutes. Nor are we quite devoid of sympathy with the men who, unsolicited, left their toil, prepared without fee or reward to do, if need be, a bit of rough and dangerous work, in order that a wronged community might recover its own. Shakespeare says—

"Blunt wedges rive hard knots."

These men displayed the rough-and-ready form of the generous, wrong-redressing element, of priceless worth, in the Anglo-Saxon race. Michel Angelo saw an angel in the unshapely marble block. So in these unchiselled blocks from the millstone grit of British manhood one can detect, in miniature, the angel of Britain's sympathetic guardianship of the oppressed and wronged throughout the world. Nevertheless, as, rough and tumble, they must in the first instance have proved destroying angels that evening, the Presbytery, at this crucial juncture, deserved well of the Christian church and the civil authorities for so wisely turning aside what Milton calls the "rough edge of battle;" and all the more because to the late Rev. J. C. Paterson, with his chivalrous ardour, it would have been easier, at any time, to lead a Balaclava charge than turn away from any part of the rightful heritage of his church. The writer knew, in youthful days, what it was to be fired by the eager glow of his perfervid spirit, and now would fain not be unworthy in tender affection to lay a fragrant bloom on his not forgotten grave.

In response to his request the crowd went up to Dundee Chapel, which was soon packed with people. Among the members of the Lancashire Presbytery present were—the Rev. J. C. Paterson, who presided, Dr M'Caw and Rev. J.

M. Ross of Manchester, the Rev. Dr Robert Lundie of Liverpool, Rev. James Cleland of Risley, and the Rev. John Gordon, M.A., of Wharton. Several members of the Presbytery addressed the people. One of the Manchester officebearers—the head of a great Manchester house—read the following letter, which had been sent by him to Mr Grant with a view to an amicable adjustment of affairs. It was not acknowledged:—

DEAR SIR,—It has occurred to myself and some other friends in the English Presbyterian Church interested in St Andrew's congregation at Ramsbottom, that before the time arrives for your acting on your notice to Dr MacLean, and before any active steps are taken by Dr MacLean's friends or congregation in defence, an effort should be made to prevent hostile proceedings on either side by meeting you and discussing the matter in a friendly and Christian spirit. I have been requested, therefore, to ask whether you will kindly name the time and place when you can receive myself, Mr R. Lockhart, Mr Robert Barbour, Mr Bryce Allan of Liverpool, and the Rev. J. C. Paterson of Manchester, without the presence of any professional man on either side, and on the distinct understanding that nothing which may pass shall be made use of afterwards. I trust that this course will commend itself to your judgment as most befitting the sacred subject on which it would appear that disputes are likely to arise; and, at all events, the friends acting with me are anxious to take every step to avoid litigation in such a matter. Begging the favour of your early reply, I am, &c.

In the course of the meeting Mr W. Wild moved the following resolution, which was duly seconded and enthusiastically carried:—

This meeting deeply regrets that Mr William Grant has shut out the congregation from the church in which they have worshipped without interruption for upwards of 35 years, and hereby appoint Messrs Robert Haworth, Joseph Strong, Samuel Wilson, John Ormerod, and Samuel Hamer, elders, with Messrs William Wild, Arthur Bentley, Lawrence Stead, and William Markland, deacons, a committee to act in conjunction with the committee of the Presbytery of Lancashire to take such proceedings as they may be advised to enforce the rights of the congregation.

During these proceedings the venerable minister, sorely stricken, was confined to his bed. He never left it again. On the morning of the twenty-fourth day after these events, on the 22d of October, he passed peacefully away, from the encompassing troubles, to where "the weary are at rest." On Wednesday, the 27th of October, he was buried, according to his own direction, at Dundee Chapel. There was a large attendance of members of Presbytery and friends, and the funeral service—conducted by the Revs. J. C. Paterson, Dr M'Caw, and Dr Lundie—was of a singularly impressive character. On the south side of the old chapel, between it and Dundee or Nuttall Lane, is the chosen resting-place, surrounded by a railing, and marked by a granite obelisk, which bears the following inscription :—

ANDREW MacLEAN, D.D.,
Forty years Minister
of the
PRESBYTERIAN CONGREGATION,
RAMSBOTTOM,
Born at
GLASGOW, 1st January 1799,
Died at
BARWOOD MOUNT,
October 22d, 1869.

"I have lived in the faith of the Gospel."
"Precious in the sight of the Lord is the death of His saints."

The funeral *cortège* started shortly before one o'clock, the coffin being carried by members of the congregation and

Rev. Andrew MacLean D.D.

teachers and scholars of the Sunday School. The procession was in the following order:—

Rev. J. C. Paterson.   Rev. W. M'Caw.
    Rev. R. H. Lundie, M.A.
S. Woodcock, Esq.   W. P. Woodcock, Esq.
Mr R. Haworth, elder.   Mr J. Strong, elder.
Mr E. Wild.   COFFIN   Mr T. M'Ghie.
Mr S. Wilson, elder.   Mr S. Hamer, elder.

RELATIVES.

W. G. MacLean, Esq.   Master A. J. MacLean.
Duncan M'Rae, Esq.   W. Wild, Esq.
R. Wild, Esq.   T. Wild, Esq.
E. Elsworthy, Esq.   Andrew M'Rae, Esq.
Graham Gilmore, Esq.   J. Marshall, Esq.

MEMBERS OF PRESBYTERY.

Rev. J. Cleland.   Rev. V. M. White, LL.D.
Rev. S. T. Dickinson.   Rev. W. T. Johnstone.
Rev. W. K. Moore.   Rev. R. Mitchell, M.A.
Rev. W. J. Gill.   Rev. J. Gordon, M.A.

CLERGYMEN AND MINISTERS.

Rev. J. H. Butcher.   Rev. H. P. Hughes.
Rev. M. Wilson.   Rev. S. Attlee.
Rev. T. Cain.   Rev. R. Maden.
Rev. J. Wheeldon.   Rev. — Yeates.

FRIENDS.

J. Halliday, Esq.   T. Bell, Esq.
Robert Crooks, Esq.   C. Stewart, Esq.
R. Lockhart, Esq.   Bryce Allan, Esq.
F. C. Calvert, Esq.   James Porritt, Esq.
W. Stead, Esq.   J. Morton, Esq.
Mr John Ormerod.   Mr G. Brown.
    J. A. Porritt, Esq.

DEACONS.

L. Stead, Esq.   A. Bentley, Esq.

Members of the Congregation, about 300 in number.

Nearly 139 years before, the mortal remains of the successor of Henry Pendlebury—the Rev. Edward Rothwell, who built the first Dundee Chapel, were laid to rest a few yards away, inside the old chapel walls.

On the following Sunday, Dr MacLean's oldest clerical friend in the Presbytery—the Rev. James Cleland—preached in old Dundee Chapel. After referring to the classical and theological equipment, love of botany, natural history, and the kind and forgiving character of the deceased, he said:—

In regard to the views which your minister entertained of divine truth, and, of course, the nature of his pulpit ministrations, I have no hesitation in saying they were decidedly evangelical. The religion prevailing throughout Scotland, the doctrines taught in her divinity halls and set forth in her national and other Presbyterian churches, are well known to be of that description. On his coming to this country and beginning his ministry amongst you, he was naturally led to enquire into your history as a congregation; and on tracing it back to its origin, he became more and more acquainted with the contendings and sufferings of the Puritan Nonconformists, and more in love with their Scriptural principles and holy lives. The numerous and sound theological volumes of the learned divines who lived and flourished in this country during the period of the 17th century were the guides which, next to the Word of God, he took most delight in consulting. Drinking at the same fountain-head with these accomplished authors, and taught by the same Holy Spirit, he embraced the same truths that they did, preached the same doctrines, enforced the same duties, and adopted the same form of worship. Need I say that he was also animated by the same hopes. Between the ministry of Henry Pendlebury and that of Andrew MacLean many days and years elapsed, but the same cleanly ground which had been chosen by the father was in after days occupied by the son. They were divided in their lives, but not in their principles. Both of them were the subject of trials, and both of them suffered ejectment from their homes and pulpits. The senior began the work, the junior took it up and carried it on; and now that they are both of them resting from their labours, their souls, I doubt not, are at this moment for ever united in the enjoyment of the same rich reward in the regions of immortality. The following beautiful lines, composed by your late pastor, on the worthies of St Bartholomew's Day, and especially on the religious hero of Holcombe Hill, seem almost prophetic of his own sad fate, which we have just seen experienced:—

The sun rose bright and clear that morn on Holcombe's heathery height;
The village church and the pastor's home shone in their gladsome light:
The lovely vale, stretching far below, smiled tranquil and serene—
Alas! that the wrath of wicked men should disturb so fair a scene.

But soon from Bury's towers rode forth a gay and glittering band,
And soon before the humble porch of the pastor's home they stand;
"Come forth, thou rebel priest—come forth! or we'll drag thee from thy den;"
And from their steeds, with ruffian shout, sprang the wild and reckless men.

Forth came a meek and saint-like man, with lingering steps and slow;
There was grief in his mild blue eye, but no fear on his lofty brow.
"I'm no rebel to my earthly king, nor traitor to his cause;
But *first* I must serve the King of kings, and honour all His laws."

Oh! it was a dark and godless deed, to quench the Gospel light,
To drive the pastors from their homes, and to put the flock to flight!
And long in perils and in prisons, in tortures and in death,
They witnessed for their risen Lord, and His pure and holy faith.

The Nonconforming fathers! they were full of grace and light;
They preserved the ark of England in a dark and stormy night;
For true liberty of conscience, for Christ's kingdom and His crown,
They preferred the cross of sorrow to worldly riches and renown.

Then high honour to their memory, and glory to their name!
The noble cause begun by them we'll build up and maintain.
The truth in Christ—the liberty wherewith He makes His people free—
May it flourish in our borders, and be the crown of Old Dundee![1]

---

[1] From a piece entitled "Holcombe Hill, 1662." "To be recited at the Anniversary of the Sabbath Schools in Dundee, September 1850."

Giving you a hasty sketch of the life and character of our departed friend, and of the labour undertaken by him, I must not overlook the numerous lectures on various topics which first and last have been delivered by him. Being enlightened and benevolent far beyond the most of men, he was unwearied in labours of love, promoting in some way or other the good of his fellow-creatures, and especially in his endeavours to elevate the character and enjoyments of the working man. It has been said, I would remark in conclusion, that two things are requisite to the making of a good minister—affliction and prayer. To neither of them was your late pastor a stranger. In the adorable providence of God, it was appointed that in running his course he should pass through various trials, but the last was the heaviest of all. As he repeatedly said to myself, it killed him by inches. Still, he was resigned to the will of his heavenly Father. When our dear departed friend was hastily driven from the comfortable mansion which had been kindly given with a promise that it should be his for life, and was driven to a humble cottage in which there was little comfort, and no convenience for his large library and museum, he was able to bear it; but when he was driven from his church he was not. Yet his sorrow was not so much on his own account as on yours. . . This year is one which by the most of you will not soon be forgotten. In the year 1819 our friend took the honourable degree of Master of Arts in Glasgow University; in 1829 he became your minister; in 1859 he received the degree of Doctor of Divinity from a learned college in America; but in 1869 he has, I trust, received the highest honour of all, that of being thus addressed by his divine Master: "Well done, good and faithful servant; thou hast been faithful over a few things; I will make thee ruler over many things; enter thou into the joy of thy Lord." Our friend did not perhaps experience the ecstatic joys which some have felt in the prospect of eternity; and this we think can be in some degree accounted for. Still he was happy. "I die," said he, "in the firm belief of those truths which I have always preached to my people." The finished work of Christ, and that alone, was the sure foundation on which all his hopes were built.

Thus bereft of the pastor who had ministered to them for forty years, the people held together, experiencing, not for the first time, something of the welding influence of adversity. They met for worship in old Dundee Chapel, which since 1834 had been used by them for Sunday-school purposes, &c.; while every Sunday morning, the teachers and scholars, in procession, had marched down after school to the morning service in St Andrew's. The ex-detective and his eighty mercenaries, undisturbed from without at least, now occupied the securely barricaded St Andrew's Church for several months, night and day, "drinking beer and playing cards," and sadly desecrating the cherished shrine of the Cheerybles. It has been said that

"Hope springs eternal in the human breast."

It did not altogether fail the people at this trying time. The fell blast that had so sorely and suddenly smitten them had not yet quite sealed up this benign fountain. Throughout 1870, and into 1871, though it might seem against hope, yet they did hope that, in some way or other, "their new church" would be restored to them. During that period, however, two events occurred which conspired to shape the future course of affairs, and, ultimately, hard and fast, to seal up the genial spring. A new bishop was nominated and elected to the See of Manchester in January 1870, and a new vicar was appointed to the parish of St Paul's, Ramsbottom, in January 1871; the old one, who had proved opposed to any diminution of his parochial area, having been translated by the bishop to a more lucrative living. The new bishop proved willing to take over this Presbyterian church; the new vicar to sanction the division of his parish. These were two governing elements in all that followed. In the course of this year, St Andrew's was received by Bishop Fraser, re-beautified, licensed and opened as an Episcopal church, in charge of an Episcopal curate. This Episcopal appropriation was not immediately followed by consecration. That function was postponed for some time. The Presbyterians, not unreasonably, had considered it consecrated enough, in the best sense, by more than five-and-thirty years of the ministration of Christ's holy Gospel, and the simple but seemly and Scriptural administration of the sacraments. Moreover, they could not forget that the dust of their venerable Presbyterian friends and benefactors—William Grant, the founder of the church, and Daniel and John his brothers—was enshrined within its walls; while dear ones from their own homes, who had fallen asleep, for ever in their eyes consecrated the peaceful graveyard around. Remembering, however, the class and character of its recent occupants and guardians, under the ex-detective, we need not wonder that there were some who deemed this a fitting opportunity for administering within its precincts whatever hallowing virtue the consecrative office of the Anglican Church might command. But the Bishop, when he came, at once dispelled the generous illusion by frankly declaring that "the validity of consecration depended not upon the prayers they had used, but it depended entirely on the legal document which they had heard read by the registrar of the diocese." Yet wisdom is justified of her children. We shall allow the distinguished prelate himself to be the historian of the event. But before listening to a part of his lordship's sermon, another voice arrests us. Midway between the Episcopal opening of St Andrew's in 1871 and the consecration in 1875, another of those events occurred which are fitted to hush for the time all human strife. In

1873, Mr William Grant, of Nuttall Hall, passed away in his 48th year. He had been ailing for some time, but the announcement of his decease came upon the community with startling suddenness.[1]

Nearly two years after this event, on the 22d April 1875, Bishop Fraser consecrated the church, which, though now called Episcopal, is still "St Andrew's." He preached on John xvii. 21, 22. In the course of his sermon his lordship said :—

There had been many difficulties which had beset the consecration of that church; and though, generally speaking, the consecration of a church was a matter of unmixed satisfaction and almost of joy to him— as testifying that the Church of England was making her way, silently but surely, and doing her duty to the population in which she was cast— he honestly confessed that they were very mingled feelings with which

---

[1] On the north side, in St Andrew's Church, a monumental tablet, near to that of his father and mother, is inscribed thus : —

✝

To the
MEMORY OF
WILLIAM GRANT,
of NUTTALL HALL,
Born August 16, 1825,
Who departed in peace
May 30th, 1873.
This monument is erected by
JANE GRANT his widow,
And ISABELLA LAWSON his surviving sister,
As a memorial of their love.
His prayer ever being—

Jesu! may Thy cross defend me,
Thro' Thy death salvation send me,
  Shield me by Thy grace and love;
When death severs flesh and spirit,
May my soul thro' Thee inherit
  Thy bright paradise above.

he engaged in the ceremony of that day. They might have noticed, perhaps, if they were following the service, that there was one prayer in the consecration service which, by an oversight, had been transferred from the ordinary form into the printed form which they were using on that occasion, and in which the blessing of God was specially invoked on those who had founded that church for the honour of God. The prayer had been transferred as though Mrs Lawson had been the founder of the church, and if she had he should have had no scruple in using it; but on the wall there he saw a tablet bearing the name of William Grant, Esq., deceased, the founder, and therefore the prayer was out of place. Mrs Lawson had carried out her brother's wishes,[1] and given effect to that bequest in his will, which he believed but for her own voluntary act might have become void. She had endowed the church with an interest of £6000, but she was not the founder, nor could she be considered as such. He was perfectly aware there had been heart-burnings in connection with that church, and he could perfectly understand them, and not only so, but sympathise with them. If he understood the history of that church aright, that fabric was erected by the Messrs Grant, who themselves came from Scotland and were in communion with the Presbyterian Church in Scotland, and he was told that they imported a considerable number of people of that persuasion to Ramsbottom. The church was built for the convenience of those people, and for many years it was used as a Presbyterian place of worship; but it was not conveyed, and so they who founded it retained their legal right to deal with the building as they pleased. A change took place in their own[2] religious convictions, and having become members of the Church of England[3] they[4] seemed to feel that the National Church had a claim on them for this building, which had been erected as a church, and had not been formally and legally handed over to any one denomination. The church was afterwards closed for several[5] years, answering no purpose whatever. No doubt this transfer-

---

[1] *Not* the wishes of the uncle, "William Grant, Esq., deceased, the *founder*." [2] Not *theirs*—their *nephew's*.
[3] Their *nephew* did. *They* were never members of any church but the English Presbyterian Church.
[4] They had long been in their graves. William, the founder, died in 1842; Daniel and John in 1855. (See pp. 92, 97, *supra*.)
[5] Over *one* year.

ence was more or less a painful circumstance, and he could quite understand how it was that somewhat exasperated feelings arose in consequence; and therefore they could easily imagine that it was with no very profound satisfaction that he witnessed the disappointment of hopes, even though the Church to which he himself belonged might be considered a gainer by it. Even now they could see at once another circumstance of embarrassment and difficulty connected with that church. There had been nothing conveyed to the Church of England that day but the site on which the church stood. The graveyard outside, enclosed within rails, was not the burial-ground of the Church of England, nor had the minister of that church any right to officiate therein. The burial-ground had not been conveyed to them. The use of it would be terminated within a certain period, but it would be allowed to be used by the survivors of those who had already laid their dead there. The work of that day had been delayed in consequence of certain legal difficulties which had to be overcome. Mr Corbould, as the vicar of St Paul's, might not have liked to see a second church so close to his own church; of course he had certain rights as vicar of the parish, and had he chosen to maintain them he might have greatly hindered and embarrassed this work to-day. If one had to start off afresh, he supposed no one would say a church standing on that hill, so close to St Paul's in the valley, was necessary to the Church of England, but they had not control of the circumstances to which he had alluded, and so the church came into their possession as it now stood, and had to be dealt with accordingly. The vicar of St Paul's, he must do him the justice to say, had waived any rights he might possess, and had worked most cordially with all those who desired to hand over that fabric to the Church of England as they saw it that day. And he (the Bishop) was glad to believe that the new incumbent of that church was one who would be anxious to work with his neighbours in the spirit of Christian brotherhood and liberality.

After the consecration a vigorous correspondence sprang up, conducted in Manchester by the gentleman — well-known at the time — who wrote under the *nom-de-plume* of " Promotion by Merit," and in Bolton and Bury mainly by "Consistency," whom we never personally knew. In answer to a letter by the latter gentleman, the Bishop sent the following to the 'Bolton Evening News':—

Sir,—Somebody—probably the author—has sent me a copy of the 'Evening News' of May 11, containing a third letter from "Consistency," in which he trusts he "will not be accounted presumptuous in asking me whether, after his disclaimer, I still adhere to the position that the Presbyterians of Ramsbottom have not been despoiled of £6000 as an endowment; and further, that it never was theirs, nor intended for them."

I do most distinctly "adhere to the position," nor do I see that anything which "Consistency" has alleged in the least invalidates it.

In his second letter—I quote from memory, having no copy at hand—on the mere authority of some anonymous correspondent, without producing a shadow of evidence, he stated that it is believed to have been the intention of the first Mr William Grant to endow the church which he erected for the use of the Presbyterian body with—not £6000, but £4000. Whatever may have been Mr Grant's intention, he apparently took no steps to carry it into effect; and in the 33 years which have elapsed since his death no claim for this endowment, so far as I am aware, has been put forward by the body who were the supposed object of Mr Grant's bounty

The second Mr William Grant, who died in 1873, and who was notoriously *not* a Presbyterian, but a member of the Church of England, bequeathed by his will the sum of £6000 for the endowment of St Andrew's Church, Ramsbottom, the site of which, together with the fabric, he had intended, if he had lived, to convey to the Ecclesiastical Commissioners. But he died before the scheme could be accomplished, and the bequest consequently became void.

It is to Mrs Lawson (Mr W. Grant's sister), who, together with the inheritance of her brother's estate, wished to give effect to his intentions, that the endowment is due. It has been her free gift, which I believe it is her intention to enlarge; and I repeat that it never belonged to the Presbyterian body, nor was intended for them.

With regard to the further charge of spoliation, as respects the building, I have already expressed my own feelings on the subject; but it is right to add that the church has long been closed as a Presbyterian place of worship. That body had built for themselves a new chapel; and St Andrew's would simply have stood as an empty building if I had not accepted it, with the offered endowment, for the uses of the Church of England, But, knowing all the circumstances, I could not, and did not, accept it with unmixed feelings of satisfaction ; and if the Presbyterians had not housed themselves elsewhere, I should have much preferred their being allowed still to occupy their old home.

I do not feel called upon to prolong this controversy with opponents who fight behind a mask; and, besides, I have nothing more to add.—I remain, Sir, your obedient servant,   J. MANCHESTER.

ATHENÆUM CLUB, PALL MALL, S.W., *May* 12.

His lordship's attitude suggests a wider application of the query of another distinguished prelate—Bishop Berkeley—"Whether my countrymen are not readier at finding excuses than remedies?"

To the foregoing letter the following answer appeared on May 17, 1875:—

THE BISHOP OF MANCHESTER AND THE RAMSBOTTOM ENDOWMENT.
To the Editor of the 'Bolton Evening News.'

SIR,—Will you be good enough to give me space in your paper to refer to the Bishop of Manchester's answer, of the 12th May, to "Consistency"? Through that gentleman I forward this to you, my only claim being that I am the "anonymous correspondent" referred to by his lordship.

First, about the endowment.

The £200 per annum was paid till 1869, so that it is simply nonsense for Bishop Fraser to speak of a lapse of 33 years, during which no claim has been put forward. It has been asserted from the moment when payment of the £200 was discontinued that William Grant provided for the *permanent* endowment of the church.

This William Grant, be it remembered, lived and died not only a member but *an honoured elder* of the Presbyterian Church. He built the church for the Presbyterians, and as a thanksgiving to Almighty God for prospering him in the Vale. This stands inscribed on its foundation stone.[1]

---

[1] Inscribed on the lithograph picture, see p. 282; and, we believe, *inserted* in the stone, see p. 291 (W. Grant's circular).

Now, William Grant told his friend and pastor, Dr MacLean, that he *had* provided for the endowment of the church, and Dr MacLean carried the conviction to his grave. William Grant, moreover, died in 1842, but Dr MacLean was paid by his successors up to 1869, when William Grant, the nephew, who, as Bishop Fraser says, "was notoriously *not* a Presbyterian, but a member of the Church of England," stopped the £200. About the same time, on a Lord's Day, he took possession of the church, and kept it garrisoned by a small army of myrmidons, who likewise "were notoriously *not* Presbyterians, but ———."

But Bishop Fraser lays emphasis on the fact that the sum claimed by the Presbyterians as set aside, in one form or another, by the first William Grant for the endowment of the church, was "*not £6000, but £4000*," while the sum received by the Church of England is not £4000, but £6000.

No doubt his lordship reads the 'Times,' and has observed occasionally in its columns an acknowledgment by the Chancellor of the Exchequer of the receipt of "*money*," which is said to have some connection with that great ethical element in human nature on which Bishop Butler was a distinguished authority. Assuming the existence of this potent and sometimes perverted principle, and remembering, what every schoolboy knows, that funds, as well as fishes, are expected to grow, there need be no difficulty in understanding how the goodly fish, lost sight of by the Presbyterians years ago, should be half as large again when his lordship succeeded in landing him at Ramsbottom the other day.

But again, the Bishop says: "It is right to add that the church had long been closed as a Presbyterian place of worship. That body had built for themselves a new chapel; and St Andrew's would simply have stood as an empty building if I had not accepted it, with the offered endowment, for the uses of the Church of England."

This, then, was his lordship's reason for accepting the church, was it? Could it be? What are the facts? They are these:—

The Presbyterians were ejected in September 1869. The church was re-pewed and beautified, licensed and opened in connection with the Church of England in the course, I believe, of 1871, and it was *not till after this event*, when the hope which some had cherished of regaining their church was extinguished by the Bishop receiving it (for it was really accepted *then*, although it has been consecrated only *now*), only then, in the spring of 1872, were steps taken for building the new church which was opened in October 1873, and on which a heavy debt still rests. His lordship must have been sadly misled. He puts cause for effect, and effect for cause. He says he accepted the church because the Presbyterians had built another, whereas the fact is they had to build another because he had accepted their church.

Is it not somewhat perplexing, in view of those simple facts, to read these further words in the Bishop's letter: "If the Presbyterians had not housed themselves elsewhere, I should have much preferred their being allowed still to occupy their old home?"

How much of pain and wrong and bitterness might have been prevented had the Bishop, when first approached on the subject, Christianly counselled those concerned to honour the memory of their benevolent uncle by restoring the church to those for whom he built it and to whom he gave it!

I enclose my card, and am, yours, &c., ROSSENDALE.

To this statement of facts his lordship never replied.

Indeed, the *intention* and provision to endow are not denied, any more than the thirty-five years' actual possession of the church, by those who know best about the matter.

Here it may be convenient to state what substantially William Grant's design was. It was threefold, embracing—

(1) A Presbyterian church and endowment.
(2) Schools, and a small endowment.
(3) A residence for the minister—a manse.

As to the *first*—the church was built and occupied, as "their new church," by the Presbyterian congregation for *over thirty-five years;* and we shall only say further that there is really no doubt or denial of this point, viz., that William Grant—the founder—provided £4000 for the endowment of St Andrew's Presbyterian Church. Dr MacLean received 5 per cent on that amount up to 1869—£200 per annum, *plus* the seat rents. As to the *second*—Mr Grant also provided £400 for the benefit of Dundee Sunday-school. The following letter, written in 1875, refers to both endowments. The cottages referred to are those with a clock in front, nearly opposite the entrance to the coal depot in Stubbins Lane. They ought to be restored.

RAMSBOTTOM PRESBYTERIAN CHURCH CASE.
To the Editor of the 'Bolton Evening News.'

Sir,—Will you kindly give me, as minister of the congregation, space in your columns to state *two facts* relative to the above case?

I give you, with his sanction, the name and address of the gentleman on whose authority I furnish them—viz., Mr Robert Haworth, Sunnyside, Rawtenstall—one who is well known and much respected not only in Ramsbottom but throughout Rossendale.

First, Mr Haworth was one of the elders of the Presbyterian Church consulted by Mr John Grant respecting the sum of money belonging to Dundee School. It was on this wise. Mr Grant stated that £400 had been left by his late brother William for the schools, that this sum was yielding only about 3 per cent, some £12 or £13, and that as the schools required a larger sum annually, it would be better to invest it in some more remunerative way. He proposed that, with their (the elders') consent, cottages should be built with the amount, undertaking, until such time as the cottages were inhabited, to pay £16 a year for the £400.

Two cottages were built—still known as "Dundee Cottages"—and from that date up till 1869 the sum of £20 per annum was paid over to Mr William Stead, the treasurer of the schools.

The cottages, however, as it happened, were built on land belonging to Mr Grant, and since 1869 they have been treated as the private property of his heirs.

Second, Dr MacLean—who, by marriage, was related to the Grants—told Mr Haworth that on the funeral day of William Grant, the elder, he saw in a book the £4000 recorded for behoof of the Presbyterian Church, and further that it was deposited in Jones' Bank, Manchester.

I write this letter simply in the interests of truth and justice and peace, and from a strong conviction that were the much-respected lady who, through her brother, inherited the wealth of her father and uncles, fairly cognisant of the facts of the case, she would not be found unwilling to do everything that fairness and honour in the circumstances might demand.—I am, &c., WM. HUME ELLIOT.

IRWELL MOUNT, RAMSBOTTOM, 8th June 1875.

As to the £400—in the Sunday-school treasurer's book the sum of "£20" appears regularly, year by year, thus: "January 7.—To cash from J. Sutor,[1] £20." "January 4.—To cash, J. Sutor, £20." "January 28.—William Grant and Brothers, £20." So it runs, sometimes in one form, sometimes another. In 1865 it is, for the first time, "February 8.—William Grant, Esq., £20." But his personal subscription also appears for the same year: "June 29.—William Grant, Esq., £5." In 1866, in addition to the "£20," we have: "June 9.—Mrs Grant, £1;" "August 13.—William Grant, Esq., £5." Up to, and including 1863, the *personal* donation of £5 is from R. D. Grant, Esq. Mr Robert Dalglish Grant died in 1863. Can there be any reasonable doubt that the £20 thus paid yearly was the rent, or the equivalent of the rent, of the two houses, according to the arrangement come to between Mr John Grant and the elders?

Of the *third* item—the manse—hitherto nothing has been said. We shall state what we know. A good many years ago, we were told by one who had known the Grant family well for half a century or more, that William Grant also designed that a manse should be built for the minister of St Andrew's. We asked—"What proof is there anywhere of that?" "Why, the very gate was put in." "What gate?" "The gate from the church to the manse." "What came of it?" "It's there yet." "Where?" "In the

---

[1] "J. Sutor" was an *employé* of the Grants.

railings." " You mean the churchyard railings ? " "Yes." " Where about ? " " Near where the manse was to stand." " Where was that ? " " On the Nuttall Lane side, towards Crowlum—a fine place for it too; the east side looking across the river to Nuttall Hall and Grant's Tower, the south side to Nuttall Lane, and the west to Dundee and Holcombe Hill." " You say the gate is there still ? " " No doubt it is. It was on the Nuttall Lane side, near the Crowlum corner." On examination afterwards, we found it exactly where and as our informant had stated. That telltale wicket, uniform with the railings, is there to-day, and any one who is curious may without difficulty verify the fact for himself. It is quite easily seen from Lower Nuttall Lane.

Now, of all that is embraced in the above beneficent scheme of Mr William Grant the elder, St Andrew's Presbyterian (Dundee) Congregation at Ramsbottom has been absolutely deprived. But the *now Episcopal* St Andrew's exists, with *endowment, schools, and vicarage*. The amount of money devoted by the toiling and benevolent fathers has, we understand, been fully disbursed by the children. Indeed, on behalf of those who have now passed away, we should prefer to say explicitly that, on this point, we do not entertain any doubt. But *our complaint*, which we here wish to state without either ambiguity or excess, is *this*—That they disregarded the sacred wish of one generation of "pious ancestors"—their grand-parents—and violated the solemn devotement of funds and the practically executed design of a second—their uncles the gentle Cheerybles, and their father—*by alienating their benefactions from the Presbyterian Church, which they had loved and served, to the Episcopalian Church, with which they never had any connection.* Moreover, that without even the common courtesy of a reference to the Presbytery, which, as it happened, had publicly and formally thanked the founder—one of its own members—for St Andrew's Church *forty years before*,[1] the Bishop of Manchester and the Ecclesiastical Commissioners *aided them in the consummation of the great wrong*.

Happily there is a higher law than the rude and ruthless

THE LITTLE GATE.

force by means of which the alienation was effected. By virtue of that diviner statute, and in the eyes of all honourable men, the property, in all its members, belongs to the Presbyterian congregation to-day, notwithstanding "the

---

[1] See p. 284, *supra*.

legal document read by the registrar of the diocese." But why did not the congregation place itself behind the broad ægis of British law, and seek restitution? This it might well have done, although, as a matter of fact, the title deeds always purposed, and more than once actually drafted, were never executed. But British law, apart from other considerations, is a very costly commodity, especially in such a case as this. And if you happen to have to dispossess one who is prepared, as Mr William Grant the younger unquestionably was, to "spend a hundred thousand pounds" of a great inheritance to enforce his will, it may eventually prove a loss, even if you win your case. In such cases, financial inequality in the subject renders the great doctrine of equality before the law practically inoperative. An ideal code might cover such a case; our actual code does not. Instead, therefore, of going to law, the ejected and now supplanted congregation set to work to build a new church. But neither change of title, nor altered ritual, nor registrar's "legal document," nor even lapse of years, can obliterate their right to the old St Andrew's and all its belongings. It was, as the hymn-paper published at the laying of the foundation stone, by the founder, declared—"their new church;" the founder was publicly and formally thanked by the Presbytery for building it, and it was occupied by the congregation for thirty-five years. The sum of £4000 was set apart by the founder for the endowment, and its interest regularly paid for twenty-seven years after his death; while the £400 he provided for the Sunday-school was transformed into cottages, and £20 yearly paid to the Sunday-school treasurer. The little gate still tells its own tale. Fact is eternal!

The consecration of St Andrew's, in April 1875, took

place just five months after the writer's induction to St Andrew's (Dundee) Presbyterian Church. At the time we were absorbed in vital spiritual work among the people, and thus preparing to grapple with the heavy debt resting upon the new church which the ejected people had been compelled

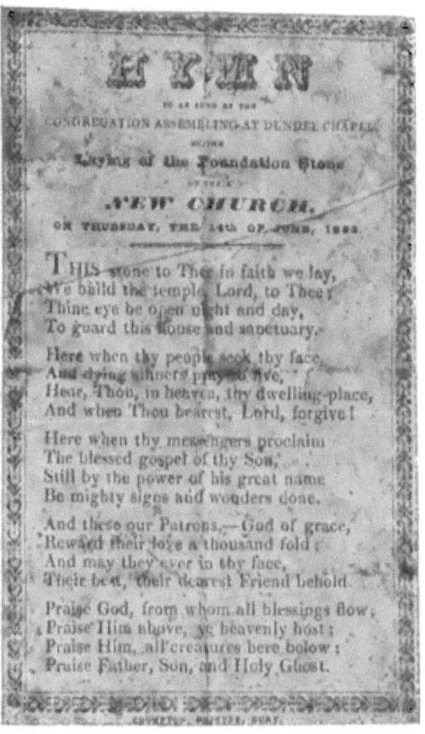

to build. We were not, therefore, in a position to do more than answer occasional queries addressed to us, and write a few letters to keep the Bishop and his opponents right as to the facts then known to us. But, in the glide of time, increasing acquaintance with the public utterances of the Bishop, and ampler knowledge of the actual facts of the case, deepened a conviction in our mind that, with fuller light, it was still possible for his lordship, should he see fit, to do something that would go far to set himself, at least, right in the eye of the Christian Church and the community at large. Accordingly, we addressed to him the following letter :—

WOODHILL, SHUTTLEWORTH, BURY,
May 11, 1880.

RIGHT REV. SIR,—As the minister of St Andrew's Presbyterian Church, Ramsbottom, I venture respectfully to approach your lordship. Five years ago I should have done this, but, for the sake of my higher work as a minister of Christ, and that peace which is so necessary to its successful prosecution, I refrained. Now, however, the calming influence of years having intervened, I think the time has come when, for many reasons, I ought to put myself in communication with you. I do so only after prayerful consideration. My object is, if possible, to bring about some action which, in the eye of the Christian Church at large, may tend to remove what, I am sure, has proved to all concerned a somewhat bitter memory. For that purpose I intended to address your lordship at length, but it has occurred to me that, meanwhile, it might be better to have a personal interview. I would, therefore, ask whether this course would be agreeable, and, if so, I shall be glad to call at any suitable time your lordship may be good enough to name. With sincere respect, and every good wish for your lordship, believe me, Right Rev. Sir, Yours most faithfully, WM. HUME ELLIOT.

We received the following reply :—

ATHENÆUM CLUB, PALL MALL, S.W.
May 13.

DEAR SIR,—I could see you at the Diocesan Registry (7 St James' Square, Manchester) on Tuesday the 25th, any time between 12 and 3. I attend there as a rule every Tuesday; but next week, being a holiday time, I shall not go down.—Yours faithfully, J. MANCHESTER.

I return home this evening.

This was followed by a post card :—

MANCHESTER, *May* 14.

Since writing to you yesterday, I find I must be in London on May 25th, but I can see you at the Registry on the following Tuesday, June 1. —Yours faithfully, J. MANCHESTER.

We went accordingly on the 1st of June. His lordship received us with frank and manly kindness. After a little conversation, he said—"You know I simply consecrated a building that had been handed over to the Ecclesiastical Commissioners, which otherwise would have stood empty, and which I might have been compelled to consecrate." We reminded his lordship that four years before that time it had been received by him, and licensed, and opened in charge of a curate. "But," he replied, "surely that must have been before my time." We said he would find it was not so. He then appealed to Mr Burder, who sat with us at the writing table, on the point. Mr Burder confirmed what we had stated. After a brief silence, his lordship said—"What is it you want me to do?" We answered that, by his lordship's action, the Church of England had received property at Ramsbottom worth, say, £12,000 or £15,000, all of which, without a shadow of doubt, was intended for the Presbyterian congregation there, and most of which had been actually possessed by it for a long series of years; that that congregation had now built a new church, and we thought his lordship might fairly be asked to take steps to provide the equivalent of the original endowment of £200 a-year. After a few seconds, he said, "Why, that would necessitate my moving the whole diocese." We replied that we had not thought it would require so great an effort. Presently he said, "I'll give you a donation of £20 if you will start a subscription for the purpose yourself." That, we answered, could not be entertained. At last he said, "Well, I'll think over it, and when I've fully considered the matter, I shall let you know my decision." We thanked him, expressing a hope that his decision might be favourable, and the conviction that, were he, in the circumstances, to take the course we had indicated, its effect would be wide-spreading and abiding good.

The following letters convey the Bishop's decision:—

THE DEANERY, WESTMINSTER, June 19, 1880.

DEAR SIR,—I have been away from home since the 7th inst., and do not return till the 26th. I have not been able to give the matter which formed the subject of our interview much more consideration than I gave it then, nor do I feel that I can advance in the direction which you suggested, further than I then proposed. I will, however, make further enquiries into the circumstances when I return to Manchester. All that I had to do with the matter was to consecrate a church, which had been built upon a site conveyed to the Ecclesiastical Commissioners, and which I probably could have been compelled by "Mandamus" to consecrate. The endowment of the church was entirely an affair between Mrs Lawson and the Ecclesiastical Commissioners.—Yours very faithfully,

J. MANCHESTER.

Rev. W. H. ELLIOT.

DIOCESAN REGISTRY, MANCHESTER, June 29, 1880.

DEAR SIR,—I am desired by the Bishop of Manchester to say that, having further considered the circumstances of the case brought under his notice by you, he can only repeat the answer given in his letter to you of the 19th June instant.

If, as asserted by you, there was any wrongful alienation of endowment, it was an act of which the Bishop had no privity, and to which he was no party; and it seems strange to him, on the supposition, that no steps were taken at the time to prevent it. He cannot therefore offer to do more than he proposed at your interview with him on the 1st June.—I am, yours faithfully, JOHN BURDER,
Secretary to the Bishop of Manchester.

The Rev. WM. HUME ELLIOT.

Thus the matter ended. The Bishop declined to do what we still believe would have been deemed to-day the brightest and most memorable act in his administrative career.

A word is necessary on his lordship's letter. Any one, not knowing who the "Ecclesiastical Commissioners" were, in reading the above letter, would be likely to think that the Bishop had no connection with them but that of subjection to their commands. It was not so. He was himself a Commissioner—the Commissioner who had personal cognisance of the Ramsbottom case, and whose knowledge and counsel, in a matter within his own diocese, would guide his brethren to whatever conclusion they reached.[1]

But we shall allow the facts to speak for themselves. We have little heart to say more on the matter, in this connection.

The worthy Bishop, as well as his Registrar, has now gone from amongst us—

"Issuing on a world beyond our mortal"—

like all the other leading actors in this strange ecclesiastical drama, leaving the wrong, unmoved and unmitigated, a sorely ravelled tangle, behind.

In closing this chapter, we simply present our claim for restitution, before the great tribunal of the enfranchised British people. "The throne is established by righteousness," and "Righteousness exalteth a nation."

---

[1] The Ecclesiastical Commissioners are: The two Archbishops; the 31 Bishops; 5 Cabinet Ministers; 4 Judges; 3 Deans; and 12 Laymen.

CHAPTER IV.

SECTION III.—1869-1891.

WE must now revert to the time immediately subsequent to the seizure of St Andrew's Church in 1869. The ejected congregation were *allowed* to occupy the old chapel at Dundee. The pulpit there was regularly supplied. In the course of 1870, Mr J. Kerr Craig, then a theological student, preached for some time with acceptance; and, after he was licensed, a call was given to him by the congregation on the 15th June 1871. He was ordained by the Presbytery of Lancashire in Dundee Chapel on the 13th of July 1871. A few days afterwards an intimation reached him from Mr William Grant "that 'Dundee' would be held at his disposal for service." About May 1st, 1872, Dundee manse was also given up by Mr Grant, but not the garden. After *many years* of investigation the writer happily found a solution of the whole difficulty with the Grants. Their deeds must have referred to a house at the foot of the manse garden, whose stones had evidently been used to build four of the seven cottages immediately below. This was our final suggestion. And fortunately, on referring to an old official Peel-plan in their agency office, they found a house faintly marked on the very spot. But

St Andrew's (Dundee) Presbyterian Church

that happy result was not reached till 1891. During Mr Craig's ministry the people determined upon a site, and proceeded to raise funds for the erection of a new church. The Synod of the Presbyterian Church made a grant of £750. Robert Barbour, Esq. of Bolesworth Castle, gave £500. Times were propitious. The foundation stone of the new church was laid in September 1872 by Thomas Matheson, Esq., Liverpool. It was opened on Thursday the 23d of October 1873. The Rev. Dr Donald Fraser of London preached on the occasion. On the Saturday evening and Sunday following, services were conducted by the Rev. Professor Chalmers, D.D., of London, and the Rev. Thomas MacPherson, M.A., of Liverpool—the Moderator of Synod. For the new church the people themselves, encouraged by the minister and office-bearers, contributed liberally; and the appeal to friends outside met with a generous response. At the time of the opening it was announced that £4030 had been subscribed. The cost of the structure was estimated not to exceed £5000. It amounted, however, to over £7000, exclusive of the site[1] on which it stands. That site is precisely the "hill-top" on which Mr William Grant said he "would like to see a fine church" planted. Soon after the opening of the new church, the Rev. J. K. Craig was translated to Chalmers Church, Ancoats, Manchester. A somewhat protracted vacancy followed. The present minister was inducted to the charge at Ramsbottom in St Andrew's Presbyterian Church, by the Presbytery of Manchester, on the 15th December 1874; and on the evening of that day the public reception meeting was held in Dundee Chapel.

---

[1] The annual ground rent is over £32.

The Rev. Charles Moinet, M.A., now of St John's, Kensington, London, had acted as *interim* moderator of session, and the Rev. Samuel Prenter, M.A., now of Dublin, preached at the induction. One of the new minister's earliest duties was, at the request of the managers, to prepare a statement showing precisely their financial position in relation to the new church. This revealed the fact that the debt on the new building was very much larger than he had been led to anticipate.

Important as it was that that debt should be dealt with, there was, the minister felt, another work of higher importance and greater urgency, which, in the first instance, had the supreme claim on his energies. Such acquaintance with the congregational history as he very soon acquired, and the fact of a tolerably prolonged vacancy, at the precise conjuncture of affairs when it occurred, led him to devote the first twelve months to direct, unremitting, and in great part personal dealing with the people on the subject of intelligent and cordial decision for Christ and a life of genuine loyalty to Him. It proved a memorable year. Not a few of those who, through subsequent years of trouble, have proved steadfast and helpful, became communicants during its course. At the celebration of the sacrament in July, fifty joined for the first time. Just then, a sum of £100 reached us from " A Friend," whose name was not disclosed by the gentleman through whom it was transmitted. In the following month another £100 came, also from " A Friend," through the same auspicious channel. At the end of 1874, the communicants numbered 84; at the end of 1875 they were 163. We then stood united, resolute, prepared to grapple with the incubus of debt. At the end of 1876, the balance at the bank against the managers—for which a number of them were jointly and severally responsible—stood at £1185, 11s. 1d. At the end of 1877, it was £176, 9s. 9d.; and on the 30th of June 1878, the balance was £5, 16s. 4d. in our favour. The debt was gone.

The cost of the church, exclusive of organ, &c., may be closely approximated thus:—

Paid up to the end of 1874.	£4536 15 4
Paid after the induction of the present minister,	2528 4 8
	£7065 0 0

By this time, however, some untoward elements had begun to appear—survivals, at first, of ancient feuds, of which the minister declined to take any cognisance; and subsequently, in the midst of the congregation's severest financial struggles, clandestinely induced, circumstances arose which involved the loyalty and good faith of certain office-bearers, who were also connected with the Sunday-school of the congregation at "Dundee," and who afterwards said they were Independents. Over these unhappy matters we would fondly draw a veil, for the sake of the persons themselves who were implicated. But eventually the whole case, after having been dealt with in the local session, came, by memorial from these men and their sympathisers, before the Presbytery of Manchester;[1] and it may suffice, instead of entering into detail, simply to give the decision of that Court of the Church. It is as follows:—

The Presbytery, having received the memorial, and having heard

---

[1] On 24th September and 8th October 1883.

representatives of the memorialists on the one side and of the session on the other, after deliberation come to the following finding:—

1st. They record their very deep sympathy with the Rev. Mr Elliot, amid all the difficulties, not only of a pecuniary but also of a personal character, with which he has had to contend in carrying forward his ministerial work, which has been so earnest and effective.

2d. They find that the teacher and the secretary of the Sabbath-school, who have been removed from their offices by the session, and for whose reponement the memorial prays, have been chargeable with such a spirit of obstructiveness in their dealings with the minister that their replacement would be injurious to the interests of both the church and school, and therefore they approve of the action of the session, and decline to grant the prayer of the memorial.

3d. They deeply deplore the condition of strife into which a section of the congregation have fallen. They would earnestly impress it on all parties concerned that such a condition is deeply sinful, and they would affectionately urge on minister, elders, Sabbath-school teachers, and congregation, that they strive prayerfully to have every breach healed, and to follow the things that make for peace.

Parties having been recalled, the Moderator intimated to them the finding as above.

These memorialists and their associates, on the following Sunday, ignored the decision of the Court to which they had themselves appealed, and, while sending in resignations, actually took forcible possession of the old chapel at Dundee, in which the week-day and Sunday schools of the congregation were held. The key of the building was refused to the minister, and his entrance on Sunday morning forcibly obstructed; and even after a solicitor's notice had been served on the offenders, they persisted in violently retaining possession by persons keeping guard inside.

The congregation were, very naturally, indignant at those who had thus betrayed their sacred trust. They had been among the foremost and loudest in their condemnation of Mr William Grant's high-handed procedure, and now, fourteen years later, they had followed his evil precedent in an aggravated form. Moreover, like him, they thought themselves secure, because they knew that the congregation, up to that time, had failed to find any trace of a trust deed of the property of which they had forcibly taken possession.[1]

Nearly three months afterwards—on the 14th January 1884—a memorial from those in forcible possession, this time bearing that it came from "The managers of the Presbyterian congregation of Dundee Chapel, Ramsbottom," reached the Presbytery of Manchester. The following was its decision :—

> The Presbytery find that the Memorialists represent a section of the Ramsbottom Congregation which was before the Presbytery in the month of October by memorial, and which, while neither acquiescing in the Presbytery's decision nor appealing to the Synod, has since taken the law into its own hands, seized by physical force the Dundee Chapel, and still contumaciously retains possession thereof, to the exclusion of the minister and the Sunday-school, and to the detriment of religion in the neighbourhood, and therefore the Presbytery finds itself precluded from receiving the memorial; but should the Memorialists resile from the false position they have taken up, restore the Dundee Chapel to the use of the St Andrew's Congregation, and come regularly through the session with a memorial couched in appropriate terms, the Presbytery will then be prepared to receive and consider such memorial, and give such decision thereon as may in their judgment seem right.

It may also be noted that two memorials of a somewhat

---

[1] Over *thirty* years ago, as we have since ascertained from indubitable evidence, the question of Dundee property and its destiny was frequently talked over by the elder portion of these men, who were then identified with Dundee school. The ground of *possible* action was—"There are no writings"—no trust deeds.

different character were presented to the session, and laid before the Presbytery of Manchester, on the 7th of April 1884. One of these was from St Andrew's (Dundee) Congregation bearing 302 signatures, the other from "the inhabitants of Ramsbottom and the surrounding district," with 392 names, including "the chairman and other members of the Ramsbottom Local Board, the vicar of the parish, the vicars of two adjacent parishes, professional gentlemen, and many employers of labour."

The Rev. W. Young, B.A., of Higher Broughton, in presenting the petitions, said he was at the meeting of Session at Ramsbottom on the previous Thursday, when they were laid on the table. He thought the Presbytery when they had heard them would have very great pleasure in receiving them. The first, which bore 303 signatures, was as follows :—

To the Reverend the Presbytery of Manchester.

We, the undersigned elders, deacons, members, and friends of St Andrew's (Dundee) Presbyterian Church of England, Ramsbottom, do hereby petition your honourable body, showing that the Rev. William Hume Elliot, minister of the said church, has laboured in this community for a period of nearly ten years, and during that time has commended himself to all by the faithful discharge of the sacred duties of his office. His high Christian character, kind disposition, and unwearied labours of love have not only endeared him to all of his own congregation but to most of the community at large; and your petitioners therefore humbly pray your reverend court to protect him from the persecution of those who are attempting to drive him from his present sphere of usefulness, and by your wise interposition to establish him more firmly in the office which he now adorns.

Annexed, your reverend court will find a summary of accounts, showing the state of church funds for the following years, 1882, 1883, 1884, which will show the progress the church has made since the seceders left us. And we, the petitioners, humbly pray that your honourable court will do all you can to protect us, now that harmony, happiness, and peace are working in concord. And your petitioners will for ever pray.

The second petition, which was signed by 392 names, was as follows :—

To the Reverend the Presbytery of Manchester.

We, the undersigned inhabitants of Ramsbottom and the surrounding district, do hereby petition your honourable body, showing that the Rev. Wm. Hume Elliot, minister of St Andrew's Presbyterian Church of England, has laboured in this community for a period of nearly ten years, and during that time has much commended himself by the faithful discharge of the sacred duties of his office. His high Christian character, kind disposition, and unwearied labours of love have not only endeared him to most of his congregation, but also to a large portion of the community of Ramsbottom; and your petitioners therefore humbly pray your reverend court not to allow him to be severed from his present sphere of usefulness, but by your wise interposition to establish him more firmly in the office which he now so ably fills. And your petitioners will for ever pray.

Mr Young thought he need say scarcely a word in laying the memorials on the table except that the movement had been, as stated in the session, a very spontaneous one. The minister, he understood, had had nothing in the world to do with it. Representative memorialists were next heard.

Dr M'Caw, of Trinity Church, Manchester, then proposed that the memorials be received, and that the Presbytery cordially agree to grant their prayer so far as it was competent for the Court to do so. The memorials, he said, must be extremely gratifying in the first instance to Mr Elliot himself. It had been well said that he had passed through a world of trouble in Ramsbottom during these ten years, and had had to contend with difficulties and opposition that no person knew so well as he knew himself. But, by the mercy of the Most High, he had been enabled to pass through these difficulties with the thorough approval not only of his congregation but of the residents of Ramsbottom. Every word of the testimony given by the 300 members and adherents as to the character of Mr Elliot he was prepared most thoroughly to endorse, so far as he knew him and the character of his work. What they could do in the future to protect him from opposition, and what was called persecution, he did not see very exactly; but anything they could do as a Presbytery in manifesting their sympathy, in upholding his hands, in strengthening, if need be, the session—in doing, in fact, what they could to show the whole community that they thoroughly approved of his work and his conduct in the past, and would do anything in future to maintain him—he thought the Presbytery would be very glad to do."

A leading member of Presbytery, known and honoured throughout the Church, in the course of his speech said: "There was even an attempt made to get letters published in ——, in order, if possible, to affect his (the speaker's) ministerial usefulness, but the editor of the newspaper did him the honour of sending him the letter after he had promptly declined its insertion. He had not mentioned the matter in public, but there had been an attempt to extend the persecution beyond Mr Elliot."

The great matter which needed now to be settled was the legal title to the property which had thus forcibly been usurped by the ringleaders at "Dundee." Unfortunately, although quest, personal and professional, had been diligently made in recent years, no trust deed of the old place was known to exist; and, to add to the difficulty, "the Roll of the Manor of Tottington," in the ["Honor of Clitheroe," in which it stood, bore, the managers were officially informed, no reference whatever to it, and this was known to those now in possession. The land is copyhold, and it came out afterwards that as for many years no appearance of, or on behalf of, any trustee had been made in the Halmot Court (hall-mote or court-baron) of the district, "Dundee" long ago had somehow been dropped from the Ramsbottom court roll—an instance of one of the evils incident to the copyhold system.

After the property was seized, and early in the week preceding the Sunday morning on which the minister's entrance to "Dundee" was obstructed, he very naturally was much absorbed with the trust-deed difficulty. It was mysterious. Dundee stood in copyhold territory within the manor of Tottington, yet it did not appear on the roll of that manor! What could it mean? Had a deed ever existed? No one knew; the roll practically said no. What could be done? To get at a trust deed, in the circumstances, seemed utterly hopeless. Such, however, was the position of affairs, when, using his wits to the utmost and seeking divine guidance in the difficulty, the suggestion shot across the minister's mind, clear as a meteor athwart the sky on a moonless night, "Try Mr ———." This gentleman was the legal representative of an old family in the neighbourhood. Without delay, the minister sought an interview, and asked the gentleman if he thought there existed, in the family[1]

---

[1] This old family was represented in the group of trustees named in the discovered deed. That deed was handed over to the rightful owners after the suit for ejectment—afterwards referred to—was gained in 1885.

archives, any documents of any kind relating to Old Dundee property. He thought not, but said he really hardly knew what there was in some of the odd corners; and, in the circumstances, kindly promised to look. Within forty-eight hours, the minister received from that gentleman by a messenger a brief extract from the *Dundee Trust Deed of 1811*.[1] It was found, he afterwards told him, in an *old and disused safe in Manchester*. With this deed in our possession, we were enabled, without further difficulty, to secure from the muniment-room at Clitheroe Castle a "certified" copy from "the Court Rolls of the Manor of Tottington," where search and inquiry for the deed had previously been made in vain.

All the trustees of 1811 were dead. It was necessary, therefore, that new ones should be appointed. This, in accordance with counsel's opinion, was now done, under the provisions of Sir Morton Peto's Act, while adhering strictly to the instructions given for such cases in the Book of Order[2] issued by the Presbyterian Church of England. The appointment took place on the 18th of November 1883. This accomplished, it was then necessary to take proceedings for the recovery of the property. A suit for ejectment might have been instituted at once. Another course, however, was deemed preferable in the first instance. It so happened that the tenant of the old manse was employed by one of the men

---

[1] See Appendix B.
[2] The "Book of Order" was prepared by a Committee of Synod acting through many years in conjunction with all the Presbyteries of the Church. The convener was the late distinguished Dr Leone Levi, a loved and honoured elder of the Presbyterian Church of England. The book bears his name as Convener, and during the protracted litigation, it was treated by Bench and Bar alike with marked attention and respect.

then wrongfully holding the old chapel. This tenant refused to pay his rent to the treasurer of the congregation, who was also one of the new trustees. He was sued for it in the County Court at Bury. The case came before the deputy judge. The real defendants were the men who had taken forcible possession of the chapel.[1] The case was considered on two separate days, and the decision given on a third—several weeks apart. The question of rent, or who was landlord, brought up prominently the further question relating to the new trustees, Were they properly appointed? That appointment the opposing counsel laboured hard and long to invalidate. The congregation stood simply and absolutely by the instructions of the Book of Order. The manse had been let by the sub-treasurer, acting as the agent of the managers. He had also collected the rent, which duly appeared, from time to time, in the congregational treasurer's book, and he had resigned some months before the difficulty arose. The decision of the deputy judge was a remarkable one. It practically constituted the sub-treasurer landlord, and gave no judgment at all on the appointment of trustees. An appeal was taken to the High Court of Justice, and in June 1884, the case came before Mr Justice Hawkins and Mr Justice A. L. Smith, in the Queen's Bench. Mr Justice Hawkins virtually settled the landlord question, incidentally, by these words—"The managers stand in the shoes of the old trustees till new trustees are appointed." The defendants' counsel then raised the question of title, and challenged the appointment of trustees. As no decision had been given on this point in the lower court, the judges sent the case back

---

[1] This was afterwards stated in court; and it was admitted that the Independents, as they called themselves, paid the costs.

for the court at Bury to "do its own work"—to investigate and give a decision on the question, Were the new trustees properly appointed?—and ordered it to come up again for final judgment. The case accordingly was referred back to Bury. This time it came before the senior judge, Mr Crompton Hutton, on July 18, 1884. He decided (1) that the trustees appointed by St Andrew's (Dundee) Presbyterian Congregation on 18th November 1883 *had been properly appointed*, and (2) gave decree for rent to the said trustees. As ordered, this decision went to the Court of Queen's Bench, and this time the case came before Mr Justice Mathew and Mr Justice Day, on December 2, 1884. They entirely confirmed the decision of Mr Crompton Hutton, and gave judgment accordingly, " with costs on the higher scale."

It might have been supposed that these decisions would be deemed sufficient, and that the property which had been so lawlessly seized and held for over twelve months, as a distinguished judge afterwards said, "without a rag of title," would now be given up. That course, however, was not compatible with the programme of those who now called themselves Independents; and, notwithstanding the above decisions and the statement of Mr Justice Hawkins, that "the managers stood in the shoes of the old trustees till new trustees were appointed," the Independent ministers of the district, as well as leading officials of the Lancashire Congregational Union, fraternised, in the old Presbyterian chapel, with the men by whom it was still forcibly held! It was on the 18th of July that the decision of Mr Crompton Hutton was given in Bury. During the same month a circular was issued, headed " Dundee Independent Chapel,"

"Proposed New Sunday-school," in which an urgent appeal was made for funds. This appeal was for day school as well, but *that* was not declared.

In seizing the Old Dundee Chapel, which is a considerable distance from the New St Andrew's Church, the usurping party assumed the absolute control of St Andrew's Presbyterian (Dundee) British School, which was conducted in it. The school documents were thus in their hands. The Education Department was deliberately and adroitly misled by a letter, written clandestinely by the ringleader of the usurpers sending *his own name* to be substituted for that of the minister, as school correspondent. An official copy of that letter, in autograph, came afterwards into the managers' hands. Here it is:—

St Andrew's Presbyterian School,
October 30, 1883.

To the Secretary, Education Department, Whitehall, S.W.

Sir,—I am instructed to intimate that from this date the correspondent for the above-named school will be [here he inserts his own name], Spring Terrace, Ramsbottom, instead of the Rev. W. H. Elliot.—I am, yours truly,

The writer of this letter, it may be noted, had left St Andrew's Presbyterian Church, and when he wrote it had not been present at a meeting of the school managers for upwards of *six years*. It may further be stated that the managers of the school knew nothing whatever of the communication. By this deceptive artifice the real correspondent was supplanted, and, notwithstanding explanation and protest, after the deception was discovered, the usurpers were recognised as *de facto* managers of the Presbyterian School, and ultimately received over £200 of the Government grants.[1] Thus while these men, under Independent auspices, were appealing for funds as "managers" of what they now called "Dundee *Independent* Chapel," they were at the same time receiving public monies as managers of St Andrew's *Presbyterian* School.

The effort to appropriate Dundee property in 1798[2] had failed, and it was becoming increasingly apparent that the present would also come to nought. But, if this time the Independents could get a building ready, *near at hand*, and therefore close to where most of the people whom they had misguided lived within a narrow radius, they could when necessary—that is, when the strong arm of the law thrust them out of Dundee Chapel—transfer to their new structure, as far as possible, the *personnel* of the Presbyterian day and Sunday schools. This was now the magnanimous work and policy of all concerned in this lawless and ignoble procedure!

The final decision in the *manse* case was given on December 2, 1884, and the tenant duly paid his rent, and gave up the key to the treasurer of the congregation, on the 15th of that month. But when, on the morning of the 16th, the trustees went to enter the house, they found its lock had been tampered with, and its doors secured, while men were in charge within. When requested to open the door, they refused, saying they were employed to keep possession, and if the trustees wanted anything they were to go to certain

---

[1] Political influence, unworthy of honourable men, was employed in connection with this matter. "My Lords" had given the assurance that no grant would be paid till the dispute "has been settled on the spot." Yet, *within a few days* of the ejectment trial (May 1885), and in the face of protest, the sum of £209, 7s. 9d. was handed over to the Independents by the Education Department.

[2] See p. 223, *supra*.

persons whom they named, and under whom they were acting.

Instructed by their solicitors, the trustees returned to old Dundee manse on the following day. The men again refused to open the door. A young man, on behalf of the trustees, then entered by a window at the rear of the building, notwithstanding the bludgeons that were flourished over his head. He opened the front door. The representatives of the congregation entered and requested the men to leave. They refused in the first instance, but one by one ultimately they disappeared. The premises were then thoroughly examined and secured. But, before leaving, one of the persons to whom the trustees had been referred from within on the previous morning came, at the head of a howling crowd, and with a sledge-hammer violently assailed the back door. Stayed, however, by his own strong barricading-handiwork within, it proved sullenly obstinate; but other hands relieved him in his arduous task, and the tough timber at length gave way in rebounding ribbon-like splinters, and forthwith the rude and noisy crowd rolled in like a tumultuous wave.[1]

The trustees—after this sledge-hammer episode—were instructed that they could proceed against a number of these Independents in a criminal court. Their object, however, was not the punishment of the offenders, however much some of them deserved it, but the restoration of the entire property to its owners, St Andrew's (Dundee) Presbyterian Congregation.

The law of England has some perplexing peculiarities.

---

[1] The old manse is built against the S.E. end of Dundee Chapel. (See p. 230, *supra*.)

The following, which was encountered at this stage of the proceedings, is one of them. If, to use a phrase of the distinguished judge who tried the Dundee ejectment case— if "any squad of people" take possession of a house, and raise the question of title, the magistrates cannot interfere, nor the constabulary force be employed to remove them! And although, as in the present case, the "squad" may be in possession "without a rag of title," yet they may tenant the house with bludgeon-men, or worse, and you are helpless, until you adopt the costly process of instituting, before the proper tribunal, a suit for ejectment.

Four days after the final decision of the manse case in the Queen's Bench, and precisely ten days before the sledgehammer episode just referred to, one of the secretaries of the Lancashire Congregational Union, who was accompanied by other Independent brethren, addressed the people who were in forcible possession, in Old Dundee Chapel. After apologising for the absence of his colleague in the secretariat, he said, "He had come to show which side he was on—(applause)—to express sympathy with them in their present position and with regard to their future prospects. When he received his invitation, he thought he would have been thoroughly destitute of backbone, and utterly lacking in enterprise, had he not responded by at once indicating that he had sympathy with the course they proposed pursuing. (Applause.) . . . They were there not simply to affirm that they enjoyed liberty, but they were there as Congregationalists, and though he and they knew little of each other, he shook hands with them as brother and sister Congregationalists, and he was not ashamed of so doing," &c.[1]

---

[1] 'Bury Times,' 13th December 1884.

The following missive, which may be given as a specimen, is dated somewhat later in the same month.—

RAMSBOTTOM, *Dec.* 24, 1884.

Right Reverend W. H. ELLIOT,

DEAR SIR,—I wish you as merry a Christmas as circumstances will permit. I should be very sorry should anything serious happen to you. I therefore wish to give you a timely and kindly warning, that should you or any of your party persist in going to Old Dundee, you will greatly suffer in your person or persons, and, what is more, I am afraid that your church will suffer also. If such should happen, I for one should feel very sorry indeed. You have the matter in your own hands.[1]—I am, your sincere friend,   A LOVER OF PEACE.

I hope you will let your ministerial brethren, friends, and supporters see this. Perhaps they may advise you. Should they fail, then look to your lawyer, and what would still be better, ask Jesus what you ought to do. I am once again yours,   XMAS.

A supply of bludgeons[2] had been prepared and distributed to the "young men," who, it was publicly boasted, "watched" the premises "night after night, in the cold," for the Independents. One of these murderous weapons is now in the writer's possession. It is of hard wood, 23 in. long, 6½ in. in circumference, heavily leaded, has 15, evidently lathe-cut, circular incisions towards the leaded end, and is stamped thus—"8 12 1884." The notable "backbone" and "enterprise" speech of the secretary of the Lancashire Congregational Union, in the old Presbyterian Chapel, was delivered on

---

[1] Precisely so. If the search for evidence to dispossess them were abandoned, and they were allowed, undisturbed, to retain possession of the old chapel and manse, then they would graciously let the rightful owners alone!

[2] They were made in the workshop of a Dundee Independent, whose lathes and anvils, not long after the achievement, became for ever motionless and silent.

Saturday the 6th of December 1884. (See p. 342.) On that day, the corner stone of an Independent chapel-school had been laid, near Dundee Chapel, " in the name of the Father, Son, and Holy Ghost."[1]

As a moderate sample of the Independent utterances current at the time, we may add that the gentleman who, in the name of the Holy Trinity, performed the function—an Independent deacon and J. P. from a neighbouring town—made the following *grossly and culpably erroneous* and misleading statement to the public on the occasion : " The Rev. Peter Ramsay . . . was followed by a minister of the name of Brown, who was a United Presbyterian, but who came as

an Independent, and continued the Independent form of worship."[2] (See Dr Brown's ordination and pastorate, pp. 259 *et seq. supra*, for the *facts*.)

On the same occasion, another speaker—he whose clandestine letter had deceived the Education Department (see p. 339)—said " that the people of Old Dundee had ever been Independent," and "the records of the church were in all times Independent"![3] Where were those records when the trial for the ejectment of the Independents came on ? They would have been useful for them then ; but they never appeared, and for the best of all reasons—they never existed.

---

[1] 'Bury Guardian,' 13th December 1884.
[2] 'Bury Times,' 13th December 1884.
[3] 'Bury Guardian,' 13th December 1884.

By the persistent iteration of such statements, however, people were deceived.

With whatever reluctance, historic fidelity compels the statement that not a few painful and unworthy episodes—acts of violence, personal threats, waylaying in the dense darkness, and other unhappy circumstances—transpired in the course of this contention, over which one would tenderly cast a veil. One illustrative incident may, however, be adduced. The chief of constabulary in the locality was good enough to warn the writer of danger. We told him frankly that while we were aware of evil machinations, we had not experienced any apprehension. It happened, however, that we had to pass through some fields to reach home from Ramsbottom, and part of the way was flanked with hedges. So, he added, "it is not so much meeting in the open that is to be dreaded, but one never knows what characters such people may get associated with them, and no man has any chance against brick-bats thrown in the darkness from behind a hedge." From that time we avoided the hedgerows at night, and struck through the open fields. One well-defined line, with partial variations, we usually followed. The hateful and almost incredible espionage practised for many months, while our quest for evidence continued, no doubt made this known; and one very dark night we were deliberately waylaid. Our way lay along the top of the rather broken and precipitous bank of a little clough, the base of which was somewhat miry and perplexing, especially in a wet season. Our would-be assailants, it seems, had got down this bank in the intense darkness, and about eleven o'clock, after we had reached home, they were heard crying loudly for help! Strangely enough, it was extended to them by one who had just left our house by the way we had reached it. He knew one of the men by name, and all they would say was—" We've had enough! we've had enough!" Subsequently the wicked purpose was divulged that had brought them into such a pitiable plight—scratched, bemired, torn, and terrified—but how and at what precisely we never knew. We had passed, it appeared, quite near to them, silently and alone, under the sable wing of night, unconscious of their presence.

But, perhaps, the most surprising and regrettable circumstance of all was the conduct of neighbouring Independent brethren—with whom there had previously existed only harmony and goodwill—and certain prominent official representatives of Congregationalism, in aiding and abetting these misguided men at "Dundee;" and, especially, might we complain of the unfraternal and insidious means they adopted for making capital out of these remarkable proceedings to promote their own denominational interests. They practically coerced unwilling brethren into co-operation. We give, in the following letter of a worthy Congregationalist minister, a specimen of what is meant. His charge was a few miles from Ramsbottom. Having called in our absence, he wrote this note:—

Thursday.

DEAR MR ELLIOT,—I have called to have a conversation about an invitation I have had to meet [here is inserted the name and official designation of a rev. gentleman well known in the Congregational Union] at Ramsbottom, in connection with the people who lately left your church. Up till this time I have refused to accept their invitations; because, apart from other considerations, I had not seen you, had not mentioned the matter to you, and did not wish even in appearance to side against you. As, however, I am *pressed officially* to meet Mr —— at the end of this month, I did not know what to do, and resolved to wait upon you and have a talk over the matter. I would on no account do anything that would either injure you or your cause in Ramsbottom, or even give you personal annoyance. But you know that, while reluctant to have anything to do with a movement, one may feel for many reasons *under pressure to go with denominational officials* and friends in their work—at least, *to stand aside* from them, after a time, has in it an element of *hostility*. But I am afraid my hurried note will only make matters worse. Yet I should have liked to have had a clear understanding with you before deciding either way. As, however, I am unable to wait longer, I must just leave this explanation of my visit, and, with best regards to yourself and Mrs Elliot, remain, yours very truly,

We called upon this brother afterwards, and talked the matter over. He entirely disapproved of his brethren going, in the circumstances, into the old Presbyterian chapel, stating that he understood he was invited to a public hall. The official pressure, however, evidently proved too strong, for soon afterwards he took his place, like his brethren, alongside Mr ———, in the old Presbyterian sanctuary. They were "not ashamed" to enter and use the premises for the attainment of their purposes—not only while the legal title was *sub judice* in the civil courts, but even after important decisions had been given in favour of St Andrew's Presbyterian Congregation—thus publicly identifying themselves with those who had taken, and were confessedly retaining, possession of the property by violence. Moreover, so held, they used it, meanwhile, as a basis of operations for founding a Congregationalist school and chapel close at hand.

All this involved the necessity of yet another and very costly trial to give effect to the decision on the manse case, and eject those men, by force of law, from the premises they so lawlessly held—chapel and manse alike.

A brief extract from the report of that Assize trial will

show the character of the claim advanced for the Independents by their counsel :—

DEFENDANTS' COUNSEL.—First of all, the legal estate was and is outstanding ; secondly, the possession has always been in the teachers and the superintendents. When the legal estate is out, and both are claiming, possession is property, and we have possession. Who is to oust us from the possession ?

HIS LORDSHIP.—That is begging the whole question. The question is whether these gentlemen have carried on a congregation for a considerable time enough to bring it within Sir Morton Peto's Act.

DEFENDANTS' COUNSEL.—This is solid ground. We, the defendants, are in possession.

HIS LORDSHIP.—If you ask me, without a rag of title. Who have the place now ?

DEFENDANTS' COUNSEL.—Those in possession of it.

HIS LORDSHIP.—Then you mean that any squad of people could go there and take possession ? You were in possession together with the rest of the congregation, but you chose to say, "We sever ourselves from you, and will have this place." So far as I can see, Dundee went over to St Andrew's in 1873.[1]

It may here be remarked that "the teachers and superintendents" of the Sunday-school of the congregation had been in possession of its old chapel, week by week, just as teachers and superintendents usually are in possession of the church or chapel premises in which the schools meet. In this sense they had been in possession, but in no other ; and had there been the faintest shadow of truth in the extraordinary claim put forward by the defendants at the trial, that "they were never under Presbyterian jurisdiction at all in Dundee

---

[1] The new St Andrew's, where the congregation now worships, was opened in 1873. (See p. 327.) At that time, having built their new church, the congregation (Dundee) removed from Old Dundee Chapel where they had worshipped since 1869, when old St Andrew's—now Episcopal—was taken from them. (See p. 298.)

Chapel," is it not very remarkable that, while the congregation was worshipping in Dundee, without a minister, in 1871,[1] and before the new St Andrew's was built, these very men should themselves describe Dundee School as "St Andrew's Presbyterian Sabbath-school?" In these or similar terms it is described on the hymn-papers for the Whit-week festival, year by year, since long before the above date. Moreover, *three of the defendants* had actually been ordained to the eldership *in* "*Dundee Chapel,*" on 12th November 1871, by the "Session of St Andrew's English Presbyterian Church, Ramsbottom,"[2] while the officiating minister had himself, not long before, been ordained to the ministry, *in the same place*, by the Presbytery of Lancashire.[3] When, at the Assizes, defendants' counsel made the astounding declaration, "We were never under Presbyterian jurisdiction at all in Dundee Chapel," his lordship said: "I have plenty of evidence in the records that you were. I have no difficulty about that." And the unbroken testimony of living members covering seventy years, with the varied mass of documents, &c., recovered both during and since the litigation, make the evidence on this point simply overwhelming and superabundant, though it is not needful to produce it here. It shows, however, that the learned judge described the defendants' position with *absolute* accuracy when he said they were in possession "without a rag of title." This was never doubted by disinterested people familiar with only the recent history of the place; while, to say nothing of Presbytery and Synod Records which go back over seventy

---

[1] During the vacancy caused by Dr MacLean's death in 1869.
[2] Minutes of Session. [3] July 13, 1871.

years, the Session Records (1818-1829)[1] and Communion Rolls (1830-1891) of the congregation now extend in an unbroken line from 1818 to the present time. And, travelling backwards through 1814, when the peace-thanksgiving sermon was "preached in the *Presbyterian* Chapel, Holcombe,"[2] we find that Dundee was Presbyterian in 1798, when the Independent brethren on the other side of the valley tried to take it, but failed;[3] in 1755, when the trust was declared;[4] in 1722, when a trust deed tells us its minister—Edward Rothwell, who gave the land and provided Dundee Chapel in 1712—was "of the Presbyterian persuasion;"[5] in 1719, when the congregation built another chapel, at Bury,[6] which, though now Unitarian, still bears, in gold letters in its vestibule, the old name, "Presbyterian Chapel." Moreover, it was Presbyterian when in 1717 it furnished its return to the historic list of Dr Evans in London; and Dr Halley, in his 'Lancashire Puritanism,' corroborates the fact in his reference to it, "in the early part of last century."[7] And, finally, it was a Presbyterian congregation during the long and chequered ministry of Mr Pendlebury, who died in 1695, but who had been ordained by the second Presbytery of Lancashire in 1650,[8] and inducted, by the same Presbytery, to the Chapelry of Holcombe, on the 16th of October 1651.[9]

The policy of the defendants, indeed, resembled that embodied in the words of Mirabeau—"De l'audace, et encore de l'audace, et toujours de l'audace"—to dare, and again to dare, and always to dare! And they encouraged the conviction, often enough expressed, that as Mr William

---

[1] See p. 250. [2] See p. 247. [3] See p. 223.
[4] See p. 218. [5] See p. 212. [6] See p. 205.
[7] See p. 205. [8] See p. 181. [9] See p. 182.

Grant the younger had not been sued in 1869, when he seized St Andrew's Church, because of the great *expense* it would involve ; so the congregation, in this case, would never face the outlay necessary to drive the defendants finally out of Dundee by an ejectment suit, if they only stuck persistently and audaciously enough to the usurped premises ! In this, as in some other matters, they made a mistake.

We shall now give the latest *genuine* trust deed for the Old Dundee property—the appointment of trustees by St Andrew's (Dundee) Congregation on the 18th of November 1883. This is the deed which passed successfully through the various courts of law as above recorded, and restored to the congregation the chapel, manse, &c., which had been so unrighteously seized.

COPY OF DUNDEE TRUST DEED, OF NOVEMBER 1883.

Memorandum of the Choice and Appointment of New Trustees of the chapel, edifice, or building adjoining to Nuttall Lane, in the Manor of Tottington, in the County of Lancaster, formerly called Little Edmund's, and afterwards called Dundee, and also of all that messuage or dwelling house adjoining the same, and also of the four falls of land by estimation thereunto belonging, at a meeting duly convened and held for that purpose in the Session House, St Andrew's Presbyterian Church, Ramsbottom, on the eighteenth day of November, one thousand eight hundred and eighty-three. The Rev. William Hume Elliot, of Woodhill, Ramsbottom, chairman. Names and descriptions of all the Trustees on the constitution of last appointment of Trustees, made the thirtieth day of April, one thousand eight hundred and eleven: Richard Rothwell, late of Chadderton, in Tottington aforesaid, Yeoman ; Edward Rothwell, late of Spout Bank, in the County of Lancaster, Yeoman ; Edward Kay, late of Little Bolton, in the said County, Yeoman ; Richard Kay, late of Lime Field, within Walmsley, in the said County, Cotton Manufacturer ; William Woodcock, late of Holcome, in the said Manor, Gentleman ;

William Grant, late of Grant Lodge, in the said Manor, Merchant; Charles Grant, late of Grant Lodge, aforesaid, Merchant; and Edward Rothwell, late of Bolton, in the said County, Painter—all long since deceased.

Names and descriptions of all the Trustees in whom the said premises now become legally vested:—

First—Old continuing Trustees, None. *Second*—New Trustees, now chosen and appointed: Henry Stead of Carr Bank, Ramsbottom, Manufacturer; Joseph Strang of Ramsbottom, Ironfounder; James Pilling of Strongstrye, Ramsbottom, Foreman; James Millership Stead of Irwell Mount, Ramsbottom, Manufacturer; Charles Henry Johnson, Palatine Road, Withington, Merchant; William D. Fairbairn, M.A., of Eccles, Minister of the Gospel; Lawrence Stead of Bank House, Ramsbottom, Manufacturer; William Stark of Chadderton, Ramsbottom, Calico Printer; John Alexander Beith of Manchester, Merchant, Justice of the Peace; Sidney Spencer of Ramsbottom, Engraver; William Young, B.A., of Higher Broughton, and William Hume Elliot of Woodhill, aforesaid, both Ministers of the Gospel, and all in the County of Lancaster.

Dated this eighteenth day of November, one thousand eight hundred and eighty-three.

Signed, sealed, and delivered by the said
William Hume Elliot, as Chairman
of the said meeting, on the day and
year aforesaid, in the presence of

WM. HUME ELLIOT,
Chairman of the said Meeting.

HUGH THOMSON, Elleray, King Henry's Road,
London, N.W.
JAMES SADLER, Square Street,
Ramsbottom.

The foregoing deed was executed under the provisions of the Act xiii. and xiv. Victoria, cap. 28—popularly known as "Sir Morton Peto's Act." The trustees named in it were appointed by the *Dundee Congregation*, which, since 1873, has worshipped in the new St Andrew's Presbyterian Church,

Ramsbottom. The Independents, at the trial, came into court armed with what, in form, were two imposing legal instruments. One of these set forth, in a very elaborate way, that the heir of the last survivor of the trustees of 1811—Mr Edward Rothwell—had assigned the Dundee property " unto the defendants, their heirs, and assigns for ever !" Here may be conveniently recorded an incident which was closely connected with the fate of this deed. On the 17th April 1885—eighteen days before the trial—a communication was received from the solicitors containing a request "*to make a search* and ascertain at what time the various persons, trustees in 1811, died," &c.—a considerable task. There were eight of these gentlemen ; two of them bore the same name— " Edward Rothwell " (p. 352), and it was not stated in the defence to which of the two the deed of assignment referred. Acting on a principle which proved beneficial throughout the varied quests that fell to be undertaken—viz., to face every task, congenial or uncongenial, without an hour's unnecessary delay, and thus prevent the accumulation of uninviting work —it was resolved to begin the search forthwith with one of the Rothwells. The *last* on the list of trustees was selected as being probably the youngest, and most likely to prove the survivor of the group—" Edward Rothwell of Bolton, painter." He proved the right one. The trustee who undertook this quest furnishes this remarkable record of it : " We started for Bolton. Arrived there, we set out for the Town Hall. An impression that it was too modern for our purpose, however, kept us from entering. Looking round in the rain and mist, we saw ' Public Library,' which seemed to bear more of the touch 'of eld.' We entered. Its stands were occupied by busy readers. Presently one entered whose face attracted us. We asked him if he knew whether there were any old directories in the place. He kindly brought one. We said—'Much further back than that.' '*How* much?' 'To near the beginning of the century.' '*This* is the oldest,' he said, handing a very small volume, for 1818. We began to peruse it. He said, 'May I ask what name you are in search of?' We told him. To our surprise, we found he knew all about the very family whose history we wished to ascertain. From genealogical research, as well as from direct personal knowledge, he was able to communicate to us *all* we needed to know. But he also kindly introduced us to a venerable friend, who stated that, when a boy, he 'lived next door to Mr Rothwell in Fold Street, in 1811.' Of singularly impressive mien, he most courteously interested himself in our inquiries, and confirmed and extended the information we had already received. This venerable gentleman was the late Mr Thomas Holden, solicitor and registrar of the County Court at Bolton; his friend, who led us to him, was the intelligent and obliging librarian of the Public Library—Mr J. K. Waite. The frank and cordial kindness of these gentlemen, to one who was an entire stranger to them, was alike creditable to themselves and the honourable municipality in which they both discharged important public functions. But what specially impressed them, as it did the searcher, was this—that he had entered the town a practical stranger, and, without speaking to a single human being, had unwittingly gone to the *one* man who, with his aged friend, was, of all its 100,000 inhabitants, best able to give him *all* the information he sought. That information was sufficient to destroy the specious deed."

When, at the close of the ejectment trial, defendants' counsel was handing over their imposing legal instrument, and other documents, with a view to a possible appeal, plaintiffs' counsel calmly intimated his intention of asking a few questions about it first. Whereupon it was eagerly snatched back, and disappeared in the black bag for evermore. The other document, which was of a still more serious and audacious kind, met with a similar fate. In it, the defendants professed and set forth that they had been duly appointed trustees according to the statute 13 and 14 Victoria, cap. 28, and that this had been done on 26th November 1883—eight days *after* the appointment of trustees by the Presbyterian congregation. It was a high-handed and somewhat perilous procedure, and deservedly proved disastrous for them. Yet, so strange are feudal ways, that, despite the decision of the civil court, that spurious deed stands " duly enrolled " amongst " the records of the Manor of Tottington " ! It might, therefore, reappear in some future generation or century and cause disturbance, should the legal proceedings of 1883-1885 ever happen to be lost sight of, as those of 1798, and the deeds of 1713, 1721, 1755, 1782, and 1811 had been. It has, therefore, been deemed advisable to insert a *verbatim* copy of it in this record, so that if it should ever again present itself, its spurious character may at once be recognised. (See Appendix C, p. 402.)

The Presbyterian Communion Rolls for the whole forty years of Dr MacLean's ministry were recovered just before the final trial. Beginning with the first year of his ministry in Dundee Chapel—1830—they are arranged thus : Minister, Elders, Deacons, Members. But no Minute Book of either congregation or schools has been discovered for that long period. There is, however, once more, *a single tell-tale leaf*, whose curious story must be briefly related. Soon after the minister had invited aid in unearthing old documents, of any kind, relating to Dundee Chapel, a faded and grease-stained leaf was put into his hands in 1884. He asked the kind donor where, when, and how it came into her possession. This was her answer: " I was getting groceries six or seven years since at Mr———'s [one of the ringleaders who had been in office], and I bought some candles. He wrapped a piece of paper round them, and when I got home and took the paper off, I happened to notice something about Dundee on it, and, instead of throwing it into the fire, and as I was in a hurry, I just pushed it into a drawer I keep private papers in, till I should have time to look at it, and thought no more about it till I heard what you said in the church. I then bethought me of it, and rummaged the drawer, and found it."

This "piece of paper" is actually *a leaf torn out of the Dundee Sunday-School Minute Book for 1849*. So strangely rescued from the oblivion which appears to have overtaken all its kith and kin during a period of forty years, it occupies precisely the middle point between the minutes of the closing year of Dr Brown's ministry at Dundee, in 1829, and those we already possessed of the last year of Dr MacLean's in St Andrew's Church in 1869. Alone it survives, like the weathered keystone of an ancient arch, telling plainly enough what had once existed, although now every stone but itself of the goodly structure has entirely disappeared. Here is its first page, which shows, clearly enough, the relationship of Dundee School to St Andrew's Church.

December 2nd, 1849.—At a meeting held in St Andrew's Church this evening, Rev. A. MacLean in the chair, it was considered requisite, to further the interests of the Sabbath-school, that a superintendent should be elected to fill the place of Mr Robert Haworth, who resigns on account of not being able to attend, from the distance of his place of residence. Mr MacLean recommended Mr Lawrence Stead as the person most fit amongst the present number of teachers, which was unanimously approved of by the meeting. After the announcement was made to Mr Stead, he expressed his sense of the honour conferred upon him by his brother teachers in being appointed to fill the office. It was also unanimously resolved that Miss Noel be teacher in the class lately occupied by Ann Brown, and that she be assisted by one of the Misses Kay when not able to attend.

The *second* page is as follows:—

December 16th, 1849.—Mr Robert Kay proposed that Mr Alexander Brown take the class vacant by the promotion of Mr Stead, and that Mr Thomas Whittle take the alphabet class. Seconded by Mr J. Schofield. Carried unanimously. Mr P. Makin proposed that a tea-party be held in Dundee School on Tuesday, January 1st, 1849; [evidently a mistake for *1850*] that the price of tickets be as usual—viz., 1s. and 9d.; that the following persons form a committee of management: Messrs James Greenhalgh, Robert Kay, James Duckworth, John Schofield, and John Mossop, and Misses Sarah Hamer, Elizabeth Bridge, and Elizabeth Wolstenholme; that the following persons sell tickets: Mr L. Stead, Mr Peter Makin, Mr Richard Hunt, and Mr James Brown. The motion, seconded by Mr Henry Stead, was carried unanimously.

December 30th, 1849.—Lawrence Stead to provide lamps for the tea-party. It was unanimously resolved that the musicians attending the tea-party should receive the price of their tickets to the number of 12.

The young Steads, of these minutes, educated in the classes connected with Dundee Chapel and St Andrew's Church, to which their parents belonged, formed in 1854 the firm of Messrs Lawrence Stead & Brother, which for nearly forty years did much for Ramsbottom (p. 148, *supra*). The partners were both trustees of St Andrew's (Dundee) Presbyterian Church, and Mr Henry was for many years, up to his last illness, congregational treasurer. Mr Robert Haworth, though resident at a distance, continued a loved and honoured elder to the end of his life—some years ago.

The final judgment in the Dundee litigation was delivered on the trial of the suit for ejectment. It was given by Mr Justice A. L. Smith, at the Assizes at Liverpool in May 1885. It is thus reported in the 'Bury Times':—

His lordship, in giving his decision, said it was true, as had been pointed out by Dr Pankhurst, that the defendants were in possession; therefore the plaintiffs must make title in order for him to give judgment on their behalf. It seemed to him the question was whether or not the plaintiffs could show that they brought themselves within the position of Sir Morton Peto's Act, or, in other words, whether they were a congregation that had acquired property as a meeting-house.

Mr Robert Haworth.

Those words would do, because a manse came within the same category. It was strenuously urged that they were not a congregation in the meaning of the section, but that they were, first, Dissenters; secondly, Scotch Presbyterians; and thirdly, in order of date, English Presbyterians; and if so, that this would not suffice, and that they could not have acquired the property as a congregation. In the first case which was quoted, the decision was that Wesleyans would not come within the meaning of "congregation" in the Act,[1] but in this case he had clear

---

[1] In the Wesleyan Church the property is vested in the "Legal Hundred." This fact, according to the decision referred to, prevents a

and definite evidence that each Presbyterian congregation held its own property and had complete control over it, and that what authority the Synod held related to spiritual matters. As a matter of fact, it seemed that Dr Pankhurst was right in saying that in 1811 Dundee Chapel, and, if they liked, the manse with it, was not used as a Presbyterian establishment; the surrender and admittance of 1811 recited that it was among other things for the "benefit of a pious, preaching, Dissenting minister," and the true meaning of a Dissenting minister was

---

Wesleyan congregation from coming "within the meaning of *congregation*" in Sir Morton Peto's Act. The trustees of St Andrew's Congregation had proceeded under that Act; and Dr Pankhurst argued that the Synod stood related to the Presbyterian congregations as the Legal Hundred did to Wesleyan congregations, and that, therefore, St Andrew's Congregation too was beyond the scope of the Peto Act. To this it was answered—"Our churches are not held by the Synod, but by trustees appointed by the members of the individual congregations, in their respective localities." Ultimately, he asked, "Can you *sell* a church without the sanction of the Synod?" We answered, "No; not if the Model Trust has been executed. But in *this* case the Model Trust has *not* been executed." This trial took place in St George's Hall, Liverpool, on the Monday after the meeting of Synod in 1885. One position taken up by Dr Pankhurst—counsel for the Independents—was that the *Book of Order*, which we had scrupulously followed, was not authoritative. He asked, "Are you aware that it was declared in the Synod last Friday that the Book of Order is not authoritative and binding?" It was answered, "No. It bears the formal *imprimatur* of the Synod on its front page [to which his lordship turned]. It was prepared by its instructions, and formally adopted by it, as useful in maintaining uniformity of procedure. Moreover, its use was formally recommended in all the Church courts and congregations. We accepted the book thus recommended by the supreme court of our Church, and have loyally and scrupulously followed its provisions. But the Book of Order did not create the administrative rules of the Church. It simply embodied substantially its immemorial consuetudinary practice; and if the Book of Order had never existed our procedure in this case would have been *substantially* the same." Counsel read, apparently from a newspaper, what might be a statement by some member of Synod, which was, of course, to be distinguished from a *resolution* of Synod, and it was replied—"Even a resolution of Synod last week could not affect our procedure eighteen months ago." The learned doctor failed in his contention. It was found, all through the different courts, that scrupulous adherence to the Book of Order—"*that book of Levi's*," as it was often called—proved wise and successful.

not that he was a Presbyterian.[1] In 1811 Dundee Chapel was used for dissenting purposes, and the old lady had given some very accurate evidence, if he might be permitted to say so, though he could not act on it— evidence on hearsay from persons who knew the place before. But to say that a lady could sixty or seventy years afterwards tell what doctrines a clergyman preached when she was between the ages of one and eight was evidence he could not act upon.[2] But he had it that, from 1817 down to 1883, when the schism took place, he had a strong cogent body of documentary evidence that the church was used for Presbyterian purposes —whether Scotch or English; it seemed to him all the same, because, as Mr Elliot said, there was no real distinction.[3] A document had been put in dated 1868, calling it St Andrew's Church of Scotland, which meant Presbyterian Church. He could not look at the records from 1817 downwards without saying that the Presbyterian religion had been carried on more or less in Dundee Chapel by Presbyterian clergymen with a Presbyterian congregation. Therefore he was of opinion that it was a congregation that would come within the meaning of the term "congregation" in Sir Morton Peto's Act. And it was proved that some time, probably in 1817, and certainly before Sir Morton Peto's Act was passed, the congregation had acquired the building for the purpose of a Presbyterian community. It was urged that the Dundee Chapel was always a peculiar of the peculiar—viz., it had jurisdiction of its own, and was never under St Andrew's, new or old; he could not find this as a matter of fact.

---

[1] Though a Presbyterian minister would certainly not be likely to so describe himself, yet the law of England renders such a description not inaccurate. But, as the *older deeds, discovered since the trial*, show, these words—"pious, preaching, Dissenting minister"—in *this* case, were an *interpolation*. They *do not exist* in the earlier deeds. See pp. 235-237, *supra*.

[2] The defendants put an aged lady into the witness-box to state that Mr Nelson was a Unitarian. The sermon published in 1814 by this minister, and discovered by the writer *since* the trial (see p. 247, *supra*), shows that this evidence as to doctrine was *erroneous*. Mr Nelson, the "clergyman" referred to, was a licentiate of the Presbytery of Edinburgh.

[3] Early in the trial his lordship asked—"What is the difference, Mr Elliot, between the Presbyterian Churches?" He answered—"All the Presbyterian Churches, my lord, are substantially the same." His lordship—"Yes. I suppose there is no other Church in which the eldership occupies the position that it holds in the Presbyterian Church?" He answered—"That is so, my lord."

Turning to the records, which had not been impugned, and were therefore accurate statements, he found that in 1817 reference was made to the "minutes of the session of the Presbyterian congregation, Dundee Chapel;" in 1819, the "elders" met (meaning of course elders of the Scotch Church); and in 1822 there was an important entry in regard to the school, to the effect that it was "very desirable, both for the good of the congregation of Dundee Chapel and of the neighbourhood at large, that a Sunday-school be established in immediate connection with the chapel." This was not the only evidence, because in 1823 there was another entry to the same effect, it being proposed to "establish a Sunday-school in the chapel;" and Mr William Grant gave consent to the establishment of a Sunday-school in connection with the church. Trustees were appointed for the school set up in conjunction with Dundee chapel, and then reference was made to a committee of management of secular affairs "belonging to this chapel and Sabbath-school." After the building of the church in 1834 by Mr William Grant the children were taken Sunday by Sunday from the school to the Presbyterian Church. This went on uninterruptedly, and he thought it was true that the school was not interfered with, because it went on in perfect harmony with the clergymen. It went on until 1869, when the benefactor, Mr William Grant, died, and his nephew, reigning in his shoes, and not being a Scotchman or a Presbyterian, thought he would like to get these Scotchmen and Presbyterians out of the church. No doubt he took legal advice, and inasmuch as they had no title Mr William Grant, being heir-at-law, got an ejectment.[1] He did not get an ejectment for the school and manse, because there would have been the difficulty of the surrender of 1811 and the occupation since. Immediately the Presbyterians were turned out of the church the Dundee school went on exactly as before the church was built, Sunday-school being held, and other services also—for the best of all reasons, that they had got nowhere else to hold them. This went on until 1873, when another St Andrew's Church was built; the school then went on as before, and the children went to church. He had to ask himself whether,

---

[1] That ejectment from St Andrew's Church was effected simply by force (see pp. 298-301, *supra*). His lordship, however, did not know this. There had been no special need to acquaint him with the *modus operandi*. William Grant, "the benefactor," died in 1842. His nephew took the church in 1869.

at any rate down to 1873—he would say to 1883, because nothing had transpired up to then to sever the continuity which was going on—whether, by the use and occupation of Dundee School under the circumstances which he had narrated, the congregation had been a congregation using the school and manse together for the purposes of their community. It seemed to him it was a "congregation" from first to last. Then in 1883 the schism took place. In that year one gentleman was said to have slandered Mr Elliot, and an inquiry was held, the persons in authority determining in favour of Mr Elliot.[1] A considerable portion of the congregation, which up to that time had kept harmoniously together, broke off, and he had some letters put in showing the different periods at which they broke off with the congregation. But having broken off they said, "We will still adhere to Dundee, and although we are the schismists we will not allow the congregation to hold Dundee Chapel," which was part and parcel of the holding of the community before. Those who were not schismists looked about to see what their title was, and then they unearthed the surrender of 1811 for the first time. No document had come to light since that, and as the board of trustees were dead, not knowing how to make title to the land which they said was theirs—and which he thought was theirs—they brought in the aid of Sir Morton Peto's Act, got a document drawn which was put in evidence, and which, if they had been one congregation and came within the Act, was a thing which would place the plaintiffs in that record. Defendants then got a document of their own and got themselves under the Act. The present plaintiffs

---

[1] At the time referred to the defendants had for some time had control of the congregational finance, and had so clandestinely depressed the funds that they had not paid *one half* of what was due for stipend for 1882. After inquiry by the Presbytery of Manchester and the Synod, the latter made a special grant of £100. Month after month passed, and no balance-sheet was forthcoming for 1882, and the "gentleman" referred to by his lordship told the young men at the Sunday-school, in the minister's absence, that the delay was caused by the minister wanting to keep back £100 from the desiderated statement of accounts. The minister had nothing whatever to do with the matter. It was entirely in their own hands. But he had been instrumental in securing the grant, which, in part, *supplied their strange deficiencies*, and *frustrated sinister designs*.

had a good title to this land, and he gave judgment for them with costs. There was also the point of *estoppel*, which would go to the Court of Appeal; he did not declare on that, but left it open. Plaintiffs had got one good thing, which was quite sufficient.

Dr PANKHURST asked for the stay of execution.

HIS LORDSHIP—Give notice within a week.

It was ordered that the books connected with Dundee Chapel should be given up.

We may here add that the old hymn-paper (p. 321, *supra*) was an object of marked interest to the distinguished judge before whom the suit was tried. Having carefully examined the antique and faded thing, and asked a few questions as to how and where it was discovered, he laid it on the bench at his side, and, as the trial went on, lifted it once and again, as he also did the inscribed communion cup of much more recent date, which one of the defendants had been compelled previously to deliver up, and asked, as the learned counsel for the Independents proceeded with his argument—"But what do you say to *this?*" quoting a few words from the heading of the hymn-paper, or the inscription on the cup; and these questions demolished forthwith the eloquent contention.

His lordship's judgment was put in force by writ of possession executed on Tuesday the 26th of May 1885.

At the appointed time the two solicitors and the sheriff's officer, with the minister of Dundee congregation and another trustee for the plaintiffs, went to old Dundee Chapel. They found there two of the defendants. The *personnel* of the day school had by this time been transferred to the still unfinished Independent premises farther down the lane. In the old sanctuary were displayed day and Sunday school apparatus, books, banners, &c., which, with the chapel, manse, and garden, were now to be formally restored, by the representative of the sheriff, to the minister and people of St Andrew's Presbyterian (Dundee) Congregation.

With a number of smaller ones, there were *three large banners*, each marking a distinct period in the history of the congregation. The *first* of these belonged to the old St Andrew's Church period, and was, we think, inscribed thus: " St Andrew's Church Sabbath-School, Ramsbottom." The *second* marked the interregnum (1869-1873) between the old St Andrew's and the new—the memorable time when, after the seizure of their church in 1869, the people worshipped again for about four years in Dundee Chapel. It is inscribed thus: " St Andrew's E. P. Sunday-school, Ramsbottom." The *third* belongs to the new St Andrew's Church period, and was purchased at a cost of about thirty-five guineas a few years after the writer's induction. One side of it bears a representation of Christ blessing the children, with " St Andrew's Presbyterian Church " inscribed above, and " Suffer little children to come unto Me " below; and the other, a picture of the new church, with the following inscription: " St Andrew's Presbyterian Church, Dundee, Sunday-School, Ramsbottom." When the writ of possession was executed in 1885, the *first* of these banners was not given up. It was not missed till the multifarious articles were gone over again later on the same day. We then applied to the solicitor of the Independents, who, after communicating with his clients, informed the trustees that they said "all the property had been given up." That well-known banner, however, has yet to be found. There is, moreover, an important set of books "in connection with St Andrew's Presbyterian Church, Ramsbottom," which, in violation of the decision of the judge and the writ of possession, has not yet been delivered up. The *second* of these large banners—like the first, of blue silk—and which bore the words "St Andrew's E. P. Church Sunday-School, Ramsbottom," was tampered with. The words were altered to "*Dundee Chapel* Sunday-School, Ramsbottom," and this banner, so altered, was carried at the head of their Whit-week procession in 1884. When the day of reckoning came, and the diversified property seized by them had to be given up, the original inscription had not been restored, but, to keen eyes, there is distinctly legible still, "St Andrew's E. P. Church" under the elaborately gilded "Dundee Chapel" of the Independents.

The minister, having examined the books, asked for the Sunday-School Minute Book[1] which was in use in 1883, when the place was seized, and which, he said, did not appear to be amongst those presented. "Oh yes, it is," said one of the defendants, stepping forward and picking out one of the books; "that's it." The minister examined it carefully and said, "It's like it, but it's *not the book.*" He was referred to the minutes in proof of its genuineness. These, he admitted, might be accurate, and they were written by the same hand,

---

[1] It was known that that minute book contained minutes sufficient to determine the case. We give one extract. It is a resolution passed at a meeting of "the teachers and superintendents," at Dundee, on 9th October 1881, at which a majority of the defendants were present, and over which the present minister presided. Some of these men were office-bearers in the church as well as teachers, &c., in the Sunday-school. Here it is—"That in consequence of the increasing requirements of the school and the inconvenience of teaching, arising from overcrowding, *we respectfully request the managers* to take into consideration the advisability of meeting this obstacle to the comfort of teachers and taught *by allowing the school to add to the available space* in the erection of additional vestry accommodation." This came duly before the managers' court of the church.

that of one of the two defendants present; but, notwithstanding that, he said, "It is not the original, and I want the *original book.*" The gentleman who was then acting as their solicitor interposed at this point, and, examining the book, asked—"What is wrong with it, Mr Elliot? Aren't the minutes right?" He said—"They *appear* to be, and to extend to the proper date, and are in the same handwriting, but *they are not the original minutes; that is not* the original book." The solicitor then turned to his clients, whose faces by this time betokened much, and asked—

"Is there *another* book?"

After slight hesitation, one of the defendants said, "Yes."

Solicitor—"How long will it take you to get it?"

Defendant—"About ten minutes."

Solicitor—"Then go and bring it *at once.*"

He went forthwith. His friends, who were outside, and who on his exit so soon disappeared, will not forget his going; nor will others who were present on the memorable occasion and saw him. The counterfeit minutes were in his handwriting. He soon returned with the *original book*. When it was examined, it was found, as they admitted, that the defendants *had written their minutes,* while in wrongful possession of Dundee Chapel, *in the original minute book*, and now their own record of their strange doings was in the trustees' hands! It is not often that men are so completely delivered into the hands of those whom they have, without cause, persistently wronged. The two defendants present confessed that the counterfeit book had been prepared and put forward to *prevent their opponents from seeing* what was contained in their minutes. Now that these minutes were in possession of the trustees, they asked that they might be permitted to take a copy of them. This, it was said, they should, at any reasonable time, be allowed to do. Their great anxiety, however, was to get back the record of their doings, which, so strangely and unexpectedly, had fallen into other hands. Their conduct, however, had not been such as readily to suggest much in the way of forbearance and consideration. Yet, bad as the conduct of these younger men had been—and truly it was deplorable and perilous enough—still there were behind them much older men, who, though now absent when the property they had profanely seized was being restored, had yet even a graver and more unenviable responsibility. But, losing sight altogether of the question of desert, that these men, younger and older alike, might know that those whom they had wronged could still treat them with generosity, notwithstanding all they had done, the solicitors were allowed by the trustees present to cut out the section of the minute book containing the desiderated minutes, on condition that they stamped and attested the transaction across the mutilated portion of the book. This, to the great relief of the defendants, was done; and at this moment the minute book is before the writer, stamped and dated "26th May 1885," and bearing, written across a fragment of 1883 minute and the clean page beyond, the signatures of the respective solicitors.

When, after the varied effects in the premises had, so far as practicable, been inventoried, and the defendants, after so long a process, been at length turned out, and doors and gates closed, the representative of the sheriff handed over the keys to the minister of St Andrew's Presbyterian (Dundee) Congregation, who, as it happened, was standing at the moment on the very spot where, nineteen months before, his entrance had been rudely obstructed by the chief defendants and their sadly deluded followers.

On the following Monday, cleansed and beautified, the old chapel was reopened, and St Andrew's Presbyterian (Dundee) British School still continues in the venerable structure, to contribute its part to the educational advancement of the town of Ramsbottom. The Dundee Sunday-school, since the seizure of Dundee Chapel in October 1883, has been, with convenience and advantage, conducted in the new St Andrew's Church.

During the autumn of 1890, the congregation once more worshipped for some time in Dundee Chapel, while the new St Andrew's was being internally decorated and its organ chamber furnished with an organ. The late Bishop of Manchester once remarked, in passing, that the new St Andrew's appeared to be one of the finest churches in his diocese. Such as it is, by the generous aid of many friends, it is the new home of the old Dundee congregation, "formerly called by the name of 'Mr Pendlebury's,'" and which has known so many vicissitudes. The new organ is worthy of the church, and a fitting enhancement of its service of praise. That service is led by a voluntary choir, which, in song-gifted and music-loving Rossendale, as well as beyond its limits, has, in choir contests, gained many prizes. It has been well and harmoniously conducted for over twenty years by Mr Robert Sharples.

The congregation, as the foregoing record reveals, stands, one fain would hope, unique in respect of the *number and variety of ejectments* that bestud its history. The Rev. Henry Pendlebury was ejected from his church and house in 1662, and the Five-Mile Act sent him forth a second time from his home

St Andrew's (Dundee) Presbyterian Church Choir

in 1665; the attempt to annex Dundee property to Park Independent Chapel in 1798 ultimately failed; the Rev. Peter Ramsay was forcibly extruded from Dundee Chapel in 1811; the Rev. George Brown, M.A., was virtually ejected in 1829; the Rev. Dr Andrew MacLean and Dundee congregation were, by force, deprived of St Andrew's Church and endowment in 1869; while the present minister and his people were, by force, barred out of old Dundee Chapel in 1883, and the old manse in 1884. In the last case—that of Dundee Chapel and manse —the evil-doers were promptly and righteously resisted, and, with exemplary costs, compelled by the majesty of British law to restore the property to its lawful owners—a just, and it may be hoped final, ejectment.

In drawing this record to a close, the mind instinctively reverts to bygone times, and we may be pardoned for our people's sake for briefly referring to once familiar forms which have passed away since the new St Andrew's Church was opened. One thinks of such respected and well-remembered names as Mr and Mrs Strong, Mr Robert Haworth, Mr Samuel Wilson, Mr William Vause, Mr and Mrs William Stead, Mr and Mrs William Wild, Mrs William Markland, and Mr Arthur Bentley. One also

MR JOHN ROE.

remembers and reveres the name of Barbara Salmon, who began to work before she was six, and worked till shortly before her death at sixty-six, in 1884. A devoted Sunday-school teacher, she wrote a hymn for the Dundee S.-S. festival about 1850. Its first verse is—

> "O list to the sound of St Andrew's bell,
> While it sends out its peal through this beautiful dell!
> Inviting poor children to school for to come,
> To learn there the safe way to Heaven's sweet home!
> Home, home, sweet, sweet home!
> To learn there the safe way to Heaven's sweet home!"

One of Barbara's last acts was to set apart a sovereign from her little store towards the expenses incurred in recovering the old property at "Dundee," with which she had so long been lovingly and loyally connected.

Of venerable mothers, whose reminiscences stretched back to the early decades of the century, such names as Mrs Gray, Mrs Murray, Mrs Whittle, Mrs Crompton, and Mrs Haslam readily occur. Nor may one forget the old friend and true, Mr John Roe, who for nearly forty years occupied a responsible post in the Square, under the Grants, and whose facile utterance and singularly accurate recollection of long past events continued till his decease in his 85th year. One thinks also of another who, though long little seen in public, was yet well known, and who bore a great affliction for wellnigh forty years with a quiet manly fortitude which never murmured, and a cheery humour-veined geniality of spirit which never grew sour—Mr Joseph Stead.

Of those mentioned one fain would say more, especially of one happy pair—genial, generous, hospitable—who, a few

years apart, passed away in the full vigour of their days—
viz., Mr and Mrs William Stead. William, like his brothers
(p. 357, *supra*), was all his life connected with St Andrew's
(Dundee) Congregation, and for many years acted most
efficiently as Sunday-school treasurer (p. 316, *supra*), while,
also like his brothers and their families, he and Mrs William
Stead (*née* Diggle) were both generous contributors towards the building fund of the new St Andrew's Church. Nor have their two surviving daughters, though resident at some distance, forgotten their early ecclesiastical home. But space forbids. Two only may be selected—both born before the close of the eighteenth century—Mr Joseph Strong and Mrs Gray. Mr Strong—*i.e.*, Strang, Anglicized—when a young man, came to manage the farming operations of the Grants. He had distinguished himself before that time as a young farmer, and been awarded the silver medal of the Highland and Agricultural Society of Scotland in 1823. He was long an honoured

Mr William Stead.

elder of St Andrew's Church. There was a fine mellowed fragrance of Scripture in his conversation, and a singularly chastened richness in his prayers. His last illness, which was about his only one, was somewhat protracted. We spent many interesting hours with him. Referring one day to the perfect provision God had freely made for men in the life and atoning death and resurrection of His Son, he said "Oh, it's a grand truth that! How comforting it is! That is indeed a *gospel* to poor sinners. Yes, that's it—one can rest there." And again, "I can never get away from that word "complete;" my thoughts wander, but I always come back to that—I am "complete *in Him*, complete in Jesus." On another occasion, he said, "I could wish to get away home if it were the Lord's will. It's not for me to dictate,—'All the days of my appointed time will I wait till my change come.' I'm often at a dead stand for a word in my devotions, but He knows my weakness and infirmity, and He will never leave us nor forsake us." Afterwards he repeated the verses beginning—

"I'm not ashamed to own my Lord."

The cough interrupted the closing lines—

"And in the new Jerusalem
Appoint my soul a place."

But before we left, he remarked, "They don't know themselves who have a high opinion of themselves—dust and ashes; even 'our righteousnesses are as filthy rags.'" His last words to us were these—"I cannot think of anything but the *atonement* now; without that what would you have? Nothing—nothing—nothing!" He died on 6th February 1877, in the old manse at Dundee.

Mrs Gray lived for nearly sixty years in the house facing what is still familiarly known, from her husband's name, as "John Gray's lodge." To deep warm motherliness she united great force and decision of character. She never thought of herself when she saw another in danger; but, as the first note of alarm found her, rushed straight to the rescue. On such occasions about the lodge, the cry was always for "Mrs Gray!" And it was no uncommon thing for children to get into the lodge in those days, for the present protecting wall had not then been erected.

A few years before her death a grandson of her own was drowned in another lodge. He had slipped down the abrupt embankment, and was found standing with soldier-like erectness at its base, with the little pitcher he had been carrying still held in his hand at his side.

Mr Joseph Strong.

It was about this time that, one day, we heard all unexpectedly from her own lips a memorable description of one of her rescues. Reference had been made to a group of young men, who, on that occasion, had stood on the bank looking on while she rescued a drowning child. One of her daughters remarked—"Ye *were hard* on these men though, mother!" The wrinkled eyelids went apart, and something of the old indignation glinted in her eyes, as in the forcible vernacular, and with an unconscious reference to one of the farming operations of her early home, after an absence of more than fifty years—she said—"*Hard* on them? *Hoo* could I help?" Then, turning to us, she proceeded thus—"There was I, wet to the neck an' dreepin' like a dippit sheep, wi' the half-droon'd bairn i' my airm, an' them stan'in' starin' at me wi' their senseless een. They made the excuse that they were gaun to their work and didna want to get wet. I *was* maybe raither hard on the lads, but *hoo* could I *miss?* I said, 'Ye great cooardly lubbards, wad 'e let a bairn droon raither than weet yer feet? Ye're no fit to be ca'ed men. Get oot o' ma sicht, ye great hertless ceephers, and *keep yer feet dry!*' I felt in my hert I could hae dookit them! I ran straight into the hoose here. Fortinately I had juist been in time, and wi' proper care the bit bairn was sune a' richt again."

MRS GRAY.

Another rescue, related to the writer by one who, as a boy, witnessed it forty years ago, was effected thus:—A child had fallen in just at the inlet, and was being quickly carried into the deeper part of the lodge by the stream, which was in vigorous flow. The mother, who was on the bank, screamed frantically, but seemed limp and helpless with terror. Presently Mrs Gray was seen rushing from her house, and making straight as an arrow, and as noiselessly, towards the drowning child. Two of her daughters, who fortunately were at hand, and divined her purpose in a moment, followed in her wake. The elder seized the skirt of her mother's dress and plunged in after her, holding on at arm's length, and the younger followed, holding similarly by the skirt of her sister. The little one was already beyond Mrs Gray's depth, and she could not swim. But the eager play of her outstretched hands and the buoyancy of her dress sustained her, until happily she seized the child as it rose to the surface, and it was saved. The child is now a man in middle life, and recently he visited the place of the memorable rescue of his childhood, but, by that time, the old arm-chair was empty in the home across whose threshold the brave and motherly woman had sped, so long ago, to snatch him from a watery grave.

There was always great gentleness and an impressive lowliness about Mrs Gray when speaking of divine things, while the fine old Saxon of her early years welled up with singular force and fluency, when, as in the above case, any strong emotion moved her. The great Gift and the precious promises of the old Book were her comfort and her stay. The last words she uttered were beautifully characteristic, "I've no money to leave you, but there's something *better* than money—love God and keep His commandments!" And having bequeathed this last and loving legacy—more precious than silver and gold to her children and her children's children—the brave and venerable pilgrim, in her 88th year, passed peacefully away. " The mountains shall depart and the hills be removed, but my kindness shall not depart from thee, nor the covenant of my peace be removed, saith the Lord that hath mercy upon thee."

Finally, of those called hence in the bloom of youth, we think of such as little Polly Stead, to whose childlike faith Christ was so real that she prayed that she might find her lost doll, and rejoiced in a speedy answer; of gentle Annie Birch, whose last words were—"I am going home;" (Appendix D., p. 404) and the late beloved secretary of our Sunday-school, gifted, untiring, systematic, and devoted —Walter Spencer, who, catching, too early for us, the

> "Murmurs and scents of the infinite sea,"

said, "I'm all right, papa—I'm all right," as he passed into the radiant realm beyond. But—

> "Death only grasps; to live is to pursue."
> While leaves are shed, the living tree remains.

Thus, in the good providence of God, preserved through shade and sunshine, storm and calm, this old Puritan tree still occupies its ancient place. And although, like the vine of the Sacred Psalter, there have been times when, unhappily, men have put forth unhallowed hands to spoil its beauty or destroy its fruitfulness, yet firmly rooted in the hill of Zion, and watered from fountains which no human hand can seal, it still bears fruit in old age; and while underneath its branches Christian youth rejoice, wearied pilgrims, refreshed by its clusters, continue to take heart of grace, and, through all surrounding shadows, undaunted, to toil on—on, till for them too, like the long line of their predecessors, "the day break and the shadows flee away"—

> "And with the morn those angel faces smile
> Which we have loved long since, and lost awhile."

CHAPTER V.

CONCLUSION.

PRESBYTERY stands in the vanguard of those forces that make for liberty and order in human society—the liberty that may not degenerate into licence, and the order that may not harden into oppression. David Hume, the historian, whom no one will suspect of Puritanic proclivities, says—"So absolute was the authority of the Crown, that the precious spark of liberty had been kindled and was preserved by the Puritans alone; and it was to this sect that the English owe the whole freedom of their constitution." We stand on the old lines—the imperishable principles of Puritan and apostolic times; those principles which, *rightly understood* and *fairly applied*, are at once the foe of licence and anarchy, and of every species of oppression. Presbytery absorbs and honours, applies and maintains, with perhaps greater fulness and more even balance than any other ecclesiastical system, the wise and benign apostolic *dictum*, given for all time, suited to all nations—"Honour all men, love the brotherhood, fear God, honour the king." Its essential agreement with the vital representative genius of Anglo-Saxon institutions, not only industrial, social, philanthropic, and municipal, but also parliamentary, is very marked. Indeed, what Anglo-

Saxon England has elaborated in her most characteristic institutions, civil and political, through centuries of ardent liberty-loving toil, the English Presbyterian Church, which is likewise Anglo-Saxon, has supplied by her polity within the ecclesiastical domain—a polity whose life-blood is liberty, whose action is order, whose method is popular representation; and which, against oppression, has been preserved to us by our fathers through blood and exile, toil and want, and tears. The sacred and the secular have thus kindred governing forces. The principles are homogeneous—in both cases representative and democratic. Their spheres of action are at once distinct, co-ordinate, and complemental—the State in the one case, the Church in the other. Presbytery, in its cardinal principle of democratic representation, answers, in the Church, to the recently conceded democratic enfranchisement in the State. Of all ecclesiastical systems, therefore, it stands pre-eminently the most English and democratic, as opposed to all that is feudal and privileged, inequitable and oligarchic. Moreover, it was elaborated from Holy Writ, on historic English soil, by distinguished English divines, and promulgated by an illustrious English Parliament.

Here we may add, as has sometimes been remarked, that it is not difficult to find in the British Parliament the analogue, in the political sphere, of the General Assembly of the Presbyterian Church. Unfortunately, however, for both this country and her statesmen, the political instrument has worked, hitherto, denuded of those subordinate members of a fully equipped system represented in the Presbyterian polity by Provincial Synods, District Presbyteries, &c. One inevitable effect of this, especially in a rapidly expanding country, is an ever-increasing over-pressure of work heaped on the supreme assembly of the nation. The natural consequences appear in periodic fag of both brain and muscle of its most faithful members; liability to slip-slop or helter-skelter legislative and executive action; and occasional dead-lock of the old Temple Bar 'bus description. A Naysmith hammer is admirably adapted for forging ordnance or armour for ironclads, but a much humbler instrument is sufficient for cracking nuts. The Naysmith, skilfully handled and with plenty of time on its hands, can of course do it, but otherwise the ordnance and ironclads suffer for the lack of fitness and proportion in organic adjustment. Quite recently an important step has at length happily been taken in the way of instituting the political analogue of the Provincial Synod; and County Councils, with well-compacted organisation and clearly defined functions, may fittingly crack many of even the larger nuts—say the cocoa-nuts—on which the parliamentary Naysmith has hitherto unwisely expended its energies. But that imperial instrument, in the past, has had to bend its potent forces to even filberts and hazels, and the dignity of even County Councils ought not to be endangered by these. We need, therefore, in some form or other, the political analogue of the *third* member of the Presbyterian system—the District Presbytery; and until that has been furnished the County Councils will not work either so sweetly or effectively as it is necessary for the wellbeing of the community they should.

He to whom we are mainly indebted for County Councils, the Right Hon. C. T. Ritchie, President of the Local Government Board, was no doubt well acquainted with the Presbyterian system of government. It is to be hoped he will not stay his hand until he has translated the lineaments of its *third* important member into the political domain. He may then, not unprofitably, contemplate the *fourth* — the Parish Session — with a view to establish something like its civil or political equivalent throughout these realms. We shall then possess a system—monarchico-democratic or democratico-monarchic—so simple and broad-based, penetrative and effective, that, wisely and intelligently worked, many of the evils which have hampered and harassed the imperial Parliament for generations will soon disappear. Moreover, while, in an adequate and inexpensive way, the smallest local wants would be promptly met, all others, up to the weightiest imperial concerns, would be clearly and sufficiently provided for; and, withal, the Throne, august and inviolable, securely buffered at every point by responsible Ministers, would remain unaffected by the movements and changes inseparable from the expansion and progress of a great and many-peopled empire.

APPENDIX.

APPENDIX.

APPENDIX A.

New Testament Episcopacy and the Future of the Church of England.

ALL Presbyterian Churches, by whatever distinctive names they may be known, and whatever distinctive purpose in the providence of God their separate existence may have been called to promote, are substantially one—one in doctrine, discipline, worship, and government. Pauline and evangelical in doctrine; Scriptural, and therefore benign and impartial, in discipline; simple and apostolic in worship; representative and democratic in government. This, it is claimed, is simply the Presbytery or Episcopacy of the New Testament, where presbyter or elder and bishop are but different designations of the same ecclesiastical officer. Bishop Lightfoot[1] puts this beyond all question for his fellow churchmen when, adducing conclusive evidence, he says: "It is a fact, now generally recognised by theologians of all shades of opinion, that in the language of the New Testament the same officer in the Church is called indifferently 'bishop' ($\dot{\epsilon}\pi\dot{\iota}\sigma\kappa o\pi o s$) and 'elder' or presbyter ($\pi\rho\epsilon\sigma\beta\dot{\nu}\tau\epsilon\rho o s$). Again, he says: "The two are only different designations of the same office." The presbyters or elders were the bishops, and there was no superior order of bishops. Thus presbytery is simply New Testament episcopacy, and Apostolic episcopacy is simply presbytery. Ordination was not the act of a prelate, but of a presbytery; not the special function of one person claiming to be of a higher order and invested with higher authority than his brethren, but the common function of the bishops or presbyters in meeting assembled,

---

[1] 'Saint Paul's Epistle to the Philippians.' By J. B. Lightfoot, D.D., D.C.L., LL.D., Bishop of Durham, Honorary Fellow of Trinity College, Cambridge. Seventh edition. 1883.

led by their president or moderator, and laying on their hands with him. As St Paul tells us, it was "with the laying on of the hands of the presbytery," not the hands of a prelate; and his instruction to Titus was: "Ordain elders"—that is, presbyters or bishops—"in every city, as I gave thee charge." When the late Bishop of Manchester consecrated St Andrew's Church at Ramsbottom, near that city, he went out of his way to say that "he did not understand how any one could read such a letter as that of Paul to Timothy without seeing that Timothy was placed in Ephesus exactly—of course allowing for difference of time and circumstances—for the same purpose as he (the Bishop) was to-day in the diocese of Manchester. That the church at Ephesus was a Presbyterian organisation he could not conceive. The presbytery had their work to do, but it was perfectly plain that Timothy was placed in a position of higher authority than the presbytery. It was an episcopally constituted church, and though the Bible did not tell him that Churches otherwise organised were outside the pale of grace, yet he thanked God that they of the Church of England rested on that sure foundation of an episcopal organisation."

Now, as his lordship on that occasion was consecrating a Presbyterian church to prelatic purposes, he might, with Christian grace, have refrained from this polemic fling. But as he did not, we may fairly be permitted to refer, with no unfriendly feeling, to his statements, and to try, very briefly, to throw some light on what he said he "did not understand," and "could not conceive." He appeals to the New Testament. We rejoice to have this goodly common ground; on that we are prepared to stand or fall. The Bishop's utterance raises two questions: (1) Was Timothy, like his lordship of Manchester, a prelatic bishop or a Presbyterian bishop? (2) Was the Church at Ephesus a prelatic or a Presbyterian organisation? This second point first. What do the Scriptures tell us? Read Acts xx.—Paul was on his way from Macedonia to Jerusalem. He was accompanied by his young disciple Timothy, and others, including Luke, the inspired writer of the Acts as well as the Gospel that bears his name. Luke says (Acts xx. 15), "We came to Miletus;" "and" (verse 17) "from Miletus he (Paul) sent to Ephesus, and called the elders (presbyters) of the church." St. Paul having thus the presbyters before him at the seaport, Miletus, he addressed them. Here is part of his ever memorable address (verse 28): "Take heed therefore unto yourselves, and to all the flock, over the which the Holy Ghost hath made you overseers (bishops), to feed the church of God which He hath purchased with His own blood." Now that word "overseers" ought to be "bishops." It is translated "bishops" everywhere else in the New Testament, and the Revised Version very properly corrects the error and removes the inconsistency. The prelatic translators, in the time of King James, did a great wrong to the English people by using the word "overseers" instead of "bishops" in this place. They did not deal fairly with the inspired text, and the ordinary readers of the English Bible have thus been prevented from seeing that the men at Ephesus, whom "the Holy Ghost had made bishops, to feed the church of God which He had purchased with His own blood," were just the elders or presbyters of that city. Yet the Bishop said "he could not conceive," precisely, what these Scriptures appear so plainly to teach—viz., "that the church at Ephesus was a presbyterian organisation." But next, Was Timothy a prelate? Did he belong to a higher order than the other bishops or presbyters at Ephesus? Had he authority to ordain, confirm, govern, adjudicate, legislate, &c., which his co-presbyters had not? The Bishop makes a general reference to the "letter of Paul to Timothy." Now, the prelatic conception about Timothy was the birth of a subsequent century. It was not known till generations after the "Pastoral Epistles" were written. We shall briefly support that affirmation, not by adducing Presbyterian testimony, but that of a distinguished prelate—the highest Anglican authority on the subject of the present century—Bishop Lightfoot. He says this: "It is the conception of a later age which represents Timothy as Bishop of Ephesus and Titus as Bishop of Crete." That may be deemed a fair and adequate answer to Bishop Fraser's "did not understand," &c. But while the Epistles to Timothy do not contain the prelatic conception, they do contain two simple statements which anybody may "understand." They tell us that Timothy was "ordained" "with the laying on of the hands of the presbytery" (1 Tim. iv. 14); and that Paul, who along with Barnabas had been ordained at Antioch, joined the other presbyters by the "laying on" of his own hands at the ordination of his young friend (2 Tim. 1. 6).

But we shall not confine ourselves to the restricted reference of Bishop Fraser.

Bishop Lightfoot says: "The duties of the presbyters were twofold.

They were both rulers and instructors of the congregation. This double function appears in St Paul's expression, 'pastors and teachers,' where, as the form of the original seems to show, the two words describe the same office under different aspects. . . . St Paul, where he gives directions relating to bishops or presbyters, insists specially on the faculty of teaching as a qualification for the position (1 Tim. iii. 2, Titus i. 9). In the one Epistle he directs that double honour shall be paid to those presbyters who have ruled well, but specially to such as 'labour in word and doctrine,' as though one holding this office might decline the work of instruction. In the other he closes the list of qualifications with the requirement that the bishop or presbyter hold fast the faithful word in accordance with the apostolic teaching, 'that he may be able both to exhort in the healthy doctrine and refute gainsayers,' &c. As each had his special gift, so would he devote himself more or less exclusively to the one or the other of these sacred functions."

He then says: "It is clear that at the close of the apostolic age the two lower orders of the threefold ministry were firmly established"—that is, deacons and "bishops or presbyters;" "but," he adds, "traces of the third and highest order, the episcopate properly so-called, are few and indistinct"—that is, the order of prelatic bishops. While, therefore, the deacon and Presbyterian bishop were firmly established at the close of the apostolic age, he frankly admits that "traces" even of the prelatic bishop —the bishop of the Church of England—"are few and indistinct." Are they really discernible? Let us see.

In the apostolic age there were what, for convenience' sake, we may call two wings of the Church — the Jewish and the Gentile. Well, what "traces" of the prelatic bishop does Dr Lightfoot find in either of these during the apostolic age? He very properly asserts that "the opinion hazarded by Theodoret," that those "who were first called apostles came afterwards to be called bishops, is baseless;" that, "in fact, the functions of the apostle and the bishop differed widely. The apostle, like the prophet or the evangelist, held no local office. He was essentially, as his name denotes, a missionary, moving about from place to place, founding and confirming new brotherhoods." "The true apostle bears this title as the messenger, the delegate of Christ Himself." He adds, "The episcopate was formed, not out of the apostolic order by localisation, but out of the presbyteral by elevation; and the title, which originally was common to all, came at length to be appropriated to the chief among them."

Now, what "traces" does he adduce of any "presbyter or bishop"—"the chief among them," that is, the president or moderator of a presbytery—undergoing this "elevation" into a prelatic bishop, during the apostolic age? First, in the Jewish wing. If his view of the origin of the prelatic order—"the episcopate properly so called"—"be true," he says, "we might expect to find in the mother Church of Jerusalem the first traces of this developed form of the ministry. Nor is this expectation disappointed. James, the Lord's brother, alone, within the period compassed by the apostolic writings, can claim to be regarded as a bishop in the later and more special sense of the term." Well, what are the "traces" of "elevation" on which this claim rests? They are these:—

(1) James's name stands first of the three in Galatians ii. 9, where Paul says, "And when James, Cephas, and John, who seemed to be pillars, perceived the grace that was given unto me, they gave to me and Barnabas the right hands of fellowship; that we should go unto the heathen, and they unto the circumcision."

(2) "In St. Luke's narrative James appears as the local representative of the brotherhood in Jerusalem, presiding at the congress (synod), whose decision he suggests, and whose decree he appears to have framed (Acts xv. 13 *et seq.*), receiving the missionary preachers as they revisit the mother Church (Acts xxi. 18, xii. 17; see also Gal. i. 19, ii. 12), acting generally as the referee in communications with foreign brotherhoods." And—

(3) "On the other hand, though specially prominent, he appears in the Acts as a member of a body." "If in some passages St James is named by himself, in others he is omitted, and the presbyters alone are mentioned (Acts xii. 17, xxi. 18, xi. 30; compare xv. 4, 23; xvi. 4). From this it may be inferred that, though holding a position superior to the rest, he was still considered as a member of the presbytery,—that he was, in fact the head or president of the college. What power this presidency conferred, how far it was recognised as an independent official position, and to what degree it was due to the ascendancy of his personal gifts, are questions which, in the absence of direct information, can only be answered by conjecture. But his close relationship with the Lord, his rare energy of character, and his rigid sanctity of life, which won the respect even of

the unconverted Jews, would react upon his office, and may perhaps have elevated it to a level which was not definitely contemplated in its origin."

Now, inferring, as the Bishop very properly says we may, that James was "still a member of the presbytery"—"in fact," its "president" or moderator—where, in all that he adduces, is there any trace of his "elevation" from the Presbyterian episcopate to the prelatic? Which, or what combination, of the facts produced raised him from a presbyter to a prelate? As president or moderator, his official action in all the cases referred to was simply ministerial, not magisterial; presidential, not prelatical. He, like presidents or moderators still, was *primus inter pares*—first among equals—but there was nothing he did in his official capacity which could not be done by any other moderator, although lacking "his close relationship with the Lord," and something of "his rare energy of character" and "rigid sanctity of life." Even if it be granted that these personal considerations might very fittingly lead to frequent or protracted occupancy of the moderator's chair, yet still he acted not as a prelate, but as a gifted and influential member of the presbytery, whose representative and official mouthpiece he was on the occasions referred to – not its master, any more than the Speaker of the House of Commons is master of that assembly. Thus, instead of finding "traces," even "few and indistinct," of the first episcopal prelate "in the mother Church at Jerusalem," Dr Lightfoot furnishes admirable proofs of the first Presbyterian president or moderator.

This appears to be plain enough from the inspired record to which the Bishop refers (Acts xv.) The delegates—including Paul and Barnabas—from Antioch "were received of the church, and of the apostles and elders, and they declared all things that God had done with them. But there rose up certain of the sect of the Pharisees which believed, saying, "That it was needful to circumcise them, and to command them to keep the law of Moses" (xv. 4, 5). This required prompt attention. Accordingly (ver. 6), "the apostles and elders together came for to consider of this matter. And when there had been much disputing" (no doubt to elicit all the facts and bearings of the case), Peter and Paul and Barnabas were heard. Then James — the president or moderator—in summing up, appealed directly to the supreme authority of Holy Scripture —the Lord's will—and very aptly pointed out that Hebrew prediction foretold the Gentile conversion reported by the apostolic missionaries present, and therefore his "judgment" was—that as God, in accordance with His gracious design, had gathered the Gentile as well as the Jew within the fold of the Church, Gentile liberty ought not to be violated by the imposition of a purely Jewish rite. Thus admirably, by simply interpreting the divine will, not by imposing his own, he conciliated the Christian Jew on the one hand, and recognised the Christian liberty of the Gentile on the other. Accordingly, to this the members of "congress" —or better, "synod"—at once agreed, just as a wise and conclusive utterance, in analogous circumstances, by a moderator of Synod now, is met usually with "Agreed! agreed!" from its members.

Moreover, as this was a constitutional matter, and therefore of great importance, very properly the concurrence of the general membership of the Church was likewise obtained. With this all that follows is in perfect harmony: "Then pleased it the apostles and elders, with the whole church, to send chosen men," &c. (ver. 22). "And they wrote letters by them after this manner: The apostles, and elders, and brethren, send greeting unto the brethren which are of the Gentiles," &c. (ver. 23). "It seemed good unto us, being assembled with one accord,' &c. (ver. 25). "It seemed good to the Holy Ghost, and to us," &c. (ver. 28).

Now, is there the remotest trace of prelacy in all this? We think not. James acts nowhere as a prelate, but everywhere as a presbyter or bishop, presiding, as moderator, over his brethren in synod assembled.

But, second, how does it fare with "the episcopate, properly so-called," in the Gentile wing of the Church in the apostolic age?

As we have seen, that office was claimed, "at least in a rudimentary form," by Dr Lightfoot for the Apostle James, and for him alone in the Jewish wing. We have also seen what it amounts to. But no claim at all is even put forward in the case of the Gentile churches. Bishop Lightfoot frankly states that "the New Testament presents no distinct traces of such organisation in the Gentile congregations." We agree. In view of all these facts, then, what we claim is simply this—that "the episcopate properly so-called" (the prelatic order of bishops) is not found in the New Testament, while Presbyterian bishops are. And this being so, the "inferior clergy," as they are called, of the Church of England are, in violation of New Testament precept and example, denied the exercise of episcopal functions, indefeasibly theirs, by the non-Scriptural and post-apostolic order of prelatic bishops.

But while this is our reading of the apostolic writings, we are no bigots; and were Dr Benson, as Archbishop of Canterbury, fairly to face a scheme of comprehension, taking as his starting-point, not the historic episcopate of his recent circular to the churches, but the common ground of the New Testament—which he and his brethren ought now fairly and fearlessly to face—it might be found possible, by the opening of the twentieth century, to see fairly under weigh, at least, one of the greatest, and, nationally considered, most salutary movements which England has witnessed in the ecclesiastical domain since the times of the Reformation. A foundation deeper and diviner than that of astute expediency on which Cranmer's ecclesiastical genius worked may be found. Happy the leaders who make it plain, and rally on it the pith and marrow and unsullied patriotism of Christian England, to hearten and help, harmonise and direct, existing forces, for both constructive and aggressive work through generations yet to come! There is room,—there is need. For one point, at least, may not unreasonably be assumed — viz., that, ecclesiastically, things cannot long continue in this country as they are at present. In the past, England has been what, for lack of a better term, we may call an oligarchic monarchy; the few, through the monarch, have controlled and dominated the many. That can no longer be. With the present Parliamentary franchise England is no longer an oligarchic but a democratic monarchy; the people, through the reigning sovereign, now govern themselves. But with this change in the State there has been no corresponding advance in the Church. It remains unchanged, with this result, that an ever-increasing force within the enfranchised and democratic State assails the still oligarchic Church. Like the "legs of the lame," these two limbs of the constitution in Church and State "are not equal." There is, consequently, an awkward limp. A man about whom the author of 'Waverley' tells us "had a stop-and-go-on sort of walk, as if ilka ane o' his twa legs belonged to sindry folk." Now the two great limbs of the Constitution obey not only "sindry" (separate) but positively conflicting principles. The one is felt by the other to be jarring and recalcitrant, and the deepening struggle is just the natural effort to restore harmony. The ultimate issue cannot be very uncertain. The shadow on the dial-plate of time cannot be put back. The Church will need to fall into line if she is to march into the future *pari passu* with the State. Oligarchic privilege will have to give way in the ecclesiastical member, as in the civil, to democratic principle and well-ordered popular representation. There is a real danger. What ought to be the most English may soon be found to be the most un-English institution in the realm. Time ought to be taken by the forelock, and, while opportunity and goodwill remain, the fitting ground and method of adjustment for the future should be found. There is no time for unconcern and delay. Rome was burning while, if some of his subjects spoke the truth, Nero was fiddling. What won't bend to-day may have to break to-morrow. Ultimately the crux may be found in this, that, while prelacy is essentially oligarchic and non-representative, the genius of the Anglo-Saxon race is essentially democratic and representative. Prevailing in many departments of its industrial and commercial life, it has at length effloresced supremely into the political sphere. But, fairly considered, it is not a foe to be feared and resisted, but a great and incalculably valuable force to be wisely regulated and impartially applied. That Anglo-Saxon genius has yet to find a fair and practicable solution of the ecclesiastical problem, which every day looms up more largely right in the line of national advance. But every principle, like every creature, acts "after its kind." English democracy will, therefore, be likely to find a solution not in conflict but in harmony with itself. In the political sphere the lordly and oligarchic element has been practically deposed, and the patient, toiling Saxon, after long centuries of endurance and effort, has at length prevailed. Will the issue be essentially different in the ecclesiastical province? It is not very likely that it will. It is not very desirable that it should.

There are two root elements closely correlated in the Anglo-Saxon character, which ultimately are likely to determine this and some other questions. The first of these is broad and common-sense reverence for the Bible. While he hates cant and sanctimoniousness, the typical Anglo-Saxon will stand by the Scriptures, and any fair and honest appeal for a legitimate purpose to their authority. The second is his love of liberty and fair play, zeal for equal citizen rights, and all-round democratic representation.

The Church of England that is to be the Church of the future must, we apprehend, have due respect to both of these elements. Its polity, as well as its creed, must have the clear and unmistakable warrant of the New Testament; and it must also afford ample scope for the rights and liberties of the Christian people, embracing their representative agency in the conduct of its affairs, which, if democratic, fortunately is likewise Scriptural and apostolic.

Now, does the Church of England as at present constituted fairly meet these requirements? With no wish but for her future stability and weal, in the best sense as a Church of Christ in this realm, we must answer, No! Anglican prelacy, or what the Archbishop of Canterbury calls "the historic episcopate," is post-apostolic, not Scriptural; exclusive, not representative. What is needed is large and fearless adaptation of her polity to apostolic precept and example, and the rights and liberties of the Christian people. Democratic representation, indeed, is amply met by New Testament provision. This, however, is disregarded by prelacy. There lurks danger. Is it wise, then, for the Church herself that prelacy, which is non-Scriptural and exclusive, should stand in the way of something else within her reach which is Scriptural and representative? Why not by timely action seek the possible common ground? With the future before the Church of England, and hostile forces of no ordinary magnitude and persistency directed against her, might not her best men fairly face this problem on broad Scriptural grounds? Or, as was the case with the Revision Committee, might they not be joined by representatives from other Churches, to attempt, at least, in that spirit of ample Christian charity which is never inconsistent with fidelity, the elaboration of an ecclesiastical polity based on New Testament precept and example? The result, one would hope, might well be the formulation of a system not less faithful to Scripture, yet, perhaps, deemed more comprehensive and flexible, than any of those with which the Churches are familiar. For the sake of the Church herself, as well as the nation in which she exerts an influence so great and bears a responsibility so weighty, every loyal and patriotic citizen may well hope that she will bend and embrace now, rather than run the risk, remote though some may think it to be, of having to break and disintegrate at some future time. And were this hope realised, as we think it might be, she would be likely to attain tenfold force, become more genuinely and adequately national, and worthily inherit the future.

[The above was originally published by the author in 'The Presbyterian.']

APPENDIX B.

1811.—MANOR OF TOTTINGTON.

The Halmot Court of the most noble Henry, Duke of Buccleuch, and Elizabeth, Duchess of Buccleuch, his wife, of their Manor of Tottington, in the county of Lancaster, holden at Holcome the first day of May, in the fifty-first year of the reign of our Sovereign Lord King George the Third over the United Kingdom of Great Britain and Ireland, and in the year of our Lord one thousand eight hundred and eleven, before John Bailey, Deputy Steward of William Carr, gentleman, Chief Steward there:

Be it remembered that, on the thirtieth day of April in the year of our Lord one thousand eight hundred and eleven, Richard Rothwell of Chatterton within Tottington, in the county of Lancaster, yeoman; Edward Rothwell of Spout Bank in the said county, yeoman; Edward Kay of Little Bolton in the said county, yeoman; and Richard Kay of Lime Field within Walmsley in the said county, cotton manufacturer (surviving feoffees in trust of the hereditaments hereinafter mentioned and intended to be hereby surrendered); in consideration of the sum of five shillings apiece of lawful British money to them in hand paid by William Woodcock of Holcome in the said manor, gentleman; William Grant of Grant Lodge in the said manor, merchant; Charles Grant of the same place, merchant; and Edward Rothwell of Bolton in the said county, painter; at or before the passing hereof the receipt whereof they do hereby severally acknowledge for renewing and extending the said Trust, and for divers other good causes and considerations thereunto moving, they, the said Richard Rothwell, Edward Rothwell of Spout Bank, Edward Kay and Richard Kay, Have and each and every of them Hath surrendered and given up, and by these presents Do, and each and every of them Doth surrender and give up into the hands of the Lord and Lady of the said manor by the hands and acceptance of James Rostron of Holcome, aforesaid gentleman, a customary tenant there and sworn, &c. All that edifice or building adjoining to Nuttal Lane in the said manor formerly called Little Edmund's, and now used as a Dissenting Chapel called Dundee Chapel, also all that messuage or dwelling-house adjoining the same for the use and benefit of the minister for the time being of the said Chapel, together with four falls of land by estimation thereunto belonging be the same more or less, of the yearly rent to the Lord and Lady of the said manor of one farthing, together with all and singular houses, outhouses, edifices, buildings, lands, grounds, ways, roads, waters, water courses, liberties, easements, privileges, and appurtenances whatsoever to the same belonging or therewith usually occupied or enjoyed. And all the estate, right, title, interest, use, trust, property, possession, claim, and demand whatsoever, both at law and in equity, of them, the said Richard Rothwell, Edward Rothwell of Spout Bank, Edward Kay, and Richard Kay, of, in, to, or out of the same, every or any part or parcel thereof.

To the use and behoof of the said Richard Rothwell, Edward Rothwell of Spout Bank, Edward Kay, Richard Kay, William Woodcock, William Grant, Charles Grant, and Edward Rothwell of Bolton, their heirs and assigns for ever to stand fined and seised thereof as feoffees or trustees in trust according to the custom of the said manor, to and for such uses, ends, intents, and purposes, as the same is now set apart, and to be continued for the service and worship of God, the interment of the dead, and emolument and benefit of a *pious preaching* Dissenting minister for the time being for ever of the said chapel, being the original intent thereof, and to and for no other use, trust, intent, or purpose whatsoever. And hereupon come the said Richard Rothwell, Edward Rothwell of Spout Bank, Edward Kay, Richard Kay, William Woodcock, William Grant, Charles Grant, and Edward Rothwell of Bolton, by the Reverend William Hampson, clerk, John Haworth Browne, Holt Browne, John Heywood, John Kay, Thomas Ramsbottom, William Hartley the younger, and James Barnes, their respective attornies, and desire to be admitted to their fine: proclamation thereof being made, and no person forbidding the same, then the said premises with the appurtenances are granted by the said deputy steward to the said Richard Rothwell, Edward Rothwell of Spout Bank, Edward Kay, Richard Kay, William Woodcock, William Grant, Charles Grant, and Edward Rothwell of Bolton, to have, and to hold to them, their heirs and assigns for ever, according to the custom of the said manor, to stand fined and seised thereof as feoffees or trustees, in trust to and for the uses, ends, intents, and purposes aforesaid and not otherwise, yielding and paying therefore yearly to the Lord and Lady of the said manor, and to their heirs, the rents and services therefore formerly due and of right accustomed, and now they give to the said Lord and Lady for fine, &c., one farthing by the pledge of John Gorton, gentleman.

Examined, J. BAILEY,
Depty. Steward of the said Court.

1782.—MANOR OF TOTTINGTON.

The Halmot Court of the Right Honourable Edward, Lord Beaulieu, and Isabella, Lady Beaulieu his wife, and the most noble George, Duke of Montagu, of their Manor of Tottington in the County of Lancaster, holden at Holcome the twenty-third day of October in the twenty-second year of the reign of our Sovereign Lord King George the Third over Great Britain, &c., and in the year of our Lord one thousand seven hundred and eighty-two, before Martin Richardson, gentleman, Chief Steward there.

Be it remembered that, the fourteenth day of August in the year of our Lord one thousand seven hundred and eighty-two, Thomas Rothwell, of Chatterton, in the parish of Bury and the County of Lancaster, yeoman ; and John Barnes, of Buckden Clough, in the parish and county aforesaid, weaver (being the surviving Feoffees, in trust of the buildings, land and premises hereinafter mentioned), for and in consideration of the sum of five shillings apiece to them in hand paid by Richard Rothwell of Bolton (son of the above named Thomas Rothwell), saddler ; James Allan of Nabbs, chapman ; Edward Kay, of Pot Green, Junior ; Richard Kay of Bass Lane, clothier ; Edward Rothwell of Spout Bank, and Thomas Rothwell of the Tanners, yeoman ; John Wood of Walmersley, shopkeeper ; and Richard Ashworth of Grain Barn, weaver ; the receipt whereof they do hereby severally acknowledge for extending and perpetuating the said Trust, and for divers other good causes and considerations them thereunto moving, Have and each of them Hath surrendered and given up into the hands of the Lords and Lady of the Manor of Tottington aforesaid by the Reverend John Smith, clerk, a customary tenant there and sworn, &c. All that one building, consisting of four Bays, adjoining to Nuttal Lane, in the said Manor, formerly called Little Edmund's, now used as a Dissenting Chapel, *and an house for the use and benefit of the Minister thereof for the time being.* Together with four falls of land by estimation thereunto belonging be the same more or less, of the yearly rent to the Lords and Lady of the said Manor of one farthing, and now in the possession of William Grindrod, clerk, and Abraham Hamer, together with all hereditaments, privileges, liberties, easements, and appurtenances thereunto belonging, or therewith usually occupied and enjoyed to the use and behoof of the above named Richard Rothwell, Edward Rothwell, James Allan, Edward Kay, Junior, Richard Kay, John Wood, Richard Ashworth, and Thomas Rothwell, their heirs and assigns for ever to be and stand fined and seised thereof as Feoffees in Trust to and for such uses as the same is now set apart and to be continued for *the service and worship of God, the interment of the dead, and the emolument and benefit of a Dissenting Minister for the time being, for ever*, and to and for no other use, intent, or purpose whatsoever, according to the custom of the said Manor. And hereupon come the said Richard Rothwell, Edward Rothwell, James Allan, Edward Kay, Junior, Richard Kay, John Wood, Richard Ashworth, and Thomas Rothwell, by the Reverend John Smith, clerk ; George Duckworth, Thomas Kershaw, Otwell Kershaw, Ralph Bridge ; Henry Aspinall, William Barlow, gentleman ; and James Barnes, their respective attorneys, and desire to be admitted to their fine ; proclamation thereof being made and no person forbidding the same ; then the said premises with the appurtenances are granted by the said Steward to the said Richard Rothwell, Edward Rothwell, James Allan, Edward Kay, Junior, Richard Kay, John Wood, Richard Ashworth, and Thomas Rothwell to have and to hold to them their heirs and assigns for ever to be and stand fined and seised thereof as Feoffees in Trust, to and for the uses aforesaid and not otherwise according to the custom of the said Manor, yielding therefore yearly to the Lords and Lady of the said Manor, and to their heirs the rents and services therefore formerly due, and of the right accustomed, and now they give to the said Lords and Lady for fine, &c., one farthing by the pledge of William Barlow.

Travelling further into the past, we found the following of date 1755 :—

MANOR OF TOTTINGTON.

The Halmot Court of the Most Noble Isabella, Duchess Dowager of Manchester, and of the Right Honourable Mary, Countess of Cardigan (Daughters and Co-heirs of the Most Noble John, Duke of Montagu, deceased), of their Manor of Tottington in the County of Lancaster, holden at Holcome the eighteenth day of October, in the twenty-ninth year of the reign of our Sovereign Lord King George the Second over Great Britain, &c., and in the year of our Lord one thousand seven hundred and fifty-five, before Lawrence Robinson, gentleman, Chief Steward there :

Be it remembered that, the nineteenth day of October in the year of our Lord one thousand seven hundred and fifty-four, Thomas Rothwell of Holcome, in the Parish of Bury and County of Lancaster, tanner (being the only surviving Feoffee in Trust of the building, land, and premises hereinafter mentioned), for divers good causes and considerations him thereunto moving Hath surrendered and given up into the hands of the Ladies of the said Manor by John Haworth, customary tenant there, and sworn, &c. All that one building lately erected, consisting of four Bays adjoyning to Nuttal Lane, formerly called Little Edmund's, and four falls of land by estimation thereunto belonging be the same more or less, of the yearly rent of one farthing to the Ladies of the said Manor and now in the possession or occupation of John Helme, clerk, or his assigns, together with all liberties, easements, and appurtenances thereunto belonging to the use and behoof of Thomas Rothwell,[1] the younger, of Holcome aforesaid,

---

[1] In front of the Chancel in Holcombe Church, two stones bear the following inscriptions :—

Here resteth the Body of Mary Rothwell,
The Daughter of Edward Rothwell of Holcome,
Who departed this Life, May the 27th 1726,
And in the 10th year of her age.

" Short was her life,
The longer is her rest ;
God takes them soonest,
Whom He loveth best."

Also the Body of *Thomas Rothwell of Harpers in Holcome*,
Who departed this Life the 22nd day of July 1781,
In the 46th year of his age.

Also, of Martha, his Wife,
Who died February 5, 1814. Aged 84 Years.

Here resteth the Body of Richard Rothwell of Ramsbottom,
Who departed this Life, December 4th 1745,
In the 43rd year of his age.

tanner; Thomas Rothwell of Chatterton; and John Barnes, the younger, of Broadwood Edge; and their heirs, the survivor of them, his heirs and assigns for ever, to stand fined and seised as Feoffees in Trust of the above mentioned premises to such uses as the same is now set apart and *to be continued for the service of Divine Worship* and to no other use or purpose whatsoever, and according to the custom of the said Manor. And hereupon come the said Thomas Rothwell of Chatterton in his proper person, and the said Thomas Rothwell the younger, and John Barnes, by John Haworth and Edward Kay, their attorneys, and desire to be admitted to their fine; proclamation thereof being made, and no person forbidding the same, then the said premises with the appurtenances are granted by the said steward to the said Thomas Rothwell, the younger, of Holcome; Thomas Rothwell of Chatterton; and John Barnes, to have and to hold to them and their heirs, the survivor of them, his heirs and assigns for ever, to stand fined and seised as Feoffees in Trust of the above mentioned premises, to and for the uses aforesaid, and not otherwise, according to the custom of the said Manor, yielding therefore yearly to the Ladies of the said Manor and to their heirs the rents and services therefor formerly due and of right accustomed, and now they give to the said Ladies for fine, &c., one farthing by the pledge of the said Edward Kay.

Still further back, in 1713, we found the *original* surrender and admittance of the Dundee property. In the old Court Rolls this deed figures in Latin; but not being perfectly Ciceronian, it may perhaps, in the less august environment of this record, minister more to general edification if it appear thus :—

MANOR OF TOTTINGTON.

The Halmot Court of the Most Noble Elizabeth, Dowager Duchess of Montagu, of her Manor of Tottington in the county of Lancaster, holden at Holcome within the said Manor the twelfth day of October in the year of our Lord one thousand seven hundred and fourteen, before Thomas Sclater, gentleman, Deputy Steward of Thomas Dummer, Esquire, Chief Steward there.

Be it remembered that, on the twenty-eighth day of September, in the year of our Lord one thousand seven hundred and thirteen, Edward

Rothwell of Tunley in the county of Lancaster, clerk, for divers good causes and considerations hereunto moving surrenders into the hands of the Lady of the said Manor, by Edward Hamer of Buckden, yeoman, a customary tenant there, and sworn, &c. One building lately erected containing four Bays of buildings adjoining to Nuttal Lane, called Little Edmund's and four falls of land by estimation, be the same a little more or loss, all which said premises are now in the tenure or occupation of the said Edward Rothwell or his assigns of the annual rent to the Lady of the said Manor of one farthing, with all profits, liberties, easements, and appurtenances thereunto belonging or in anywise appertaining to the use and behoof of Richard Kay of Chessum, Edward Hamer of Somerseat, John Romsbotham of Redisher, William Holt of Holcome, Thomas Rothwell of Strongstye, Abraham Wood of Edge, James Rothwell of Holcome, Thomas Rothwell of Holcome, aforesaid, and Richard Bridge of Spenleach, yeoman, their heirs and assigns for ever; and hereupon come the said Richard, Edward, John, William, Thomas, Abraham, James, Thomas, and Richard, and pray to be admitted to their fine, &c. Proclamation thereof being made and no person forbidding the same, then the said premises with the appurtenances to the said Richard, Edward, John William, Thomas, Abraham, James, Thomas, and Richard are granted by the said Steward, to have and to hold to them their heirs and assigns according to the custom of the said Manor for ever; paying therefor yearly to the Lady of the said Manor and to her heirs the rents and services therefor formerly due and of right accustomed, and now they give to the said Lady for fee, &c., one farthing by the pledge of Edward Hamer.

To facilitate the collection of the lord of the manor's rents, a notice was issued, signed by the late Mr "Dixon Robinson, steward, Clitheroe Castle, 16th February 1875," which contains the following simplification:—

Much inconvenience having arisen in the collection of the Copyhold rents in consequence of the minute fractional sums sometimes inserted in Surrenders of Building Land as the apportioned rents payable to the lord, it is arranged that where a plot of land is severed from an Estate which is subject to a Copyhold rent of larger amount, the apportioned rent shall be after the following scale, increasing according to the extent of the land surrendered—viz.:

> For a plot not exceeding 500 square yards, *one penny*.
> ,, ,, ,, 1000 ,, *twopence*.
> ,, ,, ,, 2000 ,, *fourpence*.
> ,, ,, ,, 3000 ,, *sixpence*.

APPENDIX C.

(See p. 355, *supra*.)

Copy of *The Spurious Dundee Trust Deed*, of date November 26, 1883.

MANOR OF TOTTINGTON.

At Clitheroe Castle, in the County of Lancaster, the residence of *Arthur Ingram Robinson*, gentleman, Steward of *The Honourable James Archibald Douglas Home*, and *Frederick Iltid Nicholl*, and *Henry Frederick Nicholl, Esquires*, Lords of the said Manor, the eighteenth day of December in the forty-eighth year of the reign of our Sovereign Lady Victoria, by the grace of God, of the United Kingdom of Great Britain and Ireland Queen, Defender of the Faith, and in the year of our Lord one thousand eight hundred and eighty-four:

Be it remembered that on the day and year first above written, and out of Court at the aforesaid Castle, come L—— L——, J—— M——, W—— S——, G—— B——, A—— B——, J—— K——, H—— P——, W—— H—— O——, J—— K——, L—— W——, T—— K——, A—— B—— C——, W—— D—— G——, D—— S——, F—— K—— A——, and J—— P——, all of Ramsbottom, in the County of Lancaster, and produce and deliver to the said Steward a certain Memorandum in writing, and desire that the same may be enrolled amongst the Records of the said Manor, and it followeth in these words, to wit :—

Memorandum of the choice and appointment of New Trustees of the Dissenting Chapel called Dundee Chapel, situate in Nuttall

Lane, Ramsbottom, in the Township of Tottington Lower End, in the county of Lancaster, at a meeting duly convened and held for that purpose in the said Chapel on the twenty-sixth day of November, one thousand eight hundred and eighty-three.

L—— L——, of Ramsbottom, aforesaid, *Chairman.*

Names and *Descriptions* of all the trustees on the last appointment of trustees made the thirtieth day of April, one thousand eight hundred and eleven:—

Richard Rothwell of Chatterton within Tottington, yeoman.
Edward Rothwell of Spout Bank, yeoman.
Edward Kay of Little Bolton, yeoman.
Richard Kay of Limefield within Walmersley, cotton manufacturer.
William Woodcock of Holcombe, gentleman.
William Grant of Grant Lodge, merchant.
Charles Grant of the same place, merchant ; and
Edward Rothwell of Bolton, painter.

Names and *Descriptions* of all the trustees in whom the said chapel and premises now become equally vested :—

First—Old continuing trustees—None.
Second—New trustees now chosen and appointed :
L—— L—— of Ramsbottom, ——.
J—— M—— of Ramsbottom, ——.
W—— S—— of Ramsbottom, ——.
G—— B—— of Ramsbottom, ——.
*A—— B—— of Ramsbottom, ——.
J—— K—— of Ramsbottom, ——.
*H—— P—— of Ramsbottom, ——.
*W—— H—— O—— of Ramsbottom, ——.
J—— K—— of Ramsbottom, ——.
L—— W—— of Ramsbottom, ——.
T—— K—— of Ramsbottom, ——.
A—— B—— C—— of Ramsbottom, ——.
W—— D—— G—— of Ramsbottom, ——.
D—— S—— of Ramsbottom, ——.

---

* Deceased.

F—— K—— A—— of Ramsbottom, ——.
*J—— P—— of Ramsbottom, ——.

Dated this twenty-sixth day of November, one thousand eight hundred and eighty-three—L—— L—— (L.S.), Chairman of the said Meeting. *Signed, sealed, and delivered by* the said L—— L——, as Chairman of the said Meeting, at and in the presence of the said Meeting, on the day and year aforesaid, in the presence of R—— B——, Ramsbottom ; G—— S——, Ramsbottom.

The above persons, who, according to the foregoing deed, got themselves enrolled as trustees of Dundee property, were defendants in the ejectment suit, and were ejected from Dundee premises, by the Sheriff's officer, in May 1885.[1]

APPENDIX D.

"Going Home."

(From 'Outlook,' August 24, 1883.)

The mortal remains of Annie Birch, a young and much-loved member of St Andrew's Presbyterian Church, Ramsbottom, were on Tuesday last interred at Holcombe. Annie was of too delicate a mould for the tear and wear of ordinary life. She had frequent illnesses, and her last—an inflammation in the region of the heart—was a protracted and painful one, but was borne with unmurmuring patience and acquiescence in the divine will. After great suffering, and just before she died, she said, " I am going ! " " Where are you going, love ? " asked her sister. " I am going home ! " She then stretched her hands eagerly upward, but presently they fell

---

* Deceased.   [1] See page 367, *supra*.

softly by her side, as a storm-tossed bird might fold its wearied wings to rest, and she was gone.

On the morning of Sunday last, at the close of a sermon befitting the occasion, on 1 Thess. iv. 14; and Ps. cxxvii. 2, "So He giveth His beloved sleep," her minister (the Rev. William Hume Elliot) read the following verses, which had been suggested by her last words:—

"I am going home!"
 From this tossing unrest
To the presence of Jesus,
 The place of the blest;
Where sickness and anguish
 Have never distrest,
Where the weak ones grow strong,
 And the weary find rest.

"I am going home!"
 From the toil and the pain,
From the task and the turmoil
 That shatter and strain;
Where the heart's fitful beat
 Ne'er shall startle me more,
Nor the eyesight grow dim,
 On yon sorrowless shore.

"I am going home!"
 From the darkness and night
To the land of the holy,
 The realm of delight;
Where the flowers never fade,
 And the leaves never fall,
And the sun never sets,
 And the joys never pall.

"I am going home!"
 But, though parted awhile,

We shall meet yet again,
  'Neath our Father's kind smile;
For the Lord, who, in blood,
  For our sins did atone,
Us in love-links enclasps
  To Himself on the throne.

"I am going home!"
  Her last words; then on high
Waved the pale wasted hands,
  As if angels were nigh;
Or the dearest of all
  Were just coming in sight,
To welcome her home
  To the mansions of light.

Home! Safely at home!
  Calm is breathed o'er her now,
Closed softly the eyelids,
  Smooth-marbled the brow.
The flower is transplanted;
  The ointment is poured;
The frail casket broken—
  The gem with the Lord.

WM. HUME ELLIOT.

WOODHILL,
  21st August 1883.

THE END.

PRINTED BY GEORGE LEWIS AND SON, SELKIRK.

Foolscap 4to, 270 Pages. Price, 6s. 6d.

Craigmillar and its Environs,

WITH NOTICES OF THE

Topography, Natural History, and
Antiquities of the District,

BY

TOM SPEEDY

(Author of "Sport in the Highlands and Lowlands of
Scotland with Rod and Gun").

WITH NUMEROUS ILLUSTRATIONS.

PRESS OPINIONS.

The Scotsman.—"In all respects, indeed, the work is a notable addition to a fascinating and fertile field of literature. . . . . No better printed book has been issued from the press for many a day."

The Evening News.—"He has roamed the highways and byeways, heights and valleys, woods and meadows, marshes and lakes of the district for many years, noting the ways of bird and beast, and the appearance of tree, flower, and weed, with the eye of a gamekeeper or hotanist and the keen intelligence of a scientific naturalist. The result is the production of several very readable chapters, with anecdotes and observations of much interest."

Evening Dispatch.—"Welcome and charming."

Manchester Examiner.—"The work is of a very exhaustive character."

Northern Chronicle.—"Mr Speedy has more than knowledge: he has enthusiasm; and, as a close and loving observer of nature whose reputation is more than local, he is able to give us, in this dainty form, history and natural history delightfully blended. . . . We have never seen a finer specimen of the printer's art."

Quiz.—"A beautiful book for the drawing-room.

Liverpool Mercury.—"An exceptionally beautiful volume in several respects; the printing is perfection, the engravings are good, the history is curious, and the chapters on the fauna, flora, and geology of the district, with which Queen Mary of Scotland's name is inseparably connected, is of enduring value."

Kelso Mail.—"It is the work of a man who has eyes to see and skill to describe what he has seen and his hands have handled."

Kelso Chronicle.—"For its literary merit, as well as for the beauty of its outward equipment, the book will doubtless have, as it deserves, a wide popularity."

Pall Mall Gazette.—"This is of the nature of a glorified guide book."

Contemporary Review.—"Neither he nor his publishers seem to have spared any pains to make the volume in every way worthy of its subject."

National Observer.—"He has the practised eye of an accurate student of nature."

GEORGE LEWIS & SON, SELKIRK.

www.ingramcontent.com/pod-product-compliance
Lightning Source LLC
Chambersburg PA
CBHW022133300426
44115CB00006B/171